Judging Obscenity
A Critical History of Expert Evidence

CHRISTOPHER NOWLIN

McGill-Queen's University Press
Montreal & Kingston · London · Ithaca

© McGill-Queen's University Press 2003
ISBN 0-7735-2518-1 (cloth)
ISBN 0-7735-2538-6 (paper)

Legal deposit first quarter 2003
Bibliothèque nationale du Québec

Printed in Canada on acid-free paper that is 100% ancient forest
free (100% post-consumer recycled), processed chlorine free.

This book has been published with the help of a grant from the
Humanities and Social Sciences Federation of Canada, using funds
provided by the Social Sciences and Humanities Research Council
of Canada.

McGill-Queen's University Press acknowledges the financial support
of the Canada Council for the Arts for our publishing program.
We also acknowledge the financial support of the Government of
Canada through the Book Publishing Industry Development Program
(BPIDP) for our publishing activities.

National Library of Canada Cataloguing in Publication

Nowlin, Christopher, 1964–
    Judging obscenity: a critical history of expert evidence /
    Christopher Nowlin.

    Includes bibliographical references and index.
    ISBN 0-7735-2518-1 (bound)
    ISBN 0-7735-2538-6 (pbk)

    1. Trials (Obscenity) – Canada. 2. Trials (Obscenity) – United States.
    3. Evidence, Expert – Canada. 4. Evidence, Expert – United States.
    1. Title.

K5293.N69 2003   345.71'0274   C2002-905504-0

Typeset in Sabon 10/12
by Caractéra inc., Quebec City

JUDGING OBSCENITY

To my family

Contents

Acknowledgments

Many individuals deserve acknowledgment for contributing to the development of this book. A much different but recognizable version was first made public as a doctoral dissertation in 1998. At that time my doctoral committee at Simon Fraser University's School of Criminology, comprised of Dany Lacombe, Robert Menzies, and Joan Brockman, had generously and patiently helped me to bring my various analyses and thoughts into a coherent and defensible form. Another colleague at this school, Ted Palys, provided me with access to the great many pages of transcripts of the 1994 *Little Sister's* trial. These enabled me to engage in argument with an extensive array of expert opinions as they actually unfolded in an important obscenity case.

I am indebted to David Paciocco at the University of Ottawa for the real enthusiasm he expressed for my doctoral dissertation, and for the constructive comments he offered in relation to it. His complimentary words inspired me to try to transform my dissertation into a book that would appeal to a broad readership.

My brother Michael's contribution can in no way go unmentioned. In the early, preparatory stages of this book, I had various questions about modern literature and American intellectual history that I discussed with Michael, who was always ready and willing to point me to a host of important and interesting materials. I thank Michael particularly for introducing me to such remarkable thinkers as Lippmann and Lasch, who served as reminders to me that in the world of ideas, "old-fashioned" can be as illuminating and relevant as the new and fashionable.

In its more recent stages of development, this book was reviewed by several anonymous appraisers and I thank them for thoughtful suggestions for the book's improvement.

I am indebted greatly to all the friendly and capable staff at McGill-Queen's University Press. I thank Philip Cercone and Joan Harcourt, the editors who dealt with my manuscript when it first arrived at MQUP, and John Zucchi, the editor who subsequently brought my manuscript to its publishable form. Joanne Pisano never tired of facilitating communication and correspondence relating to the publishing of this book over the years, even while I was teaching in England. Joan McGilvray kept the editorial process moving along most smoothly and affably. And David Schwinghamer was a most collegial, meticulous, industrious, and excellent copy editor.

I acknowledge everyone else who helped me to print off and ship one or other of the drafts of this book from Vancouver, Lethbridge, and Keele to MQUP. And finally I am grateful to those members of my family who have done what they can to assist in the completion of this project.

Introduction

At the dawn of the new millennium, Canada's highest court delivered two rulings about pornography that are among the more controversial ones to be found in the history of Anglo-American obscenity litigation. One confirmed the notion that sexually explicit gay and lesbian narratives, including sadomasochistic depictions, are socially, psychologically, and culturally more important to Canadian gays and lesbians than similarly explicit heterosexual material is to Canadian heterosexuals.[1] The other confirmed that, as a matter of their constitutionally entrenched freedom of expression, Canadian citizens should be entitled to give literal or pictorial expression to their imaginations, even where this expression looks like child pornography, as long as no one is exploited in the process and only the producers can see or obtain the expression.[2] When this latter idea was first articulated by a Supreme Court of British Columbia judge, some Canadians and parliamentarians were so outraged that they quickly attempted to pass new legislation that would permit the administrative branch of Canada's government to ignore the judge's ruling. They did so unsuccessfully.

One can find a genuine public interest in various colourful obscenity prosecutions conducted in America, England, Canada, and other Commonwealth countries. Perhaps the trials of John Cleland's *Fanny Hill*, James Joyce's *Ulysses*, Vladimir Nabakov's *Lolita*, or Bernardo Bertolucci's *Last Tango in Paris* spring to mind. This book revisits some of these trials and several others to show the importance of expert evidence to them. In so doing it notes when and how the expert opinion evidence changes and endeavours to explain why. At times it might seem as if the expert opinion introduced into a case is more or less predictable – that certain books or films had to be defended on the basis of their scientific, educational, or artistic merit. At other times, however, the evidence appears to reflect a broader historical shift in some influential segment of society's perception of pornography and understanding of art. As Vanderham has recently proposed, the liberation of Joyce's *Ulysses* from American censors in 1933, which owed much to expert literary evidence introduced in the trial proceedings, represented a dramatic legal triumph of the "esthetic" theory of art over the "moral-esthetic" theory that was prevalent until then (Vanderham 1998, 129). Arguably, the 1992 landmark prosecution of a pornographic video-retailer in Canada represented a major legal victory for an influential radical-feminist view which saw erotica and pornography as misogynistic and was itself rooted in an emergent body of social science research.[3]

As the broader analysis in this book unfolds, it should become apparent that neither the "esthetic" theory of art nor radical-feminist views of pornography bear rigorous scrutiny. The same can be said about many of the other ideas of literary criticism and much of the social science evidence about the psychological and behavioural harmfulness of reading or watching pornography that is increasingly used in obscenity prosecutions. This is a problem in itself, but the prospect that obscenity law over the last century has developed from dubious expertise and research conclusions raises other equally significant issues which this book addresses.

First, the question can be asked: why is it that North American obscenity law has been predominantly informed by expertise to date? Put another way, why do judges tend to consult experts to help them determine the moral worth or social harmfulness of some impugned book or movie? This question can be addressed in part by reviewing the history and principles of so-called "legislative-fact" evidence, as well as the more recent concept of "social fact." This book examines the substance of different kinds of legislative-fact evidence introduced in constitutional litigation since the turn of the century in North America and documents judges' responses to this evidence in particular kinds of cases. Chapter 1 looks at the evidence presented in American cases involving the so-called "police power" and in Canadian cases invoking the "reasonable apprehension of harm" doctrine. Chapters 3 through 6 focus mainly on the expert evidence introduced in American and Canadian obscenity cases over the last century.

Second, the major influence of experts upon judicial decision-making, especially in cases of constitutional importance (such as some landmark obscenity prosecutions), raises this question: Is law reform in the area of obscenity and free speech effectively democratic? Should it be? If yes, how so? And if not, why not? Chapter 2 discusses different democratic "ideals" to show how the historical hegemony of expert evidence in constitutional review is consistent with a progressivist view of democracy but antithetical to popular and pluralist views. It also argues that an expert monopoly on legislative fact-finding is inconsistent with retired Supreme Court of Canada Justice Bertha Wilson's request that, in the name of democracy, Canadian judges consult widely or "think large" when engaged in constitutional review (Wilson 1986). Arguably, the mandate of broad consultation requires judges to seek not only inter-disciplinary knowledge from university professors but also informed opinions from people of all walks of life: these include people who lack the formal training and experience of certain professionals, the publication records and academic credentials of many qualified courtroom experts, and the research skills associated with social and natural scientists. Coincidentally, American and Canadian obscenity laws require courts to consider the broader "community" standard of tolerance or decency regarding prosecuted materials, so it is inexplicable that a broad cross-section of the community is rarely consulted for this purpose. The rights and freedoms of *all* these people are at stake in one way or another in constitutional reviews, so unless there are good reasons to believe that so-called laypersons have nothing worthwhile to say, for example, about inflation, pornography, suicide, or capital punishment, the monopoly that experts have in these domains of legal decision-making is difficult to justify.

Third, the fact that much of the social science research fuelling the public pornography debates is so contentious (even on its own terms) raises the real possibility that expert evidence in this realm can only be argumentative, and therefore far from factual. Whether in the form of laboratory experiments attempting to measure the behavioural effects of watching graphic sexual images, or opinion surveys purporting to glean the moral worth of some impugned book or painting, this research is often either tied to a definite political agenda and is funded by the interest groups that maintain such an agenda, or it is professionally interpreted in a way that assists one or another party in a legal battle. These are not minor considerations. Canadian courts have traditionally distinguished between argument and opinion in the legislative fact-finding context. If a judge perceives an expert's evidence to be epistemologically contrived, she is likely to exclude or simply ignore that evidence because it is in the nature of "argument." Since expert testimony is supposed to appear epistemologically disinterested, historically courts have only asked experts to apply the recognized first principles and methods of their disciplines to a set of factual or hypothetical circumstances put before them and to explain the result. The explanation constitutes an expert "opinion," which is presumed, ideally, to be legally non-partisan or somehow neutral. Chapter 1 and chapters 3 through 6 show how frequently legislative-fact and social-fact evidence introduced into American and Canadian courts is admitted as expert "opinion" evidence which is clearly argumentative, and certainly not politically or even, at times, morally disinterested. Chapter 3 addresses the provocative idea, first raised by Leslie Fiedler, that the influential expert literary opinion evidence introduced into the 1933 *Ulysses* trial contained various "well-intentioned lies" (Fiedler 1984, 29). The same could be said for almost every piece of expert evidence to be examined in this book. Chapter 5, in particular, demonstrates the force of this claim by assessing the opinions introduced by many of the expert witnesses who testified for the plaintiffs in the *Little Sister's* case, and by situating these opinions within the context of a broader legal and political battle – and certainly intellectual *argument* – about obscenity, pornography, free speech, and equality.

Indeed, it should be said at the outset that chapter 5 offers a particularly detailed commentary on the expert testimony in the *Little Sister's* case. Available transcripts of the trial proceedings have made it possible to read exactly what each witness said, thus providing the oportunity for an analysis of the details of each witness's argument relating to gay or lesbian pornography and erotica. In turn, one can engage in one's own arguments with many of the plaintiffs' witnesses in the *Little Sister's* case, on the basis of these same witnesses' oral testimony, as I do in this book. Chapter 5 may seem much more critical of the expert opinions in *Little Sister's* than of those in preceding cases examined in the book. The more circumspect analysis in chapter 5, however, must not be misunderstood as suggesting that the expert witnesses in the *Little Sister's* case are somehow less intelligent or more politically interested than the experts who preceded them in other obscenity prosecutions. Rather, the detailed critique of the expert evidence in the *Little Sister's* case is designed to provide yet another illustration of the political and moral self-interest involved in legislative-fact evidence production, but this time microscopically, as opposed to macroscopically.

Chapter 5 also examines a couple of very recent, significant prosecutions for possessing or publishing child pornography, most notably the previously mentioned case of John Robin Sharpe, a retired city planner in Vancouver who was caught both crossing the Canada-USA border and at home with anatomically explicit photos of boys and diskettes of stories he penned under the pseudonym Sam Paloc. This case is significant here because the social science evidence introduced in it was scrutinized so carefully, whereas the literary expertise survived relatively unscathed.

Chapter 6 analyses how experts have recently tried to help Canadian courts understand the erotic or non-erotic appeal of the naked female breast and, indeed, the harmfulness of exposing the female breast in public. Moreover, the analysis of Canada's indecency laws, post-*Butler*, takes the reader behind the doors of some Toronto and Montreal sex parlours, or "bawdy-houses," to see what the experts are saying about the dangers of lap-dancing and other intimate forms of erotic entertainment for men. The evidence suggests that there is nothing harmful in just "looking" anymore (unless of course, the women baring themselves do so outside on a hot day, without an expectation of commercial gain), but "touching" is dangerous, not because some of the female dancers fear injury or molestation, but because they or their male "dance" partners might spread infectious diseases.

To assess the numerous competing knowledge claims made by all the experts who have appeared in American and Canadian obscenity and indecency trials, this book casts a spotlight on Ludwig Wittgenstein's *On Certainty*. In his book, Wittgenstein emphasized the importance of everyday, mundane human behaviour to the plausibility of empirical knowledge claims. In effect, Wittgenstein challenges the working assumption in the social sciences that a given experiment or research design can be "valid" or "reliable" according to the first principles and established methodologies of the relevant social science itself. These projects assume knowledge of some aspect of human behaviour even as they seek to understand other behaviours, but the assumptions are always contestable, both by fellow social scientists and non-scientists. Chapter 1 applies Wittgenstein's behavioural view of knowledge and his related notion of a "language game" to the world of fact-finding in law in order to encourage both a practical and inter-disciplinary approach to determining facts in constitutional law generally, and in obscenity litigation specifically.

Viewed in light of Wittgenstein, my overall objective in this book is modest. I have presented a cautionary tale aimed at disabusing North American courts of their perception that social scientific and other academic research generates "facts," however contentious, that are practically divorced from political and moral considerations. Madam Justice Southin of the British Columbia Court of Appeal recently and wryly observed in the *Sharpe* case that "legislative facts," insofar as "they are based on what is called social science, are more a matter of opinion than fact." Judges must be so apprised. Otherwise their decisions to admit or exclude important legislative-fact evidence in constitutional reviews seem arbitrary and ill-informed and the proper administration of justice is thrown into jeopardy. The expert witness who provides opinion evidence relating to certain legislative facts is engaged in the same broad process of argumentation as the activist who marches in the street, carries a placard, and speaks through a bullhorn. The argumentative nature of expert testimony is often so subtle, however, that the judiciary does not recognize it. Indeed, judges fail to appreciate in this sense that *all* legislative and social fact information is politically and morally interested because of the way the supporting scientific and academic research is funded and the conclusions are generated. The fact that a particular expert happens to be politically active does not in itself affect these broader processes.

Finally, one may argue that this book is paradoxical or even contradictory as my critique of expertise is itself grounded in several years of formal education. The reader may rest assured, however, that regardless of the number of graduate seminars and scholarly pages that have informed it, this book does not purport to offer an expert opinion about experts. As the product of scholarly research, it will surely receive the same degree of criticism it metes out to others – no more, no less. Opinions of certain experts are considered more or less "unreliable" or "inaccurate" here to the extent that other experts and interested non-experts have levelled what appear to be cogent, plausible, or fair critiques of these same opinions. At times a social scientist's research conclusion may be called "unreliable" in the narrow sense in which social scientists use that term. At other times an expert opinion may be deemed "unreliable" or "unhelpful" because it appears disingenuous or dishonest, or perhaps because it is obviously politically self-serving and clearly not aimed at assisting the court in its own fact-finding mission. Yet all the time this book bears Wittgenstein's notion of a language game in mind. *Cogency, plausibility, scientificity,* and *accuracy* are but so many terms, bearing just so many meanings, within only a select few discourses among the great variety that are practiced every day. This book properly belongs in the relatively small family of games that address problems of knowledge for knowledge's sake, and, occasionally, for political and moral reasons.

JUDGING OBSCENITY

Of course there has been an enormous increase in the amount of knowledge possessed by mankind, but it does not equal, probably, the increase in the amount of errors and half-truths which have got into circulation. In social and human matters, especially, the development of a critical sense and methods of discriminating judgment has not kept pace with the growth of careless reports and of motives for positive misrepresentation.

Dewey 1927, 162–3

Increasingly information is generated by those who wish to promote something or someone – a product, a cause, a political candidate or office holder – without arguing their case on its merits or explicitly advertising it as self-interested material either.

Lasch 1995, 174

1

The Constitutional Backdrop
for Reviewing Expert Opinions
about Pornography

AMERICA'S BIG BROTHER

For more than a century, American federal and state governments have been lawfully vested with an overarching power to act as guardians of public morals, health, and safety. Whenever affected citizens challenged the constitutional validity of nationwide or statewide regulatory schemes, the appropriate government body or agency could justify its allegedly unlawful intrusion into Americans' professional and private lives by reference to an established common law rule, conveniently known as the "police power." Around the turn of the twentieth century, state legislatures created laws, for example, that placed limits on the number of daily hours that women could work in manufacturing settings, mercantile establishments, laundries, hotels, and restaurants. When the constitutional validity of these laws was challenged by proprietors and employees who wanted unbridled freedom to contract their own terms of employment, government lawyers argued that the well-established privilege of contracting is not unfettered: rather, it requires some restriction in certain circumstances as a matter of public welfare or social interest. References to the "comfort, safety, and welfare of society,"[1] or the "welfare of society at large,"[2] readily raised the spectre of the police power in the hands of the American judiciary. For instance, the power itself was defined generally as "that power of the state which relates to the conservation of the health, morals, and general welfare of the public,"[3] or "that power which enables the state to promote and protect the health, welfare, and safety of society,"[4] and it was believed to "inhere" in the state.[5]

The generality of the police power has meant that it can be applied to many facets of social and personal life. It has been invoked to justify restrictions not only on the exercise of property rights, but on such activities as smoking opium and drinking alcohol, which, arguably, fall under an individual's right to liberty and the pursuit of happiness.[6] The police power has even been used to justify state regulation of insurance agents' commissions.[7] And in the 1917 case of *Commonwealth* v. *Allison*, the Supreme Judicial Court of Massachusetts used the police power to uphold the constitutionality of state legislation prohibiting the distribution of obscene pamphlets and the advertising of means to prevent conception.[8] Judge Rugg's reasons for judgment do not indicate what constitutional provisions were at issue in this case, but earlier and later case law shows that the First Amendment's guarantee of "freedom of speech, or of the press" lies at the heart of constitutional challenges in matters of obscenity.[9] Applying the doctrine of the police power to the statutory provisions at issue in *Commonwealth* v. *Allison*, Rugg held, "Their plain purpose is to protect purity, to preserve chastity, to encourage continence and self-restraint, to defend the sanctity of the home, and thus to engender in the state and nation a virile and virtuous race of men and women. The subject-matter is well within one of the most obvious and necessary branches of the police power of the state."[10]

The police power, like the constitutional rights restricted in its name, is also subject to restrictions, and a government that relies on the power must abide by these. One of the limitations associated with the police power can be found within the terms of the Fourteenth Amendment. It provides that no state shall "deprive any person of life, liberty, or property, without due process of law." Accordingly, if the police power is invoked to justify any such restriction, it must be exercised in conformity with legal "due process." One American judge gave substance to this idea as early as 1895. Referring to the police power in *Ritchie* v. *People*, Judge Magruder said, "Legislative acts passed in pursuance of it must not be in conflict with the constitution, and must have some relation to the ends sought to be accomplished; that is to say, to the comfort, welfare, or safety of society."[11] In *Re Jacobs*, the plaintiff challenged an act designed "to improve the public health by prohibiting the manufacture of cigars and preparation of tobacco in any form in tenement houses." In response to the challenge, the New York Court of Appeals stated, "When a health law is challenged in the courts as unconstitutional on the ground that it arbitrarily interferes with personal liberty and private property without due process of law, the courts must be able to see that it has at least *in fact* some relation to the public health, that the public health is the end actually aimed at, and that it is appropriate and adapted to that end."[12]

Sometimes the government's task of convincing a court that an impugned law was constitutionally well-tailored was easier than at other times. In *Ritchie* v. *People*, for example, Magruder was certain that "the public health, welfare, and safety may be endangered by the general use of opium and intoxicating drinks."[13] He suggested, however, that evidence was lacking of the danger to society of working in clothing factories, or even in cigar factories.[14] Years later, the Supreme Court of New York found it "clear" that "utterances inciting to the overthrow of organized government by unlawful means, present a sufficient danger of substantive evil to bring their punishment within the range of legislative discretion" because, as the court explained, "Such utterances, by their very nature, involve danger to the public peace and to the security of the State."[15] Accordingly, the Court held that "in the exercise of its police power" the State of New York could penalize the publication of a manifesto adopted by the Left Wing section of the Socialist party at that time.[16] "The Left Wing Manifesto" had been published in the *Revolutionary Age*, which was the official organ of the Left Wing.

Whether or not smoking opium, drinking alcohol, working in cigar factories, or publishing "The Left Wing Manifesto" actually endangers public health and welfare is not a matter this book can address. The key point, rather, is that as early as 1895 some members of the American judiciary wanted to see *evidence* of social harmfulness before accepting the validity of the police power in relation to some activity considered socially dangerous. This is why, for example, the state's lawyer in *Ritchie* v. *People* referred to textbooks which recognized "the propriety of regulations which forbid women to engage in certain kinds of work altogether"[17] and to an employment equality law that made an exception for women in the case of military service. The lawyer wanted to convince the court (albeit in a rather indirect way) that allowing women to work in factories, generally, posed a danger to their health, and by extension, to the public health.[18]

The judicial concern that a purported risk to society should be obviously discernable before it can be cited as a legitimate basis for infringing civil liberties has since arisen in Canada. It is addressed by what is called the "first branch" of the *Oakes* test, which asks whether the social problem meant to be redressed by the impugned legislation is sufficiently pressing and substantial to justify restricting otherwise constitutionally entrenched individual liberties and rights.

CANADA'S *OAKES* TEST AND THE "REASONABLE APPREHENSION OF HARM" DOCTRINE

The *Oakes* test is named after a 1986 Supreme Court of Canada decision which addressed the constitutionality of a so-called "reverse onus" clause embedded at that time in the *Narcotic Control Act*.[19] The Court held that a provision which required an accused person to disprove a material element of a charge against him or her was an unreasonable violation of the right to be presumed innocent until proven guilty, within the terms of section 11(d) of the *Charter of Rights and Freedoms*. For the present purpose, what is most important about the *Oakes* case is the test laid down by Chief Justice Dickson for determining the "reasonableness" (and hence constitutionality) of any government restriction of protected Charter rights and freedoms. Section 1 of the *Charter* permits governments to limit a person's exercise of guaranteed rights and freedoms "subject only to such reasonable limits prescribed by law as can be demonstrably justified in a free and democratic society." To determine whether any such restriction is reasonable in this sense, Dickson proposed that courts follow a two-fold approach. First, they must determine whether the legislative objective is sufficiently important to warrant overriding a constitutionally protected right or freedom.[20] Second, they must determine whether the legislative means chosen to achieve the objective are reasonable. As Dickson explains, this process involves three steps: "First, the measures adopted must be carefully designed to achieve the objective in question ... In short, they must be rationally connected to the objective. Second, the means ... should impair 'as little as possible' the right or freedom in question: *R. v. Big M Drug Mart Ltd., supra*, at p.352. Third, there must be a proportionality between the *effects* of the measures which are responsible for limiting the *Charter* right or freedom, and the objective which has been identified as of 'sufficient importance.'"[21]

So far the language of Dickson's analysis clearly echoes that of American judges interpreting the constitutionality of turn-of-the-century "police power" cases. Impugned governmental objectives must be "pressing" or "substantial," and the legislative means chosen must somehow be "rationally" connected or tailored to those objectives. However, Dickson departed from the American approach in some key respects. He held that the onus of proving the reasonableness of a limit rests *entirely* upon the party seeking to uphold the limit. American law is more complex here. Generally the onus of proving reasonableness is on the party challenging the constitutionality of a given law, yet the so-called presumption of constitutionality may be reversed, depending on the specific nature of the right at issue.[22] Dickson also proposed that the party defending the reasonableness of impugned legislation provide "cogent and persuasive" evidence to that effect. As Michael Peirce notes, however, this requirement has not been consistently followed at any particular stage of the *Oakes* test (Peirce 1994, 15). Indeed, Peirce cites some recent Supreme Court of Canada cases which suggest that the evidentiary requirement in section 1 analyses may be very low (17).

What is consistently held in post-*Oakes* constitutional reviews is the notion that evidence is admissible *not* to demonstrate that societal health and welfare is *actually* at risk from a particular activity, but only to inform the "reasonableness" of Parliament's belief in this regard. Evidence can be tendered, therefore, simply to support or to undermine the soundness or cogency of an already existing legislative presumption that a certain social harm, danger, or "evil" exists and is effectively redressed by the legislation being challenged. This principle, which was first formally enunciated in Canada by Justice Bora Laskin,[23] may be conveniently referred to as the "reasonable apprehension of harm" doctrine.

Elsewhere, I have reviewed the way Canadian courts have applied the reasonable apprehension of harm doctrine to a number of significant constitutional cases (Nowlin 1999). In this book, I consider three recent cases involving constitutional challenges to Canada's obscenity law. These are *Butler*, a 1992 case addressed to hard-core, heterosexual pornography; *Little Sister's*, a 1994 court challenge to Canada Customs' detentions of gay and lesbian pornography; and *Sharpe*, a 1998 prosecution that involved a challenge to Canada's child pornography law.

The 1992 *Butler* case began with the prosecution of a Winnipeg video-retailer for selling obscene materials, contrary to section 163 of Canada's *Criminal Code*. When the defendant argued that his right to free expression was unduly restricted by the law, the government presented the Supreme Court of Canada with social science evidence purporting to establish a causal relation between exposure to certain kinds of pornography and sexist behaviour and attitudes.[24] Having considered this evidence, Justice Sopinka stated that

the rational link between s.163 and the objective of Parliament relates to the actual causal relationship between obscenity and the risk of harm to society at large. On this point, it is clear that the literature of the social sciences remains subject to controversy. In *Fringe Product Inc., supra*, Charron Dist. Ct. J. considered numerous written reports and works and heard six days of testimony from experts who endeavoured to describe the status of the social sciences with respect to the study of the effects of pornography. Charron Dist. Ct. J. reached the conclusion that the relationship between pornography and harm was sufficient to justify Parliament's intervention. This conclusion is not supported unanimously ... The recent conclusions of the Fraser Report, *supra*, could not postulate any causal relationship between pornography and the commission of violent crimes, the sexual abuse of children, or the disintegration of communities and society. This is in contrast to the findings of the

MacGuigan Report, *supra* ... While a direct link between obscenity and harm to society may be difficult, if not impossible, to establish, it is reasonable to presume that exposure to images. bears a causal relationship to changes in attitudes and beliefs ...[25]

This analysis clearly accepts that the social science literature regarding the psychological and behavioural effects of pornography at that time was controversial, yet it still maintains the "reasonableness" of presuming a cause and effect relationship between pornographic images and attitudes and beliefs. One can only wonder how it is reasonable to presume that some kind of empirical relationship exists when there is so much controversy among similarly and relevantly trained and informed groups of people.[26] Perhaps it is simply the case, as suggested by the Supreme Court of Canada's judgment, that this presumption is also a matter of common sense or basic "logic," such that any conclusion to the contrary should simply be regarded as "surprising."[27]

In 1994, Little Sister's Book and Art Emporium (LSBAE) in Vancouver challenged Canada Customs's practice of "targeting" for inspection, and ultimately seizing and detaining, certain kinds of gay and lesbian erotic and pornographic publications.[28] The LSBAE lawyers introduced a great deal of social science (or legislative-fact) evidence designed to show that, in effect, the government had misunderstood a certain aspect of their social life and had legislated in respect of that area unconstitutionally. In particular, much expert and lay evidence was introduced to demonstrate that the production, consumption, and publication of gay and lesbian erotica and pornography, including sadomasochistic narratives and imagery, is not socially harmful or properly "obscene"; on the contrary, it is socially and culturally affirming as far as Canadian gay and lesbian communities are concerned. The thrust of the plaintiffs' argument was that should the court accept the idea that gay and lesbian pornography and erotica are not "obscene" within the terms of the *Criminal Code* and *Customs Tariff Act*, then the court must find that the practice of seizing such materials by Canada Customs pursuant to the relevant *Criminal Code* provisions is unauthorized and, in turn, unlawful.[29]

The federal government introduced hardly any legislative-fact evidence in reply to the plaintiffs' claim that gay and lesbian pornography and erotica have been historically misunderstood by the heterosexual community at large. It unsuccessfully sought to admit an article by a legal scholar which argued that the production and consumption of gay pornography posed social dangers similar to those associated with the production and consumption of heterosexual pornography.[30]

The government also filed a report by a prominent psychologist, Neil Malamuth, which argued in support of the generalizability of prior research findings regarding the psychological and behavioural effects of reading or watching heterosexual pornography to the effects associated with reading or watching gay and lesbian pornography.[31]

Despite the vast, interdisciplinary collage of expert and lay opinion presented by the plaintiffs – to the effect that the impugned homosexual erotic materials were central to the formation of positive social and cultural identities among gay and lesbians – Justice Smith found that Malamuth's laboratory-based opinion supported Parliament's "reasonable apprehension that obscene pornography produced for homosexual audiences causes harm to society."[32] Chapter 5 reviews much of this evidence in detail and discusses how Smith's finding has since been appealed all the way to the Supreme Court of Canada and accepted there.

In 1998 a retired civil servant, John Robin Sharpe, argued before the British Columbia Supreme Court that Canada's child pornography law unduly restricted his right to free expression and unjustly discriminated against him. The government responded with expert testimony from a police officer and a forensic psychiatrist, Peter Collins, purporting to link the possession and distribution of child pornography to increased risks of child exploitation and abuse. Justice Shaw appeared to accept much of this evidence as support for the reasonableness of Canada's child pornography law except as the law related to the private possession of child pornography produced exclusively from the creator's own imagination.

Shaw's ruling was appealed to the British Columbia Court of Appeal, where Madam Justice Rowles recognized that social science evidence purporting to establish certain "indirect" dangers of child pornography was inconclusive, and that "the debate on some of these issues has existed among behavioural scientists for many years and it is very likely to continue in the future."[33] Despite the inconclusive and perhaps contentious nature of this issue, Rowles held that the government succeeded in showing a "reasoned apprehension of harm" to children "resulting both from the potential use of child pornography by paedophiles and from the desensitization of society to the use of children as sexual objects."[34] The same could not be said, however, in relation to works possessed personally and produced from "the imagination" alone. In this context, Rowles reviewed both the expert testimony of the clinical psychologist, Collins, and the well-worn pages of Canada's *Badgley Report* and *Fraser Report*. She concluded that the available social science evidence was insufficient to show that the federal government's belief that private possession of child pornographic works of the imagination are indirectly dangerous to children was "reasoned."[35]

Shaw's and Rowles's approaches to the reasonable apprehension of harm issue in the *Sharpe* case have since been more or less accepted by a majority of the Supreme Court of Canada. Chapter 5 reviews the salient, evidentiary aspects of this case, as it proceeded from the trial stage to the Supreme Court of Canada's final ruling. The cumulative analysis of Canada's more recent obscenity cases will have shown, by this point in the book, that for most Canadian judges, *some* or *any* expert evidence purporting to link a particular activity (or "cause") with a broader social problem (or "effect") – however controversial or inconclusive that evidence might be – is enough to support Parliament's "reasonable apprehension of harm" about the problem in question.

For the moment, having reviewed the basic doctrines that govern the reception of evidence in American and Canadian constitutional reviews, it is worth taking a close look at the kind of evidence upon which governments rely when their laws are challenged in court. The following discussion shows that this evidence tends to be comprised of social science research conclusions and implications and has been legally typologised in both America and Canada as "legislative-fact" or "constitutional-fact" evidence. Although legislative-fact issues are by no means formally attached to obscenity prosecutions in general, most expert evidence introduced into American and Canadian obscenity prosecutions bears directly or indirectly upon the very issues of legislative-fact evidence that are raised in constitutional challenges to obscenity laws: Do these laws prevent the corruption of morals? Do they manage to curb misogynous attitudes or even violence toward women and children? An examination of the sources and nature of legislative-fact evidence, especially about pornography, will show why judges find this evidence to be inconclusive, debatable, or controversial. It will also lend support to this book's controversial claim that, in the final analysis, expert evidence about obscenity is not particularly edifying or cost-beneficial.

LEGISLATIVE-FACT EVIDENCE: AN INTRODUCTION

In 1942 Kenneth Culp Davis made a distinction between "adjudicative" and "legislative" facts that he thought could be useful in administrative law. He said, "When an [administrative] agency finds facts concerning immediate parties – what the parties did, what the circumstances were, what the background conditions were – the agency is performing an adjudicative function, and the facts may conveniently be called adjudicative facts. When an agency wrestles with a question of law or policy, it is acting legislatively ... and the facts which inform its legislative judgment may conveniently be denominated legislative facts" (Davis 1942, 402).

If, for example, in the course of adjudicating a dispute between a group of dairy producers and the state department of agriculture, an administrative tribunal had difficulty interpreting a specific provision in the applicable law, say *The Dairy Producers' Act*, then it might take into account various socio-economic conditions surrounding dairy production in the region that are purported to have originally informed the law or have since been affected by the law's implementation. These surrounding circumstances – perhaps an observed lack of uniformity in the quality of milk produced by competing dairies which affects the physical health or economic welfare of some segment of the consuming public – would become the legislative facts that the tribunal discerns to inform its understanding of the broader purpose or spirit of the governing law. Once the tribunal has made a careful determination of legislative intent in this sense, it is in a better position to adjudicate the more narrow issue(s) between the parties to the litigation by applying the law to the particular facts or circumstances immediately surrounding the dispute. These latter kinds of facts are Davis's "adjudicative facts."

Although Davis was writing in regard to the decision-making processes of administrative tribunals, his distinction has been widely used by courts confronted with constitutional challenges. Even before Davis distinguished legislative facts from adjudicative facts, the former were being considered by America's judiciary in the arena of constitutional review. There judges sought out similar kinds of broad social and economic facts or phenomena in order to assess the "reasonableness" of a law argued to be in violation of a specific, constitutionally entrenched right or freedom. Of course, issues of "adjudicative fact" will not normally be heard by an appellate, or reviewing court, because such issues are for trial courts to resolve; thereafter they are reviewable only under certain circumstances.[36] On the other hand, "questions of law or policy" are typically the very substance of an appellate court's mandate, and questions of "policy" are especially the substance of constitutional review. Therefore, issues of legislative fact tend to arise at an appellate level of legal decision-making, and legislative-fact evidence itself may well be tendered at this stage: there is, however, no legal principle or tradition which bars the admissibility of legislative-fact evidence at a trial which involves constitutional considerations.[37]

Although the idea of "wrestling" with a question of law or policy may not be very precise or clear, it seems Davis has in mind the picture of a judge struggling with the interpretation of some law that is relevant to the proceedings before her. Again, the judge is encouraged in this case to seek and determine relevant social and economic "facts" which, though not directly related to the specific interests of the litigating parties, may inform the broader meaning, intent, purpose, and perhaps practical effect of the law under review. The judge may want to, or even be expected to, consult one or more extra-legal opinions about such matters. And to the extent that such a fact-finding process may well contribute to a new formulation of an extant law, the process may properly be called "legislative" as opposed to "adjudicative." In this respect, the judge may be seen fairly to have struggled with a question of policy as much as with law.

Katherine Swinton has analysed the different uses of legislative-fact evidence in American civil rights cases. In light of this history, Swinton has correctly observed that in the context of constitutional litigation, evidence tendered to demonstrate certain "adjudicative" facts, especially the denial or infringement of a constitutional right, may well be the kind traditionally associated with legislative facts (Swinton 1987, 189, n.6). Swinton cites and briefly discusses the United States Supreme Court decision *Brown* v. *Board of Education* as a good case in point. In this case, some black (or at that time, "Negro") schoolchildren challenged the power of the Topeka Board of Education to establish segregated elementary schools, pursuant to a Kansas statute which permitted, but did not require, cities of more than 15,000 residents to maintain separate school facilities for Negro and White students. The plaintiffs presented social and psychological evidence to the effect that segregated education negatively affected the self-esteem of young black students and was therefore discriminatory. The evidence was presented in the form of a comprehensive social science opinion statement prepared by lawyers for the National Association for the Advancement of Colored People Legal Defense Fund, in collaboration with a small team of professional social scientists, and signed by thirty-two fellow "experts" in areas of sociology, anthropology, psychology, and psychiatry (Kohn 1960, 151–3; Cahn 1956, 157).[38] Chief Justice Warren did not refer to "The Social Science Statement" in his written judgment, but he did list several books and articles written by social scientists in a footnote and referred to these as "modern authority" concerning the psychological effects of segregation on black school children.[39] These included Kenneth B. Clark's *Effect of Prejudice and Discrimination on Personality Development*, and Deutscher and Chein's article, "The Psychological Effects of Enforced Segregation: A Survey of Social Science Opinion." Even though "The Social Science Statement" itself might not have been given much weight by the Supreme Court, Swinton observes that it was introduced to demonstrate the infringement of a constitutionally entrenched right to equality, which must clearly be considered an "adjudicative" (as opposed to "legislative") matter in Davis's sense of the word.

Legislative-fact evidence has also been used in Davis's "adjudicative" sense in Canadian administrative law. In *Mossop*, a case heard before a Federal Human Rights Tribunal, a sociological definition of "family" was introduced to help resolve a discrimination claim. Mr Mossop, the plaintiff, had applied for bereavement leave pursuant to a collective agreement made between the Treasury Board of Canada and his union. His employer, the Department of the Secretary of State, rejected his application on the basis that the individual whose funeral Mossop had attended was not a member of Mossop's "immediate family." That individual was the father of Mossop's male lover of over ten years. The collective agreement provided for bereavement leave where the bereaved employee was related to the deceased through a common law spousal relationship, but this relationship was restricted to members of the opposite sex. Accordingly, Mossop sought to have the agreement's notion of common law spouse widened to include same-sex couples.

Margrit Eichler, who was qualified as an expert witness in the area of sociology and family policy, provided opinion evidence to the effect that "family" could denote, and has historically denoted, different kinds of human relationships, depending on the function or purpose ascribed to the family unit within a given society. This evidence was largely accepted by the tribunal adjudicator: indeed it assisted her directly in her determination that the *Canada Human Rights Act* discriminated against the plaintiff by denying him a benefit provided to others pursuant to the act.

Since Davis created the expression "legislative facts," many interpretations of the concept have been suggested. In Canada, Hogg has construed legislative facts as "facts of a more general character relating to the social or economic conditions which gave rise to the legislation" (Hogg 1976, 408). More recently, the Supreme Court of Canada has remarked, "Legislative facts are those that establish the purpose and background of legislation, including its social, economic and cultural context. Such facts are of a more general nature, and are subject to less stringent admissibility requirements."[40]

Manfredi provides a more detailed definition. He says that legislative facts are about causal relationships and about the "recurrent patterns of behavior" on which policy decisions are based (Manfredi 1993, 166; footnotes omitted). Similarly, the American legal scholar Woolhandler has observed that "legislative facts are used to create law ... There is less a sense that legislative facts are true and knowable because such facts are predictions, and, moreover, typically predictions about the relative importance of one factor in causing a complex phenomenon" (Woolhandler 1988, 114).[41]

Before addressing what the Supreme Court of Canada recognized to be the relaxed "admissibility requirements" of legislative-fact evidence, it is useful to focus on the observations of Manfredi and Woolhandler about the causal element of legislative facts.[42] This is a very important consideration, yet one that tends to be overlooked in most of the relevant literature. Besides being germane to the issue of "reasonableness" discussed earlier, this matter relates to the notions of reliability and helpfulness associated with the admissibility standards, or requirements, of expert-based legislative-fact evidence.

Woolhandler explains, "A legislative fact provides evidence of the importance of one particular factor in causing a complex phenomenon. The scientist or social scientist asks a question and interprets data based on a pre-existing hypothesis about causation; this is true even for the hard sciences and especially true for *the soft sciences, which typically serve as the source for legislative facts*" (Woolhandler 1988, 119; emphasis added). Indeed, as the analysis in this book unfolds, it will become clear that legislative-fact evidence from the so-called "soft sciences" – economics, sociology, psychology, criminology, and others – routinely purports to inform American and Canadian courts about causal relationships.

For example, when the constitutional validity of two provisions of Quebec's *Consumer Protection Act* was challenged in the *Irwin Toy* case, Quebec's attorney general was required to show that the purported objective of the legislation in question was "pressing and substantial." To this end the government introduced various materials ranging from a Canadian Radio-Television and Telecommunication Commission's Decision to a number of published advertising industry guidelines and regulations which mostly expressed concern with the impact of television advertising on children.[43] Moreover, the attorney general was allowed to introduce a report commissioned by the United States government, *In the Matter of Children's Advertising*, which presumably contained a thorough review of the scientific evidence to date on this subject.[44] It is not necessary here to evaluate the so-called "validity" or "reliability" of any of this legislative-fact evidence. It is important to note only that the scientific component of this evidence purports to explain the causal relationship or "recurrent pattern of behavior" with which the impugned legislation is concerned. In other words, the objective of protecting children from the allegedly manipulative nature of television advertising is based on the idea that exposure by young children to television advertising aimed at them does in fact have a unique psychological effect upon them. In the words of the report itself, children "place indiscriminate trust in the selling message."[45] This example illustrates that what underlies most legislative-fact evidence is a broad causal assumption about human psychology and behaviour.

Another good example of the causal assumption underlying legislative-fact evidence in Canadian constitutional law is provided by the *R. v. Butler* case. This case concerned the constitutional validity of section 163(8) of the Canadian *Criminal Code*, a provision which makes culpable the publication and dissemination of obscene materials. In order to demonstrate the importance of the provision's legislative objective – interpreted as the prevention of social harm to women and children via the prohibition of publishing and disseminating obscene materials – the federal government introduced some government committee reports on the subject of pornography as well as evidence of Canada's international legal commitments in this area. Again, however, the issue arose regarding the broader social and psychological relationship implicit in the government's decision to pursue its objective by criminal prohibition. In this case the relationship was argued to be the alleged psychological and behavioural effect upon people who read or watch pornographic materials. Accordingly, much empirical social science–research evidence was introduced that either supported or challenged the validity of this broad causal proposition.[46]

Although in constitutional litigation in the area of pornography or obscenity law the social harmfulness of pornography is primarily perceived in causal terms – for example, as corruptive of morals, or as promoting misogyny – much of the relevant social science research maintains an overly simplistic view of pornography's harmfulness. Just as it is entirely feasible that pornography contributes causally to (helps to shape) sexist attitudes in broader society, it is equally possible that pornography is merely a symptom of the broader problem, and not, as it were, a contributing cause of the problem itself. The report of the Meese Commission into pornography seems to be contradictory in this regard. It insists that exposure to certain kinds of pornography bears some causal relation to misogynistic behaviour and attitudes among readers, and at the same time observes that "some of the consequences that concern us here are caused as well, and perhaps to a greater extent, by other stimuli" (*Attorney General's Commission on Pornography: Final Report*, 1986, 311).[47] Indeed, it is very possible that if the *Final Report's* own test for causality were used – eliminating exposure to pornography while keeping "everything else ... the same" (assuming such a controlled experiment could ever be achieved) – the kind of psychological and social harms identified by the report would not be "lessened" (310). The Meese Commission's approach to this problem is particularly problematic because the commission admits that its conclusion about there being a causal link between pornography and social dangerousness is a matter of practicality, which does not broach the "larger," perhaps "pervasive and intractable" causes of harmful and hateful attitudes to women observable in North American society (311). This concession illustrates Woolhandler's claim that a legislative fact "provides evidence of the importance of *one* particular factor in causing a *complex* factor." Her point is that legislative-fact evidence introduced in constitutional litigation tends to be overly simplistic or skewed insofar as it claims to explain complex social problems on the basis of a single "independent" variable (such as school segregation or pornography) – a variable which is itself selected on the basis of a prevalent ideology about society or humanity.[48]

Cases such as *Irwin Toy* and *Butler* (and, as will be explained below, the American cases *Muller* v. *Oregon* and *Brown* v. *Board of Education*) are important because they nicely illustrate the range of evidence that a court may be asked to consider under the rubric "legislative fact." From this point forward, this book concerns itself primarily with the social science research which informs the various government committee reports and expert opinion evidence introduced in North American obscenity prosecutions and in constitutional reviews of anti-obscenity legislation. As already discussed, in cases of the latter type, the social science research is used to demonstrate the reasonableness or lack thereof of Parliament's belief that publishing and consuming pornography contributes to one or more pressing social "evils." However, in trial level obscenity prosecutions, the same kind of research may be introduced in court to provide what Monahan, Walker, and others have called "social framework" evidence (Monahan and Walker 1988, 1991, 1994; Vidmar and Schuller 1989; Paciocco 1995), and what Monahan and Walker in particular have called "social fact" evidence (Monahan and Walker 1988). For Monahan and Walker, a certain social science research conclusion can be treated as a matter of social fact if it involves a particular application of a recognized social science methodology, the result being a matter of "fact" which bears no necessary relevance "beyond the particular case for which it was intended" (ibid., 469). Monahan and Walker have in mind here the use of social science surveys in trademark cases to help a court determine the consuming public's ability to distinguish between competing products. Yet they also refer in this context to the use of an opinion survey about community standards of tolerance in an obscenity case.

In chapters 3 through 6, the discussion of the different kinds of expert evidence that have been presented in American and Canadian obscenity adjudication will point out these different uses of social science. For the moment, however, it is worth raising a general epistemological question: do the social science research conclusions and other kinds of information that enter into court to assist in the finding of legislative and social facts ultimately amount to matters of fact, or are they all so much a matter of opinion and argumentation? To shed some light on this problem, this book now revisits Woolhandler briefly, and introduces the unique philosophical perspective of Ludwig Wittgenstein.

WITTGENSTEIN AND WOOLHANDLER: LEGISLATIVE FACTS ARE MORE ARGUMENTATIVE THAN FACTUAL

Various constitutionally significant cases have been reviewed so far to show how contentious the legislative-fact evidence presented in those cases is, and to show how the prevailing wisdom (of the experts) relating to specific legislative-fact issues can change dramatically in relatively short periods of time. Elsewhere I have criticized the view that such evidence should ever be treated as legally authoritative (Nowlin 2001), and the discussion so far should lend some support to Woolhandler's view that legislative facts are too complex to be considered "true or knowable" (Woolhandler 1988, 114).

Nevertheless, a different point of view is held by Monahan and Walker who expect that some social science experiments will yield more plausible results than others (Monahan and Walker 1991, 579–80), and by Donnerstein, Linz, and Penrod who share the admittedly "utopian and perhaps naive hope" that "in the end *the truth* [about pornography and its effects] revealed through good science will prevail" (Donnerstein, Linz, and Penrod 1987, 196; emphasis added). As is explained in chapter 2, this point of view seems to be shared by those judges who believe legislative-fact evidence should be generously received as it increases the potential for greater "accuracy" in constitutional decision-making. And more accuracy is supposed to enhance the so-called "legitimacy" of the quasi-political role judges play in constitutional reviews. In contrast, Woolhandler flatly contests the assumption that legislative-fact evidence contributes to the accuracy of the judicial fact-finding process. Again, she says, "The reason lies in the nature of legislative facts." These are "by their nature disputable" because they are predictive and, as already explained, "governed by pre-existing presumptions about desirable effects and their causes" which are overly simplistic or reductionistic (Woolhandler 1988, 123).[49]

Monahan and Walker argue astutely that the kinds of constitutional facts relied on by governments to support the reasonableness of their legislative schemes are more properly characterized as epistemological "assumptions," grounded in empirical research, that may subsequently be proven "implausible," depending on the nature or quality of empirical research introduced in evidence to challenge them. The challenger who introduces such research into evidence must not be seen as concerned directly with the determination of "facts," but with the epistemological plausibility of the government's legislative assumptions; thus, he or she is more properly engaged in a process of "argument," not fact-finding in the traditional sense of the word (Monahan and Walker 1991, 585).[50]

It is very important to recognize that the working assumptions behind legislative and social facts do not necessarily have any basis in fact or in experimentation. On the contrary, they are "closely tied" to what Woolhandler calls "one's beliefs about desirable effects" (Woolhandler 1988, 119). If the social science community believes, for example, that women should not work alongside men outside the home, and should instead stay home, and bear and raise children there, it will be more inclined to view women's work in industrial laundries or factories as somehow diminishing women's capacity to bear healthy children and maintain a proper home. This is the gist of much of the social science evidence presented by Louis Brandeis in *Muller* v. *Oregon*, which is discussed in chapter 3. Similarly, if the social science community believes that women should not be viewed or treated by men as sexual and social inferiors, it will look for evidence or situations in society where women *appear to* be so viewed or mistreated, such as in some kinds of pornography, and construe such phenomena as somehow contributing to the broader problem. The concluding paragraph of Donnerstein, Linz, and Penrod's *The Question of Pornography* is particularly apt in this regard. It reads:

Throughout this book we have attempted to approach the topic of violence against women in the media as objectively as possible. But as men, husbands, significant others, and fathers, *let us leave the reader with no doubt that we are personally and morally deeply offended by many of the media depictions of women we have described in this book.* We have undertaken our investigations both because we are intellectually curious about the effects of exposure to pornography and other images of women in the media, *and because we are concerned about the negative impact of these materials on the members of our society* – particularly our fellow male members (Donnerstein, Linz, and Penrod 1987, 196; emphasis added).[51]

Woolhandler's analysis of judicially received legislative-fact evidence is particularly germane here because it implies that such evidence usually takes the form of *argument*, and ultimately argument based on norms. Moreover, it invites serious consideration of Wittgenstein's broader observation that "argument" is not simply an intellectual exercise but is also a matter of everyday experience or practical living. That is to say, for Wittgenstein, the strength of an argument depends on its consistency in language with one's mundane life experience, as he explains in the following two paragraphs:

All testing, all confirmation and disconfirmation of a hypothesis takes place already within a system. And this system is not a more or less arbitrary and doubtful point of departure for all our arguments: no, it belongs to the essence of what we call an argument. The system is not so much the point of departure, as the element in which arguments have their life (Wittgenstein 1979, 16e, prop'n 105).

Giving grounds, ... justifying the evidence, comes to an end; – but the end is not certain propositions' striking us immediately as true, i.e. it is not a kind of *seeing* on our part; it is our *acting*, which lies at the bottom of the language-game (28e, prop'n 204).

In other words, Wittgenstein's belief "system" has behaviour as its source. Wittgenstein writes:

"An empirical proposition can be *tested*" (we say). But how? and through what?

What *counts* as its test? – "But is this an adequate test?" And, if so, must it not be recognizable as such in logic?" – As if giving grounds did not come to end sometime. But the end is not an ungrounded presupposition: it is an ungrounded way of acting (17e, prop'ns 109, 110).

For Wittgenstein, "[a]ll testing, all confirmation and disconfirmation of a hypothesis" is part and parcel of the nature of a broader "argument" which is settled ultimately or "comes to end" *not* by reference to intellectual constructions or "presuppositions," but by reference to everyday, mundane behaviour (16e, prop'n 105).

Human behaviour is itself governed by "rules," however implicit or even unclear, but remains "ungrounded" for Wittgenstein in the sense that people cannot be expected to provide satisfactory or comprehensive explanations for all of their behavioural tendencies, although natural and social scientists seem to aspire to such understanding. Wittgenstein asks, "Why do I not satisfy myself that I have two feet when I want to get up from a chair? There is no why. I simply don't.

This is how I act" (22e, prop'n 148). Likewise, the math teacher proceeds on the assumption that a + b = b + a, and the construction worker goes about her tasks on the assumption that concrete and steel are capable of supporting floors and ceilings. If either person begins to doubt or question their respective assumptions, they will become unable realistically to carry out their required tasks. The math teacher who seeks to explain her belief that a + b = b + a must ultimately leave the domain of mathematics proper and enter the worlds of logic, language, and perhaps philosophy (which also revolve around intellectually "ungrounded" presuppositions),[52] just as the construction worker who seeks to explain her belief in the physical properties and capabilities of concrete and steel will become a physicist and cease to be a construction worker. Similarly, as Cardozo observes of the process of judicial decision-making, in some cases a judge is simply forced to choose between principles "that shape the genesis and growth of law" (Cardozo 1924, 78). A judge may prefer history to logic, or history to custom, or "all [of these] to justice or utility as constituents of the social welfare," but this preference itself will not necessarily bear some kind of explanation beyond the mere fact that it is customary for judges to approach decision-making in that way (78–9).

Wittgenstein's approach to knowledge is concerned with the way language is used in different social contexts (such as in math class or on a construction site), such that it becomes possible to make "sense" of certain propositions by analysing their relative logical function within particular conceptual or linguistic systems. The linguistic systems or "language games" peculiar to the natural sciences and social sciences typically involve notions of verifiability, falsifiability, validity, reliability, predictability, accuracy, objectivity, and indeed certainty. Law has always been concerned with predictability and certainty, but it has borrowed notions of accuracy and objectivity from the physical and social sciences. Wittgenstein's theory of knowledge suggests that in social life generally there are many ways of knowing beyond those of the social sciences, and that, more particularly, one disciplinary knowledge-claim cannot claim any more cogency or plausibility than another by referring back exclusively to its own terms or intellectual "presuppositions."

For the moment it is important to note that, on their surface, legislative facts introduced into court do purport to be "facts," not arguments, although it is clear they are really opinions (educated or otherwise) based on many unexamined assumptions. Karst speaks in this sense of the "argumentative" character of expert-based, adjudicative-legislative fact testimony, which "rests on a chain of debatable inferences based on standards of the expert's own selection" (Karst 1960, 102; footnote omitted). Miller and Barron question references to the "facts" on contraception, abortion, and unwanted births contained in various briefs presented to the United States Supreme Court in *Roe v. Wade*. They remark that these are "legislative facts, often presented *at a level of flat assertion* unaccompanied by supporting data" (Miller and Barron 1975, 1203; emphasis added). According to Dworkin, the solicitor general's brief presented to the United States Supreme Court in *State of Washington et al. v. Glucksberg et al.* and in *Vacco et al. v. Quill et al.* did not attempt to show how regulatory schemes drafted to enable physician-assisted suicide in limited circumstances would be "porous" or "ineffective"; instead the brief relied "mainly on flat and conclusory statements" to that effect (Dworkin, Nagel et al. 1997, 46). Even the findings of the New York Task Force Report on the subject that it cited have been, according to Dworkin, "widely disputed" (ibid.).[53] In any case, Dworkin's own thoughtful discussion of the overall evidentiary significance of the empirical data and public opinion information introduced in his recent United States Supreme Court constitutional review clearly demonstrates how much more argumentative than factual the contents of these Brandeis-style briefs are.[54] The alleged facts in all of the above cases are admittedly controversial, so the judicial practice of rhetorically drawing lines between "fact" and "opinion" or "argument" is simply spurious.

Unfortunately, not only the judiciary but lawyers and legal scholars too continue to use the distinction between fact-based *opinion* and opinion-based *argument*. Karst quotes, for example, an American judge's scholarly opinion regarding expert evidence which has "primarily an argumentative character" (Karst 1960, 101; quoting Wyzanski 1952, 1296). Canadian courts have always distinguished between evidentiary opinion and legal argument or "advocacy." In the *Little Sister's* case, for example, a government lawyer sought to have an expert's legislative-fact opinion excluded on the basis that it was rooted in the expert's experience as a political activist and thus was likely to constitute a "thinly-disguised argument" as opposed to an epistemologically dispassionate – that is, legally proper – "expert opinion."[55] In the arena of constitutional law and legislative facts, however, this distinction between dispassionate, expert or "scientific" opinion and partisan argument must be abandoned. It is not a matter of some experts being more or less "biased" in the presentation of otherwise epistemologically "neutral" or "objective" information. *Most* witnesses in constitutional litigation have definite political interests, and *most* legislative fact information is compiled and prepared by recognizable social interest groups in consultation with lawyers. The overtly political and perhaps ideological character of much of the social science expertise in constitutional contests, combined with the inexactitude, tentativeness, and "inherent subjectivity that social science unavoidably involves" (Miller and Barron 1975, 1240), cries out for a reevaluation of the opinion/ argument dichotomy in this legal realm. Analyses of American and Canadian obscenity case law in this book demonstrate that all legislative-fact or social science evidence presented to courts by experts has been more argumentative than factual, although the courts appear to have treated the evidence more typically as establishing facts. This tendency has been troublesome insofar as it has perpetuated a myth which has legitimately enabled certain "bodies of knowledge" to inform constitutional decision-making at the expense of others.

The highly tentative and argumentative nature of legislative-fact evidence is not necessarily problematic in itself, but judges who are presented with such evidence, either in the form of official government reports, legal briefs, or through the oral testimony of experts, can be prone to give it too much credibility and weight. Where this has occurred in relation to so-called "social framework" evidence, Paciocco has astutely observed that judges have effectively delegated their "decision making function" to social scientists (Paciocco 1995, 4).[56] Paciocco's concern is echoed by Karst in an American context. Karst maintains, "A judge without special training finds it hard to criticize an expert's methods of gathering data or the inferences he draws from them. Yet experts are fallible." More important, Karst is aware that, at times, experts effectively "help the courts make policy" although the experts' own attitudes "on the ultimate policy issues" may well be concealed (Karst 1960, 105). Even where the judge and broader community share the same political leanings or "attitudes" or, to use Woolhandler's idiom, desire the same ends, deference to social scientific expertise undermines the judge's proper function in constitutional review: this occurs where a narrow and fairly unreliable body of opinion becomes clearly substituted for the so-called "wisdom" of the legislature, which is presumably informed by a greater variety of opinion. Justice Souter made precisely this point in the recent United States Supreme Court constitutional review of New York and Washington State anti–self-assisted suicide laws (Dworkin 1997, 42). Following a review of the aforementioned "Philosopher's Brief" on this subject, which itself canvassed statewide survey or opinion evidence, and cited international comparisons relating to government regulation of self-assisted suicide, Souter declined to declare such laws unconstitutional. He did not see it as his proper role in constitutional review to make such decisions based on recognizably controversial findings of legislative fact, especially when legislatures have access to more extensive resources for assessing these kinds of fact than judges (Dworkin, Nagel et al. 1997, 41, 46; Dworkin 1997, 42).

All of these considerations suggest that the historical relaxation of rules for admitting legislative-fact evidence in Canada is wrongheaded and that the proper course of action is for judges to be more critically "vigilant" (Paciocco 1995, 1)[57] or at least "interventionist" (Roberts 1996, 97).[58] For her part, Madam Justice McLachlin of the Supreme Court of Canada recommended this approach in *RJR-MacDonald Inc. v. Canada (A.G.)*, where she urged courts not to be deferential "to the point of accepting Parliament's view simply on the basis that the problem is serious and the solution difficult." Cahn made a similar argument with respect to the use of Brandeis-style briefs in America generally,[59] and specifically with respect to the use of social psychology testimony in constitutional review cases. As regards the latter, he points out that "the court testimony of social psychologists is concerned not so much with individual as with public issues. Hence, if accepted uncritically, it can cause immense public harm" (Cahn 1956, 183).

The potential here for harm lies in the real possibility that unreliable, oversimplified, and politically-interested social science information will "dominate" the legislative fact-finding process (Karst 1960, 106) and mostly serve as the primary intellectual basis for constitutional law reform. In other words, the opinions of a *few* specialists, representing *particular* group interests, may establish legal precedent that affects *all* citizens' rights and freedoms. Dworkin expresses the same concern in his analysis of Souter's opinion about the constitutionality of laws prohibiting assisted suicide in Washington State and New York. He says:

the question whether a factual issue is too difficult or uncertain for judges to decide, so that they ought to defer to legislative decisions for that reason, is itself a complex and difficult one, and the courts should answer it only after very careful review of the evidence, particularly when putatively fundamental rights of individual citizens are at stake. Careful review would seem particularly crucial, moreover, in the assisted suicide debate, because many of the social scientists who have compiled the relevant evidence have strong ethical opinions, including religious convictions, or convictions about proper medical ethics, that might impair their scientific independence (Dworkin 1997, 42–3).

The real potential for harm in this sense can be gleaned by looking closely at the recent *Little Sister's* case. I have attempted to show elsewhere how Justice Smith's apparently uncritical acceptance of much of the plaintiffs' expert evidence resulted in a stereotype of Canadian gay and lesbian people that could be detrimental to them in future legal contests (Nowlin 1996). A similar danger involving women's political and legal interests can be viewed by casting the historical spotlight much farther back to the turn of the century when, in *Muller v. Oregon*, social scientists largely informed the constitutionality of an employment law which clearly had an impact on women. As chapter 3 shows, this legal decision may have been heralded as a victory for some women working in Oregon laundromats, but it would be difficult to say that it was similarly perceived by all working women at that time, and for any women today. In light of such concerns, the message to be heard from a historical and critical analysis of the relevant American and Canadian case law is not that social science and other forms of highly technical or expert information should be judicially ignored, but rather that it should be accepted "with the skepticism which properly attends activity on scientific frontiers" (Karst 1960, 107). A healthy skepticism in this regard will probably result in a slower process of law reform, at least as this process occurs through constitutional review, but where fundamental rights and freedoms of all citizens are at stake, judges need to be careful.

Before observing different judges' responses to the kind of sociological and psychological information presented to them in early obscenity cases and constitutional reviews, the implications for constitutionalism of the very tradition of relying upon expertise in such cases need to be considered. Since the enactment of the *Charter of Rights and Freedoms*, Canadian judges also need to consider the democratic nature of government in Canadian society when they make determinations of legislative fact. The next chapter attempts to show just where and how Canadian judges have acted democratically in this regard.

2

Progressivism and Legislative Facts in the Shaping of Public Policy

Anyone who has ever served as an expert witness in a judicial proceeding knows that the court may spend an inordinate time "qualifying" the expert, who, once qualified, gives testimony that is not meant to be a persuasive argument, but an assertion unchallengeable by anyone except another expert. And, indeed, what else are the courts to do? If the judges, attorneys, and jury could reason out the technical issues from fundamentals, there would be no need of experts ... What is at stake here is a deep problem in democratic self-governance. Lewontin 1997, 32

Freedom is too crucial to leave to the value judgments of any elite.
Borovoy 1988, 186

HISTORICAL OVERVIEW OF EXPERTISE AT COMMON LAW

A cursory historical review of the role of expertise in courtroom decision-making indicates that common law judges maintained a fairly cooperative relationship with experts until the dawn of the twentieth century. Freckleton recalls that as early as the Middle Ages "special juries" or "struck juries" comprising experts were used by courts as an important means of acquiring expert assistance (Freckelton 1987, 232). Justice M.D. Kirby notes that judges in England were generally receptive or hospitable to experts as early as the sixteenth century (ix). In the early eighteenth century litigants were entitled to use their own special juries to try issues at bar or upon assize (232). And at the turn of the twentieth century American Judge Learned Hand proposed that special juries or tribunals be appointed by the court to assist lay jurors with matters of fact in cases involving expert evidence (Hand 1901, 56). Here either a "board of experts" or a single expert would be asked to advise the jury concerning the general propositions reached by the different parties' experts.[1]

The range of expertise recognized by the common law courts prior to the twentieth century and shortly thereafter does not appear to have been great. Professional tradesmen such as engineers were called upon to provide relevant technical information in civil suits, and doctors and other medical professionals were often relied upon in criminal proceedings to give opinions about the biological cause of a death, or about the mental state of an accused at the time of an alleged crime (Landsman 1995). The legal "formula" or rule for the admission of expert testimony in such cases was generally accepted by courts to be the actual marketability of the expert's knowledge, which translated into a measure of the witness's "qualification" as an expert (151). By the turn of the century, however, Landsman notes that professionals of different stripes had successfully forged monopolies – technically proficient professional groups or societies – that sold their special type of knowledge, technical know-how, and services to both government and the private sector alike (150–1).[2] An individual now became a member of one of these societies by successfully completing a program of specialized education and acquiring some kind of professional accreditation or licence. For Friedson, the situation is not really different today: "Explicitly connected with the idea of profession is training in higher education, the institutions of which are without doubt the major source of the transformation of the source and role of agents of formal knowledge in all advanced countries" (Friedson 1986, 15).

According to Larson, the market for specialized knowledge which developed in America was sustained by a prevalent "ideology of expertise" that accompanied the rise of professionalization (Larson 1984, 32). This ideology was "composite" insofar as "it appealed to precapitalist and anti-market elements" such as an ethic of "craftsmanship" and "community," and it purported to have a kind of transcendent basis, particularly what Larson calls "the transcendent objectivity of reason, apprehended by scientific procedures" (36). Although, as Larson observes, "Faith in science" was "not widely shared until the end of the nineteenth century," courts in particular already had other reasons for being skeptical of expert claims to specialized knowledge. Some scholars point out that common law judges had begun to show "a deep-seated suspicion" in regard to expert evidence around this time (Freckelton 1987, x; McLachlin 1993, 4). Indeed, a number of textbooks on the law of evidence that were used by lawyers and judges in the early decades of the twentieth century reflected the legal profession's distrust of expert witnesses.[3] For example, Phipson's *Law of Evidence* stated, "The testimony of experts is usually considered to be of slight value, since they cannot be indicted for perjury, are proverbially, though perhaps unwittingly, biased in favour of the side which calls them, as well as over-ready to regard harmless facts as confirmation of preconceived theories; moreover, support or opposition to given hypotheses can generally be multiplied at will" (Phipson 1921, 386). As Phipson indicates, the courts were reluctant to hear expert testimony mainly because it was considered heavily skewed or "warped" in favour of the party who paid to have it presented. This presumption of expert partisanship was so entrenched in the minds of English judges at this time that they authorized themselves the power to grant new trials in cases where juries were believed to weigh expert opinion evidence more favourably than "direct and positive evidence as to facts."[4] In jury trials, laypersons were expected to determine questions of fact in the absence of relevant expert evidence. Yet, where such evidence was present, judges tended to discredit it or at least second guess its credibility, effectively conferring upon themselves the privilege of *knowing what is worth knowing* regarding certain matters of fact.[5]

According to Landsman, the emergent professionalization of early twentieth century American society soon led to a fairly major shift in the common law's attitude toward admissibility of expert evidence. Concerned with the cogency of purported technical know-how about a new lie-detector device, an American court ruled that what was proffered as new scientific opinion evidence had to be proven to have gained "general acceptance in the particular field in which it belongs" before it could be admitted and put to the trier of fact.[6] Landsman says of the rule preceding *Frye*, "Although courts continued to use the 'qualification' standard, it is likely that the rise of professionalization led courts to consider group affiliation and credentials as part of the measure of the worth of a proposed expert witness if a relevant professional group or course of training existed" (Landsman 1995, 151).[7]

Despite its precedential value and the reams of scholarly papers addressed to it, the *Frye* test was of limited scope and was applied rarely until very recently (Landsman 1995, 153; Huber 1992, 733). It is worth mentioning here because a very real problem had emerged in American courts with respect to the heuristic validity of certain kinds of expert testimony. The question arose in *Frye*: What should a court do with a "well qualified" expert, possessing "strong credentials in his field," yet whose opinion on a particular matter appears unique, special, or somehow "novel"? (Landsman 1995, 153). As Landsman proposes, the court's formulation of the new admissibility standard was not entirely groundbreaking, but rather a "reiteration" of the progressivist belief in the expert body, commission, tribunal, board, or other "community" as the best indicator of the state-of-the-art in some area of knowledge or another. It was a test "that tended to place power in the hands of experts and the trial judge," and in "a time when jurors' capabilities were denigrated such a solution was a predictable extension of attitudes and doctrines fairly well developed" (ibid.). Huber has also noted that the *Frye* "rule came under attack ... in the 1960s and '70s" partly because it was seen as "elitist" (Huber 1992, 732).

Arguably, the flow of novel scientific information (physical or social) into courtrooms remains elitist to this day. Equally important, the notion of a "community" of experts or scientists which generally accepts certain basic principles and ideas applicable to its field may be more and more of a myth every day. Huber believes that "identifying a relevant scientific community" may simply be a matter of "common sense" (Huber 1992, 744), but Kuhn indicates that some communities of scientific researchers have historically been very specialized (Kuhn 1970, 10–11). For Kuhn, science has had its broad traditions of "'Ptolemaic astronomy' (or 'Copernican'), 'Aristotelian dynamics' (or 'Newtonian'), 'corpuscular optics' (or 'wave optics'), and so on," but the study of such scientific paradigms has also included "many that are far more specialized" than these familiar ones. Moreover, Kuhn colourfully demonstrates how the road to the development of even the broader and more familiar scientific paradigms has often been characterized by anything but consensus and understanding among communities of scientists. As he explains:

No natural history can be interpreted in the absence of at least some implicit body of intertwined theoretical and methodological belief that permits selection, evaluation, and criticism. If that body of belief is not already implicit in the collection of facts – in which case more than "mere facts" are at hand – it must be externally supplied, perhaps by current metaphysics, by another science, or by personal and historical accident. No wonder, then, that in the early stages of the development of any science different men confronting the same range of phenomena, but not usually all the same particular phenomena, describe and interpret them in different ways. What is surprising, and perhaps also unique in its degree to the fields we call science, is that such initial divergences should ever largely disappear (16–17).

For Kuhn, the development of a new scientific paradigm is ultimately accompanied by a restructuring and perhaps coalescing of an otherwise diffuse array of scientific researchers working within a recognizable general field, but even at this point, "the creative scientist" within this field will tend to "concentrate exclusively upon the subtlest and most esoteric aspects of the natural phenomena that concern his group," and the audience for this fine-tuned research will in turn become streamlined (20). The new "research communiqués" will be highly informed specialists within the generic field, "the men whose knowledge of a shared paradigm can be assumed and who prove to be the only ones able to read the papers addressed to them." Arguably, increasing specialization in technical knowledge and sophistication of theories informed by inter-disciplinary studies and research methods is even diminishing the size of those scientific communities who "share" preferred methods and research problems. This situation is evident in the social sciences,[8] which continue to enjoy relative immunity from the strict rules of admissibility that have been attached to the harder sciences.

The admissibility of expert evidence from the physical and social sciences in Canada is currently governed by rules established by the Supreme Court of Canada in R. v. Mohan, a sexual assault case. Justice Sopinka held that "admission of expert evidence depends on the following criteria: (1) relevance; (2) necessity in assisting the trier of fact; (3) the absence of any exclusionary rule; and (4) a properly qualified expert." This ruling is salient because of the way Sopinka construed "relevance." He urged other judges to consider the real possibility that some expert evidence may appear very cogent and persuasive, "particularly [to] a jury," although it is not very reliable.[9] For Sopinka, such evidence is not properly relevant and should be inadmissible.

This book has already examined various instances where *judges* – not only juries – have been overly impressed by expert legislative-fact evidence which is unable to withstand critical scrutiny. Despite Freckleton's suggestion that decades of obvious, partisan expertise in courts have made common law judges "more critical and analytical about the expert's testimony," many judges today, as surely as juries, are highly "susceptible to the aura of scientific expertise" (Freckleton 1987, 131). Justice McLachlin seems to concur. She concedes that Canadian courts traditionally treated party-paid or party-solicited expertise with skepticism or caution and, accordingly, placed strict limits on the kinds of opinions and issues about which experts could testify. However, in the last few decades, the courts have opened their doors generously to experts and loosened the strictures regarding admissibility (McLachlin 1993, 8, 12). She cites the increasing complexity of modern litigation as one reason for the hospitality shown to expertise by Canadian courts (13).[10] Another Canadian judge, Madam Justice Nicole Duval Hesler, looks more telescopically, proposing that the world has become "increasingly complex and technical" and that courts must now defer to those trained in complex and technical fields for answers to important questions of fact (Duval Hesler 1995, 208). Hagan agrees, saying, "there is no turning back from the standards of a more modern world. The social sciences have established new standards and sources of evidence that [bear] directly upon the social facts on which many important legal judgments rest. Where these standards and sources are ignored or circumvented, the judgments rendered will often become transparently inadequate" (Hagan 1987, 231–2).

McLachlin's and Duval Hesler's observations point to the real epistemological and administrative difficulties facing Canadian courts today, yet these problems can be redressed in the context of constitutional review by following Sopinka's rigorous approach to admissibility in *Mohan*. Indeed, just recently, Justice Major appears to have made the *Mohan* test even more difficult to meet, by reminding Canadian courts of the dangers associated with expert testimony, and emphasizing, therefore, that expert evidence not only be helpful but necessary as well.[11]

If judges were attuned to the methodological and conceptual limitations of much of the social science research employed in the pornography debates to date, as some have become recently, this research would fail the *Mohan* test. Presumably Canada's current anti-obscenity and indecency laws would be quite different. Though perhaps unlikely, Canadian courts might have already struck down Parliament's various attempts to regulate the publication and dissemination of pornographic materials, being unable to see the "fears" allegedly associated with these activities. For the moment, however, Canadians' constitutional rights to produce and consume pornography and erotica, women's constitutional rights *not* to be degraded by pornographic imagery, and women's constitutional rights to stroll topless along a public avenue are informed to a substantial degree by social science research and the experts who author it. The question arises then: is this democratic? If so, how? And if not, why not, and what can be done to democratize the process?

EXPERTS AND CONSTITUTIONAL REVIEW: A MATTER OF DEFERENCE OR EDUCATION, OR BOTH?

Former Supreme Court of Canada Justice Bertha Wilson has observed that, since the inception of the Charter, Canadian judges have been charged with a new responsibility. They are no longer confined to the adjudication of division-of-powers issues stipulated in the *British North America Act* – for example, whether the right to impose a tax on some mineral or natural resource in certain circumstances belongs to the federal or provincial government.[12] Courts must now answer questions pertaining to the powers of both levels of government to enact laws that infringe upon constitutionally entrenched rights of individuals. This new judicial mandate entails "developing some kind of balance between the fundamental rights of the citizens on the one hand and the right and obligations of democratically elected governments to govern on the other." In practice, "The challenge for the courts is to develop norms against which the reasonableness of the impairment of a person's rights can be measured in a vast variety of different contexts. But not only that. These norms must reflect to the maximum extent possible the political ideal of a free and democratic society" (Wilson 1986, 240–1).

For Wilson, there are at least two avenues the courts can follow for achieving the balancing act asked of them by the Charter. The first is a fundamental reorganization of the way judges and lawyers are educated and trained. She recognizes that traditional legal education has tended to develop in lawyers and, subsequently, in judges "narrow legalistic habits." These habits inhibit the ability of both judges and lawyers to "think large," which is now required of them as part of their obligation to develop social norms that reflect as much as possible "the political ideal of a free and democratic society." However, until legal education is sufficiently reformed to produce the kind of broad-minded advocates and decision-makers consistent with liberal democratic ideals, Wilson suggests that some "straightforward procedural accommodations" can be made to enable the overall balancing act (Wilson 1986, 241–2).

The first accommodation involves hospitably opening the courtroom door in constitutional cases to parties (besides those listed formally in the Style of Cause) who have and express interest in such cases. In effect, this approach entails granting *amici* or intervener status liberally, so that the "polycentricity of Charter issues" is clearly voiced and heard in the courtroom (Wilson 1986, 242). This proposal, which may be viewed as an enhanced "interest representation" proposal (Woolhandler 1988, 124–5), is very important as it relates *public* openness, participation, and accessibility, to the "legitimacy" of the courts' new role in constitutional matters (Wilson 1986, 243). As Miller and Barron observe, "Speaking generally, legitimacy refers to the right or title to rule – that is, to set the norms by which people are governed. In a nation that considers itself democratic, this right comes from the people, who through their ballots elect their rulers" (Miller and Barron 1975, 1228).[13] This book only indirectly addresses the question of legitimacy as characterized by Miller and Barron. It assumes that judges are not uniquely equipped as professionals to state "norms of general applicability," but it also assumes that judges are similarly equipped as laypersons in this regard. This book argues, more specifically, that neither judges nor legally qualified experts (in fields of social science or otherwise) are more or less competent than other people to determine matters of legislative fact. This is problematic from the point of view of "democracy" because, as already mentioned, legislative-fact evidence presented to judges by experts normally informs the very "norms of general applicability" that are produced in constitutional litigation.

Wilson suggests that a "more accessible court process" is a more representative and democratic court process (Wilson 1986, 243), which is another way of saying that a more accessible court process renders judges more "accountable" to the public in constitutional cases. This proposal is also conceptually premised on the importance of "procedural fairness" to legitimacy (Woolhandler 1988, 122, 124; Miller and Barron 1975, 1226). According to Woolhandler, "reformists" such as Wilson "claim decisions will be better procedurally because viewpoints of a wider variety of persons who will be affected by the legal rules will come to the courts' attention" (Woolhandler 1988, 122). Woolhandler disagrees with this kind of thinking,[14] but this book is concerned less with the idea of expanding the scope of (public or group) interested information available to the courts in constitutional review, and more with the working assumption that affected interests are somehow "represented" by social scientists generally, and experts specifically.[15] At this point in Wilson's analysis, her proposal appears blind to the dominant tendency of reviewing courts to divine relevant or material legislative facts through judicial notice or to receive this information predominantly through experts. As chapters 3 through 6 reveal, only very exceptionally and recently have Canadian courts actually opened the evidentiary forum to laypersons. This consideration touches upon Wilson's other "reform" proposal.

As an alternative to "liberalized intervention," Wilson suggests broadening "the base of the admissable evidence in Charter cases" (Wilson 1986, 243). This proposal is addressed to what Woolhandler calls the "substantive" component of reform in this area. She explains that "regularizing judicial reception of legislative facts" is considered by reformists to be "better substantively because decisions will be more 'accurate,' which will enhance their legitimacy" (Woolhandler 1988, 122; footnote omitted). Others have shown how this trend began years ago in Canada with the admission of evidence of legislative facts into pre-Charter constitutional cases dealing primarily with the justiciability of federal laws enacted under the special authority of the POGG power.[16] This trend continues today, the basic difference being, as Wilson's analysis suggests, that the rules of admissibility of legislative facts are now tied to a new conceptual framework. They are no longer related to the rhetoric of "peace, order and good government," but rather to administrative "reasonableness" and procedural "fairness" under section 1 of the *Charter* (Wilson 1986, 244). Swinton has analysed specific ways in which evidence of legislative facts has been introduced to support precisely the reasonableness and fairness of post-Charter laws. The immediate concern, however, is that such evidence tends to be restricted to the domain of the social sciences and is admitted generally through the voice or pen of experts. This last consideration recalls Wilson's aforementioned concern with the openness and accessibility of the judicial system to the public at large in constitutional matters. The problem may be stated simply, and it relates directly to what Lewontin calls "a deep problem in democratic self-governance" (Lewontin 1997, 32). If evidence tending to demonstrate legislative facts in Charter cases is typically informed and introduced by technically skilled individuals or groups, then it is difficult to say that the so-called "public" interest is effectively represented in these cases. It is also unclear how the process enhances judicial accountability to the public in such cases.[17] Dworkin has remarked that "wide public discussion is a desirable and democratic preliminary to a final Supreme Court adjudication" (Dworkin, Nagel et al. 1997, 42).

The increasingly generous acceptance of expert testimony in constitutional litigation may be a pragmatic antidote to the otherwise entrenched "narrow legalistic habits" of judges, but it is creating at the same time a wide gulf between expert and layperson participation in law-making. Two American legal scholars, Allen and Miller, have expressed a concern with this situation. They recall Huber's proposal that the expert scientific opinions provided on certain matters by such institutions as the Food and Drug Administration and the National Institutes of Health are "much less fallible – than a thousand juries scattered across the country" on those same issues (Allen and Miller 1993, 1143–4; quoting Huber 1992, 745). For Allen and Miller, the cogency of such a claim hinges on a certain view of "the cognitive abilities of fact finders," or more precisely of "the cognitive competence of jurors" which is grounded largely in "myth(s)." One such "popular myth" is that "judges are better equipped than jurors to make determinations of scientific consensus, or presumably to decide when scientific consensus need not be given deference." Another myth is that jurors are unable to "accurately perceive the bias" of an expert witness and to "adequately account for it." Allen and Miller are concerned that the institutional perpetuation of these myths justifies to some extent "transferring [fact-finding] authority from juror to judge," thus risking the reduction of the "scope of our common law method of juridical fact-finding by lay members of the community" (Allen and Miller 1993, 1143–6).

Allen and Miller's analysis can nicely be extended beyond the boundaries of the American common law and into Canadian post-Charter

constitutional realms. The question becomes whether increasing judicial deference to experts in Canadian constitutional matters is somehow consonant with what Wilson has called "the political ideal of a
free and democratic society" (Wilson 1986, 241–2). This very same
issue was raised in mid-century by the American judge Jerome Frank
in his "The Place of the Expert in a Democratic Society." Frank
recognized "much recent irritation and angry discussion" regarding
the "vast growth" of activity by expert-staffed administrative tribunals
since the turn of the century in America.[18] Apparently this concern was
directed mainly at the inefficiency of a process which enabled expert-
staffed commissions and administrative agencies to collect data or find
facts for the purpose of informing public policy, but which required
courts at times to review the soundness of different policies while being
bound by the prior determinations of fact. Frank's preference was to
dismantle administrative tribunals and leave the so-called adjudicative
fact-finding process of "administrative law" primarily to the judges.
As the cases arise, judges would then consult some kind of all-purpose
team or commission of experts, perhaps comprising "engineers,
accountants, and the like," or at any rate "persons who specialize in
a certain kind of fact-gathering." Frank optimistically saw this as "one
effective way of democratizing experts," and therefore of making the
judicial fact-finding process itself more democratic (Frank 1949, 23–4).

Given Frank's own admission that judges are but one of many
groups of experts (Frank 1949, 3), it is not entirely clear how calling
experts into the courtroom to inform legal decision-making "democ-
ratizes" expertise. Frank's proposal remains in this respect consistent
with the basic spirit of American progressivism and technocracy that
emerged as early as the turn of the century. Nonetheless, Frank may
be applauded for wanting to let "the public in" on what the United
States Supreme Court "is doing" (24). His insistence generally that
experts be subject to "constant criticism by the laity" in a democratic
society seems somehow inconsistent with his deferential attitude toward
the "fact-gathering" skills of certain kinds of professionals (23–4). In
any case, Frank's sober recognition that "[w]e must have specialists,"
coupled with his heartfelt prescription that "we must democratize
them," especially as they inform law- and policy-making, reveals a real
tension between two polar ends of democratic theory – what might be
called the progressivist and pluralist poles.

Justice Wilson's own proposal that "the political ideal of a free and
democratic society" requires Canadian courts to "think large" masks
the tension highlighted by Frank's analysis. It points to one pole or
"ideal" in particular: a pluralistic vision of democracy. It suggests the

importance of consulting widely, and expert knowledge is not always broad-minded. Yet courts continue to admit constitutional-fact evidence through the voices of experts, which is consistent with a progressivist ideal of democracy. In light of the growing complexity and speciousness of knowledge today, the generous invitation Canadian courts have extended lately to experts from all fields of knowledge in constitutional cases is understandable. However, it is not entirely clear that, as Justice McLachlin suggests, the judiciary is becoming "more knowledgeable and sophisticated" about the "strengths and weaknesses" of expert evidence (McLachlin 1993, 15–16). She says, "While we welcome expert evidence in new areas, we scrutinize it more carefully. We are learning more about scientific method." As this book shows, this seems to be the case for a few judges, but it does not address the concern here that constitutional law in some areas is being increasingly informed by expert opinion as opposed to non-expert opinion; and that the review process is ultimately a matter of argument, however well- or ill-informed.

In essence, the post-Charter obligation on Canadian judges to consult widely about matters of fact that touch directly upon civil rights issues exists in a real tension with the recognition by these same judges that the consultants themselves – that is, the experts – cannot necessarily be relied upon to provide sound or reliable opinions in court. Perhaps Canadian and, indeed, all judges determining difficult legal and policy-oriented issues in a highly technical world are caught in a "catch-22." They can choose to accept the increased intellectual complexity of modern litigation and accordingly defer to those experts who appear at least formally most competent to assist them with relevant factual issues. This is not only an obvious form of elitism or technocratism. It is also a kind of delegation of ultimate decision-making responsibility to non-legally trained personnel. Conversely, if judges take a skeptical position in this respect and choose to address otherwise complex factual issues without expert assistance, they run the risk of appearing distinctly arrogant or elitist, and of over-simplifying matters that others consider complicated. In either case, the accountability, representativeness, and ultimately fairness of the administration of justice is put in jeopardy. As Freckleton says, "It is important that the courts not be left powerless and unsure in the face of experts from a wide variety of backgrounds attempting to supply information that the legal system cannot deal with. So long as it is not possible to predict with confidence whether expert evidence on various subjects, although clearly relevant and probative, will be admitted, the law is deficient. Similarly, it is important in each individual case and *for the law's reputation for fairness*, that tribunals of facts not be unnecessarily subjected to barrages of difficult-to-comprehend evidence from experts who can find no basis for agreement" (Freckleton 1987, 9; emphasis added).

In order to gain a more comprehensive understanding of the proper role of the expert in democratic society, it is useful to delve briefly into the early history of progressivism in America, and then into the democratic philosophy of John Dewey. Depending on one's preferred vision of democracy, the relaxation of rules for admitting expert opinion evidence in constitutional adjudication may be seen as an unnecessary evil or a necessary good – or possibly as something somewhere in between.

COMPETING VISIONS OF DEMOCRACY

The Progressivist or Technocratic Vision

The almost natural tendency of today's Canadian constitutional courts and human rights tribunals to consult expert sociologists, psychologists, economists, anthropologists, and others, in order to help them properly review the soundness of government policy in some area of law or another, nicely recalls a view of expertise in policy-making dating back as far as the fourth century BCE. In the *Gorgias*, Plato imputed to Socrates the belief that politicians should consult technical expertise in matters of municipal construction and military organization (Plato 1964, 455–6). Laypersons were deemed simply incompetent to make informed decisions in this regard. However disagreeable this assumption might have appeared then, it has certainly not become outmoded. It clearly lies behind that important piece of early twentieth century American political and legal history wrapped up in the New Deal and the intellectual development of progressivism. There one easily witnessed a great rift between two concepts of democracy. First, a popular vision of democracy actually sought public opinion and public interest among the voices of the American citizen at large; and second, a patrician or technocratic vision eschewed popular opinion in favour of scientific knowledge and expert opinion in fleshing out the practical details of the New Deal (Lasch 1991, 365).[19]

Perhaps one of the most notable spokespersons for the technocratic camp was Walter Lippmann, who happened to be an ardent critic of the New Deal and of that variant of progressivism associated with "puritanism" (Lasch 1991, 363–5, 432; Lasch 1995, 253). At least two senses of progressivism were in use at this time. One was a varient of puritanism, meaning "uplift," and the other belonged to the philosophy of "social control," which advocated a "scientific approach to politics" (253–4). For Lippmann, increasing legal, technological, and economic complexity in the world of industry and trade called for management by someone or some "body" deemed capable of determining the collective interest of all those involved in such affairs. The elected officials or administrators entrusted with this task had the choice of consulting public opinion or expert knowledge (Lippmann 1922, 18–20; Lasch 1995, 168–9). Lippmann distrusted the heuristic validity of public opinion as it related, for example, to the so-called "common interest" of businesspeople, factory owners, and labourers because it was informed largely by distorted newspaper items and a public education system built on dogma or "the defective organization of public opinion" (Lippmann 1922, 19).[20] Moreover, the simplicity of rural life or life in the "self-contained community" made it easy and hence desirable for politically-engaged citizens to apply existing political and legal theory to new conditions, instead of testing that theory according to experience. Lippmann observed that "the public opinions of any one community about the outer world consisted chiefly of a few stereotyped images arranged in a pattern deduced from their legal and moral codes, and animated by the feeling aroused by local experiences" (174).

Accordingly, the choice of who could best determine the "common interest" in a complex economic order, and in this same vein, who could best serve the interests of democracy in such matters, was clear. For Lippmann, scientists, including social scientists, seemed the best candidates for consultation. Lippmann argued that "representative government, either in what is ordinarily called politics, or in industry, cannot be worked successfully, no matter what the basis of election, unless there is an independent, expert organization for making the unseen facts intelligible to those who have to make the decisions" (Lippmann 1922, 19). Scientists as "experts" offered the possibility for achieving a more participatory or "spontaneous" democracy, or for obtaining a "satisfactory decentralization" in government, by "supplementing" the overly simplistic and misinformed "public opinion" of individuals with more accurate and specific knowledge (or "representation of the unseen facts") in relevant political matters.[21]

Weatherly took a slightly different perspective. He also proposed a time when "both people and interests were few and simple," noting how this has changed with increases in population growth, "life complexity," and specialization. Anticipating Lippmann, he observed that by 1920 "endless complaint about the mass of ignorant voters in our political system" could be heard, and consistent with Lippmann, he distrusted "better education" as a panacea to this political problem, but for different reasons from Lippmann. Weatherly believes that "incrêasing complexity and specialization" are particularly responsible for exacerbating the problem of human ignorance in issues of social and political importance, "since the number of things that any one man may adequately know will become relatively smaller." This observation is especially important for two reasons. First, Weatherly's logic regarding the specialization of knowledge can be applied directly to the kind of evidence relevant to constitutional legal proceedings: it follows that judges can expect to be bombarded with an increasingly diffuse array of experts, testifying on increasingly specialized aspects of some more general social and political problem. And the question beckons: in what sense can judges, as specialists themselves, be expected to be competent to assess this kind of evidence? Second, Weatherly suggests that increased complexity in many facets of life will tend toward government by specialists, or what he calls "a new aristocracy." This will be a class composed of "the man who knows mining or irrigation or agriculture or education" in contradiction to the political head of state, "the man who knows merely how to influence the votes by which he shall be elected" (Weatherly 1920, 29–31). This book proposes that judges are being asked to show the same kind of deference to this new aristocracy in constitutional adjudication as any president, governor, prime minister, or premier. The problem of course, is that the judiciary in constitutional cases cannot be expected to provide an effective check on governmental behaviour when the so-called "facts" presented by many of these new specialists are so contestable.

According to Schwendinger and Schwendinger, "Elitist presuppositions have been part of liberal thought for centuries," but the dawn of the twentieth century witnessed a shift in the groups or constituents whose interests were represented by the ruling elite (Schwendinger and Schwendinger 1974, 466). Technocrats are now asked (and paid) to serve not only the interests of wealthy property holders, but also the public interest. Lippmann's own discussion of the advent of the social scientist in democratic political affairs confirms the Schwendingers' observation about the well-established technocratic basis of "liberal thought." Lippmann says that

every complicated community has sought the assistance of special men, of augurs, priests, elders. Our own democracy, based though it was on a theory of universal competence, sought lawyers to manage its government, and to help manage its industry. It was recognized that the specially trained man was in some dim way oriented to a wider system of truth than that which arises spontaneously in the amateur's mind. But experience has shown that the traditional lawyer's equipment was not enough assistance. The Great Society had grown furiously and to colossal dimensions by the application of technical

knowledge. It was made by engineers who had learned to use exact measurements and quantitative analysis. It could not be governed, men began to
discover, by men who thought deductively about rights and wrongs. It could
be brought under human control only by the technic who created it. Gradually,
then, the more enlightened directing minds have called in experts who were
trained, or had trained themselves, to make parts of this Great Society intelligible to those who manage it. These men are known by all kinds of names,
as statisticians, accountants, auditors, industrial counsellors, engineers of many
species, scientific managers, personnel administrators, research men, "scientists," and sometimes just as plain private secretaries (Lippmann 1922, 233–4).

For Lippmann, reliance on experts or technically informed individuals in political decision-making is not antithetical to democracy, but
is necessary to address a basic paradox within democratic political
theory. The paradox is that, according to classic democratic political
theory, the skills and knowledge required to govern oneself and others
belong to all human beings as a matter of instinct, yet instinct itself is
assumed to operate well in only a limited environment. Thus, the
instinctive side of humankind and the geographically specious nature
of human social organization tends to limit human beings' capacity
for the so-called "universal" knowledge required of truly participatory
or "spontaneous" democracy.[22] Referring to all schools of "political
thought," Lippmann says "the democrats who wanted to raise the
dignity of all men, were immediately involved by the immense size and
confusion of their ruling class – the male electorate. Their science told
them that politics was an instinct, and that the instinct worked in a
limited environment. Their hopes bade them insist that all men in a
very large environment could govern. In this deadly conflict between
their ideals and their science, the only way out was to assume without
much discussion that the voice of the people was the voice of God"
(Lippmann 1922, 164–5).

Thanks to some "key inventions" of the twentieth century, the
assumption last mentioned is no longer required of democratic political
theory, and the paradox may be somewhat unravelled. The "modern
newspaper, the world-wide press service, photography and moving
pictures" have served to bring geographically and intellectually more
remote matters nearer, albeit with much distortion. More important,
twentieth century science has brought new techniques of "measurement
and record, quantitative and comparative analysis, the canons of
evidence, and the ability of psychological analysis to correct and discount the prejudices of witnesses" (Lippmann 1922, 165–6). For Lippmann, these later developments in science and law serve well, albeit
with their own limitations, to promote accuracy in the kind and level

of decision-making that directly bears upon government and policy formation. The reference to legal and evidentiary developments is particularly significant because Lippmann's characterization of the self-centred and provincial opinions of members of the "self-contained" community aptly invokes the image of the stereotypical jury, whose knowledge or sense of morality was considered ideal for the articulation of the "common conscience" in early twentieth century anti-obscenity jurisprudence. It was the juridical equivalent, in this sense, of the "voice of God." Lippmann states, "In a self-contained community one could assume, or at least did assume, a homogeneous code of morals. The only place, therefore, for differences of opinion was in the logical application of accepted standards to accepted facts. And since the reasoning faculty was also well standardized, an error in reasoning would be quickly exposed in a free discussion" (174).[23]

In today's industrialized societies, however, with their increased division of labour, varied ethnic or racial composition, and large number of social interests, one can no longer assume a "homogeneous code of morals." Speaking of contemporary Canadian society, Lamont says that "the homogeneous society of nineteenth-century England is not the diverse Canadian community of the 1970s" (Lamont 1973, 144). Thus, even if there is a single or universal ethos across such a community, it needs to be demonstrated.[24] In Lippmann's terms, the picture of this morality in people's heads must be "supplemented" by outside, expert information. Referring to such an image in contemporary Canadian law, reflected in the idea of a community standard of tolerance, Lamont says, "If the community standard is truly national in scope, as the courts have clearly stated, then it is foolish to assume that a single judge or even a panel of twelve jurors drawn from one locality, and limited in their range of exposure, could adequately represent or assess the standard, even assuming they could rid themselves of their emotional reactions and ingrained personal biases on such a subjective and sensitive matter as obscenity" (141; footnotes omitted).

Consistent with Lippmann's faith in the accuracy of expert knowledge, Lamont argues the need for both expert evidence regarding the artistic value of allegedly obscene materials, and survey evidence reflecting the relevant "community" standard of decency (Lamont 1973, 141). As chapter 3 demonstrates, however, the courtroom is not the best place for receiving this kind of evidence. Judges are easily misled by social science survey evidence, so the hospitality courts have begun to extend toward such evidence must be questioned. Indeed, although Lippmann's technocratic spirit has become institutionalized in this century's constitutional case law, both in America and Canada, it was challenged on its own (extra-legalistic) terms by some of Lippmann's own intellectual contemporaries. Perhaps the most notable of these was John Dewey. His *The Public and Its Problems* published in 1927 was in part inspired by the force of Lippmann's analysis of the impact of the popular press on American public opinion, yet it directly challenged the idea that experts were pivotal to the formation of intelligent public policy in a democratic society. It is to Dewey's and similar visions of democracy, therefore, that the discussion now turns.

Popular, Pluralistic, and Perhaps "Radical" Visions of Democracy

In *The Public and Its Problems*, Dewey advocated a "popular" vision of democracy in direct opposition to the progressivist or technocratic view discussed so far (Dewey 1927, 207). Democracy is conceived here as a matter of direct or indirect participation in the political life of a community wherein all the interests and desires of individuals and groups are expressed, heard, and considered in the formation of regulations governing individual and joint behaviour (148–9). A community exists, Dewey states, "wherever there is conjoint activity whose consequences are appreciated as good by all singular persons who take part in it, and where the realization of the good is such as to effect an energetic desire and effort to sustain it in being just because it is a good shared by all."

Of course, Dewey recognized that it is empirically impossible to locate a community defined by a sense of good shared by all. In this respect, Dewey's formulation of democracy is harmonious with the more recent "radical and plural" conception espoused by Mouffe, which recognizes a "constitutive outside" or "exterior" to every community (Mouffe 1988; 1992b; 1995).[25] Like Dewey, Mouffe relates the fact of a community's outer limit directly to the "impossibility" of any given political community's "full realization" (Mouffe 1992a, 30). Dewey illustrates this point with reference to the "robber band [who] cannot interact flexibly with other groups; [but] can act only through isolating itself" (Dewey 1927, 148). Some individuals and groups of people will not accept or abide by rules of governance and conduct that the majority of persons in a given society are willing to respect. And these people are not only obvious social "outsiders," such as lawbreakers. Realistically, societies comprise individuals who have a variety of interests and desires which often compete or conflict depending on the different group associations or affiliations of these individuals. Dewey makes this point forcefully in the following passage:

Individuals find themselves cramped and depressed by absorption of their potentialities in some mode of association which has been institutionalized and become dominant. They may think they are clamoring for a purely personal liberty, but what they are doing is to bring into being a greater liberty to share in other associations, so that more of their individual potentialities will be released and their personal experiences enriched. Life has been impoverished, not by a predominance of "society" in general over individuality, but by a domination of one form of association, the family, clan, church, economic institutions, over other actual and possible forms. On the other hand, the problem of exercising "social control" over individuals is in its reality that of regulating the doings and results of some individuals in order that a larger number of individuals may have a fuller and deeper experience (Dewey 1927, 193–4).

This social utilitarian view of law and the attendant portrait of modern life's 'impoverishment' contain the seeds of what Dewey sees as the central problem of democracy. It is basically a *procedural* problem: a problem of enabling the various group interests and desires that exist in any society to become clear or "choate," and to be considered in the process of political decision-making. This is what Dewey means when he says that effective "participation in activities and sharing in results ... demand[s] *communication* as a prerequisite" (Dewey 1927, 152; emphasis in original).[26] Cooley had already emphasized the importance of uncensored speech and full communication to the practical realization of democracy (Melossi 1990, 114) and Dewey was in effect elaborating on the theme. Until different group interests could be delineated and articulated in some kind of recognized political forum, any so-called public interests must remain "inchoate," according to Dewey, and rule-making under such conditions could not be ideally democratic.

Mouffe maintains that "pluralist democracy demands not only consensus on a set of common political principles but also the presence of dissent and institutions through which such divisions can be maintained" (Mouffe 1995, 263). This proposition agrees with both Dewey's observation that democracy is not an empirical fact but a process or tendency, and that the "prime difficulty" of democracy, therefore, is one of "discovering the means by which a scattered, mobile and manifold public may so recognize itself as to define and express its interests" (Dewey 1927, 146–8). Moreover, Mouffe puts forward a purportedly "new" conception of the democratic "citizen" that, she says, "is different from both the republican/communitarian and the liberal ones, which are at the moment the only existing alternatives." Although the latter part of this claim is inaccurate,[27] Mouffe defines this citizen as "a common political identity of persons who might be engaged in many different communities and who have differing conceptions of the good, but who accept submission to certain authoritative rules of conduct." These "rules" or principles may be best understood as certain formal or procedural conditions which enable individuals and groups to have their multifarious political interests effectively communicated and practically respected. As far as Mouffe is concerned, these rules are straightforward. They simply require citizens to treat one another as "free and equal persons" not only in the process of law- and policy-making, but in "all areas of social life." (Mouffe 1992a, 28–32). Arguably, these procedural rules provide the necessary "means" of democratic citizenship that Dewey contemplates. In any case, Mouffe's view of citizenship as "an articulating principle that affects the different subject positions of the social agent while allowing for a plurality of specific allegiances and for the respect of individual liberty" resonates nicely with Dewey's observation (quoted above): "Life has been impoverished ... by a domination of one form of association, the family, clan, church, economic institutions, over other actual and possible forms" (Dewey 1927, 194).[28]

Although Dewey at least conceives of an ideal society politically organized around "free and full intercommunication" – what he calls the Great Community (Dewey 1927, 211) – the realization of such a society, he argues, has been hindered by the rise of the industrial or "machine" age. This has "so enormously expanded, multiplied, intensified and complicated the scope of the indirect consequences" of human activity, as to render the "community" in modern society virtually invisible or unrecognizable. In a word, the political and legal forms designed to regulate behaviour and serve the needs of pre-industrial society are no longer adequate, Dewey contends, in an age of enhanced technology and extended commercial relations (126–9). Thus, it is important to observe that, for Dewey, the rise of industrialization and the expansion of commercialization throughout the eighteenth and nineteenth centuries were accompanied by a transference of political power, from the hands of "landed proprietors, allied to churchly authorities," to "captains of industry" – the constitutive members of what he calls an "economic class." This class is painted as "a shifting, unstable oligarchy, rapidly changing its constituents, who are more or less at the mercy of accidents they cannot control and of technological inventions." Insofar as government under such conditions may be seen to fall far short of established democratic standards or ideals, Dewey suggests it requires a "check." This has been provided by what Dewey and Weatherly call a new "aristocracy" – an "intellectual aristocracy" comprising "expert intellectuals" (Dewey 1927, 203–5; Weatherly 1920, 30). It is the "specialist" here, or "expert in operation," whose technical, formalistic, and indeed "scientific" knowledge appears most suitable for addressing the complexity of social-economic problems arising from increased population, increased division of labour, and the influences of the physical sciences on life. As already observed, Lippmann made the same point when he referred to the various experts called in "to make parts of [the] Great Society intelligible to those who manage it" (Lippmann 1922, 234).

Perhaps mocking Lippmann, Dewey proposes that the alternative is to leave such matters to "an ignorant, fickle mass whose interests are superficial and trivial, and whose judgments are saved from incredible levity only when weighted down by heavy prejudice" (Dewey 1927, 204). However, the assumption that expert intellectuals are especially competent to govern the affairs of an "inchoate public," a society whose collective interests remain inarticulate and unrecognizable on important levels, cannot hold sway. Dewey suggests that although technically trained experts may well be competent to administer and execute extant "general policies," they cannot decide on the political wisdom of such policies. This process requires some degree of participation and information by the polity's constituents at large. In response to Lippmann's critique of the kind of propaganda-filled information the "masses" receive from the popular presses and the public education system, Dewey argues that such institutions are themselves the historical products of open communication among populations at large.[29] Paraphrasing de Tocqueville on the subject of American democracy, Dewey says, "Accusing a democracy of a tendency to prefer mediocrity in its elected rulers, and admitting its exposure to gusts of passion and its openness to folly, [de Tocqueville] pointed out in effect that popular government is educative as other modes of political regulation are not" (206-7).

Dewey also questions the assumption that "the mass of the reading public is not interested in learning and assimilating the results of accurate investigation" (Dewey 1927, 182-3). Such an assumption downplays the possibility that "results of accurate investigation" could be presented in an accessible way to non-technically trained or versed people, in which case these same people might show great willingness to learn and absorb such scientific information. This particular concern is echoed years later by Justice Jerome Frank who, as already observed, argued the need to "democratize" expertise by demanding that "experts translate their esoteric formulations into terms easily comprehensible by non-experts" (Frank 1949, 23).

It is not sufficient, therefore, to discredit the so-called "common" person's intelligence regarding the role it can play in the construction of rules and laws that serve public interests. In hindsight, most acts of political decision-making (or legislation) will reveal some degree of "folly" or unintelligence, whether the process is dominated by experts or laypersons. "The essential need," Dewey insists, "is the improvement of the methods and conditions of debate, discussion and persuasion." Again, experts have but a limited role in this process. In Dewey's estimation, they can inquire into and reveal the "facts" upon which public policy is constructed, but they are not necessarily in a position to "judge of the bearing of the knowledge supplied by others upon common concerns" (Dewey 1927, 208–9). This is primarily because experts themselves comprise a particular socio-economic class, with its own self-interest (207; Cain 1988, 70). It is also worth noting Justice Frank's armchair observation that experts tend to be "smugly authoritarian toward the public" (Frank 1949, 3) and Lasch's off-the-cuff remark that "many of the 'best people,' as they think of themselves, have always been skeptical about the capacity of ordinary citizens to grasp complex issues and to make critical judgments" (Lasch 1995, 10). In any case, knowledge produced or revealed by this special interest group will likely conflict at times with that of other recognizable social groups, each with its own conceptual tools and sets of political interests, leaving open the question as to why experts should dominate the policy-making process.[30]

Dewey's vision of democracy is especially important because it suggests that "government by experts in which the masses do not have a chance to inform the experts as to their needs" is in essence not democratic but oligarchic (Dewey 1927, 208). The trend in Canadian constitutional courts to consult experts but not laypersons in matters of obvious public interest is thus very problematic. It is consistent with the "professionalized justice" and "incorporated justice" models of most capitalist societies that Cain criticizes along class lines (Cain 1988, 66–76). Both forms effectively serve the interests of a "bourgeois class" directly or indirectly: for example, they confer or ensure professional autonomy on the part of lawyers and judges, or they privilege knowledges (such as "positivistic scientific knowledge") within the adjudicatory process that some professionals (such as 'white collar' professionals, intellectuals, and technocratics) possess and others (such as "teachers, police officers and social workers") need and are willing to purchase (66–70). In this last respect, Cain contrasts the expert-based or expert-staffed administrative agencies found in a "capitalist state" with state-run "lay justice tribunals" which purport to represent or sponsor "the collective totality" of the state's citizenry, and which at least, therefore, pose the real possibility of meting out "collective justice" in specific contexts (69–71). Unfortunately, as Cain observes, even decision-making in these ostensibly "popular" courts has tended to be governed, and perhaps dominated, by a limited group of individuals who are treated as experts or specialists, or who have some special tie to the flow of capital that sustains the agency or tribunal itself. Cain also notes here that the "ordinary lay persons" who sit on these tribunals tend to be deferential to the opinions of "the chair or experts or officials" (71–2; footnotes omitted).

The hard question remains: Do Canadian courts meet their post-Charter obligation to "think large" about the variety of constitutional claims brought before them when they consult only a "small" group of people – licensed professionals, scientists, cultural figures, and accredited academics? These people are presumed to be more capable than the mythical or stereotypical "ordinary" person to inform the courts about matters directly affecting any broad cross-section of society. But in some fields of inquiry, such as pornography, sexuality, capital punishment, and even suicide, this presumption is well worth testing. Indeed, the problem posed here is beautifully encapsulated in the domain of obscenity law, where both American and Canadian courts have sought for years to determine, case by case, the so-called "community standard" of tolerance or decency. Whereas the collective opinions of a random assemblage of jurors were once considered sufficiently indicative of this standard or Holy Grail of obscenity law, some American and Canadian courts now require a scientifically-measured standard prepared and devised by professionally or academically trained social science researchers. The irony is that the same "random" assemblage of participants or opinions is theoretically desired and empirically consulted, but the significance of the opinions themselves is now presented and interpreted through the voice of the "expert" researchers. Not only is the evidentiary process hereby complicated, but the community standard of tolerance, *as an object of knowledge,* has been removed from the broader community that originally informed it and placed in the hands of a narrow body of scientists whose special skills do not necessarily shed any extra light on the information or opinions collected.

To witness the historical unfolding of this elitist and technocratic turn in Canadian constitutional law, one must recall some early twentieth century American constitutional law and some of the juridical figures that helped to steer it this way. The progressivist bent in American constitutional law began to take shape at this time and has not been altered to this day.

3

Experts and Obscenity Law: American Rules and Innovations (1884–1990)

OBSCENITY AND THE COMMON SENSE OF THE JURY

In 1884 a New York book and art seller was charged with possessing and selling nine photographs considered indecent and obscene, contrary to section 317 of the state *Penal Code* at that time.[1] Some of the objectionable materials were photographs of paintings previously exhibited at galleries in Paris and Philadelphia. At his trial, the defendant called an artist and a person who studied art to provide in effect expert testimony regarding the nature of the photographs, or more specifically, to give an opinion as to whether or not the photographs were in fact obscene or indecent. Justice Andrews rejected the expert opinions, however, for basically two reasons. First, he emphasized that the issues of indecency and obscenity in the case at bar were not matters of "opinion" but matters of *fact* which only the so-called "trier-of-fact" (such as a judge or jury) could decide. Second, he recalled the extant rule governing the admissibility of expert opinion evidence, which stated, "The testimony of experts is not admissible upon matters of judgment within the knowledge and experience of ordinary jurymen."[2] He applied this rule to the "matters of judgment" at issue – that is, whether the impugned photographs were "indecent" or "obscene" – and concluded that such matters are clearly within the knowledge and experience of a body of jurors. In his words, "The question whether a picture or writing is obscene is one of the plainest that can be presented to a jury, and under the guidance of a discreet judge there is little danger of their reaching a wrong conclusion." Accordingly, expert opinions in this regard must be excluded as being both extraneous and largely irrelevant.

In 1891 Justice Philips of the Kansas District Court was presented with an interesting "obscene matter in the mails" case.[3] In particular, a newspaper editor and publisher was indicted for mailing a newspaper containing various philosophical sentiments but most importantly an article purportedly written by a medical doctor, revealing a number of sexual experiences related to him in the course of his practice. The written judgment says that the article discussed "abuses of women by their husbands in coercive cohabitation; of family habits of men, boys, and girls, gratifying an unnamable propensity of the father, and the unnatural intercourse between a man and beasts."[4] The defendant argued that he publicized these stories solely to correct such "abuses" and to improve married people's sexual habits.

Although the case involved the constitutional issue of the defendant's First Amendment right to free speech and press, it is important to note the legal test for obscenity that Philips employed. Briefly, he canvassed various tests (including the famous *Hicklin* formulation),[5] before establishing that the proper test is the danger to the common or public morality posed by exposure to materials alleged to be obscene or indecent. In his terms, the test is "what is the judgment of the aggregate sense of community reached by [the publication under consideration]? What is its probable, reasonable effect on the sense of decency, purity, and chastity of society, extending to the family, made up of men and women, young boys and girls, – the family, which is the common nursery of mankind, the foundation rock upon which the state reposes?"[6] Once having identified the test, Philips had to indicate where this "aggregate" judgment might best be found, or how it could best be discerned. For him, the jury is the ideal vehicle for the articulation of the "average conscience" or "judgment of the aggregate sense of the community." As he explains, "Under our institutions of government the panel of 12 are assumed to be the best and truest exponents of the public judgment of the common sense. Their selection and constitution proceed upon the theory that they mostly nearly represent the average intelligence, the common experience and sense, of the vicinage; and these qualifications they are presumed to carry with them into the jury-box, and apply this average judgment to the law and the facts."

Ideally, then, with the emergence of the so-called "community standard of decency" test, average Americans are thus far entrusted with some amalgam of literary and psychological knowledge. They can judge reliably regarding the moral worth of certain publications by gauging their "probable, reasonable effect(s)" on different people's sense of "decency, purity, and chastity." This assumption was reflected in the American rule of evidence that neither experts nor ordinary witnesses were allowed to express their opinion about "matters of ...

general human nature, or the manner in which other persons would probably act or be influenced" (Phipson 1921, 391). Justice O'Brien remarked of the relevant test in 1907, "What is the impression produced upon the minds by perusing or observing the writing or picture referred to in the indictment, and one person is as competent to determine that as another."[7] Presumably, this calculation involves some consideration of the average level of literacy or perhaps literariness of the society or readership in question. Having some understanding of the purpose for which a text is published, for example, should help to determine how it will affect someone's sense of decency.

Philips's decision in *Harmon* nicely echoes Andrews's earlier pronouncement in *People* v. *Muller* that it "does not require an expert in art or literature to determine whether a picture is obscene or whether printed words are offensive to decency and good morals."[8] And just as Andrews entrusted such matters to the "ordinary intelligence" embodied in the jury, other judges placed similar faith in the jury's ability to articulate the "common sense" in controversies regarding arts and letters during the next couple of decades.[9] In 1913 Judge Learned Hand maintained, "If letters must, like other kinds of conduct, be subject to the social sense of what is right, it would seem that a jury should in each case establish the standard much as they do in cases of negligence."[10]

Despite judicial rhetoric about the importance of the jury to obscenity prosecutions in the early part of the twentieth century,[11] juries seemed to play this role very little. In the *Harmon* case itself, Philips was sitting alone, and therefore had to determine the average conscience in the absence of a jury. He stated that the court in such a case "should try to reflect in its findings the common experience, observation, and judgment of the jury of average intelligence."[12] Of course, the evidentiary problem arose: how precisely should the judge attempt to find the so-called "common experience, observation, and judgment" of the person on the street, when twelve such people are not brought off the street and into the courtroom? Where should the judge look? To public opinion polls? To book sales or, in the case of films, ticket sales? To book reviews or newspaper editorials? To the random opinions of people on the street? Almost all of these measuring-sticks have been used at some point or another, as this discussion will reveal. Yet a series of cases arose in the early part of the twentieth century, wherein some judges argued that they had the power to declare a publication obscene as a matter of law, in the face of what *they* considered "clear and uncontradicted" evidence.[13] Despite some lack of clarity in this area of law, these cases at least demonstrate that, despite the early, finely worded rhetoric about jurors being "the best and truest exponents of the public judgment of the common sense," some American judges clearly believed themselves to be 'better' and 'truer.'

Kelly observes that for the first few decades of the twentieth century jurors were usually drawn from the middle and lower classes of American society and were "disposed to a hypocritical, undemocratic puritanism." That is to say, the working-class jurors could be presumed to have enjoyed reading obscene materials at their own leisure and in private, yet they were quick to pronounce judgment in a public court of law on those charged with publishing and reading the same. Kelly observes further that proponents of censorship recognized this tendency of juries, and that in 1923 the "Clean Books League" lobbied unsuccessfully for a bill requiring obscenity trials to be heard by juries (Kelly 1998, 117–18)

As the years passed, judicial reference to the common sense of the jury became more or less a matter of rhetorical convenience. Often judges were presiding over anti-obscenity prosecutions in the absence of a jury; so concerns about the competence of jurors to decide matters of literariness and common morality had become irrelevant. Judges purported to respect the principle that the standard of decency or morality relevant to any obscenity prosecution must be determined by the "average" conscience, but it was often the judges, not the average juror, who determined the meaning of "average." At the same time, a broader movement was taking hold in the world of law – the movement of progressivism – and this development would eventually have an impact on the way judges would come to view the role of expert evidence in obscenity cases.

POUND AND PROGRESSIVISM IN LAW

As early as 1910, the preeminent American jurist and law professor Roscoe Pound wanted to narrow the gulf that was dividing legal theory (or law "in books") and its application in court (or law "in action"). He urged fellow judges and lawyers to "look to economics and sociology and philosophy, and cease to assume that jurisprudence is self-sufficient" (Pound 1910, 35–6).[14] Although Pound appears to favour all three disciplines equally in the above quotation, most of his writings on behalf of his school of sociological jurisprudence betray his particular enthusiasm at the time for sociology, especially the sociology of Edward Ross, Lester Ward, and Albion Small (Pound 1908, 609, 621; Pound 1912, 491, 493, 509; Pound 1945; Geis 1964). Pound's concluding segment to "The Scope and Purpose of Sociological Jurisprudence" contains numerous references to all three writers (Pound 1912). The Schwendingers associate all of these thinkers with the progressivist,

and perhaps technocratic, vision of democracy that was establishing
ground in American intellectual circles at the time (Schwendinger and
Schwendinger 1974, 449, 467).[15] As Geis points out, American sociological pioneers (as professors) at the turn of the century "were gath-
ered together from a conglomerate diversity of sources," none of them
having "been trained in the field in which he was working" (Geis 1964,
269). Melossi observes more particularly,

Between the end of the century and the 1930s, American sociology was
propounded in large part by scholars who belonged biographically and intellectually to the white protestant male group ... They were often ministers or
sons of ministers, from rural areas of the Mid-West, who saw the rise of
'bigness' in American society – big business, big labor, big cities, and big
government – with a mixture of feelings ranging from preoccupation to intense
moral indignation. They often borrowed from conservative European traditions in social and political science (Melossi 1990, 108; citations omitted).

A unifying progressivist thread could be gleaned among the works of
Small, Ward, and Ross. Small stands out foremost in this regard for his
statement, "The most reliable criterion of human values which science
can propose would be the consensus of councils of scientists representing the largest possible variety of human interest, and co-operating to
reduce their special judgments to a scale which would render their due
to each of the interests of the total calculation" (Small 1910, 242).[16] A
more antithetical view of the "reliability" of public opinion (lay opinion) in matters of common interest or "values" might be impossible to
find. In any event, Small's technocratic approach or the emphatically
scientific bent to social reform that Pound labelled "social engineering"
(Pound 1920, 32; Pound 1922, 99) did not appear to concern Pound
or some of his well-reputed contemporaries (Landsman 1995, 151;
White 1972, 1007).[17] Cardozo encouraged judges to consult some kind
of "fact-finding agency" in socio-economic matters which could "substitute exact knowledge of factual conditions for conjecture and
impression" (Cardozo 1924, 117). Judge Learned Hand believed that
expert-staffed boards and commissions were the best vehicle for discerning socio-economic matters of public importance outside of the
courtroom, and in turn, for introducing such facts into court proceedings as required or desired (Hand 1901, 56).[18]

As Melossi observes, Pound conceived of law as an "instrument" of
social engineering which could be used to reach policy goals (Melossi
1990, 109). To do this properly, and simply to be able to resolve legal
conflicts fairly, Pound perceived the need for a method of identifying
different social interests (Pound 1945, 332). Referring to the difficulty

of ascertaining the so-called "social interest" in some domain of public life or another, Pound says, "There remains a method, less pretentious in itself, that may yet yield more enduring results ... Why should not the lawyer make a survey of legal systems in order to ascertain just what claims or wants or demands have pressed or are now pressing for recognition and satisfaction and how far they have been recognized or secured?" (Pound 1920, 32–3).

At the same time Pound was reading Small, United States Supreme Court Justice Oliver Wendell Holmes had been warmly absorbing the pages of Ross and Ward, and shortly thereafter would be exposed to Small's *The Meaning of Social Science*. Holmes was so enthused by Ross's *Social Control* and *Foundations of Sociology* that he "felt impelled to communicate" such a sentiment to both Ross and the president of the United States.[19] And while he was equally receptive to Ward, he was much less complimentary about Small's *The Meaning of Social Science* (Geis 1964, 277–8). Pound and Holmes differed in their opinion of Small, but their mutual appreciation for Ward and Ross clearly reveals that progressivist sociological ideas had entered the minds of some of the more influential of America's juridical figures at the time. Melossi observes, "A sociological position within jurisprudence, from Oliver Wendell Holmes to Roscoe Pound, from John R. Commons to Louis Brandeis, pleaded for a rejection of formalism, or what Pound called mechanical jurisprudence. These thinkers advocated instead the adoption of a living, processual concept of law, grounded in the actual social interests at stake" (Melossi 1990, 109; citations omitted). Holmes's dissent in *Lochner* v. *People of the State of New York*, a 1905 case rejecting the constitutionality of state regulation aimed at bakers' employment hours, and Pound's critique of *Ives* v. *South Buffalo Ry*, a 1911 case which declared unconstitutional a New York state labour law providing for workmen's compensation, reflected the influence of early sociological thinking on these figures (White 1972, 1002–5).

As White observes, the 1910 New York labour law at issue in *Ives* was a "classic Progressive exercise in policymaking" as it was the product of a commissioned report on employer liability for on-the-job accidents which also considered the cost-efficiency and validity of such legislation. The report itself synthesized "a voluminous array of statistical tables, extracts from the works of philosophical writers and the industrial laws of many countries" (White 1972, 1005). In a sense, the report was partly informed by what is now referred to as legislative-fact evidence in judicial proceedings. Although this kind of evidence has become institutionalized in cases where the courts are asked to interpret the constitutionality of any given law (in both Canada and the United States), it is important to observe that judges have always been free to weigh this evidence as they see fit. In fact, the majority of the court in *Ives* subordinated otherwise "attractive and desirable" economic, philosophical, and moral theories "to the primary question whether they can be molded into statutes without infringing upon the letter or spirit of our written Constitutions."[20]

White points out that "*Lochner* had been decided on an economic theory which a great portion of the country did not entertain. More importantly, the theory had not been empirically tested; it was merely announced as true" (White 1972, 1003). At least according to Holmes, laissez-faire capitalism was a theory many Americans had not embraced.[21] Holmes objected therefore to judges simply taking judicial notice of such contestable matters of fact, and more particularly, to "the judicial tendency to announce general social propositions as truths and to reason downward from them in the decision of specific cases" (White 1972, 1003).[22] Holmes shared Pound's concern with the "mechanical jurisprudence" of their colleagues and, in striving to bring law more into tune with the social and economic exigencies of the day, Holmes might also have urged lawyers and judges to "look to economics and sociology and philosophy" (Pound 1910, 35). Despite the express enthusiasm of Pound and Holmes for these early sociologists, it is not clear that other "cosmopolitan" legal professionals and academics were similarly receptive.[23] Tushnet maintains, "Until the New Deal, the Supreme Court's course was one of erratic opposition to Progressive reforms, a course that mirrored the inability of Progressives to sustain a political coalition that controlled the other branches of the national government," but Roosevelt "attacked" such opposition and was sufficiently influential in this regard that "the Court itself came around to support New Deal programs" (Tushnet 1990, 228). For its part, the broader, professional sociological community during this time was "condescending" toward law as a vehicle for social change, and in terms of the legal realm's understanding of society (Geis 1964, 279). Melossi even comments that Americans had begun "to develop a distaste for the role of law and the state in social control, and to appreciate instead the importance of public opinion and social relationships in general" (Melossi 1990, 109).

Both Holmes and Pound may be applauded for their desire to see that the great variety of progressivist legislative initiatives were respected by the courts, or, in other terms, for their aversion to judicial arrogance in the face of challenges to their established ways of perceiving the world. It is more difficult, however, to embrace their enthusiasm for sociology or the social sciences. Only three years after *Lochner* was decided, an action was brought in Oregon against a laundromat owner for requiring a superintendent to employ a woman for more than ten hours one day, contrary to state regulation imposing maximum daily hours of employment for both men and women.[24] Although the same kind of employment law was deemed constitutionally invalid in New York because it was held to violate an individual's right to conduct business on her own terms, it was upheld in Oregon (at least so far as it related to women) on the basis of sociological evidence supporting the idea that women have different physical capacities than men. More precisely, in *Muller v. Oregon*, Justice Brewer of the Supreme Court of the United States deferred to the "very copious collection" of legal opinions, committee reports, and sociological data contained in the "brief" of Louis D. Brandeis to support his finding that "woman has always been dependent upon man," and that "in the struggle for subsistence she is not an equal competitor with her brother." He concludes, "Though limitations upon personal and contractual rights may be removed by legislation, there is that in her disposition and habits of life which will operate against a full assertion of those rights." Thus, such basic differences in the "structure of the body," in the "functions to be performed by each," in "physical strength," and "in the capacity for long-continued labor," justified the regulation of women's but not men's hours of work.[25]

Of course, the sociological content of Brandeis's brief is not to be blamed exclusively for what may appear today to be a ridiculous finding of fact by Justice Brewer in *Muller*. Brewer conceded that the legislation and opinions contained in Brandeis's brief, although perhaps not "technically speaking, authorities," were "significant of a *widespread* belief that woman's physical structure, and the functions she performs in consequence thereof, justify special legislation restricting or qualifying the conditions under which she should be permitted to toil."[26] Moreover, the unabashedly Darwinian hue to Brewer's understanding of men and women[27] fits squarely with White's observation of the dominant current in sociology and other academic disciplines of that day. White states, "Obsession with ineluctable rules, principles, and axioms became characteristic of the academic disciplines of the time. By applying a curious combination of spiritualism and Darwinism, economists, natural scientists, and sociologists discovered universal absolutes that governed their fields" (White 1972, 1001). The main problem with *Muller*, therefore, is that Brandeis's brief, which included "extracts from over ninety reports of committees, bureaus of statistics, commissioners of hygiene, inspectors of factories, both in [America] and in Europe,"[28] presented formally as they were by a professionally competent lawyer, lent to an otherwise ignorant view of women's physical capacities an aura of plausibility or at least rationality.

Only two years after *Muller*, Brandeis appeared in the Supreme Court of Illinois to make the same factual case on behalf of hundreds of women employed by a paper manufacturing company, W.C. Ritchie & Co.[29] In this case, the differences between men's and women's bodies and physical functions observed in *Muller* were considered "so far matters of general knowledge" that Justice Hand said the courts will take judicial notice of such facts.[30] Yet feminist or "environmentalist" movements that challenged this dominant view of women's nature as servile and unchanging were already afoot in cosmopolitan American circles. Lasch treats Ellen Key's *The Woman Movement* and Charlotte Perkins Stetson's *Women and Economics* as illustrations of some womens' disagreement with the "general knowledge" accepted by Hand in *W.C. Ritchie & Co.* Lasch writes, "At this point [in American history], one begins to suspect that for many feminists the doctrine of evolution merely served to give scientific respectability to existing clichés about the nature of woman – her essential purity, her freedom from coarse or selfish motives, her 'habit of service'" (Lasch 1965, 53).

However effectively "the doctrine of evolution" was operating in America to reinforce stereotypical views of women's "essential purity" and their proper role in life, James Joyce's *Ulysses* was at the time powerfully undermining in Ireland the strictures of religious conservatism and unveiling any illusion of the essential purity of woman or man. The trip that *Ulysses* eventually made to America, for the very purpose of being prosecuted there, is an illustrious moment in the history of American obscenity cases. The case is worth considering at this point because the American prosecution of *Ulysses* encapsulates and illustrates so many of the problems that attend the use of expert evidence in obscenity cases.

ELITISM AND THE VOYAGE OF *ULYSSES*

The Emergence of the Literary Critic
and the Importance of Being "Ernst"

A distinct form of elitism was emerging in the trials of obscene publication cases, and this tendency was no more clearly revealed (and exploited) than in a 1933 libel suit brought by the United States government against James Joyce's novel, *Ulysses*.[31] More than a decade earlier, the New York Court of Special Sessions had declared the "Nausicaa" chapter of Joyce's original version of *Ulysses* to be obscene and had prohibited *The Little Review* from publishing any further installments of Joyce's novel (Vanderham 1998, 53). Just prior to the 1921 prosecution of the editors of *The Little Review*, the editors' lawyer unsuccessfully sought to have the case dropped by supplying the influential Secretary of the New York Society for the Suppression of Vice with Evelyn Scott's scholarly article that argued Joyce to be a "Contemporary of the Future" (43). Scott's expert opinion was unconvincing at this early stage of Joyce's American battle against the censors, as were subsequent literary opinions introduced into the February 1921 trial proceedings. Vanderham outlines how John Cooper Powys and Phillip Moeller of the Theatre Guild put forward erudite claims to the effect that, from a literary point of view, *Ulysses* was too sophisticated and obscure for average readers to understand (48–9). These claims were meant to support the legal argument that, if the book was by and large incomprehensible to all but the most learned readers, it could not realistically corrupt the average reader. In short, it was proposed that one could only be corrupted by the book if one understood the morally corruptive meaning contained therein.

The expert evidence was weighed against portions of Joyce's own text, which were read aloud by the prosecuting lawyer in court and in private by the judges themselves. As Vanderham recalls, Justices James McInerney and Joseph Moss conceded that Joyce's novel was unintelligible, but Chief Justice Frederic Kernochan claimed to understand the morally corrosive nature of the "Nausicaa" chapter and persuaded McInerney and Moss to find it obscene (Vanderham 1998, 52–3).

Vanderham colourfully recalls how, shortly before, Margaret Anderson and Jane Heap were enjoined from publishing installments of *Ulysses* in *The Little Review* and how, for about a year following the 1921 New York court ruling, Joyce significantly reworked *Ulysses* in order to make its publication defensible against imminent or future suppression attempts (Vanderham 1998, 77–8). Indeed, Vanderham demonstrates how Joyce purposefully elongated and embellished his original *Ulysses* according to a new literary "schema" that Joyce hoped would enable him ultimately to get *Ulysses* published in English-speaking countries (72, 74–7). For Vanderham, the changes to *Ulysses* engendered by this new schema did enable Joyce's lawyers in 1933 to make better legal arguments about the literary and non-obscene nature of *Ulysses* that could not have been made in 1921.

The 1933 libel prosecution against *Ulysses* was particularly novel for the time because the decision to have *the book* as opposed to the book's publisher tried was masterminded primarily by Bennet Cerf, then president of Random House, the prospective publisher of *Ulysses*, and the prominent New York defence lawyer and anti-censorship advocate Morris Ernst. In 1931 Cerf knew that Ernst was personally keen to instigate a legal battle on behalf of *Ulysses* and believed that Ernst was the best lawyer in the country to conduct the case (Vanderham 1998, 87). Cerf successfully solicited Ernst for this purpose and then arranged a book contract for Joyce to sign in Ireland. As Kelly recounts,

Cerf had returned from Europe with the go-ahead from Joyce, so their first order of business was to settle his contract. Joyce would get advances amounting to $2,500.00 – a thousand of which he could keep even if Ernst lost the case – on royalties of 15 percent for the first 25,000 copies, 20 percent on further sales, and 10 percent of a popular edition that would come out two years after the trade edition. Cerf and Ernst also settled their arrangement, which was similar to the terms Ernst had suggested to Huebsch in October: in addition to a $500 retainer and money for expenses and court appearances, Ernst would get 5 percent royalty on the trade and deluxe editions of the book and 2 percent on cheap reprints.

They also plotted their method of attack. Ernst preferred to test the book in a federal court, because a victory there would carry considerable weight with postal authorities and the various state courts, each of which had their own obscenity policies. So they would import one copy of the book and have it seized by customs, which, according to procedure, would forward it to the U.S. Attorney, who in turn would initiate a libel suit against the book (Kelly 1998, 106).

The plan may have been simple, but the plot thickened on a hot day in May of 1932. As Vanderham recounts, "Ernst advised Cerf to have a copy of *Ulysses* shipped from France to the Port of New York and confiscated by U.S. Customs officials" (Vanderham 1998, 88). However, when one of Cerf's agents carried the impugned copy of *Ulysses* off the *Bremen* ship in the port of New York, the front line U.S. customs officials were hardly inspecting anything that day, so Cerf's agent had to insist that his luggage be inspected. When *Ulysses* was finally discovered, the inspecting officer had no interest in detaining it, so Cerf's agent insisted further, in which case a superior was asked to judge on the matter. This officer also found the agent's persistence ridiculous but finally relented and seized the book (Kelly 1998, 109).[32]

Once the libel suit was secured, Ernst and his assistant, Alexander Lindey, plotted their complex legal strategy. Perhaps the most important element of the plan had already been set in motion. The very copy of *Ulysses* seized at the New York port was "criticism-laden" (Vanderham 1998, 89). It had been shipped purposefully from France and had a variety of supporting publicity circulars and critical articles pasted in between its front and back covers. By virtue of this fact alone Ernst and Lindey had cleverly managed to introduce favourable expert literary testimony into the proceedings against *Ulysses*. The literary opinions contained in the critical reviews would form part of the very exhibit under scrutiny. This development was critical to the defence of *Ulysses*, but not only because it made otherwise irrelevant evidence directly pertinent to the proceedings.[33] It was also motivated by Ernst's desire to have the very test for determining the lawfulness of *Ulysses'* publication shifted from its impact on the average reader to its importance in the eyes of learned critics or experts. Vanderham explains, "By virtue of the fact that the imported copy of *Ulysses* was destined to be the sole piece of evidence in the upcoming proceedings, Ernst's decision to have the opinions of literary critics pasted therein was clearly motivated by his desire to ensure that the opinions of literary critics would be the fundamental standard by which *Ulysses* would be judged" (88, 91). Once this piece of the design was in place, Ernst and Lindey proceeded to search for the most "sympathetic" judge, to have another copy of *Ulysses* sent from the United Kingdom to the U.S. Department of the Treasury, in order to have the book admitted there as a "modern classic," and to compile a weighty stock of *expert* evidence purporting to demonstrate Joyce's esteemed literary reputation in general and the literary merit of *Ulysses* in particular (Kelly 1998, 109–115).

The expert evidence introduced by Ernst and Lindey that was not pasted into *Ulysses* followed the tradition established by Brandeis years before, insofar as it was compiled in the form of legal briefs. Ernst and Lindey furnished Justice Woolsey with a "Preliminary Memorandum," a "Claimant's Memorandum in Support of Motion to Dismiss Libel," and a "Supplementary Memorandum." Kelly recalls that the "Claimant's Memorandum" was a "massive document" which "included a short biography of Joyce, a description of the book itself, a description of Random House, a narrative of recent cases (including Woolsey's own decisions in the Stope's trials), Ernst's interpretation of the law, and his arguments for dismissing libel" (Kelly 1998, 115; citations omitted).[34]

The content of the memoranda was artfully tailored to convince Woolsey, the presiding judge, that Joyce's intended reading audience was a very narrow social sector of highly erudite and wealthy individuals, and that, as Kelly proposes, the "dirty parts" of *Ulysses* would be "entirely inaccessible" to the "masses" (Kelly 1998, 117, 120). Kelly recalls,

The evidence suggests that the audience of *Ulysses* was not even as broad as "the thinking [i.e., intellectual] public." In both the Preliminary Memorandum and the Claimant's Memorandum to Woolsey and in the Petition to the Secretary of the Treasury, Ernst called the writers of the testimonials a cross section of society: journalists, professors, critics, educators, authors, librarians, clergymen, and publishers. In an other place he added psychologists. Forty-nine men and women comprise the list. Of these, three were educators. One was a psychologist, one a sociologist, another an attorney. Thirty-nine could be described as editors, writers, or publishers. Ernst drew up his list of prominent citizens almost entirely from the literary professions. He was not able to garner much support from outside the industry because, apparently, in 1932 *Ulysses*'s audience did not extent beyond a relatively small class of literati (121; citations omitted).

Kelly's description of Ernst's memoranda invites a ready comparison with the "Social Science Statement" introduced much later in the *School Segregation Cases*. Both comprised a significant number of highly-educated "authorities" in matters of literature or social-psychology, most of whom provided an opinion more or less consistent with the arguments made by the lawyer who consulted them. Ernst's case is particularly remarkable because he so flagrantly "doctored the evidence" to prove that even though, by his own account, the only people capable of reading and understanding *Ulysses* were society's elite literati, *Ulysses* had somehow become acceptable to the "average" American (Kelly 1998, 123).

Vanderham points out the selective nature of the excerpts from the critical opinions contained in Ernst's different memoranda. He notes, for example, that Ernst's collection of favourable critical opinion does not include "James Douglas's view that *Ulysses* is 'the most infamously obscene book in ancient or modern literature.'" The excerpts also quote one critic as saying simply that "[t]he book is not pornographic," even though the critic's full statement continues, "but it is more indecent, obscene, scatological, and licentious than the majority of professedly pornographical books" (Vanderham 1998, 91; endnotes omitted).

Kelly recounts how, in preparation for his case, Ernst had sent out questionnaires to hundreds of libraries across the country, and on the basis of the answers he received, furnished Woolsey with a nationwide map purporting to show that the American public in general was reading and accepting *Ulysses*. Yet, as Kelly observes further, "the survey was a sham. Ernst translated his data into the map because presenting it any other way would damage his case. The evidence indicates there was little or no demand for *Ulysses* outside "ultra-sophisticated" circles. Many librarians did dissent from the accolades, and the praise other librarians volunteered was highly suspect" (Kelly 1998, 123–4).

Not only did Ernst draw his map primarily from one statistic alone (even though the distribution of the questionnaires provided many and that statistic itself failed to "indicate a general endorsement of the book"), Kelly points out that the testimonials drawn from the questionnaire and contained in the Preliminary Memorandum left "an impression as false as that left by the map." In Kelly's words, "The brief claims the comments were 'culled at random.' This was a lie. There is no more delicate way to put it. None of the negative comments, some of which I quoted above, found their way into any of the briefs. And most of the comments that were included are unreliable, because the opinions offered by the librarians are lifted, sometimes verbatim, from the cover letter that accompanied the questionnaire" (Kelly 1998, 126–7).

So Ernst, presumably with the best legal interests of his client, Cerf, in mind, as well as his own economic interests relating to his contract with Joyce, *and* his own distrust of juries' literariness, quite properly made *Ulysses* the subject of expert opinion evidence, however greatly that evidence was distorted at trial. Another real issue for this book, however, is of course Woolsey's response to Ernst and his experts. To recall, the legal test Woolsey had to apply to *Ulysses* was its level of acceptance among America's reading community at large – not among the literati Ernst had so deftly consulted.

Judge Woolsey's "Well-Intentioned" Decision

Woolsey was careful rhetorically to apply the "average-reader" test and to read *Ulysses* himself. However, it is plain from his written judgment and other correspondence that his finding that *Ulysses* was not obscene was directly influenced by his own very erudite familiarity with the available critical scholarship on *Ulysses*, and the confidence he placed in the opinions of two "literary assessors." In short, Woolsey was no "average" reader of *Ulysses*. Vanderham observes parenthetically that, prior to rendering his ruling on *Ulysses*, Woolsey had read "virtually every book written on *Ulysses* at the time" (Vanderham 1998, 116). One can only wonder how, in light of the vast theoretical and historical information gleaned by reading these texts, Woolsey could still pretend to determine *Ulysses*'s fate by reference to the proverbial "average" reader.

Woolsey likened the average reader to the "reasonable man" from tort law and tailored this person to the issue at hand by endowing him with "average sex instincts."[35] However, recognizing the justicial "risk" in relying on such a fiction, because of the "inherent tendency of the trier of facts" to transpose "his own idiosyncracies" onto it, Woolsey took the pains to measure his sexually reasonable man (*after* making his decision) against that of two friends. Happily for Woolsey, these friends shared the same kind of hypothetical "reagent" in the circumstances. More significant, however, is the fact that the friends – "literary assessors," as described by Woolsey – were "men whose opinion on literature and on life [he] value[d] most highly."

Indeed, Woolsey does not disclose the names of his average but esteemed confidants, but they were Charles E. Merrill Jr and Henry Seidel Canby (Kelly 1998, 119). Kelly is not entirely sure whether the former was the same Merrill who founded *Merrill Lynch* and launched *Family Circle* magazine, but the latter was clearly the Canby who had once been the editor of the *Literary Supplement to the New York Evening Post*, and at the time was founder of the *Saturday Review of Literature*. Clearly then, Woolsey's ostensibly sexually reasonable man was not ultimately delineated by the average sexual instincts of a "panel of 12," but an educated elite of three, who were erudite and perhaps very much socially isolated from anyone (such as a Customs officer) who might find Joyce's *Ulysses* obscene. Kelly observes in this regard,

Merrill and Canby may or may not have had average sex instincts. There is no way to tell today. But as these short biographical sketches indicate, they were not average readers. As Ernst pointed out, the obscenity laws were really meant to keep certain books out of the hands of the lower classes and the uneducated. Woolsey did not gauge the effect of *Ulysses* on them. His method of testing the book – showing it to men like himself – merely confirmed the elitism inherent in Ernst's defence. By consulting Canby (and, for all practical purposes, Merrill), Woolsey declared that an average reader of *Ulysses* or the reader into whose hands *Ulysses* was likely to fall was equivalent to the class of experts Ernst had mobilized on Joyce's behalf (120).

As a practical matter then, it is simply implausible to propose that *Ulysses* was properly judged by Woolsey in terms of its comprehensibility to and psychological impact upon the average reader. In effect, Woolsey substituted this test for that of the learned critics' appreciation of *Ulysses*. However necessary or even laudable such a change in approach might have appeared to the publishing and reading world at the time, it involved real conceptual and theoretical problems that have since had a direct bearing on subsequent obscenity prosecutions across both the United States of America and Canada.

Drawing a phrase from elsewhere, Vanderham provocatively claims that Woolsey's decision contains four "well-intentioned lies," which are rooted precisely in the critical or erudite approach to *Ulysses* that Woolsey preferred (Vanderham 1998, 116). Before turning to the "lies" identified by Vanderham, it is important to note why he considers them to be "well-intentioned." Vanderham believes, "These misrepresentations or falsehoods were well-intentioned because Woolsey used them to achieve a legitimate and good end: the liberation of one of the greatest literary works of the twentieth century. They were nonetheless lies (or falsehoods) because they misrepresented the nature of *Ulysses* and, implicitly, literature in general." Arguably, the same could be said about much of the expert literary evidence introduced into the recent Canadian *Little Sister's* trial. Chapter 5 of this book highlights how most of the expert opinion evidence supporting the Little Sister's Book and Art Emporium tended to paint a picture of gay and lesbian erotica as emancipatory and possibly cathartic for its writers and readers. Such a bold picture is undoubtedly well-intentioned, because the liberation of gay and lesbian sexually explicit narratives and images from the grip of prejudicial or homophobic Canada Customs officials is undoubtedly a "legitimate and good end." Nonetheless, chapter 5 also tries to show that the picture painted by the *Little Sister's* experts displays theoretical or conceptual flaws, at least insofar as it is meant to be contrasted with some kind of categorical portrait of sexually explicit heterosexual materials.

Returning to *Ulysses*, Woolsey accepted that literature can somehow be clearly distinguished from pornography, erotica, or obscenity (Vanderham 1998, 121). This assumption explains, in part, Woolsey's concern with authorial intent, specifically with the question: did Joyce have any pornographic interest in writing *Ulysses*? Woolsey firmly answered "No" to this question and was clearly influenced by the variety of favourable critical commentary regarding *Ulysses* that he had consulted. Vanderham reveals, however, that if Woolsey had researched more broadly, he would have found that Joyce definitely wrote *Ulysses* with pornographic interests in mind. Vanderham draws from the historical fact that Joyce "derived inspiration from popular literary forms like the newspaper, the sentimental romance and, more significantly, pornography"; and Vanderham refers to scholars such as Leslie Fiedler and Richard Brown who have emphasized the real importance that the pornographic genre held to Joyce's own writing (117). Equally important here, Vanderham proposes that many of the sexually explicit works that Joyce had read throw into question "any distinction between literature and pornography."

Second, Vanderham questions Woolsey's belief that a singular, authorial intention can be ascribed to any work of literature. For Vanderham, Woolsey's view that Joyce's literary purpose or aspirations in writing *Ulysses* must have precluded any moral or immoral intention on his part reflects the "esthetic theory" of art, which is hardly a widely accepted theory and was certainly not one to which Joyce evidently subscribed (Vanderham 1998, 122–3). In 1990 Adler wrote a critique of American obscenity law that relies on a picture of postmodern art that is remarkably similar to the one Vanderham attributes to Joyce's writing of *Ulysses*. Adler looks at the paintings of David Salle, for example, and how "Salle uses the language of pornography to deconstruct the language of representation itself." Adler states, "To rid [Salle's] paintings of their sexual imagery would be to rob them of their power" (Adler 1990, 1374). More recently Adler has written about "the new political art," some of which uses pornography specifically to subvert existing sexist and racist social and economic hierarchies (Adler 1996). Similarly, Vanderham shows that, although Joyce was undoubtedly concerned to create a work of art in *Ulysses*, he also had clear political and moral aims that he was hoping *Ulysses* could help him achieve and consciously put pornographic ingredients into the mix in the service of these goals (Vanderham 1998, 29–31, 122–4).

For Vanderham, the third misrepresentation Woolsey makes is that *l'homme moyen sensuel* reflects the proverbial average man in the street. As discussed earlier, Woolsey's otherwise sexually average man is a literary sophisticate who, by virtue of his refined literary palate, is not likely to feel any prurient affects upon reading the more sexually explicit passages in *Ulysses*. Vanderham adroitly points out that a better exemplar of the average sexual man than Woolsey and his two literary assessors is to be found in the very character of Leopold Bloom, the protagonist of *Ulysses*, who Joyce portrays at one juncture as having a highly sensual response to the *Sweets of Sin* (Vanderham 1998, 127).

The fourth well-meaning falsehood that Vanderham locates in Woolsey's judgment is the claim that Joyce's *Ulysses* contains no obscenity whatsoever. Vanderham traces this conclusion to Woolsey's informed view that the proper approach to determining whether a book is obscene or not is to try to identify the "dominant" effect of the work as a whole. For Vanderham, Woolsey was right to find that, viewed in its entirety or full artistic context, *Ulysses* is not legally obscene, but this determination should not have led Woolsey to conclude that *Ulysses* is void of obscene elements. Joyce himself acknowledged the presence of obscenity in *Ulysses*, as did at least one of his publishers, Sylvia Beach (Vanderham 1998, 125–6).

At the end of the day Ernst skillfully manipulated expert evidence and carefully crafted arguments to the effect that Joyce's *Ulysses*, in both its sublime and "dirty" aspects, could never arouse the "leer of the sensualist" because it was intellectually accessible only to America's upper crust, which included federal justices. In the course of doing so, Ernst adroitly managed to appeal to Woolsey's well-founded self-image as a "learned, even a literary jurist" (Kelly 1998, 118). Rhetorically,

Woolsey found that *Ulysses* was not obscene according to the broader "community" standard of decency, but what is more important to observe, and what Kelly makes perfectly clear, is that Ernst and Lindey, by taking *Ulysses* to trial in the way they did, and by so blatantly misrepresenting the nature of the testimonials provided to them by American librarians, publishers, and critics, almost singlehandedly made Joyce the esteemed writer in America he has since become. Kelly observes that throughout the trial no one ever challenged "the facts," and that Lindey was entirely confident that no one would do so (128, 130). Yet the artful, "expert" appearance of the "facts" produced a dramatic result that extended beyond the frontiers of American obscenity law at that time. Vanderham argues that Woolsey's decision represents the first legal triumph in America of the mistaken "esthetic theory" of art over that "traditional moral-esthetic theory" which prevailed in earlier obscenity prosecutions (including the 1921 trial of *Ulysses*) and of which *Ulysses* itself is an illustration (Vanderham 1998, 116, 122–4, 129). As Kelly remarks, "What is clear is that before the trial Joyce was considered neither a genius nor the author of classics, and after the trial he was" (Kelly 1998, 136).

LITERARY AND OTHER EXPERTS TAKE CENTRE STAGE: THE JURY IS OUT

When the U.S. government appealed Woolsey's decision to the Circuit Court of Appeals, the legal problem of determining "obscenity" according to an average intellect and "reasonable" sexual instinct became more obvious.[36] In a majority opinion, Judge Augustus Hand downplayed the issue of the work's effect on the reader's libido, emphasizing instead the issue of artistic or literary merit, or at least balancing the issue of sexual explicitness with that of overall thematic or literary effect.[37] In so doing, he relied upon his own opinion as to the overall artistic integrity of *Ulysses* and upheld the lower court's ruling. The dissenting judge, however, rejected Hand's novel approach to the traditional obscenity test and objected to the high-brow opinion of his brother regarding the book's literary merit. Judge Manton asked, "If we disregard the protection of the morals of the susceptible, are we to consider merely the benefits and pleasures derived from letters by those who pose as the more highly developed and intelligent? To do so would show an utter disregard for the standards of decency of the community as a whole and an utter disregard for the effect of a book upon the average less sophisticated member of society, not to mention the adolescent."[38]

Whether one prefers Hand's or Manton's decision in *One Book Entitled Ulysses*, the problem remains as to how the *average* conscience, *reasonable* sexual instinct, or *community* standard of decency is to be gauged in a community that does not appear to be, in Lippmann's words, "self-contained." Manton may well criticize Hand for substituting his "more highly developed" opinion in literary matters for those "less sophisticated" opinions, but Manton, insofar as he unequivocally finds some pages of *Ulysses* too indecent to "footnote," clearly substitutes his opinion in such matters for that of the community as a whole.[39] In light of the obviousness of this problem, and its apparent intractability, it is not surprising that some judges now began to look beyond themselves for such a measure. No less surprising, but much more problematic, is the direction the courts took to address this conundrum.

Judge Woolsey's cautious reference to "literary assessors" in the state-level *Ulysses* case provided the best hint of where the courts were going. In a 1936 prosecution for sending obscene advertisements by mail, Judge Learned Hand followed Judge Augustus Hand's decision in *One Book Entitled Ulysses* regarding the "dominant effect" of the work in question.[40] He also introduced a new rule of evidence into such matters. If the work in question is "new," he held, "the opinions of competent critics in published reviews or the like may be considered." Such evidence of "qualified critics," as distinct temporarily from the oral testimony of "expert witnesses at the trial," could be assumed to be fairly probative and "rationally helpful," although Judge Learned Hand made it clear that the jury is still expected to weigh the work's otherwise literary or scientific merit against its physiological or psychological effect on the reader, and in this sense, to determine the "ultimate" issue of obscenity.[41]

The introduction of the "qualified critic" into the anti-obscenity evidentiary pot was not the only sign that Judge Learned Hand had introduced an elitist element into matters of public interest. He also agreed with the trial judge's decision to reject evidence of "a list of purchasers of the books [advertised in the impugned circulars], among whom were a number of well-known persons." Perhaps the trial judge sought merely to protect such "well-known persons" from public embarrassment. On the other hand, Hand reasoned, "Such a list taken alone told nothing of the standing of the works in the mind of the community," noting that "even respectable persons may have a taste for salacity."[42] So the literary tastes of respectable people could not be seen to reflect those of the broader community (or even part of it), but the informed opinions of "qualified critics," many of whom are presumably "respectable

persons," are "rationally helpful" in determining the literary value of
any given work. This logic suggests not only that it is technical competence, as opposed to social respectability, that "qualifies" one to offer
opinions about literariness, and by implication, depravity or obscenity;
it also marks the beginning of an interesting tendency among judges in
such matters to value opinions more than behaviour, as if sworn opinions provide a more reliable measure of community standards of decency
in such matters than people's reading habits. Yet every sociologist is
well aware of the problem of hypocrisy or "attitude-behavior inconsis-
tency" in self-report and opinion surveys.[43] This problem states simply
that, for good reasons, individuals' opinions in surveys and polls may
well appear to be inconsistent with their behaviour. And as Lewontin
has suggested, the problem is particularly acute in matters of human
sexuality (Lewontin 1995a, 28–9). So it seems Judge Learned Hand is
simply incorrect in *Levine* when he asserts that a list of readers of the
publications in question says "nothing of the standing of the works in
the minds of the community." The plain fact that certain people read
the impugned *Crossways of Sex* tells something about the community's
overall perception of the book – possibly more than what a community-
wide opinion poll would have to say about it.

The *Ulysses* and *Levine* prosecutions illustrate that judges in the
1930s clearly felt the difficult issue of whom to call and when to call
experts in anti-obscenity prosecutions. This problem could have been
rooted simply in a conservative reluctance to accept, without more,
that sexually explicit prose or imagery could contain intelligent social
criticism. Perhaps, however, the emergent willingness or even desire
among some judges to hear from putative experts in obscenity litigation at this time simply reflected a wider change in attitude toward
experts encouraged much earlier by Pound. Even if Pound, though,
was not predominantly or visibly responsible on this score, another
force was at work in the world of law that was sure to give strength
to those judges who felt experts had something to offer about the
psychological and behavioural implications of naughty books.

THE EMERGENCE OF LEGAL REALISM

By 1930 Pound's intellectual influence on his professional peers had
waned as his "sociological jurisprudence" had come under attack from
an emergent group of legal scholars called Legal Realists (White 1972,
1013ff; Llewellyn 1930; 1931). White charts many variables that combined to create a sense of disenchantment with progressivist theorizing
and institutions, most notably the human devastation wrought by
World War I. Of special interest here is a mild shift that took place in

academic and professional attention to science. White observes that "after World War I, the term 'science' increasingly included the behavioral sciences, notably psychology and cultural anthropology" (White 1972, 1014). Ogburn confirms this development, but relates it specifically to social science. In a 1934 article he claims, "Perhaps the greatest expansion of activity during the past two decades in sociology has been in the field of social psychology. In sociology the interest in psychology has been much more marked than in economics or in political science, though the social aspects of psychology have been incorporated to a greater or lesser degree in all the social sciences" (Ogburn 1934, 210).[44] Pound himself acknowledged Ward's influence on the "sociological" school of jurisprudence at that time as a kind of reorientation of sociology away from biology toward psychology (Pound 1945, 306, 330).[45] As Pound explains, "Ward did not affect jurisprudence directly. But his contention that social forces were 'essentially psychic,' and hence that the foundations of sociology were to be found in psychology, led to a change of front which took away the supports of the mechanical and biological sociological jurisprudence" (330). Moreover, addressing the "percentage" decline in biological sociology generally at that time, Ogburn says, "The causes of this possible decline may be altogether special, namely, the natural ebb of an overexpanded interest in Darwinian biology and the very great rise of interest in culture, which has caused considerable modification in the claims of social biology" (Ogburn 1934, 212).[46]

According to White, legal scholars who took an interest in psychology found theories and empirical data to support a view of human behaviour somewhat antithetical to that of progressivists. Human behaviour was not necessarily amenable to scientifically designed forms of social control, nor happily oriented to social living in general, but instead "idiosyncratic and often irrational" (White 1972, 1015). By extension, the apparently "rational" decision-making processes of judges should involve some element of idiosyncracy and irrationality. To read between the lines of a judge's text, therefore, one need only to learn to enter his mind.

By 1940 at least one American court had formally recognized the desirability, if not the necessity, of admitting sociological and psychological expert opinion evidence into anti-obscenity prosecutions for the purpose of gauging community standards of decency.[47] Obviously, no thought was paid to randomly assembling a number of people from the street or "community" to hear their thoughts on such matters. Justice Miller noted that *People* v. *Muller* challenged the assumption that social science could be helpful from an evidentiary point of view. More important, Miller referred to Spencer's *The Study of Sociology* as an indication of "the profound ignorance of psychology and sociology which prevailed generally, when those opinions were written."[48]

In *Parmelee* v. *United States*, Miller defers to the works of various "social scientists," such as Schroeder's *"Obscene" Literature and Constitutional Law*, Ellis's *Studies in the Psychology of Sex*, and Sumner's *Folkways*, to support his finding that nudity is not necessarily or inherently obscene.[49] More importantly, Miller notes the relatively primitive state-of-the-art in professional sociological knowledge and relates this to political and economic constraints placed on social science research at that time. In his opinion, "it is only because social scientists are still working under conditions of enforced self-deception, similar to those which prevailed in the early days of the medical profession, that the propriety of the present book is questioned."[50] Miller is so convinced that social scientists can intelligently inform issues of nudity in modern life that he also expresses a desire for greater "freedom of scientific research and exposition in this field."[51] And to confirm the point that the current state-of-the-art in professional and academic sociology in general is inadequate, Miller quotes from both Spencer's *The Study of Sociology*, and Sumner and Keller's *The Science of Society*.[52] The passage from Spencer criticizes the fact that, at that time, sociologists had not yet applied natural scientific principles to their study of social phenomena. The passages from Sumner and Keller criticize the state of sociological knowledge at that time for not yet having applied Darwinian principles to the functioning of societies. One can only wonder how edifying Spencer's and Sumner and Keller's sociological analyses regarding the phenomenon of nudity would prove to be.

Despite his emphatic proclamation of the importance of social science evidence in anti-obscenity prosecutions, Miller's invitation to fellow judges to consult social scientists fell on deaf ears for at least another decade. In *Commonwealth* v. *Isenstadt* in 1945, one defendant actually sought to admit expert testimony from three witnesses, one being a child psychiatrist. *Isenstadt* is a particularly noteworthy case for several reasons. First, it was likely one of the earliest anti-obscenity prosecutions to involve the use of oral expert testimony. Second, the psychological or physiological aspect of the obscenity test – that is, the psychological or behavioural effect the book has on its readers – had become the focal element of the test in this case. Third, it was held that the "attitude of the community in accepting or rejecting the book" was not a sufficiently "notorious" or "indisputable" fact that a judge could take judicial notice of it.[53]

In *Isenstadt*, the defendant sought to provide oral expert testimony from a writer and teacher of literature, a child psychiatrist, and a professor of theology. Justice Qua does not specifically indicate which expert was called in support of each of the various opinions advanced by the defendant.[54] These opinions included the view that the impugned book, *Strange Fruit*, was sincerely written, that it would elevate (as opposed to corrupt) morals, and that it would not create lustful or lecherous desires in anyone. Without knowing the theology professor's role in this, it is significant that he, like the others, was an accredited professional of one sort or another. They all evoke a sense of authority. The writer and teacher of literature probably testified regarding the overall literary merit of the book (that is, that it was "sincerely written") and possibly that it would elevate morals. The use of a professional literary person here was already foreshadowed by Judge Woolsey's personal appeal to a couple of "literary assessors" in the *Ulysses* trial. These assessors were presumed to typify the readers who would respond to *Ulysses* reasonably, as far as its effect on their libido was concerned, but their literary knowledge was also assumed to bear on the overall literariness of *Ulysses*. By the time *Strange Fruit* was being prosecuted, it seems that the "dominant effect" aspect of the obscenity test had been overshadowed by the "physiological effect" of the work on its readers, which may account partly for the defendant's decision in *Isenstadt* to call a psychiatrist. A psychiatrist is purportedly trained to understand physiological behaviour or reactivity to sexual stimuli. A child psychiatrist might have been called because the defendant was charged specifically with selling a work that, among other things, "manifestly tends to corrupt the morals of youth."[55]

Inasmuch as *Isenstadt* is an evidentiary landmark in obscenity law because it actually received expert testimony, it is equally important because Qua rejected this evidence out of hand. He reiterated the traditional, textbook rule, saying, "The principal matter about which expert opinion was sought was nothing more than the reaction of normal human beings to a kind of stimulation which is well within the experience of all mankind."[56] Assuming "the probable effect upon the general public" is a matter of "general human nature,"[57] Qua could not justify giving the expert testimony any real weight. Yet Qua's decision to reject the expert testimony in *Isenstadt* was not simply a matter of rigid application of rules or legal formalism. He introduced a kind of "flood-gates" argument into his reasons, suggesting that admission of expert testimony on the question of readers' reactions to certain kinds of imagery or narratives might lead to the reception of expert evidence in all kinds of criminal and civil cases "where issues of fact depend upon the emotions and reactions of normal persons in the conditions to which they are exposed."[58] This seems to be a problem for Qua in two respects.

First, Qua does not attribute the same "good sense" to experts, for example, in "literature or psychiatry," as he does to trial judges and juries with respect to knowledge about specific matters of human behaviour and psychology.[59] This is interesting because it suggests that experts have little to contribute to popular or lay conceptions regarding the psychological and behavioural effect of reading or watching pornography and erotica. Experts from the fields of "literature or psychiatry," or anywhere else, may well share (perhaps privately) the same "good sense" as anyone from the "general public" in such matters, but the good sense of the former is not always conveyed in courtroom proceedings.

Second, Qua proposes that if judges attribute special, probative knowledge to experts in matters of human morals and behaviour, then obscenity trials will become beset by an "expensive array of experts on both sides."[60] In this respect, Qua's decision is somewhat prescient, for he comments, "Experience in those fields in which expert testimony is now admittedly necessary does not lead us to look with favor upon such a sweeping extension. Without prejudging the indefinite future, we are not convinced that the time has come for it." As will now be explained, it was only a short time before American courts became less resistant to the opinions of other professionals besides themselves in the fact-finding enterprise, and the ensuing extension of a vast array of experts in anti-obscenity prosecutions could fairly be described as "sweeping." Today the presence of any variety of experts in obscenity proceedings is nearly institutionalized, but it is still not clear that, to construe Qua's words loosely, the time has come for this change. To understand why, it is worth taking a look at Justice Jerome Frank's contribution to this debate.

THE INFLUENCE OF LEGAL REALISM ON OBSCENITY LEGISLATION

Shortly after *Isenstadt* was decided, a very important obscenity case was heard by Justice Jerome Frank in the United States Circuit Court of Appeals. In *Roth* v. *Goldman* Frank, one of the originators of the Legal Realist movement, strongly believed that the acculturated beliefs and personal prejudices of the judge played a pivotal role in moulding the content of a written judgment (Frank 1963; White 1972, 1019).[61] In order to diminish this personal or "subjective" element in judicial decision-making, Frank proposed that judges not only educate themselves in the field of psychology (and apply psychological insights to their own judicial decision-making efforts), and abandon their naive and perhaps misguided belief in legal uniformity and consistency, but also employ experts to assist them in the determination of matters of fact (White 1972, 1020; Frank 1949, 23–4). Despite his recognition, however, of the need for expert assistance in ascertaining some kinds of facts,

mainly "adjudicative" facts at issue in "administrative law" type disputes (Frank 1949, 23–4), it is by no means clear that Frank welcomed
the kind of knowledge possessed by all branches of the so-called "social
sciences" at that time. For example, he was highly critical of the use of
social statistics to support "background" or "social and economic
facts," or what are now called legislative or constitutional facts. Accordingly, he took direct aim at the justicial propriety of the so-called "Brandeis brief," now generically named after Brandeis's formal presentation
of social statistics in the 1908 *Muller* v. *Oregon* case. According to
Frank, "The 'Brandeis briefs,' using statistical and related 'data,' were,
for a long time, used by government lawyers to win law-suits against
private corporations. Those court victories were due largely to the fact
that the opposing lawyers did not file briefs containing contradictory
data of the same kind." Moreover, Frank recalls that since corporate
executives began to retain their own "experts" who would file "contradictory" yet relevant data, "government victories have become less certain." One explanation for this situation is simply that "when 'experts'
with contrasting views collate statistics, each expert can often assemble
figures which plausibly confirm his position" (Frank 1950, 210–12).

Frank was unreservedly critical of the statistician's and social scientist's pretension to being "scientific" (Frank 1963, xxvi; Frank 1950,
212, 216; Frank 1955, 10). For him, the social world of human life
was simply too complex and multifarious to enable variables to be
"controlled" for the purposes of making meaningful correlations or
accurate predictions of social behaviour based on such correlations
(Frank 1950, 214; Frank 1955, 10).[62] And indeed, even though Frank
relied heavily on different kinds of psychology, including Freudian-
based child psychology and psychoanalysis, to provide some explanation for judges' and lawyers' occupational concern with the "illusion"
of legal certainty, uniformity, and predictability, he did not hold this
discipline out as being somehow particularly "scientific," or as being
more or less "authoritative" than other disciplines within the social
sciences generally (Frank 1963; Frank 1950, 215). This latter position
merits particular attention because it highlights Frank's main contribution to the great ongoing debate within the judiciary about the
proper role of social science evidence in American constitutional law.

Roth v. *Goldman* is significant for at least two reasons. The first
concerns its attitude toward psychological and sociological evidence.
The second relates to its view of the proper relationship between the
judiciary and the executive branch of government in obscene mail
cases. Indeed, this aspect of the case bears salient comparison with
much Canadian jurisprudence regarding the powers of the judiciary to
review and invalidate the wisdom of the legislature in areas that touch

upon the public welfare, such as the area of obscene publications. Specifically, *Roth* v. *Goldman* suggests an approach to judicial review that is comparable to the Canadian "reasonable apprehension of harm" doctrine. In both cases, a decision by a court to invalidate the wisdom of legislative body will depend on the presence or availability of various kinds of social science evidence. Ultimately, therefore, the primary focus of this comparison will be understanding how this social science evidence becomes "authoritative."

The importance of psychology and sociology to Roth's appeal against the postmaster general's exclusion of *Waggish Tales from the Czech*[63] in *Roth* v. *Goldman* lies in Frank's key observation that the prevention of "socially harmful sexual conduct," as opposed to "normal sexual desires," is the only constitutionally proper basis for suppressing obscene publications.[64] Frank thus flatly rejects earlier jurisprudence which implicitly accepted the constitutional validity of the *Hicklin* test, aimed narrowly at the moral depravity or physiological corruption that may befall some reader of an obscene publication. For Frank, the mere arousal of sexual desires or prurient interests is not necessarily socially dangerous. In the absence of evidence of a "clear and present danger" to society presented by the reading of otherwise obscene books, the suppression of books that arouse "normal sexual desires" should be deemed well beyond the scope of government regulation, especially since the right of free speech and free press is constitutionally guaranteed to all citizens.[65]

Having articulated a new evidentiary threshold in anti-obscenity prosecutions, Frank provides a glimpse as to how this threshold might be met in practice. "Perhaps," he says, referring to proof of the social harmfulness of reading sexually stimulating books, "in order to be trustworthy, such proof ought to be at least as extensive and intensive as the Kinsey Report."[66] This suggestion marks a significant development in the evidentiary approach to obscenity law to date. It newly entrusts psychological, sociological, and behavioural science research with relevant and probative knowledge in judicial inquiries touching upon matters of great public importance. As the last chapter showed, by now the American judiciary had been introduced to the Realist legal scholars, pioneered in America by Frank himself, as well as Karl Llewellyn. Both of these writers were adherents of the heuristic value of psychology and behavioural-psychology in law. So, while deferring to the otherwise "helpful" opinions of West, "a psychiatrist well versed in matters legal,"[67] Frank also refers to his own *Law and the Modern Mind* and *Fate and Freedom*, which point out the "fallibility" of psychiatry, construed as "an art still in its period of infancy" and "tainted by a superfluous deterministic philosophy."[68] This appears as either a plainly curious or surprisingly perceptive statement when viewed in light of the fact that Freudian ideas had become very influential among a wide variety of professionals (including psychologists) in America by the 1930s (Bullough 1994, 148–50). In any case, the psychological and behavioural science approach to the issue of societal harm resulting from sexual arousal is now considered heuristically valuable, but this is not necessarily true of the psychiatric approach. From an evidentiary point of view, this preferential treatment is problematic in itself, but Frank compounded the problem by turning to a couple of sociological surveys to support the view that reading obscene books may well divert a reader away from, as opposed to stimulate him or her to, anti-social conduct.[69] Frank maintains that the "statistical results" of the studies canvassed do not offer "conclusive" evidence of the proposition at issue, but they do "cast doubt upon the assertion that 'immoral' books corrupt and deprave."[70]

Frank's deference to the sociological surveys contained in Alpert's article also constitutes an evidentiary precedent in American anti-obscenity litigation. As Frank concedes, such surveys may be considered informative, but by no means conclusive, of the proposition that reading obscene books does not lead to socially injurious behaviour. Viewed conversely, however, he notes that there is no evidence in the case before him which demonstrates with certainty that socially harmful effects will likely flow from reading obscene literature.[71] And in a constitutional case, it is especially important to establish clearly the purported relation between reading obscene literature and acting dangerously. Frank observes that accuracy has been nearly impossible to obtain in such cases to date, perhaps simply "because of the primitive state of our psychological knowledge." As a heuristic alternative to discerning the social harmfulness of certain kinds of literature, lower courts have therefore preferred to identify "the current mores" or attitude of the community with respect to certain kinds of literature.[72] Yet this approach returns Frank to the original evidentiary conundrum of his brothers – namely, how to discern "community standards" of decency, or more simply, "public opinion" in such matters. Should he simply presume the reasonableness of the postmaster general's opinion? Or should he consult public-opinion surveys, experts (individually or in panels), or the collectively "average" opinion of jurors? Whatever route is followed, Frank is clear that the constitutional nature of the case before him requires him to be especially discerning. He states that where a "suppression statute approaches unconstitutionality, I would think that a reviewing court should scrutinize with more than ordinary care such an administrative determination with respect to public opinion."[73]

Frank recognizes that public-opinion polls "may go badly astray," as evidenced by the electoral polls relating to Truman's presidential election at that time. He also contemplates the reliability of opinions of fellow judges and lawyers, suggesting that lawyers should not be presumed to share a unique or exclusive opinion in such matters, as if they were "a race apart, or an intellectual elite." And, most important, he considers the usefulness of "social science" in the immediate regard. For Frank, social science data provide possibly the least reliable means of determining public opinion. Relying once again on his own scholarly writings, he concedes that "most studies of society" are not "useless for all purposes" but, to the extent that they purport to be highly accurate, they "are further away from the 'scientific' than were alchemy or astrology."[74] Perhaps here, at this stage in his reasons for judgment, Frank most clearly reveals his overall preference for a psychological approach to legal conflict-resolution and the skepticism toward other disciplines, such as psychiatry and sociology, that such an allegiance entails. Of course, this development reveals a much greater evidentiary problem brewing in American constitutional law, which is how to select among increasing numbers of conflicting scientific and social scientific opinions and methodologies. Suffice it to say, this problem has not been resolved to this day.

A FORMALISTIC PAUSE ON THE PATH TO EXPERT ADJUDICATION

Approximately five years after *Roth* v. *Goldman*, a Missouri appeal court was presented with a constitutional challenge to a state law prohibiting the possession of obscene publications "with intent to sell or circulate." From an evidentiary perspective, *State* v. *Becker* recalled elements of both *Commonwealth* v. *Isenstadt* and *Roth* v. *Goldman*. It was reminiscent of *Roth* v. *Goldman* insofar as Judge Conkling suggested that judges were capable of giving an opinion about obscenity from a layperson's point of view. And it was similar to *Isenstadt* as Conkling rejected the propriety of expert "psychological and philosophical" testimony on the subject of the "obscenity" of the nude photographs in question. Conkling's reasons for rejecting the expert evidence in this case are interesting for at least two reasons. First, he argued that the relevant terms of the prohibition – "obscene, lewd, licentious, indecent or lascivious" – were of sufficiently common usage that "most every person (and certainly the trial judge) understands their meaning." Indeed, it is fair to say that, for Conkling, the trial judge and "most every person" perhaps understand the meaning of the above terms *better than* experts in psychology and philosophy.[75] He states, "the learned trial [judge] ... knew far better than any lay professor when, under the statute controlling judicial decisions, the publications were *in fact* and in law obscene and immoral."[76] The

Southampton Solent University

Circulation system messages:
Patron in file

Title: Webworks :
ID: 464120
Due: 09/12/2013 23:10
Circulation system messages:
Loan performed

Title: Censorship.
ID: 361651
Due: 09/12/2013 23:10
Circulation system messages:
Loan performed

Title: Judging obscenity :
ID: 472600
Due: 03/01/2014 24:00
Circulation system messages:
Loan performed

Total items: 3
12/12/2013 15:15

Circulation system messages:
Missing ID and verification.

Thank you for using the
3M SelfCheck™ System.

reference to the factual determination of obscenity raises the second interesting development in Conkling's reasoning.

One precondition for admitting expert opinion evidence into court is that it be helpful or useful, by informing the trier-of-fact (judge or jury) about some matter apparently beyond their intelligence (Sopinka, Lederman, and Bryant 1992, 533–4). To the extent that Conkling felt the trial judge did not need special assistance in interpreting the ordinary meaning of "obscene," he properly upheld the trial judge's decision to exclude the "lay professor's" opinion in the matter. Yet Conkling rationalized his decision further. He argued that the "defendant could not substitute the claimed expert witness's opinion thereon for the *ultimate fact* which the trial court was compelled to find and rule."[77] Conkling is correct to point out that, according to the so-called "ultimate issue" rule, an expert is not permitted to express an opinion regarding the "ultimate fact" in issue, but only to provide opinion evidence from which the trier-of-fact can draw inferences regarding this ultimate fact.[78] Yet Conkling's strict application of the ultimate issue rule is problematic. Whether the publications in question were either offensive or inoffensive to "good morals," and whether they could or could not "arouse lustful desires, or encourage commission of crime by the susceptible man or woman, boy or girl,"[79] are "ultimate" issues, technically beyond the jurisdiction of the college professor, but the latter question broaches the arena of legislative facts, for which the ultimate issue rule has been relaxed. Conkling's analysis asks: In what sense is the exhibition of the same and similar photographs harmful to society at all? Who is at risk of harm from the "susceptible man or women?" And what kind of danger does this person face? In hindsight, Conkling's reliance on the rule in *State* v. *Becker* enabled him to rationalize his finding that the nude photographs in question were obscene, despite the contrary view held by the professor of philosophy and psychology, by substituting *his* opinion for that of the expert.

INSTITUTING EXPERT TESTIMONY IN AMERICAN FIRST AMENDMENT ADJUDICATION

Shortly after *State* v. *Becker,* and nearly six decades since the turn of the century, American courts had almost come full swing, from categorically dismissing the helpfulness of expert witnesses in anti-obscenity prosecutions to encouraging expert opinion in such matters almost as a necessary precondition for the possibility of a fair trial. In 1957 the American Supreme Court ruled that freedom of speech under the First Amendment did not extend to speech which amounted to "obscenity."[80]

A couple of years later, in *Smith* v. *California*, Justice Black and Justice Frankfurter suggested that the exclusion of relevant expert evidence regarding community standards in an obscenity prosecution would constitute a violation of "due process."[81] This idea, however, was met with only partial acceptance by the American judiciary. It was taken seriously in a 1965 case and a 1973 case, as well as in some subsequent American legal scholarship,[82] but other judges clearly repudiated it. For example, in *Paris Adult Theatre I* v. *Slaton*, Chief Justice Burger of the United States Supreme Court proposed that the use of expert evidence to demonstrate community standards in obscenity proceedings may often make "a mockery out of the otherwise sound concept of expert testimony."[83] *Paris Adult Theatre I* v. *Slaton* was the first reported United States Supreme Court decision to work with the new constitutionally accepted definition of obscenity established by the same court in *Miller* v. *California*. The so-called *Miller* test is particularly noteworthy here as it requires the court to ask whether "the *average* person, applying contemporary community standards" would find that the impugned work largely appeals to prurient interest.[84] The reference to "average" person suggests that expert evidence would be inappropriate to inform the question of prurient interest and recalls Judge Woolsey's circuitous means of discerning the average readers' behavioural response to *Ulysses*. It should not seem surprising, therefore, that shortly after the test was articulated, a high court judge eschewed the need for expert assistance on this issue. In *United States* v. *Groner,* Judge Gewin of the United States Court of Appeals observed, "The requirement that the prosecution support its proof by expert testimony on the elements of obscenity is misconceived, unnecessarily burdensome, and confounds traditional concepts of proof. It is little more than a fetishism formulated in the name of the first amendment."[85]

Gewin's opinion regarding expert evidence was met with strong dissent, indicating that, at least by the mid-1970s, the American judiciary lacked consensus with respect to the role of expertise in First Amendment adjudication. Depending on who was presiding over the case, either judges, experts, or "average" people in the street were considered to be best situated intellectually to determine matters of community standards of tolerance, issues of artistic integrity or merit, and ultimately, therefore, questions of obscenity. Indeed, the *Miller* test for obscenity also permits a defence of "serious literary, artistic, political, or scientific value";[86] and even though it is difficult to see how, logically, expert evidence should be barred from informing this aspect of the test, in 1987 one United States Supreme Court judge held that a work's seriousness should be determined by the "reasonable" person.[87] Justice Stevens dissented on this point out of concern that the new "reasonable" or "average" person standard would enable juries to downplay the opinions of experts. Bearing in mind Woolsey's earlier reliance on "literary assessors" to help him determine "average sex instincts," one still needs to be skeptical about the sincerity of even those judges who purported to seek community standards solely in the average juror. Judges may express an aversion to the opinions of experts and at the same time laud the common sense of the average juror regarding matters of morals and sexuality, but where a jury does not actually decide such matters, it is not always clear that the judges do not simply prefer their own "informed" opinions to those of the hypothetical juries. The following remark by Gewin is precisely the kind of judicial pronouncement that both criticizes the role of literary and other experts in obscenity litigation and pays lip-service to the intelligence of the average juror, only to support ultimately the competence of a single judge to determine factual issues of obscenity:

To hold, in effect, that we must turn the application of obscenity statutes over "to a collection of randomly chosen Ph.D.'s" as expert witnesses in such matters, is to require abdication of the judicial function of the judge or jury as triers of fact. Under our system of law it is the trier of fact who is responsible for the legal determinations whether the materials involved are obscene within the definition of that term as explicated in *Roth*. The jury which is drawn from a cross-section of the community embodies the average or reasonable man and that collective group is as capable as any other of making the critical determination necessary under proper instructions from the trial judge.[88]

The very live issue of laypersons' competency to know whether ostensibly obscene publications or pictures have serious artistic or other value returned to the fore in the famous 1990 criminal prosecution of Cincinnati's Contemporary Art Center and its director, Dennis Barrie. As the museum's defence lawyer explains, a number of grand jurors were assembled in court one Saturday morning in April and then taken to the Contemporary Art Center to view a retrospective exhibit of approximately 175 of Robert Mapplethorpe's photographs (Mezibov 1992, 12). Once there, the jurors were sufficiently disturbed by a small number of explicit homoerotic photographs and photographs showing nude children to issue a two-count indictment against the museum and Barrie: one for pandering obscenity and the other for displaying photographs depicting nude children.

Mezibov saw one of his primary challenges as picking a jury that had at least some exposure to museum art, particularly contemporary museum art. He discovered that only a half-dozen of sixty prospective jurors had ever visited a museum other than a local natural history museum. Originally "disheartened" by this revelation, Mezibov took some solace in discovering that the jurors expressed a real willingness to receive "the exotic opinions of carefully chosen people who looked and sounded much like" themselves (Mezibov 1992, 12–13). Mezibov must have been genuinely concerned about the "unaided" intellectual competence of the local jurors, for he argued in court that a layperson without specialized art training should be presumed to be incapable of making sophisticated determinations of artistic value without the help of expert witnesses (15, 71). He lost this argument. This illustrates that at least on this occasion the presiding judge held the intellectual powers of jurors in higher esteem than Mezibov did.

Mezibov need not have been concerned that the jurors presiding over the Mapplethorpe trial would have to make determinations of artistic value in the dark. Apparently the courtroom was well lit with a careful selection from "a seemingly unlimited number of the nation's most respected experts – artists, scholars, and critics, all with impeccable credentials – who offered their services to the defense" (Mezibov 1992, 13). As in the much-publicized Canadian *Little Sister's* trial that will be discussed in chapter 5, the 1992 Cincinnati Contemporary Art Center prosecution provided enough limelight for interested experts to render monetary compensation superfluous, and perhaps ignoble. Whereas in such a situation one need not concern oneself about expert opinions appearing partial to the party who pays the hourly or daily attendance fee, one should nonetheless question the intellectual neutrality of people prepared to incur some, perhaps considerable, expense to participate in a sensational piece of history.

Mezibov recalls that his defence team sought a balance of experts in terms of sex and geography, and eventually decided upon five people. These were the extant director of the Getty Museum in Los Angeles, a curator from the Eastman Kodak Institute of Photography, the museum director at the University of California, and the longstanding art critics of Cincinnati's two daily newspapers (Mezibov 1992, 13–14). Mezibov does not hesitate to add that the latter two critics had already written approvingly of Mapplethorpe's exhibition. The prosecution called only one expert, from the field of communications, to give an opinion specifically in relation to the two counts of displaying photographs of nude children. Someone from the prosecution's legal team suggested that it could not afford to call expert rebuttal testimony in general, but Mezibov believes that an expert with the ability to rebut the defence expert opinion evidence would simply have been too hard to find at the time. This could not likely have been the case. Without trial transcripts of the expert testimony on hand, it is difficult to analyse the relevant expert opinion evidence piece by piece, but Samaras has observed that "the defence relied heavily on the argument that a masterful command of formalism and aesthetics precluded Mapplethorpe's images from being obscene" (Samaras 1993, 81). In other words, the experts would have explained how Mapplethorpe's photographs displayed a real commitment to aesthetic formalism and possibly classicism (Mezibov 1992, 12; Adler 1996, 1535–6). Yet several years after the Cincinnati trial, Adler explains how a wider artistic and critical community has become confused by Mapplethorpe's work in general, to the point where Adler can say, "Many critics still cannot decide how to read Mapplethorpe's work" (Adler 1996, 1543). She elaborates, "Critics have given a range of contradictory political readings of Mapplethorpe's work, arguing about whether it reaffirms or subverts stereotypes about race and sexual orientation ... One of Mapplethorpe's favorite subjects was nude black men, often pictured in eroticized, classical poses. Earlier, I suggested that this work be read as a demand that the viewer see black men as heroic, worthy subjects of classical art. But there is another reading of this work that is deeply troubling: many have suggested that it draws on racist stereotypes of black men as exotic sexual objects" (1542–3).

More important than waging yet another battle of art critics here, it is worth appreciating that Barrie and the Contemporary Art Center of Cincinnati were acquitted of all charges against them by the jury which Mezibov describes as "hardly cosmopolitan" (Mezibov 1992, 13). What does such an outcome say about the intellectual competence of jurors generally – particularly of those provincial members living in Lippman's "self-contained" community? It says possibly that otherwise obtuse, technical information can be eloquently translated into terms that are familiar and comprehensible to a broad cross-section of society. It also says that, despite the distrust trial lawyers such as Morris Ernst have of jurors' abilities to put personal prejudices aside when asked to apply the black letter of the law to courtroom facts, jurors can act rationally and honestly in the face of troublesome situations. This image should at least give added force to this book's own insistence that any average community that is assembled or imagined for the purposes of obscenity litigation need not be devoid of laypersons.

POSTMODERN ART AND *ULYSSES* REVISITED

The explicit photographs of men in homoerotic and at times sadomasochistic poses which were at issue in the prosecution of the Cincinnati Contemporary Arts Center provide Adler with one of various examples of contemporary or postmodern art that cannot be judged properly by the *Miller* test (Adler 1996, 1555–6). Adler has recently criticized the *Miller* requirement that art must have a "serious" value in order to enjoy constitutional protection, as being incommensurate with the very spirit of postmodern art (Adler 1990, 1993). For Adler, postmodern artists can be identified by the different ways they "rebel" against the "stifling and idealistic confines of late Modernism," such as the "Modernist distinctions between good art and bad, between high art and popular culture, between the sanctity of the art context and real life," as well as the "Modernist demand that art be 'serious'" (Adler 1990, 1363–4).[89] Adler's concern is that if, as a matter of broad principle or theory, postmodern art effectively challenges the notion that art must be "serious," or possess "serious literary, artistic, political or scientific *value*" in *Miller*'s terms, then *Miller* cannot be applied intelligently or logically to test the legality of postmodern art, and perhaps any other genre of art. This point is especially important to consider, Adler implies, where the postmodern art in question seems to be obviously or consciously "obscene." Here the element of obscenity in the work or performance could be integral to the very nature of that work or performance as a work or piece of art.

Before turning to some ostensibly obscene, postmodern works of art that purport to challenge the very distinction between art and obscenity, it is worth recalling Vanderham's analyses of the trial of Joyce's *Ulysses*. Vanderham made clear at least two points which are of great relevance to Adler's review of postmodern art and the *Miller* test. First, Vanderham's scholarship shows that Joyce consciously incorporated pornographic or obscene elements into his writing of *Ulysses*. Second, Vanderham proposes that, in writing *Ulysses*, Joyce intended to be morally critical, political, and at any rate subversive (Vanderham 1998, 122–3).

The first observation is important as it gives strength to Adler's belief that, as a matter of art theory, a publication or performance can be both artistic and obscene. For Adler, the clearly pornographic or obscene aspects of Karen Findley's or Annie Sprinkle's contemporary stage and other public "performances" should not in themselves render the performances inartistic (Adler 1990, 1369). Similarly, the sexually explicit homoerotic or sadomasochistic photographic images of Robert Mapplethorpe, or the sadomasochistic imagery in David Salle's paintings, should not make these works categorically obscene (1370, 1373–4). This aspect of Adler's postmodern critique of the *Miller* test, especially of the basic premise "that art can be distinguished from obscenity," clearly echoes Vanderham's belief that Judge Woolsey's strict distinction between literature and pornography proper was a "well-intentioned lie." Remarkably, although Joyce's *Ulysses* can plausibly be regarded in part as a conscious literary reaction to the very kind of modernist approach to art and culture described by Adler, Joyce could not have seen himself as "postmodernist"; in fact he saw himself as a harbinger of "the new realism" (Vanderham 1998, 122–3; citing Power). This otherwise banal historical or academic point reminds the reader (and the judge) yet again of the highly tentative nature of expert evidence in the realm of art.

Power once described Joyce as a "literary conspirator, who was determined to destroy the oppressive and respectable cultural structures under which we had been reared" (Power 1974, 69). Clearly Power sees Joyce as a subversive, and according to much of the expert evidence introduced into the 1933 *Ulysses* trial, Joyce was also a very serious writer. Perhaps this latter aspect of Joyce's writing alone – his very seriousness of purpose, subversive as it might be – suffices to keep Joyce firmly out of Adler's postmodernist camp. Adler rhetorically associates real seriousness of purpose with modernist art, but a close reading of her analyses reveals that, for her, postmodern art is frivolous only in the sense that it does not take itself seriously as original or pure art (Adler 1990, 1366–7). That is to say, as a philosophy of art, it proclaims that art cannot be and should not endeavour to be pure, lofty, or original, but rather should consciously embrace its derivativeness (Adler 1996, 1518). At the same time, however, Adler states plainly that some of the more clearly obscene postmodern works of art are created and performed with a serious political or moral message in mind (1517–44), and proposes, remarkably, that only *expert* critical opinion could convince a court of this. In writing about "The New Political Art," Adler draws attention to Karen Finley's use of sexually explicit and sexually violent depictions in her performances, and to similar uses of graphic sexual and violent imagery by Sue Coe and Marlene McCarty. Adler believes they raise a real issue of "the subversive *appropriation* of pornography for explicitly activist purposes" (1526–9). Adler mentions, for example, how "many" writers see Karen Finley's live acts of on-stage defecation or graphic depictions of bizarre sexual activities "as a powerfully subversive reading of female degradation in American society" (Adler 1990, 1369, 1373; citations omitted). Yet Adler also pays heed to feminist critics who have questioned the "emancipatory" nature of Finley's work, conceding that "the reality is more complex" (1542).

Adler expresses her concern that the *Miller* test threatens "the growing body of political art about AIDS" which Adler associates with postmodern works of art (Adler 1990, 1373; 1996, 1517–18, 1531–40). Adler also draws from informed critical sources to highlight the sincerity of artistic purpose in both Robert Mapplethorpe's photography and David Salle's painting (Adler 1990, 1373–4). As mentioned above, Adler recognizes that art critics are in disagreement about the political import of Mapplethorpe's work. Does it reaffirm or subvert "stereotypes about race and sexual orientation?" she asks, and answers only that the "question has become hotly debated" (Adler 1996, 1542–4). Whether or not this question and other interpretive problems relating to postmodern art will ever be resolved is of no concern here; but, once again the lack of consensus in this field should raise an eyebrow about the alleged "expertise" of the critics involved. Perhaps more disconcerting is the way that a group of otherwise "post"–modernist artists such as Finley, Sprinkle, Mapplethorpe, Salle, and others, who by Adler's terms should appear to be somewhat cynical and self-mocking, suddenly become distinctively modernist, by virtue of their artistic sincerity and high seriousness of purpose.

Leaving academic scruples about modernism, high-modernism, and postmodernism aside, Adler's analysis of postmodern art and the *Miller* test of obscenity becomes most engaging at the very point at which it considers the role of expert evidence in determining what is and is not a work of art. Adler clearly does not want the traditional question of "artistic merit" to be decided by judges, but neither does she want this matter to be entrusted solely to the "critics, scholars, and museums" (Adler 1990, 1374–5, 1377). She explains that the latter, critical acceptance, or peer recognition, approach "would not protect undiscovered artists, developing artists, unpopular artists, or artists who are 'ahead of their time.'" The last group of artists mentioned is a curious choice, given the way that the avant-garde is problematized in a postmodern approach to art. If, as Foster describes, postmodernism is articulated in relation to "cultural" terms that are conceived "logically, [and] not derived historically" but "in terms of structure" (Foster 1994, 191), it certainly becomes difficult to imagine an avant-garde postmodern artist in traditional historical terms.

More important, just as Adler is reluctant to trust the elite world of art critics', scholars', and museums' capacity to discern the truly postmodern artist and work of art, she is as skeptical, as Mezibov was in defending the Cincinnati Contemporary Arts Center, that an uninformed jury could ever make such a designation. Adler's reason for withholding this central issue from the jury is simply that the nature of contemporary and postmodern art is somehow intrinsically elusive or at least subversive. There is no single "standard" for understanding or measuring the quality of postmodern art, she suggests, because "art" in its "recent incarnation violates any definition we give it" (Adler 1990, 1378). This final observation simply avoids the real problem that sometimes a writer or performer will publish or perform a so-called work that has little or no redeeming character except to shock, disgust, offend, titillate, or gratify oneself or a public audience. As this book has endeavoured to show so far, established critics or scholars cannot always, or even often, be trusted to view the matter comprehensively or through an aesthetically or morally liberal lens. The experts themselves, such as Adler, will openly or secretly wear their morally liberal or conservative stripes, as will the proverbial average juror. So as long as works stand to be judged by some prevalent measure of obscenity, Adler and other critics need to recognize that a so-called "community" standard in principle embraces the opinions of experts and laypersons alike. Adler at one point expresses her concern that "lay notions of what constitutes 'art'" not be allowed to prevail with respect to issues of postmodern art, but she also notes the importance of the lay audience or following to Finley and Sprinkle (Adler 1990, 1376–8). Why should the lay audience here be any more entitled to determine the legality of Finley's and Sprinkle's works than the established world of art criticism, or vice versa? Both worlds likely have something to learn from the other.

Without delving any further into the American scene in this regard, it can be said fairly that, by the mid-1970s, Canadian courts had only begun to engage in this same kind of circuitous evidentiary battle. Unfortunately, to this day Canadian judges have not fared much better than their southern brothers in terms of redressing many of the problems associated with obscenity litigation. As the rest of this book shows, the Canadian experience with obscenity and indecency law reveals a similar preoccupation with experts and social science, and a near categorical refusal to take the routine habits and stated opinions of so-called "ordinary" Canadians at face-value when it comes to determining the "community standard" of tolerance and decency. This situation cannot be treated lightly. If the "community standard" is indeed so lofty and delicate a measuring device that it requires expert handling, or at any rate is not to be left to the coarse and provincial opinions of a real "community" – a community, that is, consisting of retail proprietors, bakers, construction workers, medical doctors, engineers, students, drug addicts, artists, not to mention a few "experts" – then why call it a "community standard?" Or more important, recalling H.L.A. Hart's historic debate with Lord Devlin, if the courts' reluctance to hear from randomly selected community members is based on some fear that these people might actually be racist, sexist, puritanical, or perhaps homophobic, then why use the "community standard" as an appropriate measuring device at all?[90] The courts here could simply rise "above" the limitations of the community's knowledge of such a matter, as would be consistent with Dworkin's view of judicial responsibility, and make their determinations regarding obscenity on some other grounds. At least this approach would be more intellectually honest.

For the moment, experts and specialists continue to dominate the evidentiary scene in Canada, encouraging judges to shape constitutional law in areas of obscenity and indecency according to the latest "technical fad" (Cahn 1955, 167) or even "ideological fad" (Cahn 1956, 192). If and when a judicial determination based on such social scientific or intellectual trends appears to be undesirable, wrong, or unfair, the judge may take professional refuge or solace in the fact that she consulted the experts. In this sense, the judge is allowed legitimately to play both ends against the middle. *As a judge*, she could argue that she acted properly by consulting the experts, whose knowledge is considered helpful because it is specialized. And in any particular case, if that specialized knowledge itself appears unsound to the public, the judge cannot necessarily be blamed for weighing it more or less heavily since the knowledge may well lie beyond the intellectual competence of the judge. The classic procedural and doctrinal alternative to this situation is, of course, for the judge to take "judicial notice" of the relevant matter of legislative facts.[91] Although offensive to some judges and members of the public alike, this approach at least requires the judge to take full responsibility for legislative-fact determinations that may appear erroneous or problematic to members of the public at large. And realistically, when one takes a close look at the history of anti-obscenity and indecency adjudication in Canada, it is nearly impossible to say that expert evidence in these areas has resulted in relatively more "accurate" or "plausible" determinations of matters of legislative fact and "social framework." Arguably, much of this testimony introduced on a case-by-case basis in Canada has led to implausible and unreliable determinations of fact and, therefore, to controversial determinations of law.

4

Experts and Obscenity Law: Canadian Rules and Derivations (1942–2000)

SETTING THE STAGE: THE BAWDY HOUSE, THE BODICE, AND THE THEATRE CRITIC

On 20 May 1942, the director and manager of the Gayety Theatre on St Catherines street in Montreal was charged with showing an obscene "tableau" entitled "Spin a Web of Dreams." The Crown's evidence in *Conway* v. *The King* was that during the performance three "girls" (or "actresses") appeared at the back of the theatre's stage, "nude from abdomen to the head," standing "perfectly motionless," with actors on both sides of them. Apparently the male actors told a number of jokes with a "double meaning." The manager argued that the girls were arranged in the manner of statues. Moreover, witnesses for the manager testified that the showgirls' breasts were clothed with brassieres or bust bodices of very light material.[1]

At trial, the manager, Conway, was convicted of providing an obscene performance, but on appeal Justice Lazure acquitted him. Lazure's decision is interesting because, as Judge Woolsey did in relation to Joyce's *Ulysses*, Lazure took upon himself the role of ad hoc art critic in relation to the impugned performance. Lazure was likely influenced by evidence of a real art critic who appeared at the trial. He said in his judgment, "It is clear that the manager of the theatre wished to show a beautiful scene, some kind of an artistic background. I do not say that he succeeded; he perhaps completely missed the effect he was after, but nevertheless the object sought by the appellant was to create a beautiful background and not an immoral scene."[2] Later, Lazure commented, "It must also be said that five or six witnesses for the defence, amongst them a theatrical critic of one of our large daily newspapers, came to affirm that this tableau had nothing immoral about it but was only intended for decorative effect."

The testimony of the theatre critic in *Conway* appears to have acted similarly upon Lazure as the evidence of all the librarians and critics did upon Woolsey in the *Ulysses* prosecution a decade earlier. It appealed to what Kelly called the "class prejudice" of judges or the heightened sense of literariness some, if not many judges, associate with their esteemed social position. On the other hand, Lazure's decision is consistent with the wider tendencies of judges presiding over obscenity cases south of the border. As already shown, American judges responded in all manners to expert or lay evidence presented to them in the first half of the twentieth century. Some were highly deferential, others were highly critical, and perhaps arrogant or smug.

By the late 1950s, Canadian courts were still determining issues of obscene publications according to the British *Hicklin* test, which asked whether impugned books tended to corrupt or deprave the readers who were open to "immoral influences" and into whose hands such works were likely to fall. Artistic, scientific, and literary merit remained defences in obscene-publications prosecutions at this time, so expert testimony purporting to establish any such defence could be expected to be introduced regularly into such proceedings. As was discussed in the preceding chapter, however, despite many American judges' repeated assertions that a jury would be ideally suited to determine questions of artistic worth and "immoral influence," the judges themselves usually undertook these tasks. In 1957, *R. v. American News*, a case of possessing an obscene book for sale, was heard in Ontario. The case is interesting because the matter of the accused person's guilt or innocence stood to be determined by a jury. To recall Kelly's analysis of the American trial of *Ulysses*, a trial by jury in obscenity cases boded poorly for the accused because the jury could be expected to apply a double standard to the publications. Presumably, any assemblage of middle- and lower-class jurors were familiar with and enjoyed reading "low art" works that appealed to "prurient interest" but were hypocritically quite willing to punish writers and publishers for producing and selling similar works.

In *R. v. American News*, the jury found an Ottawa bookseller guilty of possessing several copies of an obscene book entitled *Episode*. Although the reasons for the jury's finding must always remain a mystery, the reasons given by the Ontario Court of Appeal for upholding the jury's verdict highlight all of the problems associated with American obscenity cases reviewed so far. First, in reviewing prior approaches to the law regarding obscenity, Justice Laidlaw recalled a variety of trials wherein the presiding magistrate had either declared the issue of a book's obscenity to be a matter for him alone to decide (that is, without the assistance of witnesses, expert or otherwise), rejected an offer to hear expert testimony regarding artistic merit, or minimized the importance of expert testimony tending to show a book's medical and psychological value. Laidlaw also considered the statutory defence to obscenity contained in the *Criminal Code* at that time: it stated that otherwise obscene portions of a book could be acceptable if they served the "public good."[3]

What is particularly important for the present purpose is that, at the original trial, the trial judge admitted expert testimony from six individuals purporting to establish that *Episode* had literary and artistic merit, was educational in the domain of "psychotherapy," was sincerely written, and served the so-called "public good." On the basis of this evidence, the accused bookseller's lawyer applied for a directed verdict (of not guilty), but the trial judge denied this request, arguing that "the book itself provides the best evidence whether it is or is not obscene."[4] For all practical purposes, Laidlaw agreed that "almost all of [the evidence] is irrelevant and inadmissible" and that the trial judge "was in error in admitting evidence to show the literary merit of the book and in holding that the literary merit of the book was one of the issues for consideration of the jury."[5] Ernst would have applauded this last conclusion. Yet Laidlaw went even further, saying that "the opinions expressed that the book serves a useful purpose are *simply opinions*," which do not necessarily bear on the judge's task of determining whether the public good was actually served by the sale of *Episode*, because that question is a question of law.[6] Fellow Justice Schroeder agreed with this interpretation of the law, which precludes expert opinion evidence from determining the so-called "ultimate issue" in a case (such as whether the defence of "public good" has been made successfully), even though this rule has been loosened considerably in recent years.

Ultimately Laidlaw was satisfied that the jurors, all of whom had read *Episode* themselves, were adequately instructed on the *Hicklin* test, and properly applied it to *Episode*. This finding reveals primarily how conveniently the jury continued to operate, either in practice or in concept, in the realm of obscenity law past the mid-century mark in Canada. The jury functioned as a general body of knowledge (again, with some amalgam of literary, psychological, and even behavioural scientific insight) that could be applied decisively to undermine the specialized knowledge of experts, but in a way that served a broader, puritanical, social-moral interest, as Ernst so plainly recognized. Schroeder made clear that the trial judge was perfectly entitled to remove the expert evidence purporting to establish how *Episode* served the public good from the jury because of the so-called "ultimate issue" rule. By confining the jury's attention to the question whether *Episode* tended to deprave or corrupt its likely readers, to be determined only on the basis of the book itself, the trial judge and Ontario Court of Appeal in *R. v. American News* rested assured that the bookseller would be convicted.

OUT WITH *HICKLIN*, IN WITH LITERARY MERIT

A landmark Canadian anti-obscenity prosecution was heard in 1962, when in *R. v. Brodie* the appellant called upon two prominent Canadian literary figures, Morley Callaghan and Hugh MacLennan, to give expert opinion evidence regarding the literary or artistic merit of D.H. Lawrence's novel *Lady Chatterley's Lover*. In one sense the use of literary experts in this case could have been expected. MacLellan had already testified in *American News*, and only a few years earlier a prominent American literary critic and historian, Malcolm Cowley, had testified regarding the literary merit of *Lady Chatterley's Lover* in a suit against the postmaster general in the United States.[7] In *R. v. Penguin Books,* the English prosecution of the publication of *Lady Chatterley's Lover* in 1961, Penguin Books was allowed to introduce expert evidence about the literary and ethical merits of Lawrence's novel. For all practical purposes, under the traditional British *Hicklin* test for obscenity, expert evidence was inadmissible on the issue of a book's tendency to corrupt an ordinary or average reader. The *Hicklin* test asked about the tendency or potential of an impugned book to deprave or corrupt its reader. Under the newly enacted Canadian *Criminal Code* provision, however, the court had to inquire about the degree of "exploitation of sex" involved in an impugned book (that is, whether or not it is "undue") and the extent to which the book concerned itself with sexual exploitation relative to the book's other themes or characteristics.[8] This new Canadian definition of obscenity allowed Justice Judson to consider Callaghan's and MacLennan's expert literary evidence relevant to the issue of whether the otherwise "undue exploitation of sex" in *Lady Chatterley's Lover* was a "dominant characteristic" of the novel. As Justice Judson explains, "One cannot ascertain a dominant characteristic of a book without an examination of its literary or artistic merit and this, in my opinion, renders admissable the evidence of the author and others on this point."[9]

Although Judson's express mention of the "real assistance" afforded by literary experts in *Brodie* reflects his sincere attempt to apply the new obscenity law justicially, it is worth questioning whether the "dominant characteristic" issue is always best informed by expertise.[10] In effect, Judson's approach anticipates an evidentiary problem associated with the difference between so-called "high art" and "low art," whereby expert evidence is consulted to demonstrate the literary merit of works of "high art" but not of "low art" – assuming all the while, of course, that the distinction itself is somehow generically valid or self-evident. Even where this distinction is thrown into question, however, it is worth noting that one literary expert's "high art" may well be a fellow expert's "low art." A more wonderful example of this situation cannot be found than D.H. Lawrence's urging of the legal suppression of Joyce's *Ulysses*, on the understanding that it lacked literary merit (Ernst and Schwartz 1964, 248).

The evidence of Callaghan and MacLennan in the *Brodie* case established a Canadian precedent in at least two respects. First, it constituted the first use of social-framework evidence, broadly interpreted, in obscene publications cases. As Judson observes, the literary testimony was also admitted as being relevant to the question of "undueness," which " is really directed to standards of acceptance prevailing in the community."[11] That is to say, the general question as to whether the degree of "sexual exploitation" in *Lady Chatterley's Lover* is "undue" presumably involves some consideration of the prevailing moral standards of the community; this requires the literary experts to look beyond the confines of the text in question and to speculate perhaps as to the state of the societal ethos. Although it is very difficult to see how literary experts possess some special knowledge on this issue, Rembar relates some clever testimony from the literary expert called in the American suit concerning *Lady Chatterley's Lover*. It suggests at least one way a literary expert might be able to wear both hats. When asked whether, as part of his job as a literary critic, the "most important consideration in [Cowley's] mind" was the artistic and technical aspects of a writer's work, Cowley replied, "Not necessarily, because I am also a publisher's adviser and I have to be able to guess what the public will think" (Rembar 1968, 86).

The presence of Callaghan and MacLennan in *Brodie* was also important because it represents an early form of recognition by the Canadian judiciary that literary people have something intelligent – perhaps "authoritative" – to contribute to a serious legal problem. Judson makes this recognition clear by admitting that "any tribunal" could not "get very far in an obscenity case without being influenced, either consciously or unconsciously," by the kind of information provided by Callaghan and MacLennan. Of course, Judson's hospitality toward these two experts stands in marked contrast to that shown by Justice Andrews toward art experts in the 1884 American case, *People v. Muller*, and by Justices Schroeder and Laidlaw in *R. v. American News*. The conflict here involves the use of literary or art experts for the purposes of informing a broader social reality or phenomenon

called the "community standard of tolerance." Indeed, as long as the
test for obscenity is the broader "community" standard, the issue
should be informed by much more than literary or art experts. So the
question arises, if literary experts are not necessarily qualified to
express reliable opinions about community mores, where should the
courts look for this standard?

Some answers are suggested in the early 1884 obscene photographs
case, and in both the American and Canadian cases concerning *Lady
Chatterley's Lover*. In *People* v. *Muller*, Justice Andrews downplayed
the evidentiary importance of the fact that the original paintings (from
which the impugned photographs were reproduced) had been publicly
exhibited in various metropolitan art galleries. Although this uncon-
tested fact could inform the issue of obscenity, Andrews did not believe
it to be very probative, noting the possibility that public art galleries
could exhibit indecent or obscene pictures.[12] Four decades later, Ernst
amassed a wealth of survey evidence and critical opinion testifying to
the literary sincerity of James Joyce and the artistic sophistication of
Ulysses. A couple of decades after that, in the American *Lady Chatterley's Lover* case, the plaintiff's lawyer introduced evidence indicating
the large degree of consensus among literary critics of D.H. Lawrence's
stature as a novelist (as reflected by the number of books written about
D.H. Lawrence) and attempted to introduce a number of newspaper
articles and editorials surrounding the publication of *Lady Chatterley's
Lover* in America at the time (Rembar 1968, 75, 81).[13] In *Brodie*, the
defence filed literary reviews of *Lady Chatterley's Lover* "written by
outstanding critics in the United States," tending to show "real unanimity" as regards the sincerity of Lawrence's literary and moral
enterprise.[14]

These approaches are not only interesting in their own terms, but
significant because they reveal a general tendency among the judiciary
in obscenity cases that has continued unabated to this day. This
tendency is two-fold. First, where written opinion evidence is involved
(as, for example, in the case of literary reviews or newspaper editorials), the courts have tended to accord the "higher-brow" publications
more probative value than the "lower-brow" or popular publications.
Second, evidence tending to show *actual* behaviour (for example, the
actual reading habits of people) or *matters of fact* (such as the fact
that impugned paintings are exhibited publicly, or the fact that certain
numbers of people have read a particular book or attended a particular
movie),[15] is generally accorded less weight than oral or written *opinions*.[16] Whereas the tendency first mentioned reveals a direct form of
elitism on the part of the courts hearing obscenity cases, the latter
shows a peculiar evidentiary preference for opinion over fact. As was

suggested earlier, this latter trend becomes very problematic when one considers the real problems of hypocrisy and so-called "evaluation apprehension" associated with "self-report" opinion or survey evidence (Palys 1992, 269–70). To witness how these trends develop, the case law will now be examined.

INTRODUCING THE SURVEY: *DOMINION NEWS & GIFTS*

Shortly after the *Brodie* trial, a Winnipeg newspaper and gift retailer was brought to court for selling a couple of magazines, *Dude* and *Escapade*, alleged to be "obscene" within the terms of Canada's *Criminal Code*. In keeping with the tradition of calling literary experts to edify the court regarding the broader moral (i.e., literary) value of the impugned material at bar, the defence in *R. v. Dominion News & Gifts* called Arnold Edinborough, a prominent journalist, English literature professor, and past member of the Attorney-General's Committee on Indecent Literature for Ontario. Curiously, and refreshingly, Edinborough disclaimed any pretense to being an expert on the subject of indecent literature and furnished an opinion instead primarily on the issue of the "community standard of tolerance" throughout Canada.[17] This event is significant for a few reasons. It further highlights how the voice and perhaps disciplinary knowledge of the literary community was beginning to be recognized generally as important to obscenity law. It also recalls the problematic use of literary specialists to discern loosely the psychological effect or intellectual impact of the impugned book on the "average" reader that occurred in the American *Ulysses* case, and continued through to the American and Canadian *Lady Chatterley's Lover* cases.[18] And finally it shines a spotlight on perhaps the first use of social survey information in Canada to help measure the community standard of tolerance. Edinborough had previously conducted a speaking tour through various Canadian cities on the topic "Crime Comics and Obscene Literature," and as Justice Schultz explains, "The evidence of Mr. Edinborough was, in large part, of a general nature, and related to 'pulp, picture (the so-called 'girlie' type) and slick magazines.' His testimony was based on information furnished to him as a member of a Committee on Indecent Literature appointed by the Attorney-General of Ontario ... Mr. Edinborough gave his evidence fairly but, to a degree, it was so general in nature as to be of little assistance to the Court."[19]

Thus, in a peculiar way, Edinborough ushered in the first use of "social science" evidence in Canadian anti-obscenity law, and the reaction of the judges is worth observing. Clearly, Schultz was largely unimpressed, noting in particular the unreliability of Edinborough's "assumption that community standards are the same in all parts of Canada."[20] Indeed, the empirical basis for Edinborough's "informed" opinions regarding community standards in Winnipeg may have been limited to his touring experience in Ontario (and possibly only Toronto).[21] Justice Freedman, the only judge not to declare the impugned magazines obscene, made no mention of Edinborough's "community standard" testimony, noting only his specific finding that the magazines at issue were "flippant and saucy" and treated sex "in a normal and not a perverted fashion."[22] And Justice Monnin suggested Edinborough's testimony may have been relevant, but in any case should be given very little weight.[23] For Monnin, the magazines themselves are the best evidence, and the individuals most suited to determining the factual question of the material's obscenity or lack thereof is either a panel of randomly assembled jurors or a judge, but only after reading the magazines themselves. In this vein, Monnin vividly recalls the "populist" image (and at times rhetoric) of the jury invoked in the earliest American anti-obscenity cases, such as *People* v. *Muller* and *United States* v. *Harmon*. Yet Monnin's decision is particularly significant because it implies that, as far as determining community standard of decency is concerned, a judge can sit in the same seat as any other juror insofar as a judge is "a member of the community at large."[24] At the same time, however, Monnin nearly rejects out of hand the probative value of Edinborough's opinion, suggesting that specialized opinion evidence or experience has no relevance to the community standard. What does he mean by this? That communities do not contain at least some experts, including judges?

Regardless of the ultimate use to which Edinborough's testimony was put in *Dominion News & Gifts*, it is worth making two final observations. First, the admission of survey-based evidence into the anti-obscenity court reflected an increasing willingness on the part of the Canadian judiciary to appear "objective" in such matters.[25] The plain fact that Schultz and Monnin stressed the geographical limitations of Edinborough's particular survey suggests that a more comprehensive survey might have served the court's fact-finding process better in *Dominion News & Gifts*. Second, just as Justice Freedman paid some heed to Edinborough's literary opinion, he also recognized the relevance of the impugned magazines' relatively large "readership" to the question of community standards.[26] This highlights the divide among judges at this stage regarding the probative value of marketplace evidence relative to opinion or survey evidence. The fact that so little probative value is attached to this kind of marketplace evidence seems strange at this point, especially when viewed in light of the myriad problems that have since become identified with the designs and methodologies of social science surveys and opinion research (such as "hypocrisy," "literalism," and "evaluation apprehension").

As observed earlier, judicial debate about the relevance and probative value of social science evidence in obscenity cases had been alive in America at least since 1940.[27] These courts had become concerned with finding the best way to determine community standards of tolerance. Was the jury's unassisted opinion sufficient? Was judicial notice appropriate? Or were experts needed? If experts were going to be heard on this point, the issue arose as to the kind or species of expert best qualified to do the job. Definitely psychologists and sociologists had been considered, but literary figures had not played a real part at this time. It is not surprising, therefore, that in 1963 the Manitoba Court of Appeal gave little weight to Edinborough's survey evidence regarding Canadian community standards of tolerance. Survey evidence had not been established as the best or even an appropriate means for determining community standards, and Edinborough did not purport to be a formally trained social scientist.

THE RISING IMPORTANCE OF "FREEDOM OF EXPRESSION": A MOMENT'S REFLECTION IN *R. V. CAMERON*

Shortly after *R. v. Dominion News & Gifts* was decided, the tides began to turn with respect to the relative importance of expert literary and social science evidence to anti-obscenity prosecutions in Canada. In 1966, Dorothy Cameron was charged with exhibiting seven obscene pictures in her Yonge Street commercial art gallery. In her defence, Cameron called five expert witnesses, mainly from the field of art, and in this respect *R. v. Cameron* recalls the 1884 American case, *People v. Muller*. Moreover, Justice Aylesworth (on behalf of the majority of the Ontario Court of Appeal) towed almost the same line as Justice Andrews had eighty years earlier concerning the admissibility of expert evidence in such matters. Aylesworth basically rejected the opinions of the art experts as being irrelevant because they did not purport to inform the common understanding or "average" appreciation of the works in question and instead only that of a small community of experts. He remarked, "I agree with the Magistrate in the case at bar, that the standards also are not set exclusively by those "who have an intense interest in art and for the style and method of the artist" and that "the standard must be the middle path of interest [and I would add tolerance] in the community."[28]

Justice Laskin basically disagreed with the "middle path" or "average conscience" interpretation of the community standard articulated by Aylesworth and his predecessors. For Laskin, an emergent, visible public concern with "freedom of expression" recognized throughout the American and Canadian judiciary required courts to modify the traditional community standard – to give more freedom, in effect, to artists attempting to exercise their own freedom of expression "in serious vein."[29] To this end, courts should actively consult or at least hospitably consider literary expertise. Laskin urges, therefore, that at least in cases of high art, the community standard be sought "in the higher and more developed appreciation of art than in the lower and less developed," such that "[e]xpert evidence to assist the Judge or Magistrate or Judge and jury is accordingly indispensible."[30] Now Laskin's opinion has taken on the hue of Justice Frankfurter's opinion in *Smith* v. *California* in relation to the American doctrine of "due process." A government should not be entitled to curtail an individual's right to free expression without some "clear and cogent" proof that such expression is "obscene"; to deny an accused the opportunity to prove otherwise (for example, through the use of relevant evidence provided by literary experts) may well constitute a violation of constitutionally entrenched principles of the fair administration of justice.

Although the technical relevance and broader significance of expert evidence in obscenity cases had reached a new plateau in *Cameron*, other kinds of evidence continued to be treated as they always had been. Aylesworth casually observed, for example, that thirty-five to forty people were attending the Dorothy Cameron Gallery when the police arrived to confiscate the impugned paintings. This fact would seem to suggest that at least some small segment of the community was interested at the time in the exhibit. And, insofar as there is no evidence that these people were somehow "offended" by what they saw, one might think that their attendance and possibly enjoyment was indicative of a local community standard of decency. Moreover, it is likely that this audience constituted a greater admixture of highly skilled artists and laypersons than the small body of experts who testified at the trial. Laskin appears to appreciate the relevance of this kind of factual or marketplace evidence insofar as he urges courts to consider "the range of exposure that particular art or art forms have had in the localities of Canada where art is exhibited."[31] However, he ultimately prefers oral expert opinion over practical fact, for he says that "expert evidence, which may go beyond the evidence of artists only, must be the basis upon which a finding as to community standards should be approached."[32] Again, the question should be asked: why do some judges categorically reject the viewing and reading habits of people in a community as irrelevant to "community" standards of decency, in favour of lone, expert opinions? It's always the "thought" that counts.

THE PSYCHOLOGIST ENTERS THE SCENE

By 1970, the inability of Canadian courts to settle evidentiary questions concerning community standards and obscenity had become very problematic. Judges were becoming increasingly attentive to the right of individuals to free expression and the implications of this right for rules of evidence in relevant proceedings. In *R. v. Great West News, Mantell and Mitchell*, the Manitoba Court of Appeal was asked whether the Crown had an obligation to produce evidence pertaining to community standards of tolerance in obscene publications cases. *Great West News* involved a charge of possessing two obscene magazines, *Film and Figure* and *Nude Living*. Justice Dickson ruled that the Crown bears no such obligation, but recognized that expert evidence may be desirable in cases where, for example, "a book or work of art may be predominantly characterized by an appeal to sexual interests but also embody literary or sociological or other values."[33] Thus Dickson effectively echoed the opinion of Justice Judson in *R. v. Brodie*, yet limited this to the world of what might be called "high art." At the same time, however, new kinds of experts had begun to appear on the scene.

In *Great West News* the Crown called Mr Mackalski, a "past chairman of a small interdenominational group called Citizens for Decent Literature," and at least two psychiatrists, Dr Edward Johnson and Dr Asseltine, the latter being a "psychiatrist and director of the Child Guidance Clinic."[34] The precise nature of each expert's testimony is not clear from the written judgment. Dickson says only that Mackalski "found the magazines obscene and pornographic" and that Asseltine "thought they surpassed what he understood to be the community standard."[35] As regards Johnson, Dickson suggests that he was asked about the psychological and behavioural effects of reading the magazines on readers but was prevented from answering this question by the trial judge.[36] In any case, all the expert evidence was novel in the simple sense that Canadian courts had not yet introduced either an overtly religious figure or a professional psychiatrist into the evidentiary fray of anti-obscenity proceedings. Of course, two decades had passed since the American judge Jerome Frank had paved the way for the introduction of psychiatric knowledge into obscenity proceedings.[37] To recall, Frank suggested in *Roth v. Goldman* that psychiatric and psychological evidence could intelligently inform the issue of whether exposure to certain impugned books led to "socially harmful conduct on the part of normal human beings," although he cautioned that "psychiatry [was] not an infallible science but an art still in its period of adolescence."[38] As explained above, Canada's obscenity law did not directly address this issue of psychological or behavioural effect, yet a close analysis of the cases heard by this time reveals a nagging attempt among some lawyers and judges to make the issue germane – to introduce it, as it were, from the back door.[39] For example, Justice Ritchie expressed doubt in *Brodie* that "any significant segment of the population is likely to be depraved or corrupted by reading [*Lady Chatterley's Lover*] as a whole."[40]

One can speculate about the Crown's selection of Mackalski as an expert in *Great West News*. He was clearly associated with an organized body of religious knowledge about morality or sexuality, typified by his membership in the interdenominational group called "Citizens for Decent Literature." And in light of the positive role "religious conservatives" played in suppressing pornographic materials in the late 1950s and 1960s (Lacombe 1994, 21–2), the Manitoba government might have thought it could stem the growing tide of public support for artistic freedom and personal freedom in sexual matters (including the enjoyment of "smut") with a more established, perhaps conservative opinion from a recognizable religious figure in the community.

Both psychiatrists, Asseltine and Johnson, may have been called to rebut expert psychiatric testimony introduced by the accused concerning the psychological and behavioural effects of reading pornographic materials. Although, as already stated, this kind of knowledge was associated with the outmoded *Hicklin* test for obscenity, it likely began to appear relevant in Canadian obscenity law at this time as part of a much broader trend underway in the United States toward a scientific understanding of pornography and its effects. In 1968, the American government had already created The President's Commission on Obscenity and Pornography to conduct research along these lines, in particular "to study the effect of obscenity and pornography upon the public and particularly minors, and its relationship to crime and other antisocial behavior," and to make legislative recommendations accordingly (McGaffey 1974, 226). McGaffey mentions that the commission "reviewed masses of previous research, conducted public hearings and initiated eleven major inquiries into the impact of various kinds of erotica, the background of sexual offenders and other related areas," but she also implies that much of the clinical-based information was derived from the work of psychiatrists and psychologists. Clearly, by 1970 the Canadian judiciary, as well as interested political groups such as the Canadian Civil Liberties Association, had become familiar with the kinds of debates, arguments, and concerns heard before the American committee (Lacombe 1994, 24–5).

As with Kohn's proposal about the introduction of psychological and behavioural evidence in *The Segregation Cases*, it is fair to say that evidence of this type pertaining to pornography was being admitted into Canadian courts in the late 1960s, partly because it was recognized generally as belonging to a broader, well-organized, and perhaps systemic "body of knowledge."[41] More important, as Lacombe argues, this body of social science knowledge was being "mobilized" at the time around civil libertarian interests in free speech and, to an extent, free sexuality (Lacombe 1994, 24–5). It was skewed strategically toward demonstrating the sexually liberating effects of pornography and away from the moral conservative claims that reading and watching pornography were somehow harmful and socially deleterious. Berkowitz made this point forcefully by drawing attention to the contradictory attitude of "liberals" who welcomed both evidence of pornography's lack of social harmfulness and evidence of media violence's harmful effects on viewers (Berkowitz 1971, 14).[42] Although a *New York Times* article at the time reported the latter kind of evidence as being very tentative, some prominent politicians and academics reacted strongly to this portrayal of the research conclusions. Berkowitz's point was that liberally-inclined Americans at the time wanted to hear that sexual imagery, but not violent imagery, was psychologically and socially good (or at least not bad) and that violent imagery was somehow socially bad. It is important to recognize, therefore, that anti-obscenity cases in Canada and America at this time were being prosecuted in an increasingly tolerant, liberal political climate, and as far as the courts were concerned, the government was effectively on the defensive in such cases. Justice Laskin had already alluded to the growing importance of "freedom of expression" in Canadian society,[43] and his fellow justice Dickson openly cited the "classic debate between Lord Devlin ... and Professor Hart" at the outset of the *Great West News* prosecution.[44]

TAKING THE SOCIAL SCIENCE SURVEY SERIOUSLY: *PRAIRIE SCHOONER NEWS*

Another "hard core" pornography case was brought before the Manitoba Court of Appeal in 1970. Psychiatric opinion evidence about pornography was again considered, as was survey evidence pertaining to community standards of tolerance, and the question of expertise acquired heightened significance. In R. v. *Prairie Schooner News Ltd. and Powers* a psychiatrist testified about community standards of tolerance with respect to pornography generally and specifically with respect to differences between the printed and pictorial medium. Rich's testimony was admitted as non-expert opinion evidence in this respect, but given very little weight by the trial judge because it was not related specifically to the magazines in question.[45]

The defence sought to introduce evidence about the local community standard of tolerance of magazines similar to those before the bar through a law school graduate, R.G. Carbert, who had designed and conducted a self-report style survey with a University of Manitoba sociology and criminology professor, Dr Morrison. The trial judge rejected this evidence because Carbert lacked expertise in the area of social science research methods and because his chosen sample was unrepresentative of the local community (being Canada). Clearly, this was one of the earliest obscenity cases in which the judiciary took express cognizance of some of the technicalities of social science research, such as representativeness. More important, the Manitoba Court of Appeal accepted the trial judge's decision in this regard, and Dickson set forth some preconditions for the admissibility of public opinion poll or survey evidence in future obscenity cases. These were the acceptability of the research itself as a science, the qualifications of the witness as an "expert," and the representativeness of the sample used to measure the tolerance level of the population at issue.

Despite the authoritarian tenor of Dickson's proposed rules for admissibility of survey evidence, these rules have never been formally recognized as having the force of law in Canada. Nonetheless, Dickson's approach in *Prairie Schooner News* is a landmark development in the relationship between the juridical and social scientific communities in Canada. It represents perhaps the first sign of a friendship or partnership being forged between judges and social science researchers, although clearly social scientists in America had already been actively encouraging judges to admit and use social science surveys or opinion research for over a decade.[46] In *Prairie Schooner News,* Justice Freedman consulted one early American source as support for the proposition that small samples may provide adequate representation of views in certain contexts,[47] and Dickson cited a host of American trademark cases which encouraged the admissibility of "properly conducted public surveys."[48]

At this historical moment, however, the partnership between the judiciary and the social science survey research community was founded on ignorance, "blind" trust, or faith, at least from the judges' vantage point. This is clear from Dickson's general comments regarding the heuristic value of opinion surveys in general and the admissibility of Carbert's survey in particular. For example, Dickson observes, "Basic to the admissibility of such surveys has been the acceptance of the public opinion polling as a *science* when approved statistical methods, social science research techniques, and interview procedures are employed."[49] Not only does Dickson uncritically embrace the notion here (so completely disparaged by Justice Frank) that social science research techniques such as public opinion polling can be considered "scientific" under certain conditions, he casually implies that certain statistical methods, research techniques, interview procedures, etc., are capable of being generally "approved." But by whom? By fellow social scientists? Perhaps so, but as has been shown so far, and as chapter 5 demonstrates, other social and natural scientists have forcefully challenged the general heuristic potential of social science survey techniques and methods.

Dickson also notes that a pre-condition of admissibility of social science survey evidence is the "selection of the proper 'universe,' that is, that segment of the population whose characteristics are relevant to the question being studied."[50] Again, Dickson does not formally address the very thorny question of determining this kind of "relevancy" in social science research generally, and his armchair observation that a "sample" of opinions drawn from a single city in Canada will not be representative of a Canada-wide community standard of tolerance shows his limited understanding of the issue. By the "accepted" standards of social science research, it is perfectly possible that a city-wide sample of opinions regarding the decency of some books and magazines could adequately "represent" the standard of tolerance in the entire Canadian community. To argue otherwise is to enter into a protracted and possibly fruitless debate concerning any large variety of demographic characteristics of Canadians that somehow relate (presumably best) to community standards of decency: Is age relevant? Is sex relevant? Is gender relevant? Is race relevant? Is occupation relevant? Is membership in a private association relevant? What about participation in public service? Or possession of a criminal record? Etc., etc.

In light of Dickson's limited familiarity with the technicalities of social science survey methods, and despite his apparent confidence in "properly conducted" social science surveys, it is significant that he formally issued the following "word of warning": "The findings of a poll can be deceptively simple and frequently misleading. This is repeatedly emphasized in the writings on this subject. Such evidence must, therefore, if it is to be admitted, be received with caution and carefully evaluated before weight is given to it."[51] By effectively highlighting the limited utility (or in the social science jargon, validity and reliability) of social science survey evidence generally, Dickson wants to welcome the new stock of social science professionals into obscenity courtrooms, as long as they stand no closer than at arm's length from the fact-finder.

Soon after *Prairie Schooner News* was decided, survey evidence was brought before the Ontario Court of Appeal and a District Court in Alberta.[52] Lamont paraphrases the survey evidence introduced in the Ontario case, *Times Square Cinema,* as follows: "One of the surveys consisted of the opinions of persons who attended free showings in response to newspaper advertisements, and the other was taken of persons whose names were selected at random from a telephone directory and who were invited to attend a 'controversial' film without cost. Both groups filled out questionnaires upon leaving the theatre, and these forms constituted the basis of the surveys" (Lamont 1973, 151).

The Ontario Court of Appeal mentioned its willingness to admit such evidence as a proper basis for expert opinion evidence regarding community standards, "subject to strict limits."[53] Justice Jessup suggested, for example, that the validity and perhaps reliability of the relevant opinion survey should itself be "independently proved" and recalled the same criteria for admissibility proposed by Dickson in *Prairie Schooner News* – namely, "whether public opinion polling is, in fact, a science, whether approved statistical methods were used, whether adequate social research techniques and interviews were employed and whether the questions asked were evocative of a fair sampling of opinion."[54] Again, Jessup displays the same naïveté with respect to the "scientific" character or potential of public polling and engages similar question-begging concepts, such as "*approved* statistical methods," "*adequate* social research techniques," and "*fair* sampling." Moreover, Jessup seems to be as much in the dark about representativeness as Dickson when he suggests that "an opinion with respect to the [Canadian community] standard in only a segment of such national community is irrelevant." On what terms, for example, is Jessup prepared to argue that the opinions of Torontonians regarding the impugned film *Vixen* are "unrepresentative" of the opinions of Canadians at large?

For his part, Justice McGillivray proposed that the surveys themselves should be limited to questions about respondents' behaviours, not opinions. He stated, "Questions of a factual nature such as 'have you seen nudity in other movies'; 'where have you seen it' ... would, it would seem, be permissible," but "questions as to what people felt or thought, and all questions of a subjective type would be objectionable."[55] Although this idea naively suggests that "factual type" questions are of an "objective" nature, it recognizes at least that people's behaviour is just as indicative of community standards as people's reported opinions, or is more so.

Lamont criticizes Gale, the only judge at the Ontario Court of Appeal who openly pointed to the unreliability or invalidity of the polls.[56] Yet Lamont's main point of criticism highlights the very real problem of so-called "non-respondent bias," the possibility that those people who will only participate in a survey or respond to a questionnaire for a reward of some kind are somehow different (and significantly so) from those who do not require an inducement. Lamont admits that "you cannot *force* a person to attend a showing such as the one held here." Accordingly, the "only method is to contact a random selection of persons and request them to view the film and be polled," in which case one can expect there to be "a number of persons who will refuse" (Lamont 1973, 152). But Lamont fails to consider that, when it comes to sexuality, the "number" of people who "refuse" may well, first of all, constitute a "kind" of person – such as the prude, the self-conscious, the socially cautious[57] – but also the possibility that, by offering exposure to the film for free, the survey may invite a new kind of person into the equation, namely the person who will do or see anything "for free." This last possibility raises the difficulty of identifying the relevant groups canvassed as far as the theoretical underpinning of the survey design is concerned. That is to say, the community opinion sought by the survey may now become represented by groups, for example, who are happy to watch controversial films at a price or at a cost, and by groups who are reluctant to watch controversial films in general (or in public) but who can be encouraged to do so by the removal of a fee. Yet the key issue that the survey is designed to inform – the broadest community sense of morality with respect to hard-core or soft-core films – is clearly left unanswered, because many of the people who refuse to watch the film at any cost, or for free, probably do so on *moral* grounds – that is, out of a sense of modesty, shame, and public image. One would expect that these people's opinions are clearly relevant to the broader community sense of morality in such matters. So the sample, regardless of its size, may tend to be very unrepresentative because it will not include the opinions of many of the community's members who are particularly prudish, afraid of "controversy," or somehow concerned about their public image – all good indicators of people's broader moral views.

Jessup in *Times Square Cinema* and Dickson in *Prairie Schooner News* were obviously groping in the dark regarding the heuristic fruits of social science survey evidence in obscenity cases, so it is not surprising that a member of the Canadian judiciary should quickly attempt to shed light on the matter. In *Pipeline News,* Judge Legg of the Alberta District Court deferred heavily to the expert opinions and research conclusions of three witnesses called at trial.[58] Indeed, he expressed no reservations about the qualifications of psychology professors Dirk Schaeffer and W.B. Thorngate as experts in survey design, implementation, and analysis, and of sociology professor Earle L. Snider as an expert in research methods in the fields of demography, sociology, and stratification.

The psychology professors called on behalf of the defence testified to the specific design, implementation, and results of a two-part group-administered and telephone survey aimed at garnering a community standard of tolerance with respect to a broad variety of erotic and pornographic imagery. The sociology professor called on behalf of the Crown gave an opinion mainly about the design and methodological technicalities of proper social science research generally and specifically about the surveys conducted by Professors Schaeffer and Thorngate. As recalled and paraphrased by Legg, the battle of the experts that occurred in the *Pipeline News* trial was replete with the technical jargon of social scientists: "Likert type" rating systems, "demand characteristics, experimenter effects," "social acquiescence," "probability or random sampling and non-probability or non-random sampling," "margin of error," and "confidence limits."[59] In the end, Snider reigned victorious, mainly because of his "informed" opinion that a sample taken from Edmonton is not "representative" of the Canadian community as a whole, especially when viewed in terms of the "population parameters" of "age, sex breakdown, marital status, religion, and occupation." This apparent lack of representativeness adversely affected, in turn, the "randomness" and supposed "validity" of Thorngate's and Schaeffer's surveys.[60]

The survey evidence and expert opinions provided in *Pipeline News* were hardly edifying, but they managed to mystify Legg. Without providing any explanation of the direct statistical relevance of age, sex, marital status, religion, and occupation, to any so-called "community standard" of decency, Legg was "very much impressed with the evidence of Dr. Snider who seemed much more knowledgeable on the subject of attitude surveys than were Professors Schaeffer and Thorngate."[61] Accordingly, in light of the strict requirements for admissibility of survey evidence suggested in *Prairie Schooner News* and *Times Square Cinema*, Legg opted to attach no weight to the survey results.[62] Or was the social science survey evidence reviewed by Legg at any time relevant to his decision? In the end, he simply relied on some dicta (by Justice Dickson) in *Great West News* to the effect that a judge should determine community standards in light of his own general life experience.[63] According to this rule, the answer to the question before Legg was simple: "the books and magazines in this case are nothing more than hard core pornography and far exceed the Canadian community tolerance level."

So *Pipeline News* represents a classic case of a judge deciding a socially and morally contentious issue according to his own sense of morality or decency yet rationalizing this decision (at least in part) by reference to expert, scientific evidence. On the one hand it is irrelevant to Legg that Thorngate's and Schaeffer's surveys reveal community tolerance of the impugned magazines and paperback publications, because he has been given a mandate to find community standards in light of his own experience. On the other hand he "saved face" by deferring to the expert evidence of Snider which undermined the validity, or in legalese, the "probative value," of the survey evidence. Snider's testimony, in other words, provided Legg with an ostensibly "good" reason for ignoring the survey evidence and supplanting it with his own opinion.

In light of the real evidentiary problems associated with *Prairie Schooner News*, *Times Square Cinema*, and *Pipeline News*, it is troublesome that American and Canadian courts and scholars continue to encourage the admission of professionally designed survey evidence in obscenity cases. For example, in 1990 an expert introduced the results of a Gallop poll regarding attitudes toward sexually explicit videos and the presiding judge expressed concern that, without details about the phrasing of the questions asked in the survey, the poll conclusions might not be good indicators of Canadian community standards.[64] And in the 1994 *Little Sister's* trial, the federal government submitted the results of a survey conducted by a media organization regarding Canadians' attitudes toward depictions of explicit sex and violence (Kiselbach 1995, 17). It is not clear how Justice Smith weighed this evidence in *Little Sister's*, as the written Reasons for Judgment in that case do not mention the evidence.

Shortly after *Prairie Schooner News*, *Times Square Cinema*, and *Pipeline News* were decided, Canadian courts did extend their evidentiary lens beyond surveys alone. Before looking in this direction, however, it is worth summarizing how these early 1970 "newspaper" prosecutions represented a new plateau in the juridical relationship between the judiciary and the social science community in matters of some political importance. Judges had expressed rhetorical deference to the usefulness of social scientists in determining matters of public opinion, yet they were not willing in practice to let social science research determine politically sensitive legal issues. Social scientists had obviously acquired a voice in the courts, arguably because the general discipline of social science had acquired a large "body of knowledge" akin to that on which medicine, physics, chemistry, and economics rested. In 1973 Lamont wrote, "Over the past few decades, as statistical and public opinion research methods have been refined and developed *into a science*, and especially in view of the recent introduction of computer aids, it is quite possible to determine an average community attitude with a fair degree of accuracy. Even if exact precision is not attained, any competently conducted survey would surely provide a better gauge of the standard than the faulty guesswork of a court" (Lamont 1973, 143; emphasis added). Social science opinion evidence also tended to support the popular feeling at the time that the free expression of ideas and images is more socially salutary than the suppression of pornography, even where pornography may be considered "hard-core." Yet judges themselves were obviously uneasy in their task of assessing the validity or reliability of the particular social science opinions and conclusions presented to them. They had invented strict rules for the admissibility of such evidence and emphasized that the non-expert fact-finder (judge or jury) is completely free to disregard this evidence if it does not accord, somehow, with the fact-finder's own informed opinions in such matters.

At the same time, the newspaper cases betrayed an increasing concern among Canada's judiciary that the very notion of the "community standard of tolerance" was problematic, and perhaps chimerical. This concern was best expressed by Justice Laskin, who pondered the possibility in 1966 that "a community standard is a will-o'-the-wisp, an unknown, and perhaps even an unknowable quantity despite all the expert evidence that can be adduced."[65] Approximately twenty years later, Justice Ferg astutely observed,

I am required to judge as objectively as possible, only on the basis of what I perceive the community standards of tolerance to be. A judge cannot decide on the basis of what he alone thinks, what his mother may think, what opinion a vice-squad sergeant may hold, nor, indeed on the basis of what opinion the editors of Penthouse, Chatelaine, The Winnipeg Free Press, or the Toronto Globe and Mail (or their film critics) may hold. Nor is the opinion of young or elderly suburban housewives, or the 20-year-old stags attending a party for a friend soon to be married, to govern. One must attempt to perceive the view held by all members of our Canadian contemporary society? What will the majority tolerate?[66]

Despite the rhetorical force of the community standard over the years, both Canadian and American courts in the 1970s were still at a total loss as to the means by which such a standard should be identified or discerned. This is no small technical consideration. It poses serious problems for the administration of justice on a broader scale, as a recent statement from the editors of the Harvard Law Review makes clear: "Superficially clear doctrinal standards that are in fact indeterminate nearly to the point of uselessness serve only to obscure the rules that govern the system ... This unpredictability not only tarnishes the image of the law, but also imposes costs on the system by forcing actors to make important and expensive litigation decisions on the basis of incomplete and misleading information" (Harvard Law Review 1995, 1497).[67] Survey evidence was one way of measuring community standards, yet many others had already been considered, and many more were awaiting on the horizon.

FLIRTING WITH FACTS AND FIGURES, AS WELL AS OPINIONS: A RAY OF LIGHT FOR POPULAR DEMOCRACY

By 1974, the Canadian judiciary had already begun to break away from its dalliance with social science in anti-obscenity cases. In light of a growing public awareness that reading or watching pornography was not harmful, but might well be healthy (at least with respect to erotica or so-called "soft-core" porn), courtroom psychiatric and psychological evidence pertaining to the individually and socially harmful effects of exposure to pornographic materials had become temporarily superfluous. This new perception was certainly one of the basic conclusions of the 1970 American government *Report of the Commission on Obscenity and Pornography,* which, as already observed, evoked a strong political reaction (Berkowitz 1971, 20; Fisher and Barak 1991, 69; Lacombe 1994, 24). Social scientists had also not convinced the courts that public opinion surveys were the best, or even the preferable, means for accurately determining community standards of tolerance. The courts had finally tuned into the possibility that community standards of tolerance might best be determined by somehow measuring community practices and the behaviours of individuals (as opposed to their opinions).

In *Re Regina and Provincial News,* Judge Kerans of the Alberta District Court considered the relevance of many different kinds of evidence purporting to indicate community standards of tolerance, including the availability of certain kinds of books and magazines in libraries, the market for such items in stores, the fact that the *Penthouse* magazine in question had passed Canadian Customs despite prohibition against the importation of works of "an immoral or indecent character," the actions of the Alberta Advisory Board on Objectionable Publications in regard to the *Penthouse* magazine and other "sister works," and the opinions of an established magazine distributor and an experienced librarian. Rhetorically at least, Kerans's approach to community standards here was not only somewhat unique but perhaps more democratic than that of his predecessors. He had in effect canvassed a much more representative measure of the local community standard of tolerance than his brothers and allowed for greater inclusiveness in important questions of individual free expression and state-authorized censorship. The "community" standard was not the prerogative of either distinguished literati or professional social scientists, but instead the practices and decisions of various kinds of professionals and laypersons. In this respect, the cumulative evidence approximated what Justice Aylesworth considered in the *Cameron* case to be an ideal measure of the community standard, namely "the middle path of interest ... in the community."[68]

The significance of the broad range of evidentiary materials put before Kerans cannot be understated. It recalls Wittgenstein's behavioural approach to knowledge generally, and in so doing highlights the relatively equal strength or weakness of competing empirical knowledge-claims across different disciplines. Accordingly, the mixed behavioural or marketplace and opinion-based approach to community standards of tolerance in *Re Regina and Provincial News* showed promise by indirectly acknowledging the relatively equal (as opposed to relatively greater) utility of expert knowledge in determining questions of "fact."

Unfortunately, the novel evidentiary approach undertaken by the defence in *Re Regina and Provincial News* had little practical effect on the moral sensibilities of Kerans. He flatly rejected the relevance of the public (i.e., library) and private marketplace evidence in certain kinds of books and magazines (presumably those having some similarities with the *Penthouse* magazines in question), saying, "These works may or may not be offensive to the community standards. The fact that they are bought and sold is not determinative of that question."[69] He disqualified the opinions of customs officials who had approved the magazines, on the technical basis that these did not reflect community standards but involved applications of the law. He considered the review of *Penthouse* magazines generally by the Alberta Advisory Board on Objectionable Publications but gave it no weight (although it found the magazines objectionable to an extent) because the impugned magazine had not been singled out for inspection.[70] And he seems to have readily accepted the oral evidence of a librarian, who stated that "magazines of this sort are gaining increasing acceptance." Nonetheless, like his brother Judge Legg, Kerans ultimately trusted his own, presumably better judgment regarding the question of "undueness" and found the exploitation of sex in the *Penthouse* magazine to be undue.

The attitude of intellectual superiority in matters of morals projected by Alberta judges Kerans and Legg was quickly tempered when Bernardo Bertolucci's film *Last Tango in Paris* became the subject of obscenity proceedings in Manitoba. In *R. v. Odeon Morton Theatres*, Judge Enns of the Provincial Court had an opportunity to consider the kind of marketplace or fact-based evidence offered in *Re Regina and Provincial News*. This included the number of people who had viewed the film, the restricted availability of the film (that is, to viewers eighteen years of age or older), the fact that the film was being shown in four other provinces at the time, the fact that the censor boards in those provinces had cleared the film without any deletions, and the fact that so-called "skin-flicks" were shown around the province of Manitoba "with the apparent acquiescence of the agencies of prosecution."[71] Unlike Kerans in *Re Regina and Provincial News*, Justice Freedman of the Manitoba Court of Appeal appears to have paid this evidence more than lip-service, formally recognizing its importance to his finding that *Last Tango in Paris* was not obscene. Justice Monnin, dissenting however, acted more like Kerans, finding clever ways to circumvent the fact-based evidence in favour of a conclusion that the movie was offensive to community standards. He states,

We were also told that other movies of this nature or worse were presently being shown in this city. The practice of comparing books and, for that matter, movies, was rejected by Mr. Justice Roach: *R. v. Coles Co. Ltd.*, [1965] 2 C.C.C. 304, 49 D.L.R. (2d) 34, [1965] 1 O.R. 557. Likewise, I would reject it. What is before us is a specific film and nothing else. If the film classification board or, for that matter, the Attorney General, have been remiss in their duties or lax in the exercise thereof in the past, it is not our concern at the moment. Laxity or failure to perform one's required task cannot be used to one party's advantage, nor to establish what is or is not obscene. The character of other films is irrelevant, or at least a collateral issue of little importance in arriving at the proper decision.[72]

Apparently, without any evidence on the point before him, Monnin knows when censor boards and "for that matter, the Attorney General, have been remiss in their duties." This finding is problematic not only because it appears presumptuous, but because Monnin uses it rhetorically to justify the exclusion of evidence that he recognizes is "to one party's advantage." That is to say, despite his reservations about government laxity, Monnin was willing to interpret certain pieces of opinion evidence to the *government party's* advantage, where the opportunity presented itself.

Indeed, the broader societal perception that Bertolucci's film not only had "artistic merit," but might well be an example of "high art," brought the return of the literary expert onto the Canadian anti-obscenity evidentiary scene. Among others was Arnold Edinborough,[73] the prominent journalist, editor, publisher, and English professor who testified a decade earlier for the accused in *Dominion News & Gifts*. This time he donned an expert's hat *for the Crown*, and apparently had "many harsh things" to say about Bertolucci's film.[74] Monnin recalls how, at one point, Edinborough characterized *Last Tango In Paris* as a "savage brutal movie, confused in its elements and self-indulgent in its photography."[75] Yet presented alone this statement gives a skewed picture of Edinborough's overall opinion. Monnin also points out how, for Edinborough, *Last Tango in Paris* involved "realistic grapplings simulating sex, sodomy, fellatio and mutual masturbation; and a tangled story line which by its very tangles strives to be symbolic." Edinborough even injected some Freudian psychoanalytic theory into the argument about the artistic merit of *Last Tango in Paris*, offering the opinion that "the gun is a phallic symbol turned back on the girl's tormentor; the gun belonged to her father; Brando is a father figure; he crumples up in a foetal position on her balcony because his dead wife would never provide a womb at his own inn."[76] Ironically, the suggestion that Bertolucci's film was theoretically informed (even by Freud) probably strengthened the defence proposition that the portrayal of sex and violence in the film was not "exploitative." Indeed, Justice Freedman recounted a portion of Edinborough's testimony that supported this very claim.[77]

The religious figure or theologian also reappeared in *Odeon Morton Theatres*. This time there were two such figures, one for the defence and one for the prosecution. Father Pungente, a Jesuit priest and chairman of the Manitoba Classification Board, did a kind of expert "double-duty" for the defence, and A.C. Forrest, a minister of the United Church of Canada and editor of the *United Church Observer*, testified for the prosecution. Forrest testified unremarkably that Bertolucci's film offended the Canadian community standard of decency and lacked artistic integrity. Pungente's testimony was more interesting, not only from the point of view of its substance or content, but in terms of its broader "symbolic" value. In the latter regard it is worth considering how Pungente's stamp of approval on *Last Tango in Paris* works two-fold for the accused. As chairman of the Manitoba Film Classification Board, Pungente's opinion is almost automically expected or seen to be professionally competent and informed. Yet the idea of a religious figure condoning the sincere depiction of sexually explicit behaviour, much of which is considered "sinful" within some sects of the Judeo-Christian tradition, lends a sense of even greater "objectivity" to the opinion that Bertolucci's film is not obscene. In a sense, because of the priestly underpinning to this opinion, Pungente did not merely give his secular stamp of approval to *Last Tango in Paris* – he gave it his "blessing."

The actual content of Pungente's testimony must also be addressed. Monnin observed with surprise that, despite a number of scenes in *Last Tango in Paris* which appear to conjoin sex and violence in contravention of Canada's obscenity law, Pungente found no such violence. Pungente was very reluctant, for example, to describe the scene of simulated anal intercourse between the characters Paul (played by Marlon Brando) and Jeanne (played by Maria Schneider) as involving violence, especially if "violence" referred to the kind of violence "in films today," reflected in scenes involving "sub machine guns," and the pulling of "people's stomachs apart, ripping them open, burning them alive."[78] In other words, Pungente thoughtfully challenged the view implied by the Crown attorney that the scene in question was a "rape" scene.

Pungente also made a somewhat unthoughtful, albeit passing, remark about the nature of "skin-flicks," which is not only interesting on its own terms but indicative of a broader ethos, understanding, and perhaps attitude about sexuality that could be gleaned among the Canadian judiciary at that time. According to Justice Freedman, Pungente described "skin-flicks" as "invariably" showing, "among other depictions of sex, a scene of Lesbianism as well as the inevitable wild orgy."[79] Perhaps Pungente was merely describing the substantive contents of the average "skin-flick," without suggesting that the genre was somehow "bad" or repugnant because it contained the above kinds of scenes, especially those of "Lesbianism." Yet some judges had already begun to associate homosexual sexual depictions with obscenity. In Re Regina and Provincial News, Judge Kerans observed, "On p.47 [of the impugned Penthouse magazine] there is a photograph of an apparent homosexual copulation. Such a display goes too far."[80] And in Prairie Schooner News, Freedman noted the "lurid scenes of lesbianism" in one of the magazines in question.[81] These comments reveal a subtle heterosexism, and perhaps homophobia, in judicial and social scientific expert attitudes toward pornography and erotica at this time. This phenomenon will be discussed shortly. For the moment, it is worth summarizing the general status of expert evidence in Canadian obscenity law at this time.

The decisions of Monnin in Odeon Morton Theatres and Dominion News & Gifts, Legg in Pipeline News, Kerans in Re Regina and Provincial News, and Dickson in Great West News clearly reveal that some Canadian judges still desire to be the final arbiters of community standards, regardless of how the evidence ultimately weighs in the balance. More particularly, these decisions show a real and continuing competition at that time between the Canadian judiciary and two other groups of professionals, mainly literary professionals and social science professionals, for intellectual supremacy in matters of public morals. Justice Freedman, on behalf of the majority at the Manitoba Court of Appeal in Odeon Morton Theatres, seems to have carefully weighed the opinion evidence of all ten expert witnesses sitting "on both sides of the fence" and the factual evidence pertaining to community standards of tolerance.[82] Monnin, dissenting however, took a fairly restrictive view of this evidence, preferring his "own judgment, [his] own knowledge, as well as the knowledge of the community" over the knowledge of either "film critics or University Professors of English" in matters of community standards.[83] Most other members of society (professional and lay) have little input so far in this regard, unless their words and possibly behaviour can be translated into what Jerome Frank has called "a horrible esoteric, pseudo-scientific jargon" by social scientists (Frank 1955, 10). Again, however, the literary and social science experts appear only as handmaids at this point. Their services are effectively recognized if they enable the birth of a healthy decision in the eyes of the judge; otherwise they risk being disparaged as incompetent and redundant.

FEMINISM AND HETEROSEXISM IN EXPERT PORNOGRAPHY EVIDENCE

The judiciary and the general public may have become more tolerant and indeed accepting of "smut" or "lower" forms of textual and pictorial sexual expression in the early 1970s, but this heightened tolerance remained limited largely to the world of heterosexual pornography. Justice Freedman's reference to "lurid scenes of lesbianism" in *Prairie Schooner News*, Judge Kerans finding that "a photograph of an apparent homosexual copulation" contained in a *Penthouse* magazine "goes too far," and Freedman's observation in *R. v. Odeon Morton Theatres* that "skin-flicks" typically involve a "scene of Lesbianism" clearly did not go unnoticed by Canada's gay and lesbian communities. Several years later, interested members of these communities would organize themselves, politically and intellectually, to bring their own expert knowledge regarding homosexual erotica and pornography to bear on the courts. Yet, to recall Kohn's understanding of the social science evidence presented in *The Segregation Cases*, such a "body of knowledge" first had to be produced.

For almost a decade prior to the mobilization of the gay and lesbian community around censorship and equality issues, the feminist community in Canada had begun to organize itself, intellectually, politically, and thus legally. The 1974 *Odeon Morton Theatres* case itself spotlighted a broader concern that was developing among the Canadian (and indeed North American) populace at the time – a concern, perhaps, that was shared mainly among women. This was the tendency of some heterosexual pornography to denigrate women, to exhibit scenes of violence toward women, and otherwise to depict women in "inhumane" ways. As already mentioned, various lines of direct examination and cross-examination in *R. v. Odeon Morton Theatres* attempted to demonstrate the violent character of some of the sex scenes in *Last Tango in Paris*. Significantly, those scenes that presented the greatest concern here involved depictions of "unusual" forms of sexual intercourse,[84] such as the simulated anal intercourse scene, and the scene suggesting the insertion of Jeanne's fingers into Paul's anus.[85] The perceived "violence" of these particular scenes is associated on one level with the non-conformity of the sexual practices shown there to conservative ideals of sexuality (West 1987). Thus, the *Last Tango in Paris* prosecution contained the seeds for a long and arduous debate between a burgeoning community of feminists and a concerned community of gays and lesbians. The feminists were opposed mainly to the publication of images and narratives that depict and otherwise treat women as compliant subjects of male sexual demands. The much less visible but equally concerned community of gays and lesbians opposed the ideological projection of gay and lesbian sex as not only inherently perverse and obscene, but as violent.

By the early 1980s, feminist concerns about the actual and potential harmfulness of pornography had become a matter of public knowledge, though not necessarily public acceptance, throughout North America. Both American and Canadian courts showed some degree of sensitivity to this knowledge, and with the advent of Canada's *Charter of Rights and Freedoms* in 1982, Canadian courts especially felt obliged to pour content into its formal guarantee of equality rights for women.[86] As Lacombe observes, law reformers once again turned to the social science community, which had redirected its research efforts in the area of pornography away from the liberating, or therapeutic effects of pornography, to the question of pornography's potential to bring about harmful attitudes and behaviours toward women (Lacombe 1994, 31–5). She states, "Scientists designed their experiments primarily to discover whether pornography, in both its violent and non-violent forms, caused violence to women, and whether it changed attitudes toward women to such a point that it could be detrimental to women's efforts to be treated as equal citizens" (141).

At least temporarily, then, those social scientists interested in the psychological and behavioural effects of pornography had found a new raison d'être. They were busy preparing the empirical support for the increasingly influential and theoretical "body of knowledge" articulated by prominent feminist activists, politicians, legal scholars, and other intellectuals which stated that pornographic publication and dissemination constituted a social evil insofar as it entailed women's subjugation on many planes of life (Lacombe 1994, 34–5, 49; Malamuth and Donnerstein 1982; Malamuth 1984; Fisher and Barak 1991). It would be at least another decade before the general inconclusiveness of this social science research would be explicitly addressed by the Supreme Court of Canada in *Butler*, but in the meantime the harmfulness theory had won considerable support among Canada's judiciary. Arguably, the idea first entered the Canadian courts as "legislative-fact" evidence, and only recently has a body of knowledge arisen that is dedicated to proving it wrong.

One of the first prominent feminist representatives to appear in a Canadian anti-obscenity prosecution was June Rowlands, an alderperson and member of "various committees, organizations, and boards in Metropolitan Toronto" in 1983.[87] Rowlands's presence and testimony at the *Doug Rankine Co.* trial was somewhat precedential for at least two reasons. Rowlands was one of the first women to testify in a Canadian anti-obscenity prosecution, a development that was by no means coincidental. In light of the equality provisions of the Charter and the broader feminist concerns that had begun to envelop this area of the law (or the fact that pornography had become a "women's" issue), the federal government at the time recognized the need for such concerns to be voiced in relevant legal proceedings and to be voiced by women themselves. Moreover, Rowlands was a recognized civil libertarian, so she could be expected to present a moderate or liberal feminist position on pornography. In *Doug Rankine Co.*, Rowlands testified regarding the community standard of tolerance in metropolitan Toronto at that time, and concluded generally that the community would be prepared to tolerate the publication of images of various kinds of sexual behaviour. She stated that this same community would not tolerate "scenes of men ejaculating on women's faces, penetration of the vagina by foreign objects such as corn-cobs, explicit scenes of buggery, a woman urinating into a pot, a man inserting a candle into his anus, sexual intercourse with women portrayed as young girls and scenes of sexual intercourse coupled with violence and cruelty." More important, Rowlands testified that "most women would not tolerate the distribution of motion pictures depicting sex and violence."[88] Thus Rowlands was called not only to express an opinion about the local community standard regarding pornography in general, but also in part to represent the voice of the women of that community, which had become the focal point of the legislation in question.

It was also significant that Rowlands was a politician at the time. A politician had not been called as a witness to such proceedings before, yet there are some good reasons why a politician would make a helpful witness in this kind of case. In theory at least, political figures represent the interests of a moral and political majority. They personify, in a sense, the combined interests of the different people in their community, ranging from the poorest and underprivileged, to the blue-collar worker, to the most educated and affluent. Their opinions, therefore, are expected to reflect some "middle interest" in the domain of morals and politics, which has been considered the ideal measure of the community standard of tolerance since *R. v. Brodie*. Yet a politician is also an authority figure, which suggests that an opinion offered by a politician in court may carry relatively more weight in some contexts than a similar opinion offered by a lay figure. And, indeed, Rowlands's evidence pertaining to local community standards was preferred by Judge Borins over that provided by Josephine Walker, an experienced teacher who also provided evidence regarding the community standard of tolerance.[89]

It is worth attending briefly to Borins's criticism of Walker's testimony. Walker watched five of the movies before the court and her initial opinion was that the contemporary Canadian community would not tolerate their distribution in video form. On cross-examination, however, she conceded her inability to express an opinion about Canada-wide community standards because the sources of her information were confined to Ontario. This is one reason why Borins rejected Walker's testimony as an accurate representation of the Canadian opinion and level of tolerance regarding pornographic movies.[90] More important, however, Borins seemed to be concerned with the fact that Walker was a member of the Federation of Women Teachers of Ontario and had sponsored a resolution opposing "materials depicting women or children in degrading or sadistic roles," which was itself recently adopted by delegates of that same federation.[91] This kind of political involvement seems to have rendered Walker's opinion overly "subjective" or "interested" in the eyes of Borins. He explained his decision to discount her evidence as follows: "At the very most her evidence is reflective of the views of a very small segment of society and one which holds very strong views supporting the suppression of films similar to the five which she saw. In short, Mrs. Walker represents a particular point of view and her evidence must not be given great weight."[92]

This is a particularly significant response to the kind of testimony Walker gave in the circumstances. Borins also conceded that Rowlands "advocate[d] a particular opinion," yet he considered it more reliable because she apparently "reached her opinion on a greater sampling of public views than did Mrs. Walker." Unfortunately, it is not entirely clear how Rowlands's opinion was based on a greater sample of public views. Borins emphasizes that Rowlands "did not conduct any surveys," but seems to presume that, through her own position as alderperson and involvement in "various committees, organizations and boards in Metropolitan Toronto," she "had the opportunity to meet and speak to many people."[93]

Borins's rejection of Walker's testimony is very similar to a recent decision by Judge Katie McGowan to exclude the expert opinion evidence of Kay Armitage, a film director and instructor of Women's Studies, because the latter's "research [was] not empirical and [was] conducted from a feminist point of view and so may be biased."[94] It also calls to mind the more recent attempt by a Crown prosecutor to discredit the purported expertise of Ann Scales in *Little Sister's*, on the basis that Scales's opinions were rooted partly in her experience as a lawyer and activist.[95] All of these events show that some members of the legal profession have a very naive or narrow view of expert opinion "bias," or that lawyers and judges can only recognize expert opinion bias if it is somehow obvious. For all of these decisions fail to notice the real likelihood that all expert evidence is associated with a larger body of knowledge and will bear some kind of disciplinary group bias, however opaque or subtle.[96] This point is well illustrated by the strong differences of expert opinion involved in both the 1970 American *Report of the Commission on Obscenity and Pornography* and the 1986 United States *Attorney General's Commission on Pornography* report (Downs 1987). Both reports have informed American and Canadian legal proceedings, yet it is easy to recognize their respective epistemological and political leanings. Downs comments, "Commissions are often picked for political purposes, and are expected to produce politically useful or assuring answers." Thus, despite the fact that the 1970 Commission may have seemed relatively objective, insofar as its "commissioners were drawn from a broader set of constituencies than the commissioners of the 1986 Commission," Downs notes that "some critics did point out that the *majority* of the 1970 Commission suffered from liberal bias." In contrast, "the 1986 Commission was, if anything, 'stacked' *against* pornography" (642; footnotes omitted). Carol Vance, a participant at this commission, noted that the commission was appointed to find new ways "to control the problem of pornography," and she remarked in this respect that the "list of witnesses was tightly controlled: 77 percent supported greater control, if not elimination, of sexually explicit material. Heavily represented were law-enforcement officers and members of vice squads (68 of 208 witnesses), politicians, and spokespersons for conservative anti-pornography groups like Citizens for Decency through Law and the National Federation of Decency" (Vance 1993, 32). West observes further that the 1986 Commission *Final Report* "blends the traditional and women-centered conceptions of pornography, and blends feminist anti-pornography rhetoric with conservative ideology" (West 1987, 685).

In *Doug Rankine Co.*, it is mainly Walker's affiliation with and activities within the pro-feminist Federation of Women Teachers of Ontario that undermines her objectivity or discredits her opinion as being too biased. Yet this same federation has acquired intervenor status elsewhere and played a significant role in shaping the intellectual content of other cases. Moreover, as the *Butler* case illustrates, special interest groups such as the pro-feminist Legal Education and Action Fund (LEAF) can play an immediate and direct role in reforming the law on obscenity. Clearly, Canadian courts are generally willing to admit and effectively incorporate expert evidence provided by people with obvious "special" interests, political affiliations, or belonging to professional associations, so a decision to reject any expert's evidence on that basis may be justly seen as not only spurious, but ironically quite subjective.

Although Rowlands appeared more competent than Walker to testify about local community standards of tolerance in *Doug Rankine Co.*, the precise nature of her testimony raised an important evidentiary problem that was addressed in the *Prairie Schooner News* and *Pipeline News* cases. To recall, these cases attempted to establish guidelines for the admissibility of public opinion survey evidence, especially where such evidence is introduced by experts. Technically, Rowlands did not testify as an expert in *Doug Rankine Co.*, so there was no need to qualify her as such, nor to establish independently the validity and reliability of the empirical basis for her conclusions. This development is not necessarily problematic, yet it becomes so when one considers that the kind of opinion evidence Rowlands provided was technically hearsay.[97] Judge Borins attempted to accomodate this fact perhaps by acknowledging that Rowlands's evidence pertaining to community standards "may or may not be worthy of substantial weight," yet he ultimately appeared to weigh this evidence heavily, saying, "I was very impressed with the testimony of Mrs. Rowlands when she testified and I was more impressed with it after reading the transcript."[98] So public opinion evidence had momentarily resurfaced in anti-obscenity trials, this time free of any specific legal constraints as to its admissibility. Perhaps its lack of pretense to scientific reliability and validity made the evidence more appealing to Borins. More likely, however, is the idea that such evidence functioned tacitly as "legislative-fact" evidence, thus explaining the almost complete relaxation of any kind of standard or rule for its admissibility.[99] After all, it was Rowlands's emphasis on the degrading and debasing characteristic of the pornography she sampled, and Borins's acceptance of this element as largely determinative of "obscenity,"[100] that would eventually prove highly influential in reforming the meaning of obscenity in Canada's *Butler* case. Equally important in this regard is that Charter considerations were voiced, albeit informally, opening the door for Borins to take on the quasi-political role newly granted to the judiciary in cases of constitutional importance. Borins expressly declined to exercise any such responsibility in *Doug*

Rankine Co., yet his dicta in this regard eloquently set the stage for a major post-Charter reformulation of the law pertaining to obscenity.[101] A large part of this reconstruction process would involve the relaxation of traditional rules of admissibility of expert opinion evidence concerning community standards, as well as the entrance of various new kinds of experts and laypersons onto the evidentiary scene.

For example, in a 1985 prosecution of a Calgary video-retailer for selling "skin-flicks," defence counsel called E.H. Boyanowski, a criminologist at Simon Fraser University, and J. Ezekiel, program director of the Banff Television Festival.[102] Both of these experts were of the opinion that none of the videos watched by the court would exceed the community standard of tolerance. Boyanowski commented, however, that one of the videos, insofar as it focused on incest, would have exceeded the acceptable standard of tolerance if actual incest had been shown on film. Ezekiel surmised in a very liberal vein that most members of the viewing public are conservative in their personal viewing habits but liberal nonetheless in the viewing rights of others. Indeed, Ezekiel explained further that the Canadian community will tolerate any genre of sexual conduct on the part of consenting adults in the absence of proof that it engenders anti-social behaviour. He acknowledged, however, that the liberal attitude of the majority could be flawed to the extent that those who hold it do not always watch the films that they are willing to let others watch. In response to this evidence, Justice Shannon replied, "In my view such an uninformed attitude has little value as an indicator of actual community standards of tolerance."[103]

One can only wonder how Shannon came to the conclusion that Ezekiel's opinion – which would eventually become rearticulated by the Supreme Court of Canada in *Butler* as the law of Canada – liberal as it is, was "uninformed." However, the fact that James Check, an assistant professor of psychology at York University at the time, gave evidence for the Crown in this case probably had something to do with this. He explained that modern research into pornography classified it into three sub-groups. These are (1) sexually explicit with violence, (2) sexually explicit with no violence, but dehumanizing and degrading, and (3) explicit erotica. In his opinion, the seven impugned videos that he watched fell into the non-violent but degrading and dehumanizing category, and this opinion "convinced" Shannon.[104] Indeed, in case Check's opinion might appear doubtful to others, Shannon remarked that "Dr Check buttressed his opinion by reference to sociological studies, research, and experiments that produced findings in support of his view."[105] Check might have convinced Shannon on this occasion that the plotless, vacuous, and sexist videos under examination were obscene in law, but his apparent lack of scientific candour and intellectual objectivity in subsequent proceedings in Ontario and Alberta would lead other judges to discredit him, as will be explained below.

Before turning attention away from Check's role in the *Wagner* case, it is important to note that during the case Check also took the opportunity to offer an opinion about the film, *The Story of O*, which, along with *Clockwork Orange*, was played before Shannon as part of the defence case. For Check, *The Story of O* is "[s]exually violent and degrading. It's one of the most violent and degrading films that I have come across in a long time because the woman submits to incredible brutality and abuse."[106] Apparently, as an assistant professor of psychology, Check saw no meritorious or insightful psychological message or theme to *The Story of O* – no attempt at an explanation, as it were, as to why a woman or any person, for that matter, might want to subject themselves to abuse or domination. After all, O's motivation in the film for subjecting herself to domination is not immediately or perhaps ever clear. Maybe the plot is simply a matter of male fantasy. If so, it is significant that a woman wrote the novel on which the film is based. Perhaps, then, the film is exploring a broader theme about the veiled sadomasochistic dimension to romantic relationships generally. This possibility will be raised in the context of the next chapter's discussion of the *Little Sister's* case. The issue is raised here to show how remarkable it is that a psychologist, acting as a film critic, can seem to fail to find psychological meaning in a blatantly psychological portrayal of human sexuality and inter-relationships.

In 1985, the Supreme Court of Canada heard *R. v. Towne Cinema Theatres*, a case involving the prosecution of a movie theatre company for screening the movie *Dracula Sucks*. By this time feminist concerns that exposure to pornography contributed to harmful behaviour and perhaps hateful attitudes toward women had found some support (however little) in American social science research[107] and had achieved wider scholarly and popular recognition. For example, a 1984 report from the Metro Toronto Task Force on Public Violence Against Women and Children recommended that the existing *Criminal Code* provision regarding obscenity be reconceptualized to proscribe pornography as violence in a sexual assault context. These concerns had been made sufficiently public that the Canadian judiciary incorporated them into its *Criminal Code* definition of "undue exploitation" of sexuality. Chief Justice Dickson was not prepared to draw a necessary connection between "what is not tolerated and what is harmful to society," but he recognized that sometimes what *is* tolerated is indeed harmful, so that "a legal definition of 'undue' must also encompass publications harmful to members of society and, therefore, to society as a whole."[108] Madam

Justice Wilson invoked the language of Judge Borins in *Doug Rankine Co.*, and concluded that "the undue exploitation of sex at which s.159(8) is aimed is the treatment of sex which in some fundamental way dehumanizes the persons portrayed and, as a consequence, the viewers themselves."[109] Thus "undueness," and accordingly "obscenity," had become transformed in law from a question of moral standards exclusively (or narrowly construed) to an issue of social practices, especially those that affect women's sense of self-worth and dignity.

As suggested earlier, the rights and freedoms enshrined in the Charter had also become important considerations in anti-obscenity prosecutions at this time. The Charter had not only empowered the courts to ensure that Canada's laws treated men and women equally, and formalized accused individuals' rights to a fair trial, but cemented the importance of freedom of expression to democratic political life, thus placing a historically stronger pressure on governments to justify restrictions on free speech and free circulation of the press. Accordingly, the question arose in *Towne Cinema Theatres* of whether the federal government had become obliged to adduce evidence of "undueness" in anti-obscenity prosecutions. Chief Justice Dickson answered this question in the negative, but nonetheless expressed the possible utility and desirability of evidence of community standards in some cases. At the same time, he addressed the utility and admissibility of expert evidence in such cases. He recalled both American and Canadian law on this point.[110] In particular, he cited the previously mentioned 1973 American cases *Paris Adult Theatre I* v. *Slaton* and *United States* v. *Groner*, which criticized the use of experts in obscenity cases, but he did not discuss the 1959 United States Supreme Court case *Smith* v. *California*, in which it was suggested that the exclusion of expert evidence pertaining to community standards in an obscenity prosecution would violate constitutional due process.

Dickson also turned to Justice Laskin's dissenting judgment in *R.* v. *Cameron*, reiterating the view that expert evidence pertaining to "undueness" may be admissible, and in many cases should be admissible, but that the trier-of-fact is ultimately free to weigh the evidence as she sees fit.[111] Yet Dickson added an important qualification to this principle. He held that the trier-of-fact cannot reject evidence (expert or otherwise) of community standards and undueness "without good reason."[112] In practical terms this means that a trial judge cannot reject evidence of community standards of tolerance (or undueness) without explanation, especially where that evidence stands unrebutted.[113] Wilson appears to have concurred in this finding, saying that the evidence of the Alberta Motion Picture Censor Board in the case before her "was relevant evidence and evidence which [the trial judge] was obliged to consider."[114]

Indeed, *Towne Cinema Theatres* was similar to *Odeon Morton Theatres* as both heard defence evidence from chairpersons of provincial film censor boards. These cases were also similar as both heard evidence of audience attendance figures. To recall, the probative value and relevance of this kind of marketplace evidence had already been considered in *Re Regina and Provincial News*, but mainly rhetorically. In *Towne Cinema Theatres,* the situation was not very different. Dickson merely noted the relatively sizeable attendance figures in Edmonton, Calgary, and Jasper, for the impugned movie, without indicating the relevance of these figures to the trial judge's finding that the movie was obscene.

In a sense the *Towne Cinema Theatres* case represents a small shift in, and perhaps clarification of, relations that had developed between the judiciary and extra-legal professionals in anti-obscenity litigation at that time. Judges were being encouraged, but not ordered, to abandon their pretenses to knowledge of community standards and to canvass instead the informed opinions of others, usually experts or authority figures. Wilson suggested that such an approach would not only "inspire greater confidence in the result" but possibly enhance "uniformity in the application of the law of obscenity."[115] This is important from the point of view of people charged with publishing and distributing obscene materials but also from the perspective of freedom of expression. In a broad sense, Wilson was also proposing that the kind of information relevant to Canadian anti-obscenity prosecutions was beyond the purview of a narrowly situated judiciary, and could best be obtained through broader, communal teamwork.

THE JURY AND THE EXPERTS DISAGREE ABOUT SOME *PENTHOUSE* PHOTOGRAPHS

More than a decade after the Manitoba Court of Appeal gave its learned opinion about *Last Tango in Paris*, with the film's artistic portrayal of coercive and possibly violent sexuality, juries in various courts across Canada were presented with a photo spread from *Penthouse* magazine depicting some nude and semi-nude women suspended from trees by ropes.[116] The mere fact that such images were put on trial across Canada at this time is significant. *Doug Rankine Co.* and *Towne Cinema Theatres* were clear signs that the Canadian public interest (at least as reflected in state law enforcement practices) had intensified regarding published imagery tending to denigrate women, especially if it showed them in servile or abject positions or as some-how dehumanized. The clear photographic image of semi-nude women hanging by ropes from trees certainly invited a strong response from men and women alike.

Indeed, the Crown introduced expert evidence in the Ontario trial to the effect that the impugned photographs violated the community standards of tolerance. This evidence was given by Mary Brown, then chairperson of the Ontario Film Board, and Maude Barlow, who at the time was a consultant to the Task Force on the Status of Women, founder of the Canadian Coalition against Media Pornography, and a member of Media Watch Canada. Without more, it is difficult to imagine a less "impartial" witness than Barlow in such proceedings. The defence introduced contrary expert evidence by Toby Levinson, a registered clinical psychologist and member of the Advisory Committee on Contemporary Literature (who had testified in *Odeon Morton Theatres*); Arnold Edinborough, professor of English, editor of *Saturday Night* magazine, and member of the Ontario Advisory Committee on Contemporary Literature (and veteran expert witness from *Dominion News & Gifts* and *Odeon Morton Theatres*); and Peter Webb, an art expert.

Despite the fact that by numbers alone, the evidentiary deck was stacked in favour of the bookseller, the jury hearing the evidence ruled in the Crown's favour. Of course, no one will ever know why. Perhaps what Ernst believed to be jurors' hypocritical righteousness was in itself sufficient to defeat any testimony in favour of the artistic merit of the photographs, expert or otherwise. In the Quebec prosecution of the same materials, however, the jurors could not reach unanimity regarding the acceptability of the pictures. Again, the reasons for the lack of consensus will forever remain secret.

Shortly after the *Penthouse* photographs made their way through courtrooms in Ontario and Quebec, they arrived at a Winnipeg provincial courthouse. This time the Crown did not proffer expert evidence, probably feeling confident that the Ontario decision in *Metro News*, and the photographs themselves, would lead the presiding judge to find the photographs obscene. Yet Justice Jewers had no reasons before him regarding the *Metro News* case (because it was decided by a jury), and he decided to balance his impression of the maligned photographs carefully against that of three experts presented by the defence. Levinson returned from *Metro News*, along with two fairly well-known journalists and media-figures, Alice Poyser and June Callwood. Jewers noted that that both Poyser and Callwood had previously testified as experts in Canadian obscenity prosecutions and that "the wide experience" of both would "make them better qualified than most to assess the sort of publication which might be judged obscene by the Canadian community as a whole."[117] This observation is remarkably similar to that which Judge Borins made about June Rowlands's special competency regarding community standards a few years previously in *Doug Rankine Co.* Apparently, public figures had become particularly equipped in the eyes of the judiciary at this point to gauge the collective conscience.

Justice Jewers emphasized Levinson's participation in the Government Committee on Pornography and the Fraser Committee, and particularly her ten-year membership in the Ontario Advisory Committee on Contemporary Literature. Such experiences apparently rendered Levinson especially competent to discern the Canadian community standard of decency with respect to the *Penthouse* photos. Jewers's high estimation of the literary interpretive skills of Levinson and her sister experts may or may not have been deserved, but what is more important to consider here is the plain fact that all three defence witnesses before Jewers were women, *and* all three women testified in favour of the artistic merit of the photographs. As Jewers recalls, "None of the three expert witnesses called by the defence was troubled by the photographs. Ms. Levinson said she saw nothing in the photos that implied bondage, violence, pain or cruelty, that she could see no pain or suffering in them, that they were 'serene,' and that they were neither erotic nor violent. Ms. Poyser also said she found no cruelty or violence in the pictures, which she perceived as being tranquil and surreal. Ms. Callwood also said that, to her, the pictures were strange and beautiful and that she saw no pain or cruelty in them."[118] It was likely just as difficult for Jewers to quarrel with three prominent and well-respected public female spokespersons who saw no cruelty or degradation in images of women bound or tied below trees by ropes as it was for Justice Freedman to discredit the opinion of Father Pungente, a Jesuit priest, who believed that the scenes of forced anal and digital intercourse in *Last Tango in Paris* were not violent. Had male experts given evidence like that of the women in *Arena Recreations (Toronto)*, however, it would likely have seemed much less impartial and credible. After all, *Penthouse*, like its softer sibling *Playboy*, is generally presumed to be "entertainment for men."

A closer analysis of the expert testimony in *Arena Recreations (Toronto)* also reveals a special concern with the theme of bondage suggested by the use of ropes in the photographs. To recall, it was Levinson's testimony, as paraphrased by Justice Jewers, that the photos did not evoke the theme of bondage, even though the Crown argued to the contrary. This preoccupation with the image and theme of bondage anticipates much of the prosecutorial and evidentiary attention paid to sadomasochistic expressions in Canada in subsequent years. At this juncture, however, it is worth noting that the female experts' opinions regarding the *Penthouse* bondage scenes assume what might be called the hermeneutic "accessibility" of those images to women. The testimonies of Levinson, Poyser, and Callwood implied that the photographs were not created and produced to be viewed and appreciated by men exclusively. Some men might interpret the artistic and erotic significance of the photographs differently from these female experts, as might some women, but the mere fact that the photographs (which apparently do not contain images of men, at least on any literal interpretation) were reproduced in a sexually explicit magazine marketed presumably or predominantly to men is not indicative of the way any particular man or woman will interpret and understand the images. In the circumstances, Levinson's, Poyser's, and Callwood's testimonies serve to weaken a critical aspect of the expert testimony offered subsequently in the *Little Sister's* case, which suggested that sexually explicit or erotic depictions of women in "mainstream" pornography magazines will evoke a categorically different psychological and emotional response from women viewers than from male viewers. This proposition stands to be seriously challenged.

R. V. FRINGE PRODUCT: PRELUDE TO BUTLER

Despite Canadian courts' increasing hospitality to the voices and viewpoints of women in matters of sexual equality, the broader political battle between civil libertarians and radical-feminists in the pornography arena continued to rage. Tracts of social science research supporting radical-feminist claims that hard-core and violent pornography contributed to the degradation and mistreatment of women were beginning to be produced by prominent members of America's professional social science community (Malamuth and Donnerstein 1984; Linz, Penrod, and Donnerstein 1987; Fisher and Barak 1991, 66–9). Canada and the United States had already commissioned nationwide studies into pornography, and some other countries would soon follow suit. Invariably, women's various post-Charter demands to be treated equally and with dignity by the government, coupled with the heightened public concern over the deleterious effects of violent forms of pornography on women, led to anti-obscenity law enforcement aimed specifically at stores believed to be selling or renting hard-core and violent forms of heterosexual pornographic materials.

In *R. v. Fringe Product*, when Fringe Product and some other companies were charged with unlawfully distributing obscene materials, they challenged the constitutionality of Canada's unlawful possession/ distribution laws, and the government responded with an array of social science experts and expertise regarding the purported harmfulness of pornography. This included several articles written by prominent social scientists (mainly in the area of behavioural psychology), social science–based government reports from the United States, Canada, and Australia,[119] and oral opinion evidence from two psychologists and a sociologist.[120] It is noteworthy that both psychologists, James Check and Edward Donnerstein, had co-authored some of the articles and studies entered into court and that the latter had participated first-hand in the United States's *Attorney General's Commission on Pornography*. The credibility of these witnesses could be tested by comparing their oral testimony in court with their previously written opinions regarding similar matters.

Check testified to the effect that "a causal link exists between the viewing of pornography and increased aggression toward women."[121] Judge Charron noted some of the studies filed before the court which appeared to support Check's opinion, yet ultimately criticized Check for being "less than candid with the court with respect to exposing the criticisms of his own studies" and for lacking "the degree of objectivity one expects of an expert witness" in his presentation of the "actual state of the art" in the field of pornography research. In Charron's eyes, Check was too "quick to discard" studies that tended to contradict his opinion, especially his opinion related to non-violent but dehumanizing pornographic materials. In contrast, Donnerstein seems to have "testified in a forthright and professional manner." He took issue with Check's opinion, emphasizing the significance to harmfulness of sexual violence, rather than sexual explicitness, in pornographic imagery. "More importantly," Charron said, "Dr. Donnerstein stressed the built-in methodological limitations of laboratory investigation," noting further that the "recognition of such limitations is almost universally accepted in the field of social science."[122]

As far as the "state-of-the-art" of the behavioural research into pornography's harmful effects was concerned, Donnerstein stated that "few conclusions could be safely drawn."[123] The emphasis here was, of course, on the word "safely," measured in terms of social science standards or "confidence" levels. For Donnerstein, one safe conclusion positively relates exposure to violent pornography to punitive behaviour toward women in a laboratory setting designed to measure short-term effects.[124] Although this conclusion is supported by the report of the

Attorney General's Commission on Pornography (1986), the Canadian Psychological Association, and the Joint Select Committee on Video Material of Australia (1988), it appears to be contested by the Canadian *Report of the Special Committee on Pornography and Prostitution* (1985), or what is more commonly known as the *Fraser Report*.[125] Perhaps the state-of-the-art in such matters improved in the years immediately following the *Fraser Report*. If so, it is also worth noting how much more cautious, or perhaps "enlightened," the expert or professional opinion in such matters has become since 1978, when the Canadian *Report on Pornography*, known as the *MacGuigan Report*, characterized the psychological and behavioural harm associated with pornography as a "clear and unquestionable danger" (*MacGuigan Report* 1978, 18:4).[126] According to the *MacGuigan Report*, the "clear and unquestionable danger" of pornography is precisely that "it reinforces some unhealthy tendencies in Canadian society," presumably by reinforcing "male-female stereotypes to the detriment of both sexes." This finding is particularly troublesome in light of the *Fraser Report* suggestion that, at that time, the correlation between stereotyping and reading or watching pornography had not even been tested or challenged. Seven years after the publication of the *MacGuigan Report*, the *Fraser Report* observed, "Studies demonstrating that pornography does not impede women's equality rights, for instance, are as far as we could determine, non-existent. In recasting the question to be studied we are, therefore, opening up a new area to be researched" (*Fraser Report*, 1: 98–9). McKay and Dolff's analysis of the research in this area to date was far more condemning.[127] Judge Charron recalled a portion of this analysis which is worth repeating here: "this research continues to be cited *as if* the weaknesses and limitations were incidental to the 'findings.' They are not. The level of complexity of this research, the use of deception as to method and/or purpose, the problems of reliability of measures, and the translation of operational definitions into measurement methodology render this entire area highly problematic in both interpretation and generalizability."[128]

Nowhere among the more recent materials filed in *Fringe Product* is the certainty of the *MacGuigan Report* expressed, except perhaps with respect to violent pornography in the American *Final Report*.[129] Nonetheless, it is the opinion of the 1978 *MacGuigan Report* that appears to have the greatest evidentiary effect on both Judge Charron in *Fringe Product* and Justice Sopinka in *Butler*. As already discussed, it provided the court in both cases with a "reasonable" basis for upholding the constitutionality of the impugned obscenity law.

Before discussing how virtually the same social science evidence regarding pornography that was considered in *Fringe Product* entered into the *Butler* decision, it is worth pausing to note how, once again, unreliable social science evidence was used to lend the appearance of objectivity to the legislative fact-finding process. First, Charron heard conflicting expert opinions on a single matter of fact, which may have quelled the fear of some that, in the balance, the expert opinion testimony was itself lopsided or partisan. She then weighed this evidence accordingly and found that, of the conflicting expert opinions of Check and Donnerstein, the latter deserved relatively more consideration, because it was presented in a "forthright and professional manner" and, in this respect, seemed objective. Yet here the objectivity effectively ends. Charron also canvassed the basic conclusions of various committee reports which collectively revealed dissensus within a broader social science community as to the harmfulness of pornography and a lack of confidence concerning even those opinions or beliefs widely shared in that same community. She could have relied on this broad finding of fact to challenge the wisdom of Parliament's own belief that certain kinds of pornographic publications are harmful to society, and ultimately to challenge the constitutionality of curbing freedom of expression in the name of this belief. Yet Charron made the astute observation, "Social science can only assist in a limited way on the issues at hand and many social scientists have stated so expressly. Much restraint must be exercised in generalizing from results obtained in contrived and limited experimental conditions to the real world. There certainly is no consensus among the social scientists regarding the interpretation of experimental studies or the generalization which can be made from them. Although helpful, social scientific data cannot be determinative of legislative policies or of judicial balancing of competing interests where a s.1 constitution issue is raised."[130] Despite this cautionary message, Charron deferred uncritically to the select finding of the *MacGuigan Report*, which was that the publication and dissemination of pornographic materials poses a "clear and unquestionable danger" to the psychological well-being and moral health of Canadian men and women. For those anti-pornography crusaders and onlookers, Charron legitimated her decision with the *MacGuigan Report*. For civil libertarians concerned with the power of Parliament to restrict speech without good reason, Judge Charron appears to have simply rationalized a troublesome decision in this way. In either case, the questionable use of social science expertise in *Fringe Product* readily throws into doubt any serious contention that the appearance of justice is generally enhanced by the use of expert-based, social science information in obscenity litigation.

BUTLER: A RADICAL-FEMINIST EDGE
TO *FRINGE PRODUCT*

It was to be expected that, in light of Judge Charron's express warning about the reliability and validity of extant social science research into pornography, the various committee reports canvassed in *Fringe Product* would eventually be subject to yet another bout of judicial analysis in Canadian constitutional proceedings. This occurred in *R. v. Butler*, a Supreme Court of Canada review of the prosecution of a Winnipeg video-store retailer for selling largely heterosexual pornography, purportedly in contravention of Canada's anti-obscenity provisions.

In *Butler*, the Supreme Court of Canada was presented with the same committee reports from Australia, Canada, and the United States that were introduced in *Fringe Product*, as well as similar materials from New Zealand and a number of scholarly articles and treatises on the issue of pornography and civil liberties. Moreover, a number of interest groups intervened in the proceedings, most notably the Legal Education and Action Fund (LEAF). The presence of LEAF in *Butler* was particularly important as its submission to the court was informed significantly by the prominent American "radical-feminist" legal theorist and activist Catharine MacKinnon. The latter had already actively influenced the enactment of ordinances in Indianapolis and Minneapolis which identified the production and publication of pornography as a discriminatory sex practice and provided civil redress for women who felt victimized in certain ways by pornography.[131] By the time *Butler* was before the Supreme Court of Canada, MacKinnon was well known in both American and Canadian academic and professional legal circles for her view that the very act of heterosexual intercourse within a patriarchal society, despite any claim that it was consensual, is an act of physical violence by a man against a woman, as well as an expression of political domination by a man over a woman (MacKinnon 1989, 172; MacKinnon 1984, 340). This situation was only exacerbated by the production, publication, and consumption of pornography, a genre of literature and imagery which itself reflected and reproduced patriarchal social relations between men and women (MacKinnon 1989, 204). Without discussing the intellectual merits of this particular "radical" view here, it is important that MacKinnon helped LEAF to convince the court in *Butler* that certain types of pornography, especially those presenting images of sex and violence in association, and those involving sexual practices with children, were harmful to society. Accordingly, these materials needed to be banned from publication and distribution (Busby 1994, 175). This claim was purportedly supported by some of the large amount of social science research that had by now been conducted across the world, and had been summarized in the various committee reports mentioned above. As Busby observes, "The fact is that social scientists are not capable of proving whether there is or is not a *direct* link between pornography and other forms of violence including sexual assault. Clearly there is a need for further study on the causes of pervasive sexual violence, but in the meantime, LEAF chose not to ignore the substantial body of empirical research indicating that pornography is implicated" (170).

The Canadian *Fraser Report* was particularly influential insofar as it divided pornography into three categories which the Supreme Court of Canada used in interpreting Canada's *Criminal Code* anti-obscenity provisions. Precisely, these are "explicit sex with violence," "explicit sex without violence but which subjects people to treatment that is degrading or dehumanizing," and "explicit sex without violence that is neither degrading nor dehumanizing." Justice Sopinka asked whether any of these kinds of pornography were "harmful" in the sense already contemplated by the Supreme Court of Canada in the *Towne Cinema Theatres* case. He concluded that the first kind "will almost always constitute the undue exploitation of sex," whereas the second type "may be undue if the risk of harm is substantial," and the third category "will not qualify as the undue exploitation of sex unless it employs children in its production."[132] Sopinka's conclusion with respect to the first two classifications of pornography is particularly germane because it relies on social science evidence which is admittedly inconclusive in important respects. Indeed, on the general question of whether a causal relationship exists between obscenity and the risk of harm to society at large, Sopinka writes, "it is clear that the literature of the social sciences remains subject to controversy."[133] Despite this controversy, however, Sopinka refers to the social science evidence presented to the American Meese Commission, and to the "common sense" logic of that Commission's *Final Report*, in partial support of his own finding that graphic depictions of sex and violence will "*almost* always" be undue, in the sense of predisposing people to mistreat women and possibly men.[134] This finding is problematic because, as West points out, the *Final Report* was quick to reach the conclusion that Class 1 materials cause violence against women based on "women's testimonies of victimization, on social science, on feminist arguments, and on 'common sense,'" yet it displayed much confusion regarding the definition of "violent pornography" itself and lacked any statistical data to support the claim that sado-masochistic pornography causes violence (West 1987, 701–3). Carol Vance, who participated in the Meese Commission, observed that much of the material depicted at "early slide shows and educational events" organized by anti-pornography feminists "focused very heavily on sm pornography," which occupies a "very small percentage of the actual pornography market."[135]

As for the second category of pornography and its relation to harmfulness, Sopinka is clearer. He expressly acknowledges the lack of a certain or exact demonstration of the risk of harm posed by "degrading" pornographic materials, but he cites *Fringe Product* and the various committee reports from Canada, the United States, New Zealand, and Australia as constituting "a substantial body of opinion" in support of the claim that "the portrayal of persons being subjected to degrading or dehumanizing sexual treatment results in harm, particularly to women and therefore to society as a whole."[136] The third category of "soft-core" porn was not at issue in *Butler*, but that subcategory of soft porn which employs children in its production would eventually have its own day (week and months) in court.

Apparently the state of the social science art regarding the psychological and behavioural effects of pornography had not notably changed since *Fringe Product*, but evidence supporting hard-core pornography's harmfulness may have been given increased weight in *Butler* through MacKinnon's direct participation in the preparation of LEAF's Brandeis-style brief. In effect, MacKinnon added significant intellectual and perhaps theoretical support to empirical research that was admittedly "inconclusive" by some social scientists, as well as members of the Canadian judiciary. As Lacombe observes, anti-pornography feminists, and MacKinnon herself, heralded the *Butler* decision as a landmark legal victory for women's equality (Lacombe 1994, 136). The problem with this particular development is that, shortly after *Butler* (and indeed, shortly prior to *Butler*),[137] MacKinnon's own position on pornography had found increasing opposition and criticism from sister feminists and reputable academics engaged in analyses of text, film, and other kinds of imagery. In a word, MacKinnon's intellectual treatment of pornography has in some key respects been shown to be overly simplistic, at least insofar as it tends to treat much mainstream pornographic imagery and text as literal expressions or reflections of otherwise real social relations. This so-called "literalist" approach toward pornography's psychological and behavioural effects, which seems to have informed much of the empirical research cited in *Butler*, has since become the subject of serious critique in the *Little Sister's* trial, which will be discussed in detail in the next chapter.

R. V. HAWKINS ET AL.:
BUTLER BECOMES UNHINGED

Shortly before and after *Butler* was decided, a number of prosecutions were brought against owners of private residences and businesses across Ontario for possessing pornographic videotapes for sale or distribution that appeared on their face to fall into the second category established in *Butler*.[138] To recall, this category comprised materials that depicted "explicit sex without violence but which subjects people to treatment that is degrading or dehumanizing." Expert evidence was introduced by the accused people in most of these cases, mainly from Robert Payne, then chairperson of the Ontario Film Review Board, to the effect that many of the videotapes would meet the national community standard of tolerance test. And in almost every case, particular attention was paid by the judges and the experts to depictions of women being spanked in the videotapes.

In one of these cases, *R. v. Ronish*,[139] the Crown introduced oral and written psychiatric evidence from William Marshall. Marshall's oral testimony purported to show a correlation between the commission of sex offences and the use of pornography, but Marshall's own writings on the subject conceded that, in the manner of *Butler*, no definite proof existed of a link between exposure to pornography and negative attitudes or behaviour toward women. Judge Cole reviewed both Marshall's written and oral evidence and read a series of articles from a special issue of the *International Journal of Law and Psychiatry* entitled "Socio-Legal Studies of Obscenity." Cole noted that a couple of these articles undermined the force of Marshall's oral evidence and strongly supported the view that the psychological state-of-the-art in obscenity research is unedifying and primitive at best.

Cole also watched some of the impugned videotapes himself and, in light of his own perception informed by all of the relevant expert evidence at hand, including 1990 "Gallop" poll results purporting to show that a majority of Canadians tolerated sexually explicit videos and the 1985 *Fraser Report*'s conclusion about the inadequacy of pornography research, Cole concluded that the Crown failed to establish the requisite level of harmfulness. In his words, "I am entirely satisfied that I have no proof, let alone legally sufficient proof of harm before me."

Cole's decision is particularly significant not only because it results from a careful and indeed critical assessment of the social science evidence presented there, but because it carved out a specific legal rule relating to the depictions of explicit sex without violence. Cole followed the logic of the post-*Butler* decisions in *R.* v. *Hawkins* and *R.* v. *Laliberte*[140] that in cases involving depictions of explicit sex without violence, proof of social harm *must be established, not assumed.* This rule set a troublesome precedent because it has centralized the importance of social science evidence to legal determinations of obscenity. In other words, Cole deserves to be applauded for so vigilantly examining the social science presented in *Ronish*, but by making such evidence necessary to a successful prosecution, he has inadvertently placed social science research evidence at centre stage of every future courtroom proceeding regarding obscene publications in Canada. While this invitation acknowledges that social science evidence may or may not have probative value relating to the lawfulness of obscene materials in particular cases, history has yet to provide any good reason for believing that social science research could *ever* inform this enigmatic domain of human experience.

On appeal, Justice Robins of the Ontario Court of Appeal followed Cole's reasoning and confirmed that the harmfulness of pornography (belonging to *Butler*'s second category) is "now an element of obscenity-based crimes," and, "Like any element of a criminal allegation, it must be proved beyond a reasonable doubt and that proof must be found in the evidence introduced at trial."[141] Although Robins accepts various kinds of evidence as being indicative of community standards of tolerance, such as film board approval or disapproval, or the public availability of images or depictions similar to those being prosecuted in court, he clearly suggests that social science evidence will be required to establish the requisite, proverbial "link" between exposure to sexually explicit materials and hurtful behaviour toward women and children. Robins observed, "The further argument is made in *Ronish* that the trial judge dealt with the nature of the proof required to establish the harm in such a way as to require the Crown to prove a direct causal link between a specifically discernable societal harm and the films referred to in the indictment. I would agree that such proof is not required. It is sufficient for the Crown to prove the requisite harm by reference to films of the same genre."[142] Robins does not say here that the Crown need not prove a causal link. He says only that the link need not be "direct." Moreover, he does not suggest that the films themselves can establish the required link. He suggests that the link must be between exposure to the actual films in question, or films of the same genre, and harmful behaviour flowing from such behaviour. Social science research remains pivotal here "to prove to the satisfaction of the judge that social harm could result from exposure to the films."[143]

Robins's position in *Hawkins et al.* was subsequently reaffirmed by Judge James of the Provincial Court of Alberta in *R. v. Erotic Video Exchange Ltd. et al.* Some familiar expert evidence resurfaced here. William Fisher and Augustin Brannigan, who had both published articles considered by Judge Cole in *Ronish*, appeared for the defence and testified to the effect that social science research purporting to correlate exposure to "nonviolent but degrading and dehumanizing pornography and societal harm" was to date inadequate or insufficient.[144] Moreover, Check returned from *Fringe Product*, where he had been largely discredited by Charron, to say in effect that some of the impugned videos contained sexually violent scenes and that non-violent degrading and dehumanizing pornography did create a substantial risk of harm for society. Not surprisingly, Judge James also declared that he "was not overly impressed " with respect to Check's evidence.[145] James even commented, more remarkably, "I could not help but be left with the impression that [Check] was more of an advocate than an academic or social science researcher." This statement provides yet another illustration of Canadian judges' mistaken belief that some experts, when they appear in court as academics, social science researchers, or literary professionals are not "advocates." One has only to recall Judge Charron's preference for Donnerstein's evidence over Check's evidence in *Fringe Product*, and to view this preference in light of Donnerstein's plain admission in *The Question of Pornography* that his research is driven by social-moral concerns of the negative effects of pornographic materials on men, to realize that all research and academic opinion is so much advocacy (and indeed, to recall Woolhandler, *argument*).

James's opinion in *Erotica Video Exchange* also addressed the theme of sadomasochism that was apparently conveyed in a couple of the impugned videos before him, particularly *Dr. Butts II* and *Lesbian Bondage and Black Jack*. A director of classifications for the British Columbia Film Board felt that a particular depiction of spanking in the *Dr. Butts II* video was not "violent" and was acceptable to the Canadian public. James disagreed with this view and found all of the videos at issue to contain scenes of pornography and violence. With respect to *Lesbian Bondage and Black Jack* in particular, James concluded that "the visitation of various sado-masochistic practices upon the servant constitutes the combination of sex and cruelty or violence, and is obscene within the meaning of s.163(8)."[146]

For decades Canadian judges have singled out lesbianism as a significant indicator of the moral and social acceptability of a novel or film. Since the 1928 English prosecution and 1929 American prosecution of Radclyffe Hall's *The Well of Loneliness*, and the prosecutorial attention paid by Canadian authorities to *Women's Barracks* in *R. v. National News* in 1953, some judges have openly stereotyped the less artistically redeeming and perhaps more morally repugnant kinds of pornography – "skin flicks" – as involving scenes of lesbian sexuality, gay sexuality, and "unusual" forms of sexual expression such as anal penetration.[147] Yet *Butler*'s finding that combined images of sex and violence will almost always be obscene seemed to give a green light to those prosecutorial agents across Canada who viewed "sado-masochistic" depictions precisely as interwoven images of sex and violence. The next chapter examines the post-*Butler* fallout on Canada's gay and lesbian communities who read, write, film, and publish sadomasochistic depictions.

5

From Sadomasochism to Child Pornography: Experts Narrow Their Focus While Canadian Courts Broaden Their Horizons

In my view, common to all feminist denouncers of lesbian s/m porn and practice is the standpoint of *not knowing*. In the place of knowledge, we find conjecture about what lesbian s/m fantasy is, how it works, and whom it 'harms.' But on what grounds might 'harmful materials' be distinguished from 'non-harmful materials'? Who decides?

Ross 1997, 186; emphasis in original

If a blind man were to ask me "Have you got two hands?" I should not make sure by looking. If I were to have any doubt of it, then I don't know why I should trust my eyes. For why shouldn't I test my *eyes* by looking to find out whether I see my two hands? *What* is to be tested by *what*? (Who decides *what* stands fast?) And what does it mean to say that such and such stands fast?

Wittgenstein 1979, prop'n 125

... social scientists and psychiatrists like Dr. Collins are not men from Mars observing the world and recording what they see from a vantage point of pure detachment. Nor, for that matter, are judges. To a greater or lesser degree, we all view the world encumbered by our own education, values and experiences.

Madam Justice Southin in *R. v. Sharpe*, para. 66

PHILOSOPHICAL AND HISTORICAL BACKDROP TO GAY AND LESBIAN CHARTER LITIGATION

The emergent prosecutorial and judicial concern with images that combined sex and violence, or with graphic expressions of gay and lesbian sexuality, reflects in part a wider conservative and indeed heterosexist ideology prevalent in society to this date which conceptually links sexual intercourse with the institution of marriage (Downs 1987, 651) and species reproduction (West 1987, 691). To the extent that gay and lesbian acts of sexual expression are not procreative, and until only recently bore no relation to marriage, they have been seen as debased, or as not having any cultural value or significance. Again, these considerations help to explain why specific scenes in *Last Tango in Paris*, such as the scene where Paul asks Jeanne to insert her fingers in his anus, and the scene of simulated anal intercourse between Paul and Jeanne, became the special focus of attention in *Odeon Morton Theatres*. It is not simply that they appeared unduly violent by "traditional" standards, or that (in the case of the latter scene) they suggested the social propriety of coercive sexual behaviour. They were also activities that occurred outside the institution of marriage, they suggested infidelity, and they were without purpose from the point of view of species reproduction.

A conservative, heterosexist ideology regarding human sexuality was shared by more people than judges at the time. Anal intercourse, for example, was categorically a criminal offence, and section 159 of Canada's current *Criminal Code* makes anal intercourse an indictable offence unless it is committed in private between husband and wife or between any two consenting persons aged eighteen years or older. In 1985, Canada Customs produced an internal memorandum that empowered front-line customs officers to seize and detain materials depicting various kinds of sexual practices, including "anal penetration."[1] As a result, some Canada Customs ports began to seize and detain gay and lesbian erotica and pornography arriving from the United States and destined for gay and lesbian bookstores. One book that was seized under this regime was *The Joy of Gay Sex*, which was *en route* at that time to Jearld Moldenhauer's Toronto bookstore. In response to this detention, Moldenhauer brought a legal action against Canada Customs (Fuller and Blackley 1995, 11–12). The Ontario Provincial Court Judge ruled in Moldenhauer's favour, finding the book in question not to be obscene. The Canada Customs ban on *The Joy of Gay Sex* was accordingly overturned in 1987, but Canada Customs continued to seize and detain other sexually explicit gay and lesbian literature.

Another challenge was brought in 1987, this time by the gay and lesbian Little Sister's Book and Art Emporium (LSBAE) and the British Columbia Civil Liberties Association (BCCLA), both located in Vancouver. This case did not make it to trial because, almost a year after the proceedings had commenced (and just weeks before the trial was scheduled to begin), the federal government conceded that it had misapplied its anti-obscenity provisions to the magazines at issue (ibid., 12). Frustrated by their inability to set a precedent in favour of the general acceptability (and indeed legality) of gay and lesbian sexually explicit literature, both the LSBAE and the BCCLA launched a much greater legal challenge to relevant provisions of the *Customs Act* and the *Customs Tariff* in 1990. Here the gay and lesbian bookselling community would argue that the system of "prior restraint" used by Canada Customs, whereby customs officials were authorized to seize and detain publications, and to require the importer to establish the conformity of these same publications with the relevant *Customs Tariff* provisions, was a violation of Canadians' constitutionally entrenched right to free expression.

Before the LSBAE went to trial in 1994, however, its lawyer, Joseph Arvay, became involved in the *Butler* case as an intervenor representing the BCCLA. It was clear to Arvay that the *Butler* case could have significant legal ramifications for *Little Sister's* (ibid., 39–40).[2] The Supreme Court of Canada could have deemed section 163(8) of the *Criminal Code* constitutionally invalid, in which event the *Little Sister's* case itself would be bolstered. More realistically, the Supreme Court of Canada would uphold the constitutionality of Canada's obscenity law, but carve out its breadth of application carefully. In this event, Arvay would want to know specifically what kinds and genres of pornographic imagery and text Canadian law was going to allow publishers to publish, booksellers to sell, and readers to read. Most likely, Arvay and the LSBAE were concerned that the Supreme Court of Canada would exclude certain kinds of gay and lesbian sexual expression, such as anal intercourse, but also gay and lesbian forms of sadomasochism, from the ambit of tolerable, and hence legal, pornography and erotica. Again, Canada Customs did not remove "anal penetration" from the scope of images and depictions officers could seize and detain until just a few days before the *Little Sister's* trial began. But gay and lesbian sadomasochist literature and film had also become a focal point of anti-obscenity law and its enforcement. According to Fuller and Blackley, "Nothing seemed to bother Customs as much as gay and lesbian s/M" (57).

Before addressing how "queer" s/M came to play such a pivotal role in the *Little Sister's* trial, it is instructive to return to the mid-1980s, particularly to the aforementioned Attorney General's Commission on Pornography which identified s/M pornography generally as a genre of "violent pornography" deserving of strict censorship. This categorization is particularly interesting to West, who explains that "like the commissioners, anti-pornography feminists define sado-masochistic pornography as 'violent' in spite of the fact that the practices depicted are consensual, not violent, and in spite of the lack of evidence linking sado-masochistic practice or pornography with acts of violence against women ... Sado-masochistic pornography is harmful, according to anti-pornography feminists, and even 'violent,' *whether or not it actually causes particular acts of violence*, because it encourages women to accept and even enjoy sexual inequality" (West 1987, 703; emphasis in original; footnotes omitted). These observations are particularly significant for at least three reasons. First, West's emphasis on the lack of "evidence," particularly "social science data," suggests that social science experiments conducted with a view to assessing the harmfulness of s/m could somehow support or undermine the assumption that reading or watching s/m pornography brings harm to individuals, especially to women (702–3, 705). Social science is yet again held out as an important determinant in this area of inquiry, despite the almost complete fruitlessness of social science experiments to date regarding pornography and harm. As it turns out, the broader historical inability of social scientists to demonstrate pornography's harmfulness, according to indigenous standards of proof or predictability, may well explain why the kind of expertise about s/m introduced in the *Little Sister's* case was rooted primarily in the humanities, not in the social sciences. As far as the LSBAE was concerned, social science had become part of the problem, not the solution.

Second, West's paraphrase of the radical-feminist view of s/m must be taken to refer mainly to heterosexual s/m involving a male dominatrix (or "top") and a female masochist (or "bottom"), although West does briefly explain how both lesbian s/m and heterosexual s/m involving a female dominatrix and male subjugant could be relevant.[3] From a literalist perspective,[4] the male ("top")–female ("bottom") kind of imagery simply reproduces in concentrated form the dangerous double-message of heterosexist, patriarchal society, that male-dominant acts of sexual aggression committed upon women are socially acceptable and that women find these acts committed against them by men pleasurable.[5] From the same perspective, however, this message does not seem to be so clearly conveyed in lesbian and gay s/m, and in heterosexual s/m involving a female dominatrix and a male subjugant. Thus, as already mentioned, Vance pointed out in *Little Sister's* that the slide shows presented by anti-pornography feminists in the 1970s focused heavily on male dominant and female submissive s/m, even though there existed a "great body of material that showed the reverse in sm pornography" because the latter "did not fit with their analysis."[6] Here women are either literally absent from the imagery or text altogether (in the case of gay s/m), or appear to be inflicting pain or violence upon men, or are seen as both inflicting and receiving pain, in which case the otherwise clear message that women enjoy receiving pain is clouded by the message that women also enjoy inflicting pain on other women.

All of these possibilities pose a significant intellectual challenge to the kind of radical-feminist theorizing and conservative ideology about human sexuality and pornography that informed the Meese Commission's 1986 *Final Report* and the 1992 *Butler* case in Canada. It is not insignificant, therefore, that many gay and lesbian scholars and literary theorists, novelists, and artists were invited to raise these issues on behalf of the LSBAE in 1994, as will be discussed shortly.

A third consideration which arises from West's analysis of S/M, as it was treated by the Meese Commission, is that it anticipates or perhaps foreshadows the importance of S/M generally (that is, whether heterosexual or homosexual) to the continuing legal debate about pornography's harmfulness. West observes that "the report's unequivocal denunciation of sado-masochism could easily become a vehicle for needless persecution of an entirely powerless and harmless sexual minority. The deeply entrenched conservative inclination to persecute sexual minorities, evidenced throughout the Attorney General's Report, has, by virtue of the feminist-conservative alliance, simply been bolstered by the confused feminist claim that sado-masochism is violent and harmful to women" (West 1987, 709). As became clear in the *Little Sister's* trial, the genre of S/M functioned as the empirical fulcrum for a highly contentious theoretical discussion about the so-called "message" of pornography itself. It was claimed that S/M was not about harm and was not to be interpreted literally, but was ultimately about mutual trust and the sense of "empowerment" achieved or experienced by those who willingly extend their trust to others who appear capable of hurting them. In other words, S/M, particularly "queer" S/M, is argued to be unique. West implies this when she claims, "In content, effect, and meaning, pornographic depictions of sado-masochistic sexuality are as different from depictions of non-consensual violence, battery, assault, and rape as sado-masochistic sexuality *itself* is different from rape and battery" (708). To demonstrate the plausibility of this claim, the LSBAE enlisted some old-fashioned literary experts, but also some relatively "new-fashioned" literary experts schooled in the philosophies and lexicons of deconstruction and hermeneutics, and interested personally and professionally in gay and lesbian fiction and pornography including, of course, sadomasochist expression. As far as the diversity of expertise heard so far in Canadian constitutional adjudication was concerned, the *Little Sister's* trial marked another watershed, mainly because of the S/M issue. What is of particular note in this regard is, first, what was actually said about S/M by the experts in *Little Sister's*, and second, the peculiar role played by the behavioural and psychological experts there. Before embarking on this discussion, however, it will be fruitful to review the relatively brief history of the

Canadian gay and lesbian community's courtroom struggles with Canada's obscenity law and customs officials prior to *Little Sister's*. This shows the gradual transition in the courtroom of the nature and species of so-called expert knowledge about pornography and relates this to the special interest of a particular community. In so doing it again raises the question: In what sense is expert-based legislative-fact evidence "objective," reasonable, and perhaps reliable, if at all? If it is not, why do Canadian courts continue to be so receptive to it?

The Gay and Lesbian Expert Enters Canada's Anti-Obscenity Battle: Glad Day Bookshop

Some years before both *Butler* and *Little Sister's* were decided, gay and lesbian pornography and erotica had already become the target of Canadian anti-obscenity law enforcement officials, who were concerned about depictions of human beings in apparently "degrading" and "dehumanizing" positions, which included images of s/m. As a result of having some shipments of his books detained by Canada Customs in 1989, Jearld Moldenhauer, owner at that time of Glad Day Books in Toronto, appealed to the office of the Deputy Minister of National Revenue for Customs and Excise, challenging its tariff determination of the books in question as "obscene."[7] At the appeal level of this action, the government did not call evidence in support of its opinion that the gay magazines and short-story publications in question were "obscene," but the appellant bookstore called three witnesses to challenge this opinion.

Robert Payne, then chairman of the Ontario Film Reform Review Board, testified to the effect that explicit sex scenes in film, including scenes of either vaginal or anal penetration, were acceptable for publication, as long as they did not involve violence or minors, and as long as they were not degrading. Most notably, Payne took issue with Justice Wilson's dicta in *Towne Cinema Theatres* that "sub human" and "merely physical" portraits of human life must somehow contribute to a process of "moral desensitization" and be "harmful in some way."[8]

Kyle Rae, then city councillor for Ward 6 in Toronto and a director of the community centre for the lesbian and gay community, testified that gay sexual activity is essentially non-violent, although it sometimes involves practices that are called "rough sex," such as spanking, fisting, and sexual activity where one party is restrained. He also testified that "rough sex," in his opinion, was not "degrading." Although the presence of Rae in *Glad Day Bookshop* is remarkably similar to that of Rowlands in *Doug Rankine Co.* from a logistical or tactical point of view,[9] Rae's opinion received very little attention from Justice Hayes. It is difficult to understand why. Clearly Rae represented a specific "voice," namely that of the gay community in Canada,[10] but Rowlands's presence in Doug Rankine Co. also symbolized a particular point of view, namely that of Canadian women. It is conceivable that Hayes did not feel the same kind of political pressure to heed gay and lesbian legal concerns at this moment in Canadian history as Justice Borins did with respect to feminist concerns a decade earlier. It is also noteworthy that, like Walker in Doug Rankine Co., Rae had some personal history of political activism.[11] This fact might have tainted Hayes's perception of Rae's "objectivity."

A third witness for Glad Day Bookshop was Barry Adams, a professor of sociology at the University of Windsor who testified as an expert on various subjects pertaining to gay sexuality. Perhaps more than the others, Adams's opinion was addressed to the issue of s/m which had risen to such importance since the Attorney General's Commission on Pornography, but more recently in light of a crucial, albeit obiter, remark made by Justice Sopinka in Butler. There Sopinka surmised, "Among other things, degrading and dehumanizing materials place women (and sometimes men) in positions of subordination, servile submission or humiliation," but he then added, "In the appreciation of whether material is degrading or dehumanizing, the appearance of consent is not necessarily determinative. Consent cannot save materials that otherwise contain degrading or dehumanizing scenes. Sometimes the very appearance of consent makes the depicted acts even more degrading and dehumanizing."[12]

Canadian courts had already shown themselves willing to place limits on the legal importance of consent in some kinds of actual assault,[13] and the English House of Lords was well divided on the precise issue of whether sadomasochistic behaviour constitutes a form of criminal assault.[14] Yet these were not the immediate concerns before Sopinka in Butler. He was informed by certain feminist analyses of pornography that said images of sexual domination by a male over a female in which the female appears to be consenting only reinforce the false, sexist view that women naturally desire to be, or take sexual pleasure in being, dominated, if not violated, by men.[15] And clearly this contention – that the appearance of consent to some form of physical domination or perhaps violation exercised by a sexual "partner" in pornographic imagery may well reinforce a socially prevalent view that women (and sometimes men) enjoy being dominated or violated – has since become one of the major topics of concern in Canadian anti-obscenity adjudication. Adams himself remarked at the Glad Day Bookshop trial that "obviously I am not a lawyer, but my understanding of [Sopinka's remark about consent] is that there is a concern that has come out of the woman's movement that there are forms of pornography that function as a kind of hate literature which give warrant to providing, encouraging, and affirming violence against women, and this is a literature that is written by men from a male viewpoint, impugning pleasure into woman to allow men to exert that domination."[16] This concern has become alloyed with a focus on S/M almost as a matter of definition, because "masochism" connotes taking pleasure in subjugation and pain.

This brief historical and philosophical backdrop should help to explain why Adams testified in *Glad Day Bookshop* that there exists "coercive sex in the gay community in the form of sadomasochism and bondage but if there is there is underlying consent *and it is sexual theatre.*"[17] The idea of sadomasochism and bondage constituting forms of "sexual theatre" appears to have been novel to Canadian courts at this time, although it was familiar to some literary and sociological scholars interested in human sexuality.[18] It is particularly significant here because, despite any concern Justice Hayes and others might have regarding its validity, plausibility, or cogency, it so obviously serves a tactical purpose; and this purpose partly explains the shift in the nature of expertise about pornography and human sexuality that has occurred since *Butler.* The purpose, already suggested, is to combat the feminist-informed notion that the "appearance of consent" in pornographic imagery and text may well render otherwise (or apparently) healthy expressions of sexuality "degrading and dehumanizing" and therefore criminally obscene. To this end, gay and lesbian litigants have introduced into court the notion that sexually explicit gay and lesbian text and imagery, especially that which contains scenes of sadomasochism, bondage, and so-called "rough sex," is qualitatively unlike graphic depictions of heterosexual sexuality (perhaps with the exception of heterosexual sadomasochism), such that Sopinka's comment in *Butler* about the "appearance of consent" should be deemed irrelevant to gay and lesbian pornography. This is evident in the following exchange between Adams and his cross-examiner in the *Glad Day Bookshop* trial:

Question Since you have just raised the issue, Professor, isn't it correct to say that the principle enunciated by Justice Sopinka will appear to apply to all people, not just heterosexual people or to women but to all people?

Adams Yes, I don't think that is what we are talking about here in excepting gay men, but rather that *the nature of this particular form of erotica does not conform or does not fall into the problem that was identified in the quote that you just read.*[19]

Now the Canadian courts are presented with a new epistemological quagmire. Suddenly s/m – the apparently most deleterious form of pornography because it obviously depicts human beings in positions of willing subjugation and subservience and enjoying the wilful infliction of pain upon themselves – is argued to be perhaps the least harmful of all since it is understood by its readers, observers, and indeed participants, to be pure "theatre." Traditional approaches (or at least radical-feminist and literalist approaches) of textual and pictorial interpretation are argued to be irrelevant to the theatrical and ritualistic nature of s/m. Equally important, the hitherto dominant social science approaches to pornography's harmfulness – namely, behavioural-psychological laboratory experimentation and opinion sampling – are now expected to take a back seat. Arguably, s/m expression plays a much different (and indeed, much less harmful) role in the social lives of its participants and observers than non-s/m pornography plays in the lives of its participants and readers. It is not characterized as appealing to so-called "prurient" interests or as replicating and reinforcing prevalent social attitudes, but is portrayed rather as operating on some kind of spiritual plane. So until social scientists can redesign their experiments and methodologies in light of this understanding of s/m text and imagery, it is suggested that they have relatively little to contribute to the harmfulness debate.[20]

Unfortunately for Moldenhauer and the broader community of gay and lesbian writers and readers of erotica, Hayes retained the Canadian judiciary's strong appetite for laboratory or clinical-based research into the psychological and behavioural effects of reading or watching sexually explicit materials. The mere fact that Adams's evidence lacked any support in such kind of research enabled Hayes to reject it handily. He said, "I have reviewed the evidence of Professor Adam[s]. His research and opinions are generally not based on recent original research. In addition, his views are largely restricted to the gay community and oriented around consensual activity which he indicates should be allowed. His evidence does not assist the Court with respect to *the effect of the publication of descriptions of homosexuals' sexual activities as it might relate to harm.*"[21]

Adams's key claims about the consensual and theatrical nature of gay and lesbian s/m would eventually be accepted by Justice Smith in *Little Sister's*, likely because they formed part of what Kohn refers to as a recognized and systemic "body of knowledge" by that time. Prior to this moment in the gay and lesbian legal struggle for social equality and free expression, however, the laboratory-based approach to pornography's harmfulness continued to be the dominant body of knowledge that Canadian courts appeared willing to recognize. At the same time, bearing Miller and Barron's observation about judicial "political" sensitivities in mind, it appears that Canadian judges at this time intuitively felt politically safe in rejecting alternative "knowledges" and points of view. This feeling is reflected in the next gay and lesbian obscene publications prosecution to arise in Canada.

Bad Attitude Raises Good Questions

The consent issue and gay and lesbian s/m came to the forefront of the Canadian legal consciousness just shortly after *Glad Day Bookshop* was decided. In *R. v. Scythes*, Judge Paris of the Ontario Court of Justice, Provincial Division, was required to rule regarding the legality of the possession and sale of a magazine (again, at Glad Day Bookshop) of a "lesbian sadomasochistic nature" entitled *Bad Attitude*.[22] According to Paris, "Bad Attitude consists of a series of articles where the writers fantasize about lesbian sexual encounters with a sadomasochistic theme. Photographs loosely complement some of the articles."[23]

Expert evidence regarding homosexual pornography was given by Neil Malamuth, the prominent American professor of psychology and communications, Jonathon Freedman, a University of Toronto psychologist, and Becki Ross, a recent doctorate in lesbian studies recipient. Non-expert evidence was provided for the defence by a law student and a lesbian photographer whose photographs were contained in the particular *Bad Attitude* publication at issue.

Malamuth's presence at the *Scythes* trial was important not only because it so clearly reflects the continuing thirst of Canadian lawyers for laboratory-based research conclusions in matters of legislative fact (especially in the area of pornography), but also because, ironically, it was practically superfluous. The latter argument has been made plausibly by Ross, whose non–laboratory-based sociological knowledge, which is specifically concentrated in the areas of feminist theory and gay and lesbian studies, was expected in *Scythes* to challenge the validity and credibility of Malamuth's otherwise "expert" opinion about the social harmfulness of gay and lesbian pornography (including gay and lesbian s/m). As Ross recalls, "Over the course of his testimony, Malamuth flatly repeated that he had never studied lesbian and gay erotic material made specifically for members of the lesbian, gay, and bisexual community" (Ross 1997, 155; footnotes omitted). Nevertheless, Malamuth was permitted to offer an opinion about the harmfulness of such materials, and Judge Paris accepted this opinion.[24] Indeed, Ross points out that Paris had already decided there was no need "to make a distinction between [representations of] heterosexual sex and homosexual sex," as far as the problem of these representations' harmfulness was concerned, before Malamuth was even qualified as an expert in such matters (154–5). To the extent that this opinion revealed itself to be entirely consistent with Malamuth's evidence during examination, Ross has every reason "to wonder why it was necessary for [Malamuth] to testify at all."

This book has already suggested some of the more plausible explanations for Malamuth's presence in Scythes. The clinical or laboratory element of Malamuth's research lends it an aura of scientificity, which in turn appears to enhance the desired "objectivity" of the fact-finding process. Ross herself recognizes that "Malamuth's work in large part supplied the 'scientific' foundation for the Butler decision, and it appears as the 'Truth' about pornography in the factums submitted by the Attorney General of Manitoba, Attorney General of Canada, and the Group Against Pornography" in that same case (ibid., 154). Moreover, the positivistic nature of Malamuth's research envelops the conclusions in a cloak of epistemological legitimacy from a broader, social point of view. Insofar as any judicial pronouncement of legislative fact in a constitutional review also strives to be legitimate in this sense, it makes sense that Paris's relevant determination of legislative fact would ultimately be supported by the scientific observations of Malamuth. To use Cahn's idiom, the fact that Malamuth shares the same opinion as Paris on the record also enables Paris to "save face" in the event that his opinion is challenged as unsound, biased, unfair, or somehow politically insensitive.

Marketplace evidence was also introduced by the defence in Scythes to make the point that lesbian s/M images do enjoy "mainstream" circulation, and in this sense are not offensive to so-called community standards of tolerance if they are produced by the right (i.e., heterosexual and mainstream publishing) people. In particular, Paris was presented with a highly popular book by American popstar Madonna containing at least one depiction of a lesbian sadomasochistic theme. He stated, "Madonna's book called 'Sex' was offered to show the public tolerance to this type of material. One photograph of particular relevance shows a so called playful rape scene in a school gymnasium."[25] In keeping with judges' reluctance to consider marketplace evidence in Canadian obscenity proceedings, the large market for Madonna's book did not seem to inform Paris's conclusion about the community standard of tolerance for lesbian sadomasochist literature, but he was attuned to the possibility that the "sexual orientation of Bad Attitude" was a relevant concern in the proceedings before him.[26] Paris ultimately rejected this idea, however, saying "The community tolerance test is blind to sexual orientation or practices. Its only focus is potential harm to the public."

With this finding, Paris categorically rejected the emerging "body of knowledge" or opinion regarding homosexual erotica that was put forward by the defence in Scythes and by the plaintiffs in Glad Day

Bookshop. To the extent that Paris appears to have paid no mind to these opinions, his categorical claim about sexual orientation and community standards is problematic. One might describe it as wilfully myopic. On the other hand, in its very simplicity and apparent ignorance, it reveals a remarkable evidentiary problem regarding homosexual erotica and pornography that has yet to be addressed seriously by Canadian courts in obscenity litigation. Simply put, Paris saw no good reason for categorically distinguishing homosexual pornography from heterosexual pornography from the point of view of societal harmfulness, especially where scenes of bondage and sadomasochism are involved. Referring to Trish Thomas's short story of lesbian sexuality involving bondage scenes and what might be called "rough sex," Paris commented, "If I replaced the aggressor in this article with a man there would be very few people in the community who would not recognize the potential for harm. The fact that the aggressor is a female is irrelevant because the potential for harm remains."[27]

As various gay and lesbian experts in *Glad Day Bookshop* and *Little Sister's* testified, the fact that an "aggressor" is female or that an aggressor and recipient of apparent physical and sexual abuses in gay and lesbian erotica are of the same sex is very relevant to the issue of social harm. These experts, in other words, argue that there is every good reason for categorically distinguishing between the two genres of pornography or erotica along these lines. Yet in the final analysis the expert opinions presented in *Little Sister's* are not entirely convincing. The following discussion of the *Little Sister's* case will demonstrate that these opinions can be readily and intelligently challenged on their own terms – indeed, in a way that lends some support to Paris's otherwise controversial point of view. Hence, despite obvious limitations to Paris's interpretation of the community standard of tolerance test, this view is very important from an evidentiary and epistemological perspective. The idea that depictions of so-called "rough sex" between women pose the same kind of danger to society as images of a man committing "rough" sex against a woman indirectly challenges the theory espoused by Adams in *Glad Day Bookshop* that otherwise "violent" homosexual sexual depictions are quite safe, or at least harmless, because they are not only *consensual* but *theatrical*. It throws into question the assumption that violent theatrical presentations do not have, as a matter of principle, similar psychological and behavioural effects on audience members as violent non-theatrical depictions have on readers. It also questions the unexamined but working assumption that non-s/M portrayals of human sexuality (whether homosexual or heterosexual) are not themselves "theatrical," or understood to be such by their readers or watchers. Finally, it asks simply why otherwise "violent" or "rough" sexual depictions between individuals should become "non-violent" and perhaps "playful" where the individuals are of the same sex but remain "violent" and "harmful" where the individuals are of opposite sexes. Much of the expert evidence introduced in *Little Sister's* is aimed at identifying the conditions under which superficially violent depictions of sexual behaviour become really harmless. Ultimately, however, there appears to be some cogency in Paris's comment about substituting a male aggressor for a female aggressor in the context of sadomasochist or violent pornography. Therefore, Paris may appear to be ignorant in simply suggesting that the community standard of tolerance should be blind to the "sexual orientation" of pornographic magazines, but he has unwittingly acted judiciously in questioning the categorical claim that sexual orientation is necessarily relevant in such considerations.

Before turning to the *Little Sister's* case, however, it is worth reviewing one other evidentiary development in *Scythes* – the fact that one of the women who had photographs published in the impugned *Bad Attitude* magazine testified as a lay witness. The appearance in court of artists whose works are the subject of obscenity proceedings is itself a very recent development in Canadian anti-obscenity law. It is especially important insofar as it serves to counterbalance the almost exclusive reliance on art critics and other informed academics as experts. Paris effectively ignored Jennifer Gillmore's lay testimony about her photographs in *Bad Attitude*. Yet the fact that Gillmore was allowed to speak about impugned materials that she produced at least stands for the possibility that lay witnesses can make an important evidentiary contribution in matters of so-called "social fact" and possibly legislative fact. More important, Gillmore's presence in *Scythes* raises the question of why experts are considered necessary at all in such proceedings where lay persons are available to testify on similar matters. Ross makes it clear that in *Scythes* she and Gillmore *both* "strove to stress the particularities of lesbian-produced sexual texts" (Ross 1997, 166). As the following discussion of the *Little Sister's* case will reveal, various artists testified for the first time in Canadian law about the nature or meaning of the artworks they create and have created. And though much of this evidence is clear, thoughtful, and intelligent, there is a sense that it remains merely supplemental to that of the experts, who are predominantly social scientists or academics. This phenomenon suggests that the legislative fact-finding process in anti-obscenity and free speech adjudication continues to be elitist and not entirely democratic from a popular democracy perspective. Moreover, to the extent that much of the expertise provided by the plaintiffs in *Little Sister's* can be demonstrated to be unclear and unthoughtful at times, it becomes a matter of wonder not only why Malamuth should be called to testify (again), but why any of the experts should be called to testify when the authors and artists of the impugned works appear entirely capable of testifying on their own behalf.

LITTLE SISTER'S RECRUITS A BATTALION OF EXPERTS

In 1994, a Vancouver gay and lesbian bookstore, Little Sister's Book and Art Emporium (LSBAE), brought an action against the federal government, alleging generally that Parliament's legislative scheme prohibiting the importation of obscene books and magazines violated Canadian citizens' guaranteed rights to free expression.[28] LSBAE also argued that the practical implementation of Canada's *Customs Act* and *Customs Tariff Act* was unjustifiably discriminatory to the extent that disproportionately more gay and lesbian books were detained by Canada Customs officials than were pornographic materials produced by and for a heterosexual audience. From a purely evidentiary point of view the *Little Sister's* case was novel as a Canadian anti-obscenity case. The plaintiffs called approximately thirty witnesses from across North America to testify about gay and lesbian sexuality, literature, and community life in general. Several of these witnesses were laypersons who provided what might be called "anecdotal" evidence, and approximately twelve of the witnesses were academics who were culled from a wide variety of disciplines. These individuals were typically qualified as "experts" and were expected to provide the court with the theoretical underpinnings of the plaintiffs' discrimination arguments.

Out of the Lab and Into the Fields – of Sociology, Semiotics, Anthropology, Ethnography, Cultural History, Literature, and Gay and Lesbian Studies

As a preliminary observation, the *Little Sister's* trial represents a dramatic development from the point of view of the history of legislative-fact evidence in Canadian constitutional law. The legislative fact-finding process here was informed by both experts *and laypersons*, thereby diminishing temporarily the hegemonic hold on this process by lawyers, academics, and social scientists. At the same time, the intellectual content of most of the experts' opinions was historically novel, as far as courtroom adjudication was concerned. Bart Testa provided expert testimony in the area of semiotics, a post–World War II "science" relating to communicative signs.[29] Becki Ross testified as an expert in women's studies and in lesbian representations and also gave expert evidence comparing and contrasting lesbian and heterosexual sexual imagery and text.[30] Thomas Waugh provided expert opinion evidence regarding gay and lesbian cultural history, including the role of eroticism in gay cultural and social life.[31] Carol Vance offered her opinion as an expert anthropologist and epidemiologist about sexuality, gender, the body, the historical and cultural aspects of the regulation of sexual material, the interpretation of sexual images in text, and the evolution of feminist ideology.[32] Ann Scales gave expert testimony regarding the nature and extent of lesbian pornography in the United States, and regarding the political worth or value of lesbian pornography both in general and in particular.[33] Gary Kinsman expressed his opinion as an expert regarding the history of the regulation of gay sexuality in Canada, and the sociology of gay sexuality in Canada.[34] And Lorraine Weir testified as an expert in literary theory, specifically with respect to hermeneutics and deconstruction, two relatively recent developments in that domain.[35]

This roster of LSBAE experts also shows that the social science evidence itself was not confined to clinical or laboratory-based research but was mainly scholarly in substance. Many of the other kinds of evidence that managed to enter obscenity proceedings to date, such as readership figures, movie attendance figures, and social science surveys were notably absent from *Little Sister's*, or at least only indirectly discernible. This is because the legal contest and concern of *Little Sister's* was primarily theoretical, and only secondarily empirical.

LSBAE argued that Canada Customs officials lacked both the physical and intellectual resources to make proper tariff classifications and decisions regarding homosexual literature and film. This argument hinged on the ability of *Little Sister's* to convince the court of the plausibility of the various theories articulated by its sociological and literary experts concerning sexually explicit gay and lesbian reading and viewing materials. Again, these theories were introduced precisely to inform the issue of "apparent consent," as highlighted in *Butler*, and the unique nature of gay and lesbian erotica and pornography, from a broad literary, social, and cultural perspective. Gay and lesbian social history, as well as literary and cultural theory, and history generally, would make the case for the *consensual and theatrical*, and hence non-injurious, nature of graphic gay and lesbian sexual expression (especially s/M).

Refreshingly, laboratory-based social science research data was absent from the *Little Sister's* courtroom. It is likely to return in future obscenity trials, but in the meantime, the same questions posed in relation to the expert evidence that has spanned the last twenty-five years of anti-obscenity adjudication in Canada must be posed in relation to the expertise offered in *Little Sister's*: Is it reliable, valid, cogent, plausible, helpful, relevant, etc.? It is nearly impossible to answer these questions, perhaps only because much of the information presented by the experts appears so novel. Yet much of this evidence does bear the mark of political self-interest and, in a sense, does not present an epistemologically compelling account of lesbian and gay pornography's uniqueness within the vast world of pornographic imagery and script. Yet the reader will have the opportunity to be the judge here, as this book now turns to each of the different LSBAE witnesses.

Hermeneutics and Deconstruction as Novel Legislative-Fact Evidence

The LSBAE experts had a philosophical case to meet in response to Justice Sopinka's finding in *Butler* that "the portrayal of sex coupled with violence will almost always constitute the undue exploitation of sex."[36] Until *Glad Day Bookshop*, S/M was viewed by the Canadian judiciary as being prototypical of such "undueness." Adams testified to the contrary in *Glad Day Bookshop*, but his testimony failed to convince Justice Hayes. As far as the gay and lesbian reading and publishing community was concerned, therefore, more theory, or at least more intellectual support, was needed.

University of British Columbia English professor Lorraine Weir was called to testify as an expert in literary theory about two particular theories of literary interpretation – hermeneutics and deconstruction – and to apply these theories to four impugned books: *Urban Aboriginals, Leading Edge, My Biggest O*, and *Different Loving*. Before addressing some of the particulars of this evidence, it should be noted that Weir's testimony clearly had characteristics of both legislative-fact and "social-fact" evidence. It was intended to inform the broader policy issue at stake: Is S/M a genre of "harmful" literature within the terms of *Butler*[37] and therefore deserving of proscription within Canadian anti-obscenity law and customs legislation? It was also expected to inform some of the more specific factual issues at bar – namely, whether some of the books shipped to LSBAE but detained by customs officers had been inappropriately classified as obscene.[38]

According to Weir, hermeneutics and deconstruction theory can inform the broader policy question by shedding light on the different ways of interpreting texts, and especially by dispelling or at least challenging the notion that any given text has a unitary message, or "meaning," regardless of "context."[39] In a sense, this aspect of Weir's testimony also challenges the established wisdom of Justice Wilson's pronouncement in *Towne Cinema Theatres* that the particular readership of a book or dominant audience of a film should be considered irrelevant to the community standard of tolerance of that book or film.[40] Weir makes it plain that, according to hermeneutic theory, "accuracy" in textual interpretation or meaning is dependent on the "personal background, education, and so on" of readers.[41] Applying this notion to the realm of s/M literature, hermeneutic theory implies that the intended meaning, import, or message of any given s/M text will be recognized more obviously by those readers who are personally and culturally familiar with the literary conventions and terms of the genre.[42] Other experts at Little Sister's described some of these conventions and terms more idiomatically as "codes."[43]

Once Weir provided the court with a general introduction to hermeneutics and deconstruction theory, she moved straight to the focal problem of Little Sister's, namely discrediting the hitherto persuasive yet wrongheaded (radical) feminist analysis of s/M and substituting this with an alternate, indeed more "accurate," account. The stage was nicely set for this undertaking when Weir was asked to apply her expert understanding of hermeneutics and deconstruction theory to Geoffrey Mains's book Urban Aboriginals. She stated that this book, subtitled "A Celebration of Leathersexuality," is not just an ethnographic exploration of the elements of "transcendence" and "ritual" associated with s/M practice, but is also in part an argument for the relatively different cultural meanings associated with gay and heterosexual genres of s/M literature and practice.[44] According to Weir, Mains is interested "in making it clear that what, let's say, mainstream culture classifies as the negative side of SM experience in a heterosexual context in fact should not be applied in the context of leathersexuality because [Mains] wants to argue ... that SM practice is not the same thing in one context and in another."[45] In case there should be some confusion as to how "mainstream culture" does in fact classify "the negative side" of s/M, Weir states that Mains has the "feminist approach" in mind and explains,

inside an SM relationship practised between two people, man and woman in a straight context, the woman retains that posture [of a "one down position"], that status that she has inside mainstream society. But she's also entered into a set of sexual practices which have a fantasy element ... that has to do with domination and submission practices. But what Mains wants to say is that the woman who is already in a posture of submission in her society, does not enter the fantasy relation of, let's say, submission in the same way as one who is the gender equal in a man-to-man relationship, the gender equal of his partner in sexual practice, performing what might appear to an onlooker – performing much the same kinds of manœuvres.[46]

So far then, Weir has loosely applied hermeneutic theory to Mains's Urban Aboriginals in such a way that the court, until now an outsider or "mainstream" observer of gay s/M, becomes more intimately exposed to its real meaning (as more readily recognized by gay practitioners of s/M), which is about transcendence, spirituality, and "nobility," but certainly not violence or degradation.[47] Yet to make Mains's point, Weir has introduced another interesting idea, that of gender equality within different kinds of sexual relationships, especially gay relationships and heterosexual relationships. She implies that some kind of "gender" inequality exists within a "mainstream" sexual and domestic relationship between heterosexuals which is absent from a gay sexual and domestic relationship. This claim is too categorical to accept without further analysis, especially when viewed in light of certain feminist arguments which claim that gay sexual relationships are characterized by the same kind of "gender" difference and perhaps inequality as heterosexual relationships. Again, MacKinnon has suggested that homosexual sexual and social relations are affected by the existing "gendered sexual system": thus, whatever the sex of the participants in sexual activity might be, one partner will be recognized as "feminine" while the other is recognized as "masculine" and these designations themselves are defined in terms of "dominance and submission" (MacKinnon 1989, 141–3). Weir, however, did not hold herself out to be an expert on this particular point. This issue was left for Gary Kinsman, a professor of sociology at Laurentian University.

A Sociological Approach to Gay s/M

In one sense, Kinsman may be seen as the star witness at the *Little Sister's* trial. Apart from the relevant general expertise he brought to bear – that is, on the subject of "the history of the regulation of gay sexuality in Canada" and "the sociology of gay sexuality in Canada" – he was expected to address one of the specific and key legislative-fact issues at bar. *Little Sister's* lawyer Joseph Arvay put the question in the following way: "Would depictions of sex between men and, in particular, consensual s/M activity be characterized as demeaning, dehumanizing or degrading even if the same depictions as between a man and a woman might be so characterized."[48]

This was the question raised indirectly by *Butler*, with its categorization of combined sex and violence imagery as "obscene." It was also the question raised directly by Weir's analysis of Mains's *Urban Aboriginals*, which suggested that gay s/M, but not necessarily heterosexual s/M, is anything but "dehumanizing," "degrading," and indeed, ultimately "obscene." For Kinsman, the "key" to answering this question lies in the notion that gay sexual relationships (but not heterosexual

sexual relationships), including those involving s/m practices, are characterized by "gender equality."[49]

Kinsman proposes that there is a "major difference" in the "social organization" of heterosexual sexual relations and homosexual sexual relations. This difference lies primarily in the differential "access to social power" between men and women in a male-dominated, sexist society. Men have relatively more access to "social resources" than women in such a society and, presumably, this differential access flows more or less directly into heterosexual sexual relationships. By this very logic, however, this power or access differential should be absent from gay sexual relationships, simply because the partners to the relationship are both men who enjoy similar, or perhaps equal, "access to social power" in a "broader social context," that is to say, in a male-dominated society.[50] In sum, despite other possible "lines of social differences" within gay sexual relations, such as lines of age, race, and class,[51] as far as the "question of gender" is concerned the participants are equals. This is what Kinsman means when he says that the sexual relationship between gay men generally is "fundamentally a relationship between gender equals."[52]

Despite real problems with this smooth translation of "social power" into the specific realm of sexual relationships, it is important to observe how Kinsman relates this phenomenon of gender equality between gay males to gay pornography. He says first that the analysis applied to "mainstream" (that is, heterosexual) pornography, which may construe its "degrading" and "dehumanizing" aspect in terms of the "gender differences" of its participants or models, "wouldn't work because the social organization of the sexual practices is actually quite different."[53] A new kind of analysis must therefore be applied. It must consider the fact that gay male pornography is produced and viewed mainly by men, and uses male models exclusively.[54] These factors suggest that gay male pornography "provides some positive support and reinforcement for gay sexuality in the context of a society that historically and to a degree socially still does not see homosexual sexual activity as legitimate." So far, then, unlike the negative and indeed "degrading" view of woman's sexuality presented by mainstream, heterosexual pornography,[55] gay male pornography presents a positive image of gay male sexuality to its readers.

When the issue is boiled down to gay s/m pornography, however, Kinsman is thankfully not so categorical, but neither entirely clear nor convincing. He stresses the variety of gay s/m, underscores the importance of taking an ethnographic approach at this early stage of inquiry into the field, and introduces the notion of "symbolic interactionism" to explain how gay people have developed their own "sexual script" out of the combined influences of their historical interactions with gay and heterosexual people alike. It is at this point of his analysis that he recalls the notion raised by Adams in *Glad Day Bookshop*, which is that some gay s/m may be aptly understood as "erotic theatre." Indeed, the focal point of Kinsman's testimony from here on may be seen as the contention that, despite the range of practices of gay s/m across gay communities, "what is actually being eroticized is not the actual infliction of violence on other people or the actual infliction of pain on other people in the sense in which people might conceive of that, but, instead ... the eroticism of forms of pressure, the use of certain props and paraphernalia in the context of sexual relationships to which people who are involved in s/m cultures and communities have given particular types of meanings."[56]

Whatever these "meanings" may be, the thrust of Kinsman's opinion is that they are not to be taken literally according to traditional notions of violence and pain. The real exertion of pressure by a dominatrix (or "top") on a submissive (or "bottom") is not a literal expression of nonconsensual violence or "sadism," but illustrates rather the terms of a skillful, trusting, and ritualist "negotiation" between two consenting and presumably equal partners or actors on stage.[57] Accordingly, insofar as he is treated as a contractual equal in the particular s/m ritual, the "bottom" is not perceived by the "top" or by any member of the gay audience to be in a position of "degradation" or "humiliation." On the contrary, as Mains has already explained, the humanity of both "bottom" and "top" is enriched, and their spirits are elevated, via the very process of going through the s/m ritual. This, essentially, is the gay community's argument in *Little Sister's* against the hitherto dominant (that is, heterosexual) belief that gay or any other form of s/m is "obscene" within the terms of Canada's *Criminal Code*.

The main problems with, or at least limitations to, Kinsman's expertise appear under cross-examination from government lawyers. There Kinsman concedes, "When I was talking about sadomasochism in the context of gay male culture I was not referring to the dynamics of domination or power that might work in individual relationships. I was talking about the specific practices of gay male s/m. That's actually engaged in by gay men as specific erotic sexual practice. I was not talking about all the problems that could exist in relationships between two gay men."[58] Realistically, any number of "problems" could beset gay relationships and, as will be discussed shortly, many of these are likely to involve "dynamics of domination or power" however subtle and however different these may appear from those operating in heterosexual relationships. Busby appears to make a similar point when she observes, "Lesbians and gay men are not exempt from expressing or modelling the coercive sexual practices deeply embedded in the gendered, homophobic, and racist culture that has shaped us all" (Busby 1994, 183). Thus, when confronted by the suggestion that "not all homosexual relationships are models of social and sexual equalities," Kinsman frankly responds, "That's certainly the case and I was not suggesting that they were."[59] Kinsman seems sincere at this point, but his admission under cross-examination that gay relationships are indeed troubled by social inequities of their own does undermine his earlier argument that gay male pornography production is qualitatively different from mainstream heterosexual pornography. The government tried to introduce a scholarly article that challenged this argument, but this was rejected by Justice Smith as being "argument," not expert opinion proper.[60]

In addition, Kinsman never clearly explains just how the broader "gender equality" among gay men in society informs the particular issue of gay S/M's "moral" worth. To recall, this question seems to be answered by reference to gay S/M's ritualistic and theatrical nature, which focuses specifically on the particular rules of the game and the element of mutual trust and partnership which is familiar to participants and observers. It is also informed by the fact that, historically, gay men have been made to feel ashamed of their sexuality, whereas gay S/M affirms or celebrates it. Yet these considerations are not necessarily related to the fact that men generally enjoy a position of political, social, and economic privilege in a so-called male-dominated society. This observation only serves to problematize Kinsman's otherwise reductionistic suggestion that gay S/M can be given a neat cultural context. Under cross-examination, Kinsman accepts that some of the heterosexual "icons and images" of masculinity created in a "more mainstream" society "might be used in the context of gay S/M."[61] This concession does not necessarily bear, once again, on the particular obscenity issue at stake, yet it does bear directly on the particular issue the lawyer for *Little Sister's* said Kinsman would address, namely, whether (and if so, how) depictions of consensual gay S/M differ from depictions of consensual heterosexual S/M as far as their cultural and social significance for the respective gay and heterosexual communities (and audiences) across Canada is concerned. At the end of the day, Kinsman does not seem able to address this question satisfactorily. He recognizes certain "common features" between the two genres of S/M but he again resorts ultimately to the notion of "social organization." Kinsman suggests that, because men and women are not "gender" equals in broader society, the requisite or desired element of mutual consent in S/M "might actually be more difficult to secure" in a male ("top") and female ("bottom") s/m scenario. Yet Kinsman cannot support even this contention. He states merely that "in some of what I have seen there are some significant problems around the seemingly lack of consent on the part of the women who are in those ["bottom"] positions. Also in the case of heterosexual pornography sometimes a woman is the top." Kinsman practically admitted his lack of expertise on this point. When asked whether he would agree that "most depictions of heterosexual s/m purport to depict consensual relations between the man and the woman," Kinsman responded, "Okay. In terms of my areas of expertise I was not sort of – I mean I have not done, you know, an amazing amount of research on hetero-sexual s/m."[62]

Kinsman's evidence served to enlighten the court about gay sexual imagery and text in terms of its historical regulation across "main-stream" society and its cultural significance for gay people generally, yet Kinsman was not in a position (as an expert or otherwise) to comment reliably about differences between gay and heterosexual s/m. LSBAE needed an authoritative voice to comment on precisely this point (along with one other),[63] so it appears that the expert knowledge professed by Kinsman in this regard was consciously moulded or even contrived to suit the narrow legal issue of s/m's harmfulness as mea-sured according to the *Butler* standard. Of course, expert construction of knowledge for purposes of litigation is hardly novel in other legal contexts. On this level of analysis, therefore, Kinsman's testimony at *Little Sister's* represents just another example of the argumentative nature of expert evidence in constitutional adjudication. And even if Justice Smith is prepared to reject argumentative evidence from experts when he sees it as such (as he did, for example, with Kendall's article), he accepted Kinsman's and other expert witnesses' evidence for LSBAE as more or less cogent or at least uncontentious.

A Literary View of s/m: New and Old

Should Kinsman's sociological evidence about the positive message of gay s/m not be sufficiently convincing, more expert evidence was prepared to support this claim. Bart Testa, a professor of cinema studies and semiotics at the University of Toronto, was called on behalf of LSBAE to speak as an expert about "messages and codes" in books, magazines, films, and videos, but also to apply this general knowledge to four impugned works, three of which involved gay s/m depictions and themes.[64] Nino Ricci, an award-winning novelist and creative writing teacher, was also called to express his opinion about the "artistic and literary value" of three impugned books, one involving gay s/m themes and another involving lesbian s/m themes.[65] Testa's evidence in particular provided the plaintiffs with a somewhat unique form of literary support regarding the broader (political) and deeper (psychological) significance of gay and lesbian s/m writings, namely, a scientifically-based literary support. Ricci echoed many of the same themes in a literary jargon likely more familiar to most observers of the *Little Sister's* trial, as well as the presiding judge himself. Justice Smith expressly recognized the heuristic contribution of Ricci to the legislative fact-finding process in *Little Sister's* but did not give explicit mention of Testa. One may infer from this that Smith did not consider Testa's evidence helpful, or perhaps even relevant. It is also conceivable that Smith either had difficulty translating the technical jargon of semiotics into language he could use, or that Smith was fully capable of applying Testa's evidence to the factual issues at hand and simply considered Testa's particular lexicography somehow unnecessary, perhaps in the sense of it being unnecessarily complex. The former possibility raises the important questions already explored in this book about judicial competence to receive expert legislative-fact evidence generally. At what point must judges defer to such expertise? Should judges educate themselves in unfamiliar technical matters and languages in order to make intelligent findings of fact? The second possibility broaches the issue of judicial accountability with respect to fact-finding in a democracy. That is to say, if Smith understood Testa's technically worded evidence generally and simply preferred to analyse the impugned books in the more familiar terms of Ricci, he has made a conscious choice to keep the legislative fact-finding process in *Little Sister's* accessible, and in a loose sense, popular. Such a decision would reflect an anti-elitist tendency in Smith's ultimate fact-finding endeavour.

Testa's Semiotic Approach to Gay s/m   What is perhaps most noteworthy about Testa's testimony from the outset is the way it appears to reflect (like Weir's testimony) a real advance in the state-of-the-art of literary knowledge since, for example, Morley Callaghan and Hugh MacLellan entered the courtroom in *Brodie*. Those literary figures were also presumed to have some special knowledge of the way "messages" were revealed and concealed in literary texts, but their treatment of this subject at that time lacked any formal pretense to scientificity. By contrast, semiotics purports to offer a sophisticated and indeed scientific account of communication generally.[66] It treats communication systematically, as a function of shared "codes" between "senders" (for example, authors) and "receivers" (for example, readers) of "messages."

Testa explains that "when we utter a message, we are uttering complex utterances using signs. Each of those signs is coded, that is to say that there has been a join between an idea and its vehicle like the example of 'cat'. Now, when we speak a complicated message, the signs that we use and therefore that message is coded at a higher level than simply the individual word like 'cat' that we use."[67] What among some literary persons, then, is simply a "metaphor," with a certain literary significance from the point of view of its author, becomes for Testa an integral part of a complex message, or at any rate not a "unary message,"[68] and a system of signs that can be explained away or "decodified" by a proper application of semiotic tools and methodology.

Testa's semiotic expertise was important for *Little Sister's* in a few respects. First, it offered to the Canadian judiciary a hitherto (judicially) unexplored manner of distinguishing s/m from "pornography" proper. Indeed, it is not insignificant that Testa uses Roland Barthes's example of "a hypothetical pornographic photograph" to explain how pornography proper contains only a single or "unary" message.[69] One of the works Testa interprets uses the image of "a Polaroid snapshot of genitals" as an example of a non-serious treatment of gay sexuality.[70] The "unary" message in some such explicit depictions of "sexual organs" or "sexual acts" is simply the concept of whatever image is portrayed in those depictions.[71] In Testa's words, there would be no "doubling" of the depicted "reality" here, no "making it vacillate, no duality, no indirection, no disturbance." Presumably, with this view, a semiotician is especially competent to identify the "reality" so depicted, or to understand when an image represents one or more concepts.

In principle, semiotics itself ultimately lacks the tools for distinguishing between simple and complex messages. A semiotic analysis of a text or image must itself *assume* the simplicity or complexity of a given message. Testa suggests as much when he says, "I would like to propose something like a semiotic baseline for pornography, which I believe – I have the opinion pertains to our common sense of emotion of an (*sic*) pornographic message." Referring to the aforementioned photograph of genitals, Testa maintains that for Barthes "the pornographic message is [the] literal depiction of genitals, a sign whose idea is the concept of the thing itself with no other – no other message really involved."[72] The problem here is that any observer of this same photograph might "really" or plausibly find another message "involved" in it, and semiotic theory alone may not be able to convince that observer that her "complex" rendering of the photograph is somehow erroneous. Nevertheless, Testa was expected to apply semiotic methodology to some pieces of gay literature, mainly of the s/m genre, with a view to demonstrating the complexity of their respective messages. Once it has been argued that pornography proper involves only a unary message, proof that some of the s/m works detained en route to LSBAE involve complex messages should lead directly to the conclusion that such works are not pornography so defined. This is the second important aspect of Testa's expert testimony in *Little Sister's*.

Testa readily conceded that John Preston's books, *I Once Had a Master* and *Entertainment for a Master*, involve "explicit sadomasochistic depiction[s]." Yet these depictions purportedly serve a broader, indeed "political" purpose. According to Testa, Preston's s/m writings themselves serve as a kind of "vehicle" or medium for challenging "the [effeminate] stereotype of gay men."[73] They do this by drawing upon certain "narrative codes," the "cultural codes" of Preston's gay "subculture," as well as "sub-codes" of s/m such as "handcuffs" and "licking leather," which in turn "represent a gay ideology," the latter being that "gays are masculine."[74] Following a recitation of an s/m scene in *I Once Had a Master*, Testa explains that "we can multiply examples from this book, that constantly the message is masculinity, that to be gay and to be realized as gay is to be masculine and s & m becomes the vehicle of the expression of that."[75]

In one obvious sense, Testa's testimony is simply meant to demonstrate the so-called "artistic" or "literary" merit of Preston's works. Canadian courts should view it as representing a new theoretical or intellectual angle on this aspect of the obscenity question – that is, the issue of whether the depiction of explicit sexual scenes in any given work constitute the "dominant characteristic" of that work. It clearly recalls MacLennan's and Callaghan's role in the *Brodie* case, and more recently, Edinborough's and Pungente's role in *Odeon Morton Theatres*. In all cases, the expert literary opinions were offered to show that, despite the obvious presence of sexually explicit (and in some cases, violent) depictions in *Lady Chatterley's Lover*, *Last Tango In Paris*, and *I Once Had a Master*, these depictions either contributed necessarily to the artistic value of the work in question or served to articulate some broader political message.

The problem with Testa's testimony is that, in light of existing literary theory or knowledge, it presumed as much as it informed and in that sense was extraneous. Certainly the introduction of a language of "codes," "subcodes," "ideolects," and "unary" and "multiple" messages presents a new way of talking about texts and imagery, but the general idea that some works have more complex messages or layers of meaning than others – reflected in the use of such literary devices as metaphor and metonomy, the author's "tone," or the work's overall "mood" – remains at work. Weir reiterates this same idea by warning the reader and the court against reading Preston's works out of "context" and judging or interpreting them according to notions and beliefs held by those uninitiated into the rites of leather s/m. In her parlance, a good "hermeneut" would make the effort at some point in her analysis to learn the literary conventions associated with s/m fiction and non-fiction, and the broader significance of these conventions for the s/m community.[76] This is entirely consonant with Testa's own view that, given sufficient resources, Canada Customs officials could plausibly understand "the mixed messages and mixed codes" in the works of Preston.[77] In any event, both Weir's and Testa's messages were ably conveyed by Ricci in more accessible language.

Ricci's Literary Approach to s/m   Ricci basically confirmed Testa's opinion about Preston's *I Once Had a Master*, albeit in a more familiar idiom, and extended the literary evidence desired by the plaintiff, LSBAE, to the domain of lesbian s/m. Ricci focused, for example, on the literary "structure," the "internal consistency," and the "use of language" in Preston's *I Once Had a Master* and found that it treated the theme and depiction of gay s/m seriously and with complexity.[78] More specifically, Ricci claimed that the fictional component of Preston's book argued for an acknowledgment of gay s/m within the gay community and across the wider world.[79] Drawing from the non-fictional epilogue, Ricci rearticulated Testa's earlier opinion that Preston himself saw the writing of sexually oriented materials (however "simple") by gay writers as a "social and political act."[80]

What is notable about Ricci's testimony is, first, its similarity in spirit but not in language to Testa's evidence. Ricci employs the language of "recurring motifs"[81] and "themes"[82] to demonstrate Preston's complex treatment of gay s/m. Ricci also recognizes that gay s/m bears its own "special codes"[83] but expressly rejects the suggestion that he was consciously using this notion in the way Testa treated it.[84] Ricci had in mind the literary conventions of the gay s/m genre whereas Testa had in mind the cultural conventions of gay s/m rituals. Ultimately, however, Ricci's testimony is simpler and clearer than Testa's and seems to render Testa's testimony almost superfluous or redundant. Ricci says, "Often texts which at first glance seem quite simple can reveal themselves to be quite complex when they're examined at the deeper level in terms of some of the tensions that are underlying the material, some of the dichotomies that are introduced through the juxtaposition of various situations, various images in types of characters."[85] Again, the idea that apparently "simple" texts may be found to have more "complex" meanings and messages upon further examination of cultural contexts and closer attention to linguistic conventions does not seem to require expert (scientific or otherwise) evidence, whether from the field of semiotics or according to deconstruction and hermeneutic theory. Perhaps because of its clarity, Ricci's testimony was more persuasive in this regard than Testa's evidence, which is consistent with the fact that Justice Smith favourably quoted Ricci in his reasons for judgment but made no express mention of Testa.

Clearly Testa's and Weir's technically loaded evidence is meant to shed light on the deeper psychological and broader cultural significance of certain gay s/m literature but this dimension is made clear by the words of some of the impugned texts themselves. Ricci, for example, recites from the epilogue of Preston's *I Once Had a Master*, which plainly conveys the author's intentions with respect to his own writings and those of other "gay writers."[86] These are basically the same intentions Testa, Weir, and Ricci attribute to Preston. Moreover, Preston had already supplied the court with a written account of his evidence, based on a 1993 public lecture he delivered (Fuller and Blackley 1995, 88). These considerations suggest strongly that the plaintiffs felt the need in *Little Sister's* to "legitimate" or somehow validate Preston's own voice with expertise. If so, LSBAE was merely keeping with a long tradition of reliance on literary expertise to defend sexually explicit materials against criminal sanctions and other state powers of detention and prohibition. The concern remains, however, that this expert information is ultimately a matter of argument, not fact, and needs therefore to be viewed with a critical eye.

A Cultural-Historical Approach to Sexual Imagery

Vance's Anthropological Analysis of Pornography Carol Vance's appearance at the *Little Sister's* trial is particularly germane on various levels. Years before the trial began, she had provided the government with a written account of her testimony, but unexpected evidentiary problems posed by Ross's testimony at trial caused the LSBAE lawyer to call Vance to take the witness stand in Vancouver "at the last moment."[87] Apparently the federal and provincial governments' cross-examination of Ross had undermined somewhat the "reasonable face of anti-censorship feminism," and Vance, an open anti-censorship proponent, was expected to repair some of the damage (Fuller and Blackley 1995, 49–50). The selection of Vance as an "expert" witness is important simply because it suggests that she could provide more reasonable testimony than Ross did in this respect. This suggestion seems to have been borne out in the courtroom, not only with respect to Ross but with respect to Scales as well, as will be discussed shortly.

Vance's testimony at the *Little Sister's* trial is also significant because she is an anthropologist, and Canadian courts have only recently begun to receive legislative-fact evidence in matters of human sexuality from the field of anthropology.[88] In the *Little Sister's* case, Vance's anthropological training was applied specifically to the issue of the regulation of sexual imagery in certain societies, especially "English-speaking" societies.[89] In this respect, she emphasized the relatively greater "intensity of concern" in such societies for the regulation and potential "danger" of sexual material.[90] This concern is associated with the religious histories and philosophies of these societies, as well as with changing demographics and the political and economic self-interest of the upper class. Vance also briefly discussed the concept of "sexual panic" and indicated moments in Canadian history where sexual panics occurred.[91]

Vance was also an interesting choice of expert at *Little Sister's* because she is an anti-censorship advocate who had participated in the American Meese Commission, which has been so highly influential in Canadian anti-obscenity law to date. Vance's testimony about the Meese Commission paralleled both her own and West's published observations concerning the skewed political composition of the commission and the undue emphasis placed by anti-pornography feminists at that time on heterosexual s/m involving male dominant and female submissive/subordinate participants.[92] Vance's testimony in this regard emphasized the real lack of consensus among witnesses at the Commission hearings concerning pornography generally. Her testimony should therefore have served as yet more evidence of the argumentative (as opposed to factual) nature of the social science evidence introduced into American and Canadian courts in obscenity proceedings.[93] As it turns out, Smith ruled that Vance's testimony relating to the Meese Commission was inadmissable because it was hearsay evidence purporting to give a truthful account of what Vance heard at the commission.[94] In effect, Smith was content with the conclusions of the Meese Commission as adopted by Justice Sopinka in *Butler*, but Smith did not want to hear from an actual participant about how those conclusions were obtained. Moreover, even though Smith recognized that Vance's testimony pertaining to the Meese Commission was "in the nature of social science evidence" and was "relevant to the rational-basis" issue,[95] he found that this evidence was merely "anecdotal" and as such failed to meet the tests of reliability and necessity associated with expert evidence.[96]

Vance also discussed how there was once a great degree of dissensus within the American feminist community relating to the ideas behind the previously mentioned Minneapolis and Indianopolis anti-pornography ordinances authored by Catharine MacKinnon and Andrea Dworkin, and related how this divisiveness has since diminished. Vance noted that while there is continued disagreement regarding the propriety of state-controlled censorship there is a tendency away from viewing pornographic literature as posing a "special danger" to society.[97] Apparently Smith accepted this evidence and any other testimony Vance provided which was unrelated to the Meese Commission at face value.

Of particular relevance here is Vance's emphasis on some feminists' concerns that "female dominant–male submissive SM pornography" was excluded from early S/M slide shows orchestrated by anti-pornography feminists.[98] It has already been suggested how female ("top") and male ("bottom") S/M imagery could upset the radical-feminist anti-pornography analysis, according to a literalist reading. More important here, however, is Vance's suggestion that heterosexual S/M imagery is deserving of the same kind of analysis traditionally applied by gays and lesbians to gay and lesbian S/M expression. Vance said, "Other feminists found the omission of female dominant–male submissive SM pornography a bit of dishonesty and others said, because of knowledge gained in other ways about SM, that this characterization of SM is a non-consensual, brutal force on people and also literal as opposed to being a theatrical play in which people were engaged, they felt that that characterization was not correct."[99] This observation at least raises the possibility that heterosexual S/M imagery shares some of the so-called "codes" and "messages" of homosexual S/M. As will be shown below, Ross advanced the claim in *Little Sister's* that lesbian S/M is *sui generis* or somehow "radically" specific. Vance's testimony does not directly address this claim, but her recognition that "viewers of sexual imagery have very different reactions to and interpretations of images, sexually explicit images, depending on a variety of social and personal factors,"[100] implies that categorizing pornographic imagery in terms of the sex, positions, and behaviours of the participants, as well as the sex and sexual orientation of the observers, may not always be an intelligent or fruitful exercise.

Although much of the evidence Vance provided was clearly insightful, helpful, and relevant to the legislative-fact issues at bar in *Little Sister's*, Smith's general receptivity to Vance is ultimately quite curious. As stated earlier, Vance is clearly an anti-censorship advocate. Her jointly authored publication in *Women Against Censorship* (Duggan, Hunter, and Vance 1985) reflects her anti-censorship stance, and in direct examination at *Little Sister's*, Vance said that she still held such a position.[101] Presumably, Arvay laid Vance's political cards on the table *before* cross-examination, in order to preclude the government from arguing that Vance's expert testimony masked a particular political and perhaps moral bias. Skilled lawyers reveal potential legal concerns associated with their witness's testimony in direct examination in order to demonstrate that the witness has "nothing to hide" and can be relied on to provide credible and comprehensive evidence. Nonetheless, it is very curious that Vance's overt political and moral leanings with respect to pornography did not appear to concern Smith. As has already been shown, several Canadian judges have readily discredited and discounted expert testimony where the expert obviously has a specific political affiliation or history of activism.

This book has argued that judges are wrongheaded in presuming that the opinions of politically active or associated experts are any more or less trustworthy than other kinds of purportedly neutral expert evidence, especially where legislative facts are at issue. Vance's evidence in *Little Sister's* is an excellent example of how a politically interested individual can provide plausible expert evidence, just as the discussion of Ann Scales later in this chapter reveals how an expert's obvious political self-interest can nearly preclude her from testifying helpfully and reliably. The concern here is not the difficulty of choosing between intellectually trustworthy, politically active experts, but of fully appreciating that all expert evidence pertaining to legislative-fact issues is argumentative, and in that sense somewhat "political," and that political neutrality in this context is a matter of each expert's real willingness to hang her political interests on the hook outside the courtroom door. Unfortunately for Canada's judiciary at large, no scientific means are available for detecting those interests that are smuggled inside.

Waugh Casts a Cinematic Spotlight on Gay and Lesbian Cultural History   Thomas Waugh was another relatively unique figure to testify at the *Little Sister's* trial by virtue of his academic speciality – namely, film studies. Chapter 6 will discuss how, in a recent indecency proceeding, a documentary filmmaker provided legislative-fact testimony about female sexuality which was rejected because of the witness's perceived political biases. As it turns out, Waugh's academic training in film studies was not entirely germane to the testimony he provided in *Little Sister's*. His major contribution to the LSBAE lay in his scholarly knowledge of the cultural importance to gays and lesbians throughout history of gay and lesbian erotic imagery generally. His expert opinion in this respect was meant to bolster the opinions of other plaintiffs' experts that gay and lesbian sexual expression, including gay and lesbian s/M, is an integral aspect of gay and lesbian culture, and more specifically, plays "a very important educative and social and political function" within that culture.[102] To this end Waugh discussed, for example, the growth of licit male body builder magazines from the turn of the century through the 1950s and 1960s, and the circulation of illicit photographs and films after the late nineteenth century and into the 1920s and 1940s.

Waugh's testimony was similar to the other gay and lesbian experts' opinions regarding the "cultural and social" differences between homosexual and heterosexual sexual expression. To recall, Kinsman distinguished the two kinds of materials primarily in terms of the "social organization" of the sexes involved in the representations. Gay erotica and pornography portray the participants as "gender equals," whereas heterosexual pornography necessarily portrays a hierarchical sexual-social relationship, simply because women are socially subordinate to men in a male-dominated, sexist society. Similarly for Waugh, there appears to be no gender hierarchy in the content or production of gay male erotica, in the sense that the sexual activities it portrays are less "predetermined by gender divisions"[103] or in the sense that there is no "silencing of the woman as object."[104] A close analysis of this issue along various lines would show it to be contentious. For example, psychoanalytic theorists since Freud have typically distinguished between "gender" and "sex" with a view to understanding how individuals of different sexes acquire particular gender orientations and identifications. Although such a fundamental distinction is highly relevant to much of the *Little Sister's* testimony being discussed here, it was barely addressed by the *Little Sister's* witnesses, none of whom claimed to have any expertise in the field of psychoanalysis. Waugh simply defers to the "argument that feminists *always* make about heterosexual material about women being silenced in heterosexual pornography," and he observes that this element is absent because of the "production system" involved in gay erotica.[105]

Waugh also claimed that gay readers of gay pornography consume such materials differently than heterosexual readers consume heterosexual materials. For Waugh, gay pornography and erotica are consumed more communally than heterosexual materials are by heterosexual readers and watchers.[106] Again, this claim is meant to support the broader claim of the plaintiffs that gay and lesbian pornography are crucial, empowering elements of gay and lesbian culture and society. This may well be the case, yet the government makes it clear that Waugh is well outside his area of expertise (and presumably experience) when he expresses his opinion about the way heterosexual readers or observers of heterosexual pornography consume such materials.[107] Even if heterosexual videos in fact "tend to invite individual and isolated consumption," as Waugh believes,[108] it is important to note here that Waugh's expert opinion on this legislative-fact issue is not necessarily based on any kind of fact and is more likely a matter of speculation.

Waugh is yet another expert witness for LSBAE to claim that gay and lesbian S/M is primarily "a kind of [consensual] theatre," but, significantly, Waugh admits that S/M "extends across boundaries of sexual orientation into heterosexual society."[109] This latter concession cannot be overemphasized here. Waugh explains his view mainly in terms of the role of fantasy and documentation in sexual imagery generally. For him, "S/M practices play out or reconstruct fantasies that individuals might have," such as "fantasies of submission or domination," but "*all* eroticism draws on both fantasy and documentation."[110] This proposition echoes Vance's careful discussion of the role of fantasy in understanding sexual imagery. Vance suggests that some images "are meant to be fantasies," but she also implies that fantasy plays at least some "role in sex" generally.[111] Waugh explains that "there's a kind of oscillation" between fantasy and documentation, or between "realism and the imagination,"[112] and this principle applies as much to heterosexual materials as it does to gay S/M. He claims that S/M "eroticizes exchanges of power, and submission and dominance in intimate relations" adroitly adding that "a lot of people have fantasies about unequal relations, and I think a lot of eroticism addresses these – those – fantasies, just as Hollywood movies and just as Cinderella and saints' lives do."[113]

Waugh, supported by Vance, cuts against the grain of his expert colleagues in *Little Sister's* by admitting that S/M in gay materials is depicted as both fantasy and "reality," and that S/M motifs are not peculiar to gay S/M literature and film but derive from the broader stock of popular culture generally. Waugh's insistence that S/M fantasy or imagery is an integral part of most intimate relationships is bolstered further by the writings of distinguished psychoanalyst and feminist theorist, Jessica Benjamin (Benjamin 1988; 1980). She applies Hegel's classic "master-slave" analysis to the psychological-social relationship an infant child has with his or her parents (or parent) in order to understand why infants sometimes wish to destroy their parents (or parent) and at other times desire to submit wholly to their parents' overwhelming sense of authority and power (1988, 31–6). This sadomasochist tendency carries forward into intimate adult relationships to the extent that the respective partners continually strive both to be "recognized" as independent and self-asserting persons in their own right and to "lose" themselves, figuratively speaking, in the person of their partner or lover. While Benjamin's thesis need not be elaborated here, it is significant that Benjamin relies heavily on Pauline Réage's *The Story of O* as an insightful "allegory for the struggle of recognition" that characterizes sexual relationships generally (1988, 55–62). This novel explores the sadomasochistic dimension of human desire mainly through specific heterosexual relationships; in so doing, it lends credence to the idea suggested by Waugh in *Little Sister's* that regardless of sexual orientation S/M imagery is an integral part of the erotic life of many human beings on at least some level, conscious or subconscious, in fantasy or in reality. If this view is accepted, then the categorical nature of much of the other plaintiffs' expert opinions about gay and lesbian S/M begins to appear contrived.

Furthermore, under cross-examination Waugh inadvertently debunked the myth about gay and lesbian "gender equality" that many of his expert colleagues promulgated in the *Little Sister's* trial. Kinsman's and Weir's analyses of gay S/M, for example, relied heavily on the notion of "gender equality" between males, and Ross's analysis of lesbian pornography emphasized the same kind of "gender equality" between females.[114] Yet Waugh soberly sees such a notion as an unrealistic "ideal." He explains that, in North American culture, "no relationship is this pure, equitable, balanced, mutual relationship that was dreamed of by feminists in the 1970s." More specifically, for him, "that [notion of social-sexual equality] was a kind of naive ideal that was espoused by a certain movement, a certain phase of the lesbian feminist movement in the 1970s."[115] Perhaps Waugh is correct to say that some degree of sexual-social "hierarchy" characterizes "gay male relationships" and by implication, lesbian relationships, as much as heterosexual relationships.[116] In any event, as some of the following discussion will reveal, the "naive ideal" that Waugh attributes to the 1970s "lesbian feminist movement" is still very much alive today – or at least it was in the *Little Sister's* courtroom.

Lesbian S/M

The category of sexually explicit lesbian imagery posed perhaps the most interesting intellectual challenge to the plaintiffs in *Little Sister's*. Viewed superficially, it may have appeared to be the least harmful genre, at least from the radical-feminist perspective of pornography which influenced *Butler*. This emphasized the structurally inherent male "dominant," female "subordinate" character of heterosexual sexual imagery.[117] Accordingly, if men are not in the picture, literally, then such an analysis does not necessarily apply. As MacKinnon has noted, "Some have argued that lesbian sexuality – meaning here simply women having sex with women, not with men – solves the problem of gender [in pornography] by eliminating men from women's voluntary sexual encounters" (MacKinnon 1989, 141; footnote omitted). For MacKinnon, however, the broader social stereotype of women as inferior to men is not avoided by merely substituting women for men in pornographic scenes where men are typically "on top." She explains that "women's sexuality remains constructed under conditions of male supremacy; women remain socially defined as women in relation to men; the definition of women as men's inferiors remains sexual even if not heterosexual, whether men are present at the time or not ... It may also be that sexuality is so gender marked that it carries dominance and submission with it, whatever the gender of its participants" (141–2). For MacKinnon, lesbian sexual representations superficially appear to subvert the male dominant–female subordinate sexual paradigm in a heterosexist society; however, the cultural meanings attached to the image of women in this same society ensure that women will continue to be seen (on some deeper, psychological level) as sexual and social inferiors to men. In other words, lesbian sexual representations are as harmful as heterosexual sexual representations, within the terms of *Butler*. One of the challenges for LSBAE was to undermine this argument. If LSBAE could be successful here, it might also be able to convince the court that lesbian s/m was equally unharmful.

Ross's Sociology of Lesbian Sexual Imagery Revisited   A number of witnesses, expert and lay, testified on behalf of the plaintiff bookstore about lesbian sexual imagery, including lesbian s/m. Ross testified as an expert in various fields of inquiry and on various topics. To recall briefly, she was presented as an expert in both women's studies and lesbian representations, and as an expert "who can express an opinion on the nature and importance of lesbian sexuality imagery and text, and the differences and similarities between such material and heterosexual imagery and text."[118] Although the field of inquiry in which she obtained her doctorate degree was a Canadian novelty, her presence as an expert in anti-obscenity litigation was not.[119] As already observed, Ross provided opinion evidence in the *Scythes* case and apparently "was very much in demand at obscenity trials" (Fuller and Blackley 1995, 95). According to Fuller and Blackley, Ross's task in *Little Sister's* was clear: "it was essential that Ross establish a sociological defence of s/m practices, in order to upset the heterosexist premises about consent and degradation that the Crown, and *Butler*, relied upon" (97).

As Fuller and Blackley see it, Ross's credentials as a "sociologist" and, more significantly, a "social scientist" were pivotal in the *Little Sister's* case, presumably because they could be used to "prove" the

"Little Sister's accusation of homophobia within Canada Customs" or at least rebut "the Crown's claim that pornography had harmful effects" (ibid., 95). The laboratory-based social science battle staged between the plaintiffs' experts and the Crown in *Little Sister's* will be explored later in this chapter. Ross's testimony is important here mainly for the opinions it contains regarding lesbian sexual imagery and text, especially lesbian s/M sexual imagery, and regarding differences between lesbian sexual imagery and heterosexual sexual imagery.

For Ross, lesbian sexual expression in the form of imagery or text is anything but degrading and dehumanizing. On the contrary, it validates lesbian sexuality as "healthy, as meaningful and as empowering" and contributes to "the positive formation of lesbians' consciousness, community and culture." Lesbian s/M is similarly enriching to both lesbian and heterosexual communities. According to Ross, it "expands, deepens and enriches our knowledge of female sexuality and female sexuality fantasy in general," and "the larger heterosexual society benefits if lesbian sexual subcultures are healthy and proud and robust."[120]

There can be no doubting the wisdom of Ross's argument that increased knowledge and tolerance of lesbian sexuality enhance the greater good of society generally, but it is worth noting how the notion of community, moral, and political empowerment through unrestricted sexual expression by lesbians (and gay men) became the standard line among the plaintiffs' lesbian experts and non-expert witnesses. Are there really so few gay and lesbian people who would quarrel with this view that their opinions were not worth consulting in court? Pat Califia testified that she wrote lesbian s/M fiction and non-fiction because doing so fosters recognition and a sense of self-respect among sister sadomasochists, and at any rate helps her from going "crazy."[121] Jane Vance Rule, an author and anti-censorship advocate, stated that *Bushfire: Stories of Lesbian Desire*, a collection of erotic short stories by lesbian writers, helps to redress feelings of shame and alienation among lesbians living in a "homophobic" culture.[122] And Ann Scales reiterated this view in her own parlance. She referred to lesbians as a "disenfranchised sexual minority" and found that *Bushfire* contributed to "the communication matrix amongst lesbians and increases lesbian visibility and acceptance."[123] Generally these lesbian witnesses had the same opinion about lesbian sexual expression, whether "soft," "hardcore," or s/M, as the gay witnesses had about similar forms of gay sexual expression: it all fosters pride and recognition (both on an individual and community level); it is dignifying, not degrading; it is fantastical and theatrical (where harmfulness might be an issue), not "real;" and it is personally, sexually, and intellectually liberating, not only for gays and lesbians, but for the heterosexual community as well.

Like much of the other gay and lesbian expert testimony which takes the above perspective, however, Ross's testimony becomes problematic precisely where it begins to differentiate homosexual sexual expression from heterosexual sexual expression at the level of imagery and text (as opposed, for example, to the manner of production). Indeed, for Ross, lesbian imagery and text are unique, and "radically" so, which she explains in the following way: "The gender of the female actors/ models in lesbian-made sexual imagery is fundamentally relevant and defies the mental practice of substitution or translation. A reading that denies gender relevancy irreparably ruptures the integrity and intention of lesbian texts made explicitly for lesbian viewers/readers, and the particular context/s in which the work is received. In so doing, it discounts the radical specificity of a lesbian sub-genre that exists outside of, heterosexual male imagining of lesbian sex" (Ross 1997, 176–7). So far this claim makes sound logical sense only if one accepts that the variety of contexts in which lesbian sexual imagery is received is limited and excludes that of "heterosexual male imagining," whatever that may be.[124] Presumably there is an expert psychologist somewhere in a university or clinic who could nicely detail all the elements of such a condition. When she is found, it will be interesting to see if this categorical "heterosexual male imagining" is also radically "specific" (as if the adjective does not become redundant at some point). Until she is found, however, it is fair to characterize this line of Ross's expert thinking as somewhat simplistic.

One concern here is that Ross, a qualified sociologist, is offering an expert opinion on a primarily psychological matter, one which is difficult at best for a trained psychologist to make. Yet on a purely intellectual level, Ross's reference to "heterosexual male imaginings" raises an even deeper issue. It suggests basically that every person's imagination is limited, perhaps as a function of biological make-up or as a function of sexual orientation. But why stop here? Why not make an analogous case in terms of class or race? To perceive the real intellectual danger with this kind of thinking, it is worth reading Lasch's discussion of the emergent "politically correct" humanism in North American academia contained in his essay "Academic Pseudo-Radicalism: The Charade of 'Subversion'" (Lasch 1995, ch. 10). Lasch makes the point there that withdrawing texts written by white males from the reading curricula, for example, of "women, blacks and Hispanics," on the basis that such texts are somehow "inaccessible" to these groups of students, ultimately shows "little respect for these groups' intelligence or their powers of imaginative identification" (184). Indeed, when Waugh was asked in *Little Sister's* whether the viewer (male or female) of heterosexual s/m involving a dominant male "identifies" with that male, Waugh said the matter "can be quite complex." He said more specifically that "some of the assumptions about the heterosexual male spectator may be a little bit reductive," such that we do not necessarily know "whether a heterosexual male spectator really only identifies in a scene with a male active figure."[125] Other LSBAE witnesses clearly suggested that some degree of acculturation with respect to a text's codes, symbols, tropes, and meanings may well enhance what Lasch calls the reader's powers of "imaginative identification," but this is a far cry from suggesting that such powers are limited by one's anatomy and sexual desires.

In any event, Ross's own "postmodern insistence that pornography has many meanings" and her belief in the "*fluidity* of sexual desire" (Ross 1997, 174) are not entirely consonant with the notion of a radically specific genre of lesbian sexual imagery. Waugh implied (and Califia suggested, as will be explained shortly) that the particular codes, meanings, and messages, of lesbian and gay pornography (S/M or otherwise) are drawn to some extent from imagery familiar to many readers and writers, lesbian, gay, and heterosexual alike. So different aspects of the "imaginings" of lesbian authors and producers of lesbian S/M explicit materials, as well as of lesbian consumers of such products, may well intersect at some point with "imaginings" of gay and heterosexual males. For her part, Jessica Benjamin provides a developmental psychological account of the way men and women could "identify" erotically with members of the opposite sex, in the sense of imagining themselves as either the subject of love or recipient of affection of another person, regardless of that person's sex (Benjamin 1988, 111–14). This point need not be belaboured any further. It suffices to say here that this aspect of Ross's testimony is very problematic and, as with most of the legislative-fact evidence considered by Canadian courts in obscenity cases, needs to be assessed critically.

Regarding lesbian S/M, in particular, Ross emphasized in *Little Sister's* that often the so-called "bottom" (female participant) "actually dictates the scene," thereby "disrupt[ing] popular conception that she is passive, a victim, submissive and exploited."[126] At least MacKinnon's and Scales's conception is disrupted so far.[127] Yet Ross goes further. In her opinion, "The objective at the top by contra is to provide her bottom with sexual pleasure. Importantly it's the top's own sexual needs and desires that are then dependent on the pleasure experienced by the bottom and may even be sacrificed in the process of providing pleasure to the bottom."[128]

So the "top" now becomes effectively servile to the demands of the "bottom" and, despite, or indeed in light of the appearance of consent, the "top" begins to look a lot like MacKinnon's "bottom" in mainstream heterosexual pornography.[129] The lesbian dominatrix here, despite her leather trappings and other paraphernalia, becomes a willing, imaginary, theatrical vessel for the masochist's pleasure, just as MacKinnon's female "bottom" in heterosexual pornography becomes the vacuous, willing, and certainly consenting supplicant of the male dominant's aggressive and perhaps sadistic desire – except for this problem of the "codes" and "subcodes." Or is it a real problem?

Ross was asked to distinguish between some lesbian s/M spreads in an issue of *Hustler* magazine, presumably aimed at a heterosexual male readership, and some of those found in a volume of *Bad Attitude*, published by lesbian and gay people, and presumably intended for lesbian readers. According to Ross, the two kinds of spreads use different "photographic and compositional conventions."[130] The *Hustler* pictures project what Ross construes as "the masculine fetishization of hyper-caricatured femininity."[131] The women in these lesbian pictures "tend to have large, pouty mouths, large breasts, lots of facial makeup, ... long lacquered fingernails with often red nail polish, a big lacquered style hair, stiletto heels" and even "colour enhanced ... pussies," but more important, they are typically "constructed as to be primed or ready for *heterosexual* intercourse initiated and controlled by the male reader."[132] That is to say, for Ross, the male reader is but a "voyeur" who is "invited into the scene" by various lighting techniques and production values, and the women's bodies are positioned to maximize his arousal and suggest their compliance with his sexual needs.[133] By contrast, it would appear that a "water shot" in *Bad Attitude*, in which one woman is "lying on her back" in a state of "some ecstasy" while her sexual partner performs cunnilingus on her, is not aimed at satisfying a male voyeur's prurient interest and does not even likely consider his imaginative condition.[134] At this stage of the analysis, it is unclear, however, why the male reader is not psychologically invited into the *Bad Attitude* scene, nor is it clear why the female models in the *Hustler* lesbian spread are primed for "heterosexual" intercourse, except for the banal likelihood that their scene will be witnessed mainly by men. One wonders, though, whether the anticipated intercourse in the *Hustler* spread will become truly "lesbian" if and when the scene is viewed by a woman, perhaps accidently, when it is left open and exposed on her and her male sexual partner's coffee table. Ross appears to reject even this possibility, suggesting elsewhere that lesbians and non-lesbian women could find "straight lezzie spreads" educational, but not necessarily arousing (Ross 1997, 167). Ross argues that, if such spreads met lesbian readers' desires, there would be no lesbian consumers of, and hence no market in, lesbian-produced images. But is it really that simple? Does Ross actually want to say that all lesbians desire only lesbian-made images? Perhaps so, but it is plausible that the erotic appeal of explicit lesbian sexual imagery, whether in *Hustler's* "lezzie spreads" or those of *Bad Attitude*, will sometimes lie more in living room "lighting" and an observer's mood than the latter's anatomy and sexual orientation.

Ross does not shed much more light on the matter before the court when asked about another spread from the *Hustler* issue mentioned above, this time a heterosexual series of images called "Fan-Fucking-Tastic." Most of the images in this spread portray a woman literally on top, and for Ross, the woman is even in a "superior position," "taking quite a lot of control over the sexual scene," and "asserting her sexual needs and desires." Ross proposes that this series of images is atypical of heterosexual pornography, and she conjectures that the spread "exhibits the beginning of an emergence, a new conceptualization by heterosexual pornographers of heterosexual woman and heterosexual female pleasure."[135] According to this view, heterosexual women's sexual desire (or desires) is "reconceptualized" by men as, or as including, a kind of sexual-social superiority, dominance, and control, mainly by virtue of the fact that the women are depicted "on top" of their male partner in a heterosexual pornographic publication.

As already mentioned, some radical-feminists have had conceptual difficulties with dominant female–submissive male images for years, because it appears to upset their simplistic (i.e., literalist)[136] view that male dominated, heterosexist society prefers to view women in the "bottom down," sexually submissive and yielding position. Yet Ross's own analysis also appears to treat heterosexual and some homosexual (especially lesbian) sexual expression this way. The picture from *Bad Attitude* seems palatable to Ross because it does not portray "explicit violence" or "coercion" against a woman (by a man), or at any rate, does not portray a woman as being "subordinated and victimized by [a] male sexual partner."[137] This also appears to be the case with the female dominant–male submissive depictions in *Hustler*. In other words, a closer examination of Ross's analysis of lesbian s/m imagery and heterosexual sexual imagery (involving a female "top" and male "bottom") suggests that, for her, *the* distinguishing feature between these genres is not necessarily "production values," readership, or so-called "publishing environment,"[138] but the kind of sexual behaviour being portrayed. So, for example, portraits of women models (with or without "pouty lips," "lacquered styled hair," "red nail polish," and "stiletto heels") performing and receiving cunnilingus may positively affirm and esteem female and lesbian sexuality, while women models who are presented in the missionary or any other obviously "lower" position, "happily" being penetrated by a man's penis, do not necessarily appeal to women's sense of sexual pleasure and self-identity but, more likely, to men's prurient interest. Such visual permutations and combinations invite one to ask how Ross would analyse the scene in *Last Tango in Paris* where Jeanne inserts her fingers in Paul's anus. Does Jeanne simply comply with Paul's request out of fear of some kind of physical reprisal or does Bertolucci want to suggest that Jeanne also can take some undiscovered, and perhaps more complicated, pleasure in the act? And what about the various acts of sexual subservience and degradation O apparently undertakes willingly in Réage's *The Story of O*? For Benjamin, "*Story of O* confronts us boldly with the idea that people often submit not merely out of fear, but in complicity with their own deepest desires. Told from the point of view of the woman who submits, and representing, as it does, the fantasy life of a gifted woman writer, the story compels the reader to accept the authenticity of the desire for submission. But the narrative also makes clear that the desire for submission represents a peculiar transposition of the desire for recognition" (Benjamin 1988, 55–6; citation omitted). Whether or not one agrees with Benjamin's broader analysis of *The Story of O*, the complexity or ambiguity of the graphic sexual depictions there (and for that matter in *Last Tango in Paris*) serve well to reveal the heuristic limits of Ross's broader analysis.[139]

Of course, by attempting to show where Ross's testimony here is of limited utility, this chapter does not want to understate Ross's real assistance to the court in exposing the positive importance of lesbian pornography generally to lesbian communities across Canada. This point was made earlier, and it is significant therefore that Justice Smith quoted a portion of Ross's evidence proclaiming the cultural, moral, and political significance of lesbian-made sexual materials (including s/m) to lesbian communities and sub-communities in support of his finding that "a society committed to the values underlying freedom of expression, as our society is, cannot defend the automatic prohibition of descriptions and depictions of homosexual sadomasochism."[140] Ross, along with some of her fellow and sister expert witnesses for LSBAE, clearly assisted the legislative-fact finding process in this respect[141] and effected a breakthrough in at least one Canadian judge's understanding of pornography and its harmfulness to women.

Indeed, before moving on to analyse some other LSBAE expert testimony relating to gay and lesbian pornography, it is essential to bear in mind that such witnesses as Ross, Testa, and Kinsman cumulatively presented a formidable intellectual challenge to the dominant epistemological mode of understanding pornography in Canadian constitutional law. This is important because, just as Ross's, Waugh's, and

Kinsman's expert sociological and cinematic or literary evidence is contestable along certain lines, so has been *all* the empirical, laboratory-based, and social survey–based evidence implemented in American and Canadian constitutional challenges to obscenity laws to date. And, ultimately, there is no good reason why the empirical research should be most persuasive.

A Legal "Expert" on Lesbian Sexuality Invites One More Waltz with Last Tango   The inability of the plaintiffs' experts in *Little Sister's* to differentiate clearly between homosexual and heterosexual sexual expression (in both its textual and pictoral forms), and homosexual and heterosexual s/M, was highlighted further by the testimony of Ann Scales. Before addressing her testimony directly, it is worth observing how peculiar or striking the presence of Scales at the *Little Sister's* trial seems. First, she openly admitted her professional alignment with the so-called "radical anti-pornography feminism camp" of MacKinnon and Dworkin – the enemy camp, that is, of most of *Little Sister's* other witnesses. Second, she freely described herself as "primarily a lawyer" and "political activist," which would normally make any judge or trier-of-fact think twice about her intellectual neutrality or "objectivity" as an expert witness. Third, although proffered as an expert on certain issues (to be discussed below), she did not seem to possess any kind of expert qualifications with respect to those issues. This possibility inspired the government lawyers to object formally to her being presented as an expert at all. Fourth, the actual substance of her otherwise expert testimony is so problematic that her presence as an expert may be treated as an exemplar of all the problems this book has associated so far with the use of experts in constitutional litigation. So why was she invited to appear?

In the words of Fuller and Blackley, "Arvay aimed to present Scales as an expert witness on three matters: (1) the nature of lesbian porn in the U.S.; (2) the evidence of whether lesbian porn creates a substantial risk of harm; and (3) the political worth of porn, particularly certain works by Pat Califia" (Fuller and Blackley 1995, 62). Before addressing each of these matters in turn, it is important to discuss the real concerns of LSBAE and the prosecuting government lawyers that, besides being a qualified lawyer and law professor, Scales was a political activist who was publicly known for her general anti-pornography stance.

LSBAE was well aware of "how well [Scales] could articulate a persuasive case *against* the bookstore, if she so desired" (ibid., 63; emphasis in original), and the government's lawyers were concerned that Scales's experience as an activist undermined her ability to provide the court with detached, expert evidence.[142] Indeed, Scales's generous admission of her political activism was perhaps the only spark in the *Little Sister's* case to reignite the traditional, technical, evidentiary issue concerning political or partisan bias, or more specifically, the substitution of argument for expert "opinion." Following a recital of Scales's expert qualifications, the province's Crown prosecutor, Nina Sharma, made the following submission to the court: "it seems to me [Scales's] evidence is that her opinions, her inferences are drawn not only from her academic legal experience, but from her role as advocate. In that sense it does potentially impact on whether this is a thinly-disguised argument or truly an expert opinion."[143]

Obviously for Sharma here, and for the legal profession at large, the issue is "either-or." Presumably, expert opinions are not supposed to take the form of "argument," whether thinly-disguised, deeply-concealed, or patently obvious. Yet most of the legislative-fact evidence reviewed in this book so far has been part and parcel of "argument," usually "thinly-disguised" as the object of social scientific hypothesis testing, just as Wittgenstein has maintained that "[a]ll testing, all confirmation and disconfirmation of an hypothesis" belong to a "system" in which "arguments have their life" (Wittgenstein 1979, 16e, prop'n 105). As already mentioned in chapter 1, many of the legislative facts introduced in the landmark American abortion decision *Roe* v. *Wade* were presented in the form of simple assertions without any supporting data[144] – as if "supporting" data would be sufficient to transform assertion into fact anyway. Similarly, the myriad social science research conclusions about the harmful effects of exposure to pornography have been shown to be simply empirically-based pieces or points of argument that reading pornography is sexually liberating, morally corrupting, or socially harmful. Even expert opinions about the literary merit of *Ulysses, Lady Chatterley's Lover,* and *I Once Had a Master* are inherently argumentative, not factual. So what is Scales's particular argument about lesbian erotica?

Scales argued for the "political" importance of certain books depicting lesbian sexuality, particularly Karen Barber's *Bushfire*, and Pat Califia's *The Lesbian S & M Safety Manual* and *Doc and Fluff.*[145] Like Testa in relation to Preston's works, Scales claimed, for example, that the portrayal of sex (and violent sex) in Califia's *Doc and Fluff* bears a specific political importance, in this case the diminution of violence against women.[146] *Bushfire* fosters social and personal recognition among lesbians. And *The Lesbian S & M Safety Manual* "clearly advances the political purpose again of increased visibility of sexual minorities" while simultaneously promoting women's sexual health.[147]

Once Scales had discussed the political merits of the above books, she chose to offer her opinion about the lesbian pornography or erotica industry. According to Scales, the very small number of sexually explicit lesbian publications available, the relatively small market in these materials, as well as the small size of the companies that produce such magazines and films, suggest that there is no "industry" proper in sexually explicit materials.[148] Elsewhere Scales described the world of lesbian erotica production in more detail, arguing that it can be distinguished from the "mainstream" pornography industry only under certain conditions (Scales 1994, 374–5). Presumably women (and perhaps preferably lesbians) must be the producers; the models must be "consenting;" the industry must perceive itself as "as a small group of dissident radicals;" the models should not be "victims of prior sexual abuse;" and lesbian producers should exist *"in opposition"* to mainstream producers, in the sense that they should be wary of portraying "women proclaiming delight in being used as objects of sexual consumption." Although some of this evidence clearly assists the court in better understanding the nature of lesbian pornography production, like much of the expert evidence presented by the LSBAE witnesses, key aspects of it are too categorical and require critical scrutiny.

The issue of when models are "consenting," for example, could be very difficult to resolve in many cases, whether these involve the production of lesbian or "mainstream" pornography. And the idea that women models in lesbian-produced pornography should not appear to be taking "delight in being used as objects of sexual consumption" seems difficult to reconcile with some of the analyses of lesbian S/M depictions offered by other LSBAE witnesses. It is arguable, for example, that the lesbian "water shot" from *Bad Attitude* that Ross reviewed favourably expresses "delight" insofar as it portrays a woman in a state of apparent "ecstacy" at the mouth of her female lover. Scales might well reply that the ecstatic female in the *Bad Attitude* shot is not an "object" but a "subject" of sexual consumption, as is clear from "the context" which includes any variety of "codes" and possibly a consideration of Ross's "production values." In any case, the legislative-fact finder here, as in all the prior obscenity cases reviewed so far, needs to be attuned to the elements of epistemological overstatement and sometimes oversimplification, as well as political self-interest, that tend to accompany expert opinions of legislative fact, social framework and social fact.

When it comes to the matter of distinguishing sexually explicit lesbian text and imagery from sexually explicit heterosexual materials, Scales reveals most clearly not only the serious weaknesses of her own purported expertise, but the overly categorical or reductionistic aspect of much of the plaintiffs' expert testimony in *Little Sister's*. As should be clear by now, one of the clarion cries of the plaintiffs' experts has been the need to read sexually explicit lesbian and gay materials (including s/m) in context – whether cultural, social, literary, political, economic, etc. Whereas much effort is spent thereby contextualizing these same materials, *very little is expended with respect to heterosexual materials*. These are consistently and categorically "mainstream." Scales's testimony accentuates this categorical divide insofar as it is informed by "radical" anti-pornography analyses. But the imposition of this perspective on the legislative fact-finding process hinders as much as helps Justice Smith.

During her testimony, Scales was asked to comment on certain passages from *Bushfire* mentioned above, as well as Kate Allen's *Tell Me What You Like*. One story in *Bushfire* describes a sexual encounter between two female electricians wherein at one stage of the encounter one of the women puts her finger in the other woman's anus. Scales points out that the narrator used the word "shocked" to describe how she (as the woman penetrated) felt regarding this apparently novel experience.[149] In *Tell Me What You Like* the author describes an s/m scene between the protagonist female police officer and what Scales refers to as a professional "lesbian sex worker/dominatrix."[150] After reciting some of this scene directly from the book, Scales draws the court's attention to the following words:

'Oh, that's not a good idea,' crooned Anastasia [the dominatrix]. She spread the lube over the tight outside of Allison's asshole. Her fantasy made it into chilled butter ...

'I mean, you can tighten that sweet little asshole all you want, but I am going to fuck it anyway and it will just make it go harder on you.' She inserted just the tip of one finger inside as she spoke. It was not the first time Allison had been buttfucked and almost against her will she opened up in pleasant anticipation.[151]

These scenes have been isolated here not because they somehow represent the average substance of lesbian erotica (s/m or otherwise), but because of their similarity to two particular scenes in *Last Tango in Paris*. One scene involves the spreading of "lube" (particularly "butter," but not obviously "chilled") by the male protagonist, Paul, presumably around Jeanne's "asshole" for lubrication purposes. The other scene is where Paul asks Jeanne to fetch some finger-nail clippers so that she can digitally penetrate his anus without tearing his skin.

As regards the "butter" scene, it should be noticed first that, despite the clear suggestion that Jeanne is being "buttfucked" by Paul, it is a heterosexual encounter. According to a radical anti-pornography analysis, this last element should easily suffice to render the scene degrading and perhaps dehumanizing in its portrayal of Jeanne's humanity and sexuality. According to Justice Sopinka's decision in *Butler*, this suggestion could be compounded, of course, if the scene portrayed Jeanne as somehow consenting, or even enjoying the encounter. For what it is worth, the scene appears ambiguous on this score, just as Allison's reaction to having her anus penetrated by Anastasia's finger(s) evokes a certain element of emotional uncertainty. To recall the narrator's words, *"almost against her will* [Allison] opened up in pleasant anticipation." There seems to be no room for ambiguous expressions of sexual desire, female or male, in Scales's analysis, yet it is precisely this sense of ambiguity which appears to have informed Pungente's testimony in *Odeon Morton Theatres* that the anal intercourse scene did not involve violence. In other words, looking at the context in which the anal intercourse scene in *Last Tango in Paris* occurs, including the so-called "production values," Pungente did not necessarily see a woman being violated or "raped" by a man, just as Allen does not necessarily portray Allison being victimized by Anastasia. Yet Scales is categorical on this point.

Scales disagrees, for example, with Judge Paris's suggestion in *Scythes* that the sexual composition of models in bondage scenes is "irrelevant" to the issue of obscenity because, in his words, "the potential for harm remains" (Scales 1994, 368). Again, "social context" does matter here (369), assuming that the expression bears any meaning whatsoever. For Scales, a "positive-outcome" rape scene involving a male aggressor and female recipient must conform to some kind of male dominant, heterosexist notion of female sexuality; that is why such scenes "in mainstream pornography" hold so little "prosecutorial interest for any of the powers-that-be" (ibid.). The "positive-outcome" rape scene in *Tell Me What You Like*, by contrast, does not so conform but, more likely, "resists" such a notion. But how so? Is the male point of view resisted, challenged, or opposed simply by the fact that men are not literally depicted in the scene?

Again, MacKinnon argues forcefully that the sexual composition of the actors or models in s/m depictions is irrelevant, as far as the harmfulness of s/m imagery to women's sense of equality and self-worth is concerned (MacKinnon 1989, 141–2). For MacKinnon, a heterosexist, patriarchal society associates femininity and womanhood with subjugation and submissiveness and these associations are at work in sadomasochistic imagery and behaviour. Accordingly, it does not matter who is "on the bottom," whether biologically male or female, because any observer or participant who has grown accustomed in a sexist society to making such associations will also tend to perceive that person figuratively as a "woman." The central problem with s/m generally on this view is, therefore, the simple portrait of a socially unequal relation – being, indeed, one of domination and subjugation.

Scales is concerned that some lesbian materials could "practice sexual exploitation of women *by women*" (Scales 1994, 374), presumably by sending misogynistic messages, or by physically and economically exploiting the female models involved. In this respect, she recognizes clear "disagreement about whether the mere fact of the sex of the participants should ... be legally relevant or dispositive."[152] Elsewhere she has quoted MacKinnon to support her own position that, "Though the genders may be rearranged in gay and lesbian pornography, if the turn-on requires domination and subordination, then those materials affirm the social hatred of women ... The value enacted ... even in some gay and lesbian materials, is that it is socially acceptable, indeed, desirable to turn women (or their surrogates) into things, to deprive us of our selves, and to screw us to death" (365). Yet even Ross recognizes the difficulty of maintaining this position consistently. She observes that "Scales maintains a paternalistic position in speaking for the 'victimized' bottom instead of letting the bottom speak for herself" (Ross 1997, 185). This is half-true. Ross's comment is directed at Scales's disparaging portrait of a so-called "positive outcome rape" story written by Trish Thomas, which was itself deemed obscene in the *Scythes* case.[153] Yet, as is clear from Scales's favourable interpretation of the lesbian anal penetration scene in Allen's *Tell Me What You Like*, Scales is prepared to let the "bottom" speak for herself on occasion. Scales's problem, therefore, consists in presuming to know when the "bottom" does and does not speak for herself, and when the "bottom" is and is not a victim. This problem is caused partly by the fact that, at times, Scales brings a purely literalist approach to pornographic expression to lesbian materials. As Ross observes, one of the "multiple, unpacked assumptions at work" in Scales's post-*Butler* reflections – Scales 1994 – "is the claim that the image itself does the screwing: a literalist reading of pornography as a practice innately harmful to women" (Ross 1997, 185).

Ultimately, however, Scales has inadequate tools for discerning a misogynistic message in a lesbian sexual script. For her, lesbian sexuality has its own ethics, reflected in the way sexually explicit lesbian materials (including lesbian s/M) assure the reader "that the participants are doing what they are doing because they *really* want to, because they are ... equals" (Scales 1994, 376; emphasis added). This lesbian sexual ethos, which applies equally to lesbian s/M, is categorically different from the "legalistic idea of consent" associated with heterosexual materials, including heterosexual s/M.[154] For Scales, lesbian materials involve a "deeper interrogation of ... the actual quality, comfort, and well-being of the parties involved." In other words, whatever the context, it is clear to Scales that lesbian sexual partners really want to do what they do even though, for example, Allison experienced pleasure from Anastasia "almost against her will" and the narrator in the *Bushfire* story was initially "shocked" by the insertion of a finger in her anus.

According to Scales's analysis, women depicted in lesbian sex scenes somehow know one another's minds. By contrast, women in hetero-sexual sex scenes do not really know their own minds. This is why Justice Sopinka emphasized the relevance of "apparent consent" in *Butler*. And heterosexual men in heterosexual depictions are clearly single-minded. They just want to penetrate women's vaginas and anuses, which is obvious to the women in the scenes. Yet if this is the standard script, then why, in *Last Tango in Paris*, does Paul asks Jeanne to insert her fingers in his anus? Is it simply another gratuitous, pornographic illustration of man's desire to "consume" women?[155] Or does this request reflect Paul's own, perhaps masochistic, desire to be consumed – indeed, to have his ego deflated, to be consumed by the power of women? Certainly it is plausible that on some personal level, Paul really wants to have Jeanne's fingers inserted up his anus; and viewed "in context," Paul looks a lot more like Allison than Anastasia.

Again, why does Jeanne comply? Before asking Jeanne to get the fingernail clippers, Paul accuses Jeanne of dating her fiancé, Tom, only to avoid loneliness and insecurity. Then Paul says, "You're alone. You're all alone and you won't be able to be free of that feeling of being alone until you look death right in the face ... Until you go right up into the ass of death, and find the womb of fear. And then, maybe" (Caputi 1994, 19–20). Perhaps there is an imaginative or "fantasy" element associated with Jeanne's compliance; particularly associated with a confrontation with and perhaps transcendence of a fear of "death." It is possible at least that, on some personal level, Jeanne really wants to put her fingers up Paul's anus.

The possibilities last mentioned should bring to mind the role psy-choanalytic theory played in the *Odeon Morton Theatres* case. Even if such an approach to understanding gay and lesbian pornography was not considered informative or helpful in the *Little Sister's* case, the different interpretive problems associated with much of the imagery reviewed in *Little Sister's* suggest the importance of canvassing as many disciplines as possible in the legislative fact-finding process of obscenity adjudication. As a lawyer, political activist, and experienced lesbian porn analyst, Scales clearly brought more epistemological variety to the fact-finding process engaged in by Canadian lawyers and courts since *Brodie*. At the same time, however, Scales's testimony regarding the literary and political merit of certain lesbian s/m publications appeared stubbornly reductionistic and univocal at times, which again highlighs the importance of maintaining a critical attitude toward all expert evidence in such matters.

Balancing Scales: Lesbian Sexuality Viewed and Expressed by Non-Experts   If Scales's expert testimony about lesbian erotica seems unreliable or incredible along theoretical lines, it is even more readily challenged by the opinions of some of the lay witnesses at *Little Sister's*. Pat Califia, the author of many of the impugned lesbian s/m works and the "subject" of much of the legal debate in *Little Sister's*, indirectly challenged the notion that, thematically, lesbian s/m sexual expression can always be categorically distinguished from mainstream (heterosexual) sexual expression. She recalled, for example, how one of her stories in *Macho Sluts* makes "compassionate" light of the great difficulty some sexual partners have in bringing one another to orgasm and, in so doing, points to a sadomasochistic element in sexual intercourse generally.[156] She intimated that her audience for this kind of work extends to gay men and heterosexuals. She also referred to another story she wrote entitled "Daddy," which both explores "incest fantasies" and analyses the social implications of incest for some individuals and communities, but more important here, plays with gender roles. She explains, "I play with gender in my stories ... to say, okay, if we are acting like men what does that mean? What does that imply? What might that look like? Is that in fact true? Are we acting like men or are we trying to be more complete human beings? ... I'm interested in the question whether there is anything useful in the masculine repertoire that women can appropriate to achieve their own lives and similar questions."[157] Thus, Califia appears to consider gender constructs used in heterosexual sexual depictions to be relevant (at least artistically or conceptually) to lesbian sexual depictions, and not necessarily in the "negative" or harmful sense portrayed by Scales and MacKinnon.

The aspect of Califia's testimony about "the masculine repertoire" recalls the evidence of Persimmon Blackbridge, a performance artist who testified regarding sexual imagery in general and a photographic-textual exhibit for which she had modelled. As Fuller and Blackley observe, Blackbridge's testimony allowed the plaintiffs' lawyer "to humanize the dry legal and theoretical discussions of sexual imagery" and at the same time "do justice to the complexity" of her own artistic endeavours (Fuller and Blackley 1995, 71–2). Her most notable opinion concerned this very complexity. For Blackbridge, "Sometimes, as women, we are acknowledged only as victims, or only as self-affirming subjects ... Neither position reflects our actual lives. Our sexuality is far more complex. We respond to sexual images in very individual and sometimes conflicted ways. And it's not because we've learned our sexuality from pornography" (72). This statement is so clear and compelling in and of itself that, to borrow a word from Justice Burger in *Paris Adult Theatre I* v. *Slaton*, it almost makes a "mockery" of much of the literary opinion offered and social science research ever conducted regarding pornography. It is an uncluttered statement about the complexity of all sexual imagery in terms of its so-called "codes" and "effect" on people who look at it. It challenges not only the literal approaches to mainstream pornographic imagery taken by Scales and at times Ross and Weir, but also the "social equality" or "social power" analysis of pornography provided by Kinsman. Equally important, it reflects an intellectually mature perspective on the topic, or one that sees itself as having grown beyond ideology. Blackbridge commented during her examination-in-chief that, as one of three members in the artistic group *Kiss & Tell*, "All three of us ... were involved in the anti-feminist pornography movement at one time or another ... But in the process of looking at and discussing imagery with other feminists, we realized that we had more questions than answers" (71). This perspective is particularly germane in a legal context where some experts such as Scales and Ross openly wear their ideological colours.

As mentioned in the previous section, Scales testified about the political significance of Califia's *Doc and Fluff*. She emphasized the way Califia addressed the problem of male violence against women in contemporary society. Yet Scales also injected some of her own political concerns into Califia's treatment of this theme. Scales noted, for example, that *Doc and Fluff* "does a very good job, in the context of an important political story, of showing the sexualized nature of the violence," such that the book can be viewed as an "important commentary on pornography because one of the feminist critiques of pornography is that it eroticizes violence for the sake of sexual pleasure."[158] For her part, Califia outlined various political themes in *Doc and Fluff*, including "environmental damage, the rise of the New Christian right, homophobia and racism," but nowhere in her discussion does she suggest that it is about pornography.[159] Elsewhere Califia is overtly against censorship,[160] so either Califia is simply silent about the "anti-pornography" theme of *Doc and Fluff* or Scales sees a message in the novel that Califia herself did not envision. In any case, the fact that Scales (and for that matter, Rule) was called to express an expert opinion about Califia's writings, over and above Califia's own lay opinion on similar issues, should raise an eyebrow about the political and legal self-interest of the expert evidence called in *Little*

Sister's and about the law's perception of lay intelligence in general. The latter issue is of the most concern at this stage in the book. Why, for the first time in Canadian legal history, was an author's courtroom testimony about her writing supplemented (and nearly supplanted) by the voices of experts? Perhaps it is not simply a matter of expert versus non-expert knowledge here, but that the sexually more "mainstream" lesbians, Scales and Rule, were perceived to be more "objective," credible, or even palatable to the court than the proud s/m performing Califia. Fuller and Blackley's analysis of the trial suggests, however, that Califia was well-received by the courtroom players (Fuller and Blackley 1995, 60).[161] And indeed, as already mentioned, Justice Smith appeared to give considerable weight to the very literal and clear words of Califia's introduction to *Macho Sluts*.[162]

One plausible way of assessing the plaintiffs' decision in *Little Sister's* to call expert upon expert to testify in relation to Califia's works, even though Califia was present and able at the trial to perform the same duty, is simply to see it as a strategic manoeuvre based on a philosophy of "strength in numbers" or "the more, the merrier" philosophy. Yet, as has already been observed in this book, expert opinion has traditionally been reserved for issues that cannot be properly understood without it. All in all, Rule and Scales did not contribute much in *Little Sister's* to the court's understanding of Califia's writings beyond Califia's own testimony; and, indeed, as already mentioned, Smith quoted Califia's own words in support of his finding that homosexual s/m writing can empower and dignify homosexual communities. So this particular aspect of the *Little Sister's* trial is very significant and cannot be overlooked here. By duplicating and triplicating the main aspects of Califia's opinion in the language of expertise, the plaintiffs have encouraged (albeit perhaps unwittingly) the elitist tendency of Canada's legislative fact-finding process.

LSBAE's belief that Califia's lay opinion needed to be bolstered by expertise clearly reflects the general, legal understanding that first-person, lay opinion, will likely lack sufficient probative value in and of itself to be convincing in the Canadian legislative fact-finding process. This contention is supported somewhat by Fuller and Blackley's observation that "In fact, the Crown and the Attorney General (AG) [in *Little Sister's*] treated the writers and artists as essentially irrelevant to their case, saving their most vigorous cross-examination for the expert witnesses – the sociologists, the law professor, the anthropologist" (Blackley and Fuller 1995, 60).

As it turned out, even though the Crown and the attorney general did concern themselves with the lack of organized, empirical research tending to support the legislative-fact and "social fact" opinions of many of the LSBAE witnesses (expert and non-expert alike), in some key respects the ultimate fact-finder in *Little Sister's*, Justice Smith, did not so concern himself, and neither did Justice Macfarlane, who reviewed Smith's ruling at the British Columbia Court of Appeal. The next section of this chapter examines Smith's response to the experts, and the British Columbia Court of Appeal's response to Smith, in order to show how, despite the varied judicial responses given to the social science expertise introduced in the *Little Sister's* case, such expertise will continue to be a pivotal consideration in the near future at least.

THE FINAL SAY: THE COURTS' VIEWS OF THE EXPERT EVIDENCE IN *LITTLE SISTER'S*

The trial judge in *Little Sister's* accepted that the kinds of sexual depictions in question affirmed gay and lesbian sexuality in a way that brought a sense of dignity and self-worth to gays and lesbians generally. Using very curious logic, however, he reasoned from this view that the impugned *Customs Act* and *Customs Tariffs Act* were not unconstitutional. Justice Smith acknowledged first that legislation is not necessarily discriminatory just because it affects different groups of people differently. Some differences in legislative effect are reasonably related to specific goals of legislation. In this regard Smith recognized that gay and lesbian booksellers across Canada seem to incur relatively more obscene publication prohibitions and detentions than their heterosexual counterparts. Yet this phenomenon could be understood, Smith reasoned further, in terms of the relatively greater significance of sexuality and sexual expression to the broader gay and lesbian community.[163] In his words,

The defining characteristic of homosexuals – the element that distinguishes them from everyone else in society – is their sexuality. Naturally, their art and literature are extensively concerned with this central characteristic of their humanity. As attested by several of the plaintiffs' witnesses, erotica produced for heterosexual audiences performs largely an entertainment function, but homosexual erotica is far more important to homosexuals. These witnesses established that sexual text and imagery produced for homosexuals serves as an affirmation of their sexuality and as a socializing force; that it normalizes the sexual practices that the larger society has historically considered to be deviant; and that it organizes homosexuals as a group and enhances their political power. Because sexual practices are so integral to homosexual culture, any law proscribing representations of sexual practices will necessarily affect homosexuals to a greater extent than it will other groups in society, to whom representations of sexual practices are much less significant and for whom such representations play a relatively marginal role in art and literature.[164]

In other words, it is precisely because sexual expression is so important to gays and lesbians (as opposed to heterosexuals) that the latter should expect to have proportionally more sexually expressive materials prohibited by anti-obscenity legislation. According to this logic, Smith ruled that the impugned customs legislation, which is not discriminatory on its face, was not discriminatory in effect.

Despite obvious problems with the above reasoning,[165] the immediate question is, how does this same thinking, which implies a judicial acceptance of much of the legislative-fact evidence presented by *Little Sister's*, jibe with Smith's finding that Parliament's proscription of gay and lesbian pornography and erotica is reasonably informed? Either the evidence firmly "established" the non-harmful, affirmative nature of gay and lesbian sexual expression, as Smith's above words and logic seem to say, or it did so only more or less, subject to the contrary and more weighty evidence of Malamuth. Indeed, for Smith, it appears that the single expert opinion of psychologist Malamuth that "homosexual pornography may have harmful effects even if it is distinct in certain ways from heterosexual pornography,"[166] constituted enough "social science evidence" to support the constitutional "reasonableness" of the *Customs Act* and *Customs Tariff Act* provisions at issue in *Little Sister's*.[167]

Yet a close review of Malamuth's written expert opinion in *Little Sister's* does not support Smith's confidence in Malamuth's research or the judge's view that the expert witnesses for the plaintiffs "generally acknowledged that [Malamuth] is a leading researcher in the field." Malamuth wrote in his report, "As in virtually all areas of media effects, it is likely that the existence and degree of impact upon subjects will vary considerably as a function of various parameters, including the cultural and individual background of those exposed."[168] Elsewhere in the same report, Malamuth noted that one of the problems in the relevant research literature is "the use of over-simplistic models, including the lack of sufficient consideration of the role of the individual and cultural differences as moderators of media influences."[169] Accordingly, Ross and Kinsman challenged the validity of Malamuth's research conclusions regarding homosexual pornography. In the course of her oral testimony, Ross was presented with a passage from an expert report prepared by Malamuth and tendered in evidence at an earlier trial.[170] According to the passage, the psychological processes involved in reading or watching heterosexual pornography are comparable to those involved in reading or watching homosexual pornography, and homosexual communities and heterosexual communities experience similar kinds of social problems associated with exposure to pornography.[171] Under cross-examination by a government lawyer, Ross categorically denied the validity of both conclusions. The exchange proceeded as follows:

Falzon As a social scientist, do you accept that this is a reasonable statement by Dr. [Neil] Malamuth?

Ross I do not. I think there is absolutely no scientific validity to the statement whatsoever.

Falzon As a social scientist, Professor Ross, I put it to you that it would be at best, given the state of social science research, it would be at best premature to express the categorical statement that you have just made.

Ross I fundamentally disagree. As a social scientist, one of the principles that we operate from is the principle that we do not generalize from research carried out in one specific context for a specific set of purposes and objectives to another context. This is an absolute violation of the principles of social scientific research.

Falzon Notwithstanding any similarities between those two contexts.

Ross Exactly.[172]

Kinsman also agreed that generalizing from research done "in a certain area with a certain population ... to another grouping, another population" is "quite suspect and is often challenged within social science research."[173]

Smith did not seem to have reservations in *Little Sister's* about the admissibility of evidence, nor about the justiciability of legislative facts. However, his illogical finding regarding Parliament's rational basis for fearing the social harmfulness of gay and lesbian pornography definitely implies some concern about the justiciability of protecting such materials from the watchful eye of the Customs department. Arguably, Smith felt, but did not express, that the Canadian public at large is not yet prepared to accept the unhindered importation and distribution of gay and lesbian pornography and erotica across Canadian bookshelves. If so, the reasonable apprehension of harm doctrine enabled him to maintain this moral status quo while appearing sensitive to the political interests of Canada's gay and lesbian communities.

At the British Columbia Court of Appeal, Justice Macfarlane found Malamuth's expert opinion to be almost irrelevant, while Justice Finch believed it to be relevant but of very little "probative" value. Macfarlane observed, "[Smith's] comments on the research of Professor Malamuth were not necessary for his decision. In the end it is open to Parliament, even in the face of inconclusive evidence, to entertain a reasoned apprehension of harm from the proliferation of obscenity, whether heterosexual or homosexual, and to prescribe a standard for determining the question whether particular material is obscene."[174] Macfarlane's deference to the wisdom of Parliament is contrasted greatly by Finch's circumspect review of Malamuth's evidence and his resulting observation that, in light of this evidence, Parliament has little or no "reason" for proscribing gay and lesbian pornography and erotica. Finch actually reproduced Malamuth's expert report in his reasons for judgment and, referring back to this report, concluded,

I am unable to find in Professor Malamuth's tentative and qualified opinion the sort of evidence that would show a reasonable basis for a finding by Parliament of a "pressing and substantial" objective. To say that "it would be desirable to have more information", that "consideration of these complex issues is beyond the scope of the present analysis" and that "I am not aware of any published systematic content analysis of gay pornography" is to acknowledge that available social science evidence does not disclose a pressing and substantial objective. Professor Malamuth's concluding sentence in answer to question "a", which I have underlined, is nothing more than an assumption, and an equivocal one at that.[175]

In effect, Smith tried to have his evidentiary pie and to eat it too, by applying the reasonable apprehension test in the manner of the *Anti-Inflation Act* reference, while at the same purporting to give much weight to the sociological evidence provided by the LSBAE witnesses. He could have simply applied the reasonable apprehension test more favourably toward the plaintiffs, as did Finch, and concluded that Parliament does not have a reasonable apprehension of harm with respect to gay and lesbian expression. Yet Smith clearly felt obliged to "balance" the competing interests, values, and visions at stake in *Little Sister's*. What is so confusing about Smith's decision is his finding that the impugned customs laws were not discriminatory against gays and lesbians in the face of legislative-fact evidence that was so clearly tipped in favour of the LSBAE.

Smith must not have taken the evidence seriously – for example, of Ross, Kinsman, and Califia – even though he formally recognized its helpfulness in determining the legislative-fact issue of gay and lesbian obscenity. In effect, Smith's deference to Malamuth's laboratory-based research in the face of Ross's, Testa's, Ricci's, and Califia's literary evidence reveals the ultimate contradiction or at least confusion in Smith's finding of legislative fact. For Smith, gay and lesbian sadomasochist depictions could avoid the prohibitive arm of the *Customs Tariff*

Act if the sexual and violent elements contained in the material can be proven "necessary" to the broader political, educational, artistic, and indeed cultural dimension of the same works.[176] Yet this is precisely the point or claim the LSBAE witnesses were making in *Little Sister's*. Earlier in his judgment Smith found, "The plaintiffs established that sado-masochism is a theatrical, ritualistic practice in which the consent of the participants is inherent, although they conceded consent is not necessarily always present."[177] This finding is entirely consonant with the idea that the combined images of sex and violence in gay and lesbian S/M are categorically "necessary" to the broader artistic merit or cultural meaning of such images, which was more or less the point of much of the plaintiffs' legislative-fact evidence in *Little Sister's*.

The fact that Malamuth's opinion was determinative for Smith of the legal issue of obscenity is consonant with Canadian courts' nagging need to appear objective in deciding matters with clear political and moral overtones. Justice Finch's criticism of Malamuth also serves the same purpose, because in examining the evidence so closely Finch implies that such evidence should be taken seriously. In addition, the fact that Malamuth, referred to by Smith too casually as a "leading researcher in the field" of pornography, won the battle of the clinical-oriented experts in *Little Sister's*, is illustrative of the trend for Canadian courts to defer to whoever appears to be the most technically qualified, or to possess the most professional credentials, from the perspective of the scientific community in which the expert works. This is problematic to the extent that, as the *Little Sister's* case so colourfully demonstrates, there may be many scientific and non-scientific communities who have different opinions on the same subject matter, and that a scientific "community" concerned with any particular issue may itself be more mythical than real.

Smith's broader analysis of the different legislative-fact opinions in *Little Sister's* does signal a slight break with tradition: Smith considered the importance of some lay opinions regarding the self-affirming and empowering nature of gay and lesbian depictions of sexuality to gay and lesbians as individuals and members of a recognizable community in Canada. Most notably, Smith referred to Pat Califia's testimony and quoted sympathetically a passage from her own writing which spoke perhaps more eloquently and forcefully to the above phenomenon than the convoluted and at time hyperbolic opinions of some of the plaintiff's academically-minded witnesses on this same issue.[178]

In one important regard, Smith's attentiveness to Califia (however legally inconsequential as far as his broader findings of fact are concerned) should be contrasted with Judge Payne's treatment of Gwen Jacob just a few years before. Jacob's lay opinion about the nature of her (impugned) behaviour was effectively disregarded in favour of some published and well-recognized medical opinions about female sexuality, and only subsequently, when further opinion evidence was introduced by experts from other fields, was this hitherto authoritative medical opinion decisively challenged, if not completely rebutted.

By formally recognizing the evidentiary contribution of the plaintiff's numerous witnesses in *Little Sister's*, including some of the lay witnesses such as Califia and Blackbridge, Smith has laid down a footpath for future consideration of lay opinions in constitutional review cases, particularly where those opinions are proffered in regard to legislative facts. Such a development will not only serve to check the otherwise privileged status and indeed reliability of expert opinion in such cases, but to render the legislative-fact decision-making process more democratic in the sense conveyed by Dewey and Mouffe.

It is also significant that Smith omitted express reference to certain experts for LSBAE, particularly Lorraine Weir, Bart Testa, and Ann Scales. As already discussed, the expert testimony of Weir and Testa was highly theoretical and purportedly scientific and, although relevant to certain adjudicative issues in *Little Sister's*, it seemed intellectually redundant for the most part. It is conceivable but not likely that Testa's and Weir's evidence was too complex for Smith to sift through properly, even though the theoretical jargon was translated at times almost simplistically. In any case, similar insights were provided in less abstract and technical terms (including those of some other experts, such as Ricci), and the fact that Smith quoted Ricci on germane points indicates that Smith was somehow more comfortable with Ricci's less technical jargon. Regarding this same area of testimony, it is worth noting further that, if deconstruction theory, hermeneutics, and semiotics were introduced by LSBAE to give theoretical support to its own expert literary opinions – that is, to combat the contrary empirical social scientific claims of Malamuth – this strategy was clearly unsuccessful, at least at this stage of the litigation. Smith's finding in this respect highlights our courts' current amenability to the social, but not the literary, sciences.

As for Scales, it is significant that she openly advertised herself as a political activist and that her qualifications or credentials as an expert were challenged at the very outset of her testimony. Given her genuine lack of expertise in most of the issues put before her, it is significant that Scales's testimony had to be "stage-managed" by the plaintiffs' lawyer "with superb agility and finesse, even during the rough and tumble of cross-examination" (Blackley and Fuller 1995, 63). Although

Smith did not preclude Scales from testifying because of her experience as an activist, this same experience may have been responsible (at least in part) for Smith's decision not to recognize Scales's evidentiary contribution explicitly. If so, Smith was simply acting cautiously and traditionally, by ascribing little weight to the opinion of an expert who is clearly seen to be partisan, biased, and argumentative. As already suggested, however, the traditional legal distinction between the intellectually impartial expert witness and the partisan, argumentative expert witness is naive and stands in need of serious reconsideration.

The Supreme Court of Canada's decision in *Little Sister's* was relatively uneventful, at least as far as its treatment of the expert evidence introduced at trial was concerned. The lengthy reported decision only occasionally paraphrases some of the key findings that Smith made and that the Court of Appeal confirmed. Justice Binnie accepted without much analysis, for example, Smith's earlier findings that much of the gay and lesbian materials seized by Canada Customs were not obscene in law, and were detained and examined in amounts that were very disproportionate to the size of the readership of those materials.[179] Binnie also accepted without question Smith's highly problematic finding of fact to the effect that "sexual practices" are much more "integral to homosexual culture" than to "other groups."[180] In a law journal article published shortly after Smith made this finding, I endeavoured to show that this finding was rooted in an unsupportable generalization and was an example of the very kind of stereotyping that the Supreme Court of Canada has become loathe to accept.[181] It is worth noting that my argument was not considered by the Supreme Court of Canada even though it was readily available to any competent legal researcher. This is significant because the court did consult a wide variety of relevant scholarly articles that were not made available to Smith or the British Columbia Court of Appeal.

Perhaps the Supreme Court of Canada's most notable and problematic ruling in relation to the expert evidence presented to Smith was Justice Binnie's and Justice Iacobucci's decision that the research conclusions of Malamuth regarding heterosexual and homosexual pornography supported the federal government's "reasonable apprehension of harm" about such materials.[182] Binnie actually reproduced a portion of Malamuth's highly tentative research conclusions to support his ruling. As already discussed, however, at the British Columbia Court of Appeal, Justice Macfarlane commented that Malamuth's research was more or less irrelevant to the issue of apprehended harm, and Justice Finch flatly dismissed the same research as having any probative value in regard to this harmfulness issue. Ultimately, therefore, despite

the real challenge made to Malamuth's research by ostensibly competent experts in the field, and the pejorative comments made in relation
to that research by appellate justices, the Supreme Court of Canada
has effectively rendered the controversial research of a single social
scientist central to the free expression interests of all Canadians.

FROM SEX AND VIOLENCE TO SEX AND CHILDREN: WHERE TO DRAW THE LINE

By the time the experts had their days in court in *Little Sister's*, at least
one golden rule could be gleaned from Canada's history of obscenity
prosecutions: where there is pornography, any pornography, there is a
self-proclaimed pornography expert. The rule applies equally to heterosexual erotica and smut, to "vanilla" and "hard core" sexual imagery,
to sadomasochism, and certainly to child pornography. *Butler's* own
particular emphasis on the special dangers of pornography for children
(as well as for women) must surely have been welcomed by the behav-
iourists and psychologists in this area, who by this time surely needed
some good reason to obtain funding for further research in an area that
has consistently yielded bruised fruit. Why not rely on a high court
legal ruling? Even during the *Little Sister's* trial, which was ostensibly
aimed at adult homosexual sadomasochistic literature and imagery, the
federal government attempted to undermine the credibility of LSBAE
witness Jearld Moldenhauer for carrying the North American Man-Boy
Love Association (NAMBLA) newsletter in his Boston bookstore (Fuller
and Blackley 1995, 25). The *Little Sister's* trial is particularly remarkable in this respect because, just as the issue of child pornography strad-
dled the margins of the greater pornography debates conducted there,
both the LSBAE and its lawyer, Joseph Arvay, made a point of drawing
the line of acceptable sexual imagery and expression short of child
pornography (Fuller and Blackley 1995, 24).[183]

  In light of Moldenhauer's frank admission that he would not censor
the NAMBLA bulletin because he does not consider that images of
"man-boy" love could be obscene, and in light of the way *Little Sister's*
so craftily attempted to distinguish gay and lesbian sexual expression
categorically from heterosexual sexual expression, one is forced to ask
what makes child pornography so distinct from all the other genres
that it alone remains as the special subject of Canadian law enforcement on the obscenity front? After all, even *Butler* held that the
otherwise innocuous "third category" of pornography, that which
portrays explicit sex that is not violent and neither degrading nor
dehumanizing, will generally be tolerated by Canadians *unless it
employs children in its production.*[184]

The Harmfulness of Child Pornography

There is no revelation in the thought that children who are seduced, tricked, manipulated, or exploited one way or another by adults so that the children pose for sexually explicit or suggestive photographs, are hurt, degraded, and demeaned. In some or many cases, children who have been victimized in this way may suffer long-term psychological and behavioural repercussions. Yet these realities and possibilities are surely not the proper subject of expert evidence. As both Cahn and Dworkin remarked of the social science evidence introduced in the *School Segregation Cases*, this type of knowledge is acquired by people as a matter of everyday practical experience. So what do the experts have to say about child pornography that is "special" or "special knowledge?" And do such expert opinions have any cogency in the final analysis? Since *Butler*, Canadian courts have had a few occasions to hear from the child pornography experts. A couple of the judges have accepted the expert opinions that this genre is dangerous in the way discussed in *Butler*, but others have assessed the evidence critically, and, as might be expected at this historical juncture, found it unenlightening.

The first case to interpret Canada's most recent child pornography laws, *R. v. Langer*, involved the seizure of a number of paintings and drawings from the *Mercer Union* art gallery in Toronto in 1995. Justice McCombs describes the paintings and sketches as having generally depicted children explicitly engaged in a variety of sexual activities, often with adults (or with adults in the background), and remarks that "as a whole, the subject-matter is deeply disturbing."[185] Eli Langer, the artist, challenged the child pornography law itself as being a violation of his freedom of expression under the Canadian *Charter of Rights and Freedoms*. Looking to section 163.1 of the *Criminal Code*, and following *Butler's* approach to obscenity where relevant, McCombs saw his task as determining a number of issues, including: the nature and extent of pornography; whether exposure to child pornography increases the danger that children will be sexually abused; whether the seized paintings and drawing posed a "realistic" risk of harm to children; and whether these same paintings and drawings had artistic merit.[186] Clearly, the way these issues were characterized invited to the *Langer* trial all the experts Canadian courtrooms had hitherto hosted, and more.

To address the recurrent "causal link" questions, a number of behavioural psychologists were called by the Crown and the defence. The Crown called three psychologists, Howard Barbaree, William Marshall, and Richard Berry. To recall, Marshall had testified for the

Crown in *Ronish* and it was Marshall's research on Canadian Customs inspection agents that was the subject of much debate in *Little Sister's*. The Crown also called Peter Collins, a practicing psychiatrist who specializes in treating persons with so-called "sexual deviancy" problems. Langer's counsel called evidence from psychologists Jonathan Freedman and Ronald Langevin. The latter had given evidence in the *Arnold* case regarding the erotic nature of public female nudity and would soon again give evidence about child pornography in *R. v. Stroempl*.

With such an impressive line of "psy" experts to do battle on fairly fresh terrain, Justice McCombs's approach was relatively straightforward: give each expert his due, then weigh the evidence carefully in the balance and arrive at the appropriate finding of facts. As McCombs recalls, Freedman and Langevin testified that "there is no sound scientific basis for concluding that exposure to explicit depictions sexualizing children increases the likelihood of sexual abuse of children." Yet Collins, Barbaree, and Marshall testified generally that "some paedophiles use child pornography in ways that put children at risk." In particular, "[child pornography] is used to 'reinforce cognitive distortions' (by rationalizing paedophilia as a normal sexual preference), to fuel their sexual fantasies (for example, through masturbation) and to 'groom' children, by showing it to them in order to promote discussion of sexual matters and thereby persuade them that such activity is normal."[187] So the consensus at this point seems to be that, for all people who are not paedophiles, and even for some paedophiles, exposure to sexually explicit imagery of children will not increase rates of child sexual abuse, but for some paedophiles, exposure to such materials puts children at risk in the ways mentioned above.

Although McCombs appeared to assess the expert evidence evenly, he did consider the clinically-based evidence of Marshall, Collins, and Barbaree pertaining to paedophiles generally more relevant than the results of "scientific studies." Like Justice Sopinka in *Butler* and Justice Smith in *Little Sister's*, McCombs saw no need to establish scientifically a "clear link" between child pornography and the sexual abuse of children. Remarkably, however, when it came to the issue of the harmfulness of the particular paintings and drawings in question, McCombs preferred Langevin's evidence over that of the Crown "psy" experts. He noted how the Crown's experts "each expressed the opinion that the seized materials would be of interest to paedophiles and would increase the risk that they would act on their fantasies." The paintings and drawings might reinforce a paedophile's perception that sex with children was not wrong, or a paedophile might not interpret the children depicted in the paintings as being in a state of distress.

Yet McCombs observed further, "In Dr. Langevin's view, paedophiles would be more aroused by photographic images, even relatively innocuous mainstream advertising images, such as children modelling swimwear or underwear, than they would by the seized paintings and drawings, which, in his view, would have a frightening quality that would be disquieting to paedophiles."[188] McCombs preferred Langevin's expertise pertaining to the paintings and drawings in question and accordingly found that these materials did not pose a "realistic" risk of harm to children.

As has become customary in prosecutions involving the issue of an impugned painting's, movie's, or book's artistic merit, McCombs was presented with an array of evidence from artists, art experts, art critics, and art historians. McCombs does not recall in detail the evidence of these literary people. He observes merely, "With varying degrees of enthusiasm, each of the art experts described Mr. Langer's work as having artistic merit. At one end of the spectrum of enthusiasm, an expert said that while he did not think much of the paintings, he nevertheless thought they were works of art. At the other end of the spectrum of enthusiasm, Langer's work was described as 'important, serious, and passionate' and 'of quality and significance.'"[189] McCombs accepted the general opinion of the art experts that Langer's paintings had artistic merit, and this determination was enough to require the government to return the paintings to the gallery. As in *Little Sister's*, the art critics, historians, and artists, were clearly influential, and they possibly helped to persuade McCombs to prefer Langevin's evidence over the Crown's own expert psychologists. Yet McCombs was obliged to inquire further to determine whether section 163.1 of the *Criminal Code* violates, as a matter of principle, Canada's constitutional guarantee to its citizens of freedom of expression. And in this regard, McCombs reverted to the scientific and clinical psychological evidence, just as Justice Smith in *Little Sister's* and Justice Sopinka in *Butler* turned to the laboratory evidence of Malamuth.

Canada's child pornography laws and obscenity laws are conceptually linked, so McCombs was obliged in part to follow Sopinka's interpretation of obscenity in *Butler*.[190] This means that McCombs was required to assess the harmfulness of child pornography, as a matter of both attitudinal and behavioural harm resulting from exposure to images of children in sexually evocative poses and situations. This book has suggested that the actual harm to children exploited and abused in the production of child pornography is self-evident, and McCombs did not seem to require evidence in this regard. Moreover, McCombs and counsel for the prosecution and the defence agreed that the protection against such harm is a "pressing and substantial" objective within the terms of *Oakes*.[191] But one of the purported legislative objectives of section 163.1 of the *Criminal Code* is the protection of children who are *not* involved in pornographic production from the harmful effects of possessing and distributing child pornography to others.[192] McCombs recognized that this objective might be "overbroad" for constitutional purposes but accepted the evidence mentioned above of Marshall and Collins regarding the dangerous ways paedophiles might use child pornography and concluded that the wide breadth of this objective "is necessary in view of the pressing and substantial objectives of the legislation."[193]

In effect, McCombs treated the behavioural science evidence regarding child pornography in precisely the same way Justice Sopinka and Justice Smith treated the social science evidence about pornography in *Butler* and *Little Sister's*, respectively: it all supports Parliament's "reasonable apprehension of harm." As McCombs observes, "In my opinion, in light of the evidence which I have accepted concerning the use to which child pornography is sometimes put, and the consequent risk of harm to children, Parliament had a reasonable basis for criminalizing not only the creation and dissemination of child pornography, but its possession as well."[194] McCombs formulated this opinion despite the following recognition at the outset of his judgment: "There is considerable controversy within the behavioural science community about the effects, if any, of child pornography upon behavior. The main reason for the controversy appears to be that it is virtually impossible to conduct studies with sufficiently rigorous adherence to proper scientific method to produce statistically reliable results. After all, paedophiles are not anxious to identify themselves or to co-operate with researchers. The problems of small sample size, false reporting, interviewer distortion, and a myriad of other inherent difficulties contribute to the difficulty of scientific study."[195]

The last quoted statement is particularly remarkable for at least two reasons. First, it suggests that people who read, watch, or even produce child pornography may not be affected whatsoever by so doing, at least as some segment of "the behavioural science community" has examined the problem. But McCombs is not entirely clear here as to whether the studies have been conducted on anyone who willingly or unwillingly is exposed to child pornography, or to paedophiles exclusively. McCombs presumes that paedophiles are difficult research subjects, and that this fact poses real problems for the methodological construction and statistical reliability of scientific analyses into paedophiles and child pornography. Yet, presumably, tests of the effects of child pornography on human behaviour could be conducted using non-paedophiles, who likely would not be too difficult to find. Indeed, as already discussed, even McCombs's review of the legislative intent behind section 163.1 of the *Criminal Code* does not suggest that Parliament had paedophiles in mind as the only group of people who might realistically cause harm to children through the possession, production, or distribution of child pornography.

In any case, it is significant that McCombs even mentioned some of the methodological problems associated with social science research about paedophiles and recognized that a "myriad of other inherent difficulties contribute to the difficulty of scientific study."[196] This book has attempted to show that the particular limitations McCombs identifies in relation to paedophile research, such as sample size, false reporting, and interviewer distortion, are applicable to all social science research and for the most part render such research far more unreliable than most social scientific communites are likely to concede. Even in *Langer*, Langevin, who McCombs described as a "respected clinician and academic," disagreed with the other psychologists and psychiatrists about the psychological and behavioural effects of the Langer paintings and drawings on paedophiles. Unfortunately McCombs did not reproduce or paraphrase any of the expert evidence of "lecturer and social scientist" Varda Burstyn, who testified regarding "sexual expression in popular culture" on behalf of Langer.[197] As an anti-censorship advocate, Burstyn's testimony likely served further to show the limited utility of the behavioural scientific evidence introduced by the Crown in *Langer*.

McCombs's positive conclusions about the dangers of child pornography posed by paedophiles who possess, produce, or distribute it were subsequently considered in *R. v. Stroempl*, the prosecution of a sixty-seven-year-old man in Ontario for so-called "simple possession" of a substantial collection of child pornography. The Ontario Court of Appeal relied on the idea that paedophiles use child pornography in three ways identified in *Langer* to justify giving primacy to the principles of general deterrence and denunciation in sentencing the convicted person. Although the Ontario Court of Appeal reduced Stroempl's sentence from eighteen months imprisonment to ten months in jail, the case is particularly noteworthy because Stroempl was psychologically assessed by Langevin before the original sentencing hearing in order to determine whether Stroempl was a "danger to the public." Langevin's report concluded, among other things, that Stroempl (1) presented a "pro-social, non-criminal and non-violent history"; (2) did not abuse alcohol or drugs; (3) had been gainfully employed throughout his adult life; (4) reported a conventional sexual history; (5) denied having ever engaged in sexually deviant activity; (6) acknowledged the development of a recent interest in nudism which included a curiosity about female minors; and

(7) denied having paedophilic interest. Overall, Langevin's report concluded that "Stroempl is not a violent or aggressive person. The major signs of dangerous sexuality are absent and, in this sense, he presents a low risk for criminal sexual behavior. However, his mental confusion and neuropsychological disorganization place him at risk for inappropriate and out of character behavior in general. Treatment of his condition may reduce the risk and he should be followed up after further medical investigation."[198]

Langevin's "risk-assessment" of Stroempl nicely highlights the chicken and egg nature of the behavioural science conclusions put forth in *Langer*. According to Langevin, Stroempl is "at risk *for inappropriate and out of character behavior in general*," whatever that might be, because of "mental confusion and neuropsychological disorganization," not necessarily, or even probably, because he reads child pornography. Moreover, his acquired interest in nudism and curiosity about female minors may well be considered "out of character behavior" for a sixty-seven-year-old man, and therefore entirely symptomatic of "mental confusion" or "neuropsychological disorganization." But this conclusion is a far cry from suggesting that either Stroempl acquired a curiosity about female minors through reading child pornography or that Stroempl sought to acquire a substantial collection of child pornography in order to satiate or explore an extant curiosity about young girls. Perhaps Stroempl is simply the exception that proves the behavioural science rule.

Indeed, two of the Crown behavioural science experts in *Langer* returned to a British Columbia courtroom a few years later to reiterate in *R. v. Sharpe* the view that child pornography placed in the hands of paedophiles (and this time, child molesters) poses a substantial risk of harm to children. Collins reappeared for the Crown, this time to explain four ways that child pornography poses a risk of harm. The "grooming" and "cognitive distortion" notions from *Langer* were reiterated. The self-evident proposition that children are abused in the making of pornography was put forward again. And Collins introduced the idea that "pornography excites some child molesters to commit offences."[199] The last view was supported by two published studies, one authored by Marshall (who testified in *Langer*) and another penned by D.L. Carter, R.A. Prentky, et al. The presiding judge, Justice Shaw, emphasized that Marshall's study focused exclusively on the impact of hard-core child pornography on rapists, child molesters, and non-offenders, and that the study by Carter et al. examined the impact of exposure to a wide range of pornographic images on convicted rapists and child molesters only. Curiously, the subject or target group of the relevant research has shifted from paedophiles in *Langer* to child molesters and sex offenders in *Sharpe*, even though there was no evidence that paedophiles were visiting the Mercer Gallery in Toronto to see Langer's paintings, or that Sharpe was a paedophile, sex offender, or child molester.

In any event, as Shaw recalls, the study by Carter et al. found "that child molesters have a greater exposure to pornography than rapists and use it more often than rapists in association with criminal offences. The study also showed that child molesters use pornography more often than rapists to relieve impulses to commit offences."[200] Presumably, the "criminal offences" contemplated here do not include property offences such as theft or fraud, or motor vehicle offences, such as careless driving or driving while impaired. Shaw expresses, though he does not overtly state, a real interest in the research finding by Carter et al. that "child molesters report that they were more likely than rapists to employ pornography as a means of relieving an impulse to act out."[201] It would be interesting to know how child molesters themselves could know how often rapists use pornography to relieve impulses to act out, but Shaw is particularly advertent to the logical implication of the mere finding that child molesters sometimes use pornography to relieve sexual impulses. According to the study by Carter et al., pornography does not necessarily inhibit "sexual acting out" but, rather, because pornography may be used by child molesters to fuel "an already active, and in many cases rich, fantasy life," exposure to such imagery is more or less irrelevant to the desire child molesters have to act on their fantasies – whatever these might be (Carter, Prenky, et al. 1987, 207).[202] In other words, some child molesters sometimes find relief from sexual tension in pornography, and some child molesters – possibly even the same ones – sometimes use pornography to strengthen their tendency to act out sexual fantasies involving children. Moreover, Shaw points out that studies cited by Carter et al. from 1974 and 1977 purported to show that "mildly erotic stimuli" inhibited "aggression" whereas "highly erotic stimuli" increased "aggression" in a laboratory setting.[203] Given the analytic beating that studies of the variety last mentioned have taken throughout North America prior to and since Canada's Fraser Committee report, it it not surprising that Shaw is unable to draw any edifying findings of fact from the study by Carter et al. In his conclusion of facts derived from the evidence, he states, "'Highly erotic' pornography incites some pedophiles to commit offences. 'Highly erotic' pornography helps some pedophiles relieve pent-up sexual tension." But he adds, "*It is not possible to say which of the two foregoing effects is the greater.*"[204] Indeed, it is not even a case of understanding which of the two effects – relief versus incitement – is "greater," because the conditions under which either "effect" may be produced and recognized as such are likely so complex, and probably vary so much between individuals who experience them, that it is impossible to devise a standard measure for determining the relative size or strength of a "good" or "bad" effect[205] – presuming, all the while, of course, that sexual relief or incitation to act out sexual fantasies are "effects," rather than, for example, correlatives or symptoms. Indeed, it is the explicit conclusion of Carter et al. that "if an individual is prone to act on his fantasies, it is likely that he will do so *irrespectively* of the availability of or exposure to pornography."[206]

Collins reiterated the expert evidence from *Langer* that paedophiles often use pornography as an aid to masturbation. This evidence, which resonates with much earlier research or survey findings that some heterosexual couples use pornography to enhance their sexual lives together, appears fairly innocuous and perhaps irrelevant to the issue of dangerousness in *Sharpe*. Significantly, however, Collins informed Shaw that Langevin was currently attempting to gauge whether the "relieving" or "inciting" effect of pornography was greater – as if the social science research community (and any other community for that matter) stands to benefit somehow from yet another such study.

Sharpe did not have a lawyer representing him at trial. Accordingly, he was guided by Shaw in the niceties of introducing and eliciting evidence. Despite his lack of polish as a barrister, Sharpe showed himself to be erudite on the subject of child pornography, and subjected Collins to a lengthy and at times devastating bout of cross-examination. Sharpe managed to get Collins to concede that some paedophiles can be troubled by their behaviour and recognize that it is wrong; that stress in different forms, such as financial, occupational, and marital, contributes to "paraphilic acting out"; that some paedophiles suffer from low self-esteem; that Collins does not know how fantasies originate in a person; and that there are more questions about the cause of paraphiliac behaviours like paedophilia than answers.

Justice Shaw's hospitable attitude toward Sharpe's rough-edged but effective cross-examination of Collins is particularly significant because it may have enabled Shaw to reach a different conclusion from Justice McCombs in *Langer* regarding the constitutionality of section 163.1 of the *Criminal Code*. To recall, McCombs found that the expert evidence introduced in *Langer* supported Parliament's "reasoned apprehension of harm" regarding the effects of child pornography, but McCombs also found that there was no evidence presented to him showing that the practical realities of executing section 163.1 "are so deleterious that they outweigh the pressing and substantial objective of the legislation."[207] For Shaw, however, the expert evidence failed to establish that the "simple possession" of child pornography offence under section 163.1(4) was a sufficiently effective means of redressing the putative risks of harm to children, especially given the "profound" nature of the violation of freedom of expression permitted by that section. Indeed, in assessing the detrimental effects of executing section 163.1(4) of the *Criminal Code*, Shaw found, "First and foremost, the invasion of freedom of expression and personal privacy is profound. Further, the prohibition extends to all persons including those who make no harmful use of pornography. They may be collectors of pornography, whether out of prurient interest or simply out of curiosity, but with no harmful intent. The prohibition also includes pedophiles who, instead of preying on children, use pornography for very private purposes, such as relief from their affliction by masturbation."[208] Although Shaw applied a more elaborate proportionality test than McCombs employed in *Langer*,[209] the nub of the difference between Shaw's and McCombs's reasoning lies primarily in Shaw's more comprehensive interpretation of the Charter right violated by section 163.1(4) and his more careful finding, based on the evidence, that the "beneficial" or "salutary effects" of Canada's prohibition of simple possession of child pornography are "limited."[210]

Shaw's decision in *Sharpe* immediately sparked a national outcry, fueled by fear-mongering politicians who saw the decision as an official, state-sanctioned condonation of paedophilia, child exploitation, and the sexual abuse of children. The government's appeal was fast-tracked to quell the fears and anger of those citizens and politicians opposed to Shaw's ruling. And Shaw even received an anonymous death threat.

The British Columbia Court of Appeal received further social science evidence and "extrinsic" materials (such as international committee reports, treaties, and legislation). Madam Justice Southin approached the constitutional issue logically in part by recognizing that a prohibition against the possession of images of certain sexual acts that are themselves legal is "unreasonable." Yet she upheld Shaw's decision mainly because the social science and extrinsic materials were not "compelling evidence" of the need to criminalize the "private possession" of expressive materials *of any kind*.[211] In this last respect, it is noteworthy that Southin commented, after reviewing RJR-*MacDonald* v. *Canada (A.G.)* on the topic of legislative-fact and social fact evidence, "With respect, it does appear to me that the so-called 'legislative' facts, insofar as they are based on what is broadly called social science, are more of a matter of opinion than fact."[212] Southin may well be the first Canadian judge to make this astute observation so candidly in a written judgment.

Madam Justice Rowles also addressed the social science evidence purporting to establish that the possession of child pornography is "indirectly" harmful to children insofar as it reinforces cognitive distortions, facilitates the "grooming" of children, and fuels paedophiles' sexual fantasies. She found that, although the available social science evidence was "inconclusive" with regard to some of these correlations or causal relations, it supports the government's "reasoned apprehension" that children are at risk of harm from "the potential use of child pornography by paedophiles and from the desensitization of society to the use of children as sexual objects."[213] The evidence did not adequately establish, however, that the possession of "works of the imagination" as opposed to the possession of visual depictions (such as photographs or drawings) of actual children, posed any real risk of harm to children,[214] so the government failed to show that it had a "reasoned apprehension of harm" with respect to such materials. In light of the "profound violation of freedom of expression and privacy" made possible by the impugned child pornography law, Rowles agreed with Justice Shaw that Parliament's manner of minimizing the indirect dangers to children resulting from the mere possession of child pornography was unreasonable.

The British Columbia Court of Appeal decision was quickly brought before the Supreme Court of Canada for final resolution. Unfortunately for the government, the majority of the court followed the majority of the British Columbia Court of Appeal's thinking and held that certain kinds of visual and written materials depicting children could not be regarded as posing a sufficient risk of harm to children to justify making their private, personal possession criminal. These are written materials or visual representations created from one's imagination and which are held by the creator alone; and visual recordings which depict lawful sexual activity between adolescents, where one or more of the participants might look like a child, and where the recording is possessed exclusively by the creator of the recording or any of the participants in it.[215] Madam Justice McLachlin and the majority of the justices also agreed largely with Rowles that the relevant social science evidence introduced at trial and on appeal regarding cognitive distortions, grooming, and fantasy-fueled incitement, supported Parliament's reasonable fears about the dangers of child pornography in general. Remarkably, McLachlin conceded that some of the social science evidence presented by Collins, in particular that relating to cognitive distortions and fantasy-fuelled incitement, was weak. In this respect, she made clear that "unanimity of scientific opinion" was not necessary to validate the government's fears about child pornography, and she implied that the issue of whether reading or viewing child pornography makes the reader or viewer more likely to offend against a child is a matter of "[complex] human behavior." Nonetheless, where social science research is incapable of convincingly establishing empirical correlations between exposure to child pornography and acts of child abuse, the court can rely on "experience and common sense"to "buttress" this inconclusive evidence.[216]

On behalf of the minority decision, Madam Justice L'Heureux-Dubé also deferred heavily to Collins's trial evidence about cognitive distortions and grooming, and to police evidence regarding the impact of computers and the Internet on the distribution and circulation of child pornography. The evidentiary importance she gave to the police evidence is problematic in its own right. She recalled Detective Waters's evidence that the ready availability of computers and the Internet to people possessing or creating child pornography has recently led to a dramatic increase in the distribution of child pornography.[217] Indeed, at trial Waters explained how United States Customs had once set up a phony Web site advertising child pornography which attracted some 40,000 hits in eight weeks.[218] L'Heureux-Dubé does not mention, however, that when Sharpe asked Waters about the way 'hits' are generated, the witness conceded that she could not answer such questions and that "other experts" dealt with the computer side of such covert operations.[219] In any case, L'Heureux-Dubé saw fit to bolster Waters's evidence with an extract from Criminal Intelligence Service Canada's Annual Report on Organized Crime in Canada (2000) that makes the armchair and perhaps trite observation, "The distribution of child pornography is growing proportionately with the continuing expansion of Internet use. Chat rooms available throughout the Internet global community further facilitate and compound this problem. The use of the Internet has helped pornographers to present and promote their point of view."[220]

It is unfortunate that L'Heureux-Dubé chose to breathe new life into the clearly partial and indeed morally-interested police evidence introduced at Sharpe's trial. When Sharpe asked Waters whether she would describe her practice of giving presentations and lectures about reforming Canada's child pornography laws as "advocacy," she replied, "I don't consider it anything other than a part of my job to – in the protection of children."[221] L'Heureux-Dubé also put evidentiary stock in a statement made by Monica Rainey, a spokesperson for Citizens Against Child Exploitation, purporting to link exposure to child pornography directly to an increased risk of harm to children. The statement maintains in part that "fools" would believe "that 90 minutes of viewing adult sex with children will have no negative influence on those who are already addicted to children." The other part, which apparently provides the logic for the former, implies that "advertisers [sell] billions of dollars of advertising for 90-second commercials" because "90 seconds work in advertising."[222] It's all so simple, is it not? Advertising works! People purchase products on the basis of 90-second commercials, just like people who are "addicted to children" change their attitudes toward children by exposure to child pornography – indeed, just like adults who watch and possibly enjoy violent movies leave the cinema with a slightly greater inclination for violence than they had previously. One can only wonder how Malamuth's research into adult pornography failed to make an appearance here.

The Literary Merit of Child Pornography

After Sharpe succeeded in convincing the Supreme Court of Canada to decriminalize the possession of child pornography in narrowly limited circumstances, he had to return to trial in Vancouver to find out whether the circumstances in which he was originally found to be in possession of diskettes and photos depicting children were lawful or criminal. Sharpe argued that the boys depicted in the photos seized at the border were likely fourteen years of age or older and that there was nothing unlawful about any sexual activity in which they might have appeared to be engaging. Moreover, these photos were kept in his private possession and were intended exclusively for his personal use. For these reasons, the photos fell within the exception just created by the Supreme Court of Canada. Justice Shaw disagreed.[223] There was no evidence before him that Sharpe kept the photos in strict privacy, nor was there any evidence presented that the photos were intended for the private use of the boys depicted. As for the photographs seized at Sharpe's home, Sharpe accepted Shaw's ruling that Sharpe's possession of these was unlawful.[224]

Sharpe's own written works which were the subject of prosecution consisted of a short story collection entitled *Sam Paloc's Boyabuse: Flogging Fun and Fortitude – A Collection of Kiddiekink Classics* and a short story entitled *Stand By America, 1953*. The stories in *Boyabuse* cover a range of plots, most of which involve boys at some point along the way engaging in sexual acts with men or other boys – as having "man-boy" or "boy-boy" sexual relations, as sometimes described – or being beaten, flogged, or strapped by men. Sharpe provided his own description of *Stand by America, 1953* in a note below the title, part of which reads as follows: "Two sadistic brothers posing as KGB agents intercept a small group of boys while they are on a hike. The setting is 1953, during the time of the Senator McCarthy witchhunt of Americans with present or past Communist affiliations. Under the ruse that the boys have found a briefcase containing important secrets, the two men subject the boys to torture and sexual relations and force the boys to participate in similar activities between themselves. The fortitude shown by the boys plays a large role in this story. There are obvious parallels between parts of this story and the film Stand by Me."[225]

With Sharpe's purported exploration of themes of McCarthyism, fortitude, and the film *Stand by Me* at stake in these proceedings, it is not surprising that his lawyer and the Crown counsel alike lined up their experts to debate the artistic merit of *Stand by America, 1953*. Insofar as the theme of fortitude also appeared to be present in some of the *Boyabuse* stories, the experts could presumably assist the court in this regard as well. The Crown called Paul Delaney, the Chair of the Department of English at Simon Fraser University, and Shaberhan Lohrasbe, who Justice Shaw described as "a forensic psychiatrist with considerable experience in the assessment and treatment of sex offenders."[226] Sharpe's lawyer, Paul Burstein, called James L. Miller, a professor of English at the University of Western Ontario, and Lorraine Weir, the University of British Columbia professor of English who gave evidence about hermeneutics and deconstruction theory at the *Little Sister's* trial.

Before analysing the opinions of these experts, it needs to be noted that they were in one sense largely superfluous to the outcome of the trial. An essential element of the Canadian crime of writing child pornography, whether for private possession or for publication, is that the written material must *advocate* or *counsel* unlawful sexual activity with a person under eighteen years of age.[227] Canadian law requires that the notions of advocating or counseling in this context be interpreted "objectively" and "purposively," such that, put simply, "the prohibition is against material that, viewed objectively, sends the message that sex with children can and should be pursued."[228] The Crown argued that Sharpe's stories did indeed send this message, but Shaw disagreed. He stated,

While *Boyabuse* and *Stand by America, 1953* arguably glorify the acts described therein, in my opinion they do not go so far as to actively promote their commission. The descriptions may well be designed to titillate or excite the reader (if the reader is so inclined) but these descriptions do not actively advocate or counsel the reader to engage in the acts described.

Nor, in my view, do *Boyabuse* and *Stand by America, 1953* send "the message" that sex with children can and should be pursued. If that were the case, then literature describing murder, robbery, theft, rape, drug use and other crimes in such a way as to make them appear enjoyable would likewise be said to advocate or counsel the commission of those crimes. In my opinion, such literature is not what the "advocates or counsels" requirement is intended to capture.[229]

In those few words Shaw capably rejected a simplistic, literalist approach to discerning meaning, by recognizing that the message of a text does not always or necessarily equate with the depiction of events in that text. For him, the sexual and violent depictions in Sharpe's stories are not presented in such a way that they could be said to encourage people to try "man-boy" or "boy-boy" sex, or to believe that flogging children is desirable or acceptable, even though some readers might be sexually aroused by such imagery. At this point in his reasoning, Shaw does not venture to articulate the message or messages contained in Sharpe's stories, but insofar as they do not appear to advocate or counsel unlawful behaviour, they cannot, in Shaw's view, amount to child pornography. Accordingly, Sharpe was found not guilty of possessing or publishing child pornography in relation to these writings.

Just in case someone (such as an appellate court justice) might disagree with his analysis of the advocating and counseling point, Shaw considered the expert evidence that was presented to him on the subject of "artistic merit" and asked himself whether Sharpe's stories could be defended as having artistic merit – notwithstanding, that is, the possibility that they advocate or counsel unlawful sexual behaviour. Indeed, the availability of an artistic merit defence in Canadian child pornography law effectively pays recognition to what others such as Vanderham and Adler have proposed, namely, that writing can simultaneously be pornographic or obscene and literary or artistic.

As mentioned, three English literature experts testified about the literary merit of Sharpe's writings. A fourth expert, the "forensic psychiatrist" called by the Crown, did not pretend to be properly qualified to talk about literary matters, but he did mention that in his work with sex offenders he has observed that such persons use pornography for sexual stimulation and as masturbatory aids.[230] Given the obvious irrelevance of this last piece of information to the issue of literary merit, it is significant that it was introduced at all in the proceedings. This book has already shown how a similar observation pertaining to paedophiles was introduced in the *Langer* and *Stroempl* cases, and how research into the use of pornography by child molesters and rapists was considered by Shaw himself in Sharpe's earlier constitutional challenge to Canada's child pornography laws. Moreover, the Supreme Court of Canada accepted in Sharpe's case that clinical research with sex offenders and child molesters, despite its real limitations, supports a reasonable fear that children are placed at risk of harm by the creation, publication, and dissemination of child pornography. Although this well-worn social scientific approach to understanding pornography appears to have become stale or unedifying for some lawyers and judges, for others it still manages to keep its lustre.

With Lohrasbe having effectively disqualified himself from speaking in an informed way about the literary merit of Sharpe's *Boyabuse* and *Stand by America, 1953*, the Crown was left to battle the two literary experts for the defence with Delaney alone. As Shaw recalls, Delaney, being "well-versed in literature and literary criticism," reviewed Sharpe's stories from numerous perspectives and concluded that they lacked literary merit. For Delaney, Sharpe's writings were characterized by a host of literary weaknesses and failings. Shaw summarized many of these in his judgment. He recalls that, for Delaney, the plots, narrative, characterizations, and style of Sharpe's stories are crude or simplistic. As well, the motivations behind Sharpe's characters are typically simple or implausible, and the stories lack a coherent philosophy or even fail to make philosophical inquiry at all. Delaney appeared to have difficulty finding evidence of parody in Sharpe's stories and was not prepared to say that Sharpe used allegory in the strict sense. Where Sharpe might have used allegory in a broad sense, he was incompetent and contradictory in Delaney's view.[231]

So far, depending on the merit Shaw was prepared to find in Delaney's litany of criticisms, the Crown's case might have been more than adequately served by their sole literary expert. As it turns out, Shaw expressly acknowledged his "great respect" for Delaney and recognized that Delaney "brought to bear considerable skill and learning in his analysis of Sharpe's works." However, in Shaw's view, Delaney's expert opinion was flawed or in any case unhelpful because it was informed to a significant extent by moral considerations.[232] Whereas the moral aspect of a body of writing or imagery is relevant to an assessment of the community standards of tolerance, as is the case, for example, where adult pornography is being reviewed,[233] the Supreme Court of Canada made clear in relation to Sharpe's own constitutional challenge to Canada's child pornography law that child pornography is to be understood differently (as was explained above).

Despite Shaw's concern that the difference between the legal tests for adult and child pornography be understood and upheld, his rejection of Delaney's opinion as moralistic in part is highly problematic. In effect, Shaw subscribes to the view that a piece of writing, particularly one that appears to depict children in sexually evocative or provocative manners, can be pornographic or obscene and at the same time artistic.[234]

As this book has shown, other individuals of some reputable literary aptitude and knowledge accept this view at least in relation to adult pornography. Yet the question of whether one can properly talk about the literary merit of a book, while at the same time being moralistic (or even political), is distinct from the question of whether one should import moral considerations into assessments of pornography or obscenity, or indeed, the harmfulness of pornographic works. The former question invites a consideration of competing theories of art, such as the "aesthetic theory" and the so-called "moral-aesthetic theory" at play in the trial of *Ulysses*. In rejecting Delaney's evidence as being moralistic, Shaw appears to have preferred the former theory over the latter. This is especially remarkable if one accepts, for example, that Joyce's *Ulysses*, being both literary and obscene, can still be viewed reasonably as a "moral-aesthetic" piece of art.

This book has also endeavoured to show that most if not all experts who testify in pornography trials across North America bring some kind of moral or political inclination to bear upon their evidence, and that this often goes unnoticed by judges. Shaw recognized the moralistic dimension of Delaney's evidence (even though under cross-examination Delaney maintained that his literary opinion was free of morality), but failed to see how it also pervaded Weir's and Miller's testimony. One aspect of Sharpe's writing to which Weir, Miller, and Shaw apparently gave serious consideration was the theme of fortitude that ostensibly pervaded many of the stories. The theme must not have been hard to detect, for in his own note to *Stand by America, 1953*, Sharpe referred to the large role that the "fortitude shown by the boys" plays in the story.[235] In a letter written in 1993, Sharpe wrote how "the thrill is the fortitude of the boy, testing rather than crushing the spirit."[236] And in various summaries to the short stories contained in *Boyabuse*, Sharpe points out that fortitude is the predominant or significant theme.[237] But why should this theme of fortitude somehow come to inform the literary merit of Sharpe's stories any more or less than, for example, other themes that might have been present in these works, such as sadomasochism, transgressive sexuality, or McCarthyism?

In Shaw's paraphrase, "Professor Miller found an *ethical theme of fortitude* throughout *Boyabuse*. This fortitude is primarily physical, in the sense of endurance of boys who are beaten and whipped. *While not purporting to pass moral judgment* upon Mr. Sharpe's writings, Professor Miller expressed the view that *the theme of fortitude adds to the literary value* of the stories in *Boyabuse*."[238] Indeed, later in his reasons, Shaw explains that for Miller "Mr. Sharpe's *ethos of fortitude* was his 'special twist' on the Sadean tradition" of transgressive literature.[239]

So the "ethos" or "ethical theme" of fortitude appears to add literary quality to Sharpe's stories, which bear some hallmark of literariness, in any case, to the extent that they seem to belong to an established genre of transgressive literature typified by the writings of the Marquis de Sade.

According to this analysis, it seems that the moral predilections of Miller do inform his analysis of literary merit, despite his attempt to stay somehow morally impartial. Something about Sharpe's choice of ethos or ethic in relation to images of spankings, floggings, or torture of boys seems in Miller's eyes to be meritorious from a strictly literary perspective. Yet this should not seem surprising. Literary merit does tend to be measured, at least partly and perhaps unconsciously, by the extent to which a depiction or series of depictions of human behaviour fosters or promotes broader understanding, awareness, and openness, rather than, for example, sexism, racism, or hatred. Had Sharpe chosen to depict, for example, the "spirit" of the different boys who receive the spankings or floggings as being "crushed" or defeated, and nothing more, one could ask fairly what Sharpe meant to achieve through such imagery – assuming, of course, that his depiction was meant to convey a point or message.[240] Sometimes an artist will describe or depict a beating in graphic detail for the simple purpose of evoking a feeling of revulsion in the observer.[241] This is considered a laudable aim and it is, without doubt, moralistic. If successful, from an artistic point of view, the message driven home to the reader or viewer is that tortuous or cruel behaviour is intolerable and never to be condoned or encouraged.

For Sharpe, at least one of the objectives of his depiction of torture in a *Boyabuse* story is erotic stimulation. To this end, the theme of fortitude seems critical, as Sharpe explains in a letter written in 1993: "For me the thrill is the fortitude of the boy, testing rather than crushing the spirit. Ali in the Rites of Port Dar Lan #1 expresses this idea. I doubt if I would find it erotic if a torture kept a boy well beyond his endurance, out of control – convulsions. Mindless torture is a turnoff."[242] Titillation through exposure to images of torture, circumcision, and floggings of boys might not be the noblest of aspirations for a writer, but in principle it is a far cry from enticement or encouragement to commit unlawful acts, and to this extent, as has already been observed, Sharpe cannot be faulted from a legal perspective.

Weir also drew attention to the theme of fortitude in *Boyabuse* and *Stand By America, 1953*, although it is not directly apparent from Shaw's decision whether, and if so how, Weir regarded this theme as contributing to the literary merit of Sharpe's stories. As she did in the *Little Sister's* case, Weir explained for the court how hermeneutic theory could be applied to texts. She explained that a hermeneutic approach to understanding a written work required an analysis of the literary skills present in the text itself as well as an assessment of the text in relation to other works written by the same author, relevant works of other authors, and one's knowledge of the subjects treated in the text itself.[243] So, in addition to reading the short stories before the court and becoming familiar with "relevant" nineteenth century literature, Weir read two novels written by Sharpe. In one of these, *Algernon at Eton*, Sharpe appears to have drawn from an established Victorian historical context which included "the practice of flogging in Victorian boys' schools, as well as the themes of apprenticeship and fortitude." One learns that, for Weir, Sharpe's exploration of the theme of fortitude in *Algernon at Eton* could cast light on the significance of this theme to Sharpe's broader corpus.[244]

Weir was called in Sharpe's case to give expert literary testimony about various stories depicting, among other things, an uncle spanking his young nephew with a leather strap[245] and exploring (by Sharpe's own concession) "heavy sadomasochistic themes."[246] It is perhaps sheer coincidence that she was also called in the *Little Sister's* case to edify the court about Geoffrey Mains's *Urban Aboriginals (A Celebration of Leathersexuality)*. After all, Justice Smith learned from Weir about the spiritually emancipatory nature of some sadomasochistic practices or rituals in the *Little Sister's* case, and in Sharpe's case Shaw was educated about the importance for Sharpe, as an aspiring writer of literature, that the young boys show fortitude in his stories when they are portrayed as being tortured, sexually or otherwise, by men. These are quite different tasks undertaken by Weir (and again, it is not entirely clear from Shaw's judgment just how Weir saw the centrality of the fortitude theme as contributing to the literary merit of Sharpe's writings). More important here, however, is the possibility that, however different the stories and texts written by Geoffrey Mains and Sharpe might be, they are similar in a significant respect, and this relates to their overarching moral character. According to Weir in the *Little Sister's* case, Mains wrote about sadomasochism to explain it and to reveal its emancipatory and possibly ennobling potential. For many, this aim will seem meritorious and perhaps laudable. Similarly, if one accepts Miller's evidence about the ethos of fortitude that pervades Sharpe's stories, then one can conclude plausibly that Sharpe's aim or message in writing his stories is not harmful and indeed, is possibly praiseworthy – at least in part.[247] So, even though Weir appeared in Sharpe's eyes to be "careful not to judge the morality of Mr. Sharpe's writings,"[248] it needs to be asked why she considered the theme of fortitude in Sharpe's writings to be relevant to the literary merit of those writings. A likely answer is that fortitude or courage in the face of torture, just like emancipation or transcendence through sadomasochistic ritual, has a positive moral connotation in Weir's mind, as it also likely does in the minds of Miller and even Shaw. Whether or not this amorphous moral consideration can effectively be divorced from literary criticism is probably an impossible question to answer.[249] In pornography cases, judges should bear this real difficulty in mind before categorically preferring one expert literary opinion over that of another just because the latter clearly or expressly bears a moral aspect.

Ultimately the *Sharpe* case is particularly significant because it illustrates so plainly the deeply embedded tendency among Canadian judges to determine controversial issues of social policy, especially those directly involving sexuality and morals, by reference to social science and other disciplinary forms of expertise. In the course of the constitutional challenge, Justice Shaw, Justice Southin, and Justice Rowles courageously displayed what Paciocco would call a critically vigilant attitude toward social science evidence. Yet more recently, Shaw appeared to give much weight to the testimony of literary experts who appeared to be somehow amoral in their approach to Sharpe's child pornography stories. Still, the simple fact that such expert evidence figured so prominently one way or another – that is, as something to be rejected outright, weighed lightly, or taken seriously, but in any case analysed and addressed – testifies to the increasing dominance of the role social science and other forms of expert evidence play in judicial fact-finding about sexual offences and offences against morality across Canada. The question remains pressing: When history demonstrates that the opinions proffered be experts are often less than edifying, cogent, or even trustworthy, not simply because of technological and methodological limitations, but because of political and moral influences, how desirable is the institutionalization of such expertise in Canadian courts?

6

Indecency Law:
Microscopic and Macroscopic
Views of the Female Breast
and Lap-Dancing in the Dark

Canadian courts have traditionally applied to the law of indecency the same "community standard of tolerance" principle associated with obscenity. In the 1970s this principle was applied to a case of "streaking" in Ontario, where the nude culprit was apparently en route to buy a case of beer at the Brewers Retail store. In the 1980s certain individuals in Ontario and the Yukon Territory had the legality of their acts of "mooning" determined by the same principle. Shortly before and after *Butler*, however, some women in Ontario caught the attention of the entire Canadian public by exposing their breasts to the full view of the sun, as a matter of comfort and protest. With the great influx of human sexuality experts into obscenity proceedings by this time, it is no surprise that they should appear either in different stripes to defend or challenge the moral propriety (and indeed harmfulness) of these women's behaviour, when it was placed on trial.

Similarly, the sex experts have found a new home in indecency prosecutions involving the newer "dancing" techniques found in some of Canada's private entertainment parlours. In these cases, however, the expertise extended itself to the medical or health professional realm, and the proverbial "risk of harm" issue from *Butler* was broadened to redress the world's increasing concern with sexually transmittable diseases, particularly AIDS. The following discussion reviews the role experts played in these indecency prosecutions which relate to the bold exposure and indeed free expression of one's physical self, in private and public, for money and for protest.

Jacob and Arnold: Sexologists, Doctors, and Anthropologists
Take a Close Look at the Female Breast

Shortly before *Butler* was decided, a young woman strolled barebreasted through various streets in Guelph, Ontario, on a sweltering summer day. Along the way, Gwen Jacob was arrested for committing an indecent act, contrary to section 171(1)(a) of the *Criminal Code*. At her trial, Gwen Jacob challenged the constitutionality of the law which purportedly made it an offence for women, but not men, to bare their breasts in public. Defence evidence was presented by Jacob, by onlookers at the scene, and by a local newspaper editor. Crown evidence was introduced by passers-by and in the form of specific sexological treatises and medical works in the area of human sexuality.

Gwen Jacob testified at her trial in Guelph. She emphasized that the above-average heat on the summer day in question warranted her decision to bare her breasts, and she argued otherwise that, just as men could walk barebreasted in public places, so section 15 of the *Charter* should permit women to do so. Furthermore, to show that her behaviour in the circumstances did not offend the so-called community standard of tolerance, Jacob's lawyer called some lay opinion evidence and some published or recorded "survey" evidence. In particular, a Guelph lawyer who drove past Jacob at the time testified that he was not offended by Jacob's actions in the circumstances. A mother of two children testified that, although she did not observe Jacob's behaviour, she would not have been offended by it. And Rolf Pederson, a local newspaper editor who penned an editorial pertaining to Jacob's case also gave evidence.[1]

Pederson's presence at Jacob's trial is particularly significant for at least two reasons. As an editorial columnist of a local newspaper, Pederson's opinion was held out to be somewhat reflective of the local community opinion in matters of public interest. In this respect, he evoked more or less the same kind of public figure or image in the *Jacob* case as Rowlands did in the *Doug Rankine Co.* case. Both individuals were well known and enjoyed a certain popularity in their respective communities, but neither purported to have any specialized information or expertise on matters of community morals. The fact that Pederson was allowed to give his opinion as a lay witness at Jacob's trial was illustrative, therefore, of a mild departure from the tendency of Canadian courts at that time to restrict such evidence to experts in opinion-polling and survey-collection techniques.

At the same time, however, Judge Payne suggested that Pederson's oral evidence, which was intended to explain the contents of his previously published editorial piece, was ultimately very unintelligent and at any rate most unhelpful to the court. Payne wrote, "It soon became apparent that the author had no idea what he was talking about and repeatedly made [statements] of fact about the subject when he had no factual basis at all."[2] Not only does this statement belie Payne's own aversion to Pederson's liberal views on the matter at hand, it also reflects the Canadian judiciary's broader, undying appetite for a "*factual* basis" to all matters of opinion. As should be clear by now, tradition dictates that the latter can and should only be supplied by experts in the field.

Accordingly, Payne canvassed the results of a telephone survey conducted by the *Guelph Daily Mercury* newspaper. This showed that the large majority of callers disagreed with Jacob's conduct. Even though this "majority" opinion is consistent with Payne's finding of fact (as will be made clear shortly), it is telling that he appears to have given little weight to it, possibly because it was "poorly conducted."[3] This concern with the proficiency of the survey design and implementation is consistent with Justice Dickson's ruling in *Prairie Schooner News*, but for this very reason it further entrenches the centrality of social science experts in legislative-fact decision-making.

In response to the lay opinion evidence provided by the defence in *Jacob*, the prosecution produced two of its own lay witnesses and introduced a variety of published medical and psychological treatises on the subject of human (and in particular, female) sexuality. One of the laypersons who lived on the street where Jacob walked nude stated that it is "dirty" for women to expose their breast publicly. Another, who had actually confronted Jacob at the time of the incident, described the exposure of female breasts in public as "disgusting."[4] Among the published works contained in the Crown's contemporary Brandeis-style brief were Kinsey's *Sexual Behavior in the Human Female*, Masters and Johnson's *Human Sexual Response*, and medical treatises entitled *Fundamentals of Human Sexuality, The Medical Self-Care Book of Women's Health*, and *Every Woman's Health, The Complete Guide to Body and Mind*. Although not admitted under the guise of expert evidence, strictly speaking, Payne referred to these various "reports and articles" as having been penned by "recognized *authorities*."[5] In this respect, the judge recalls Chief Justice Warren's treatment of the psychological treatises introduced in *Brown v. Board of Education* as "modern authority." Warren did not expressly indicate how the materials in *Brown v. Board of Education* influenced his ultimate finding of facts, but Payne selected certain passages from the works mentioned above that he believed supported his finding that Jacob's conduct in the circumstances was indecent. He discovered from *The Medical Self-Care Book of Women's Health*, for example, that the female breast serves a "primary" function in the production and delivery of milk to infants and that female breasts are accordingly equipped with nipples, which "are amply supplied with nerve endings and blood vessels" and which bear minute "oil glands" to lubricate and protect the breast during breast feeding. This particular scientific or medical revelation resembles that of Jonathan Swift's miniature Brobdingnag adventurer, whose close, physical encounter with a female breast (which appears magnified and gigantic from the point of view of tiny Gulliver) caused him a greater sense of "disgust" than beauty or wonder. But Swift's encounter with science is both an illuminating parody and serious polemic.

Payne also extracted a notable passage from Kinsey's *Sexual Behavior in the Human Female* relating to "breast stimulation." It reads: "Males, and particularly American males, may find considerable psychological stimulation in touching and manipulating the female breast. Many males are more aroused erotically by observing female breasts, or by touching them, than they are by the sight of or manual contacts with female genitalia. In actuality, many females are not particularly stimulated by such breast manipulations, but some of them are aroused. A female may even reach orgasm as a result of such contacts."[6] This passage is reproduced not because it is especially edifying, but because it appears to inform most directly Payne's opinion that, in light of the physiological effect women's exposed breasts may have on men, whether touched or merely seen, the female breast is not "a part of the body that ought to be flagrantly exposed to public view."[7] It seems to lend scientific support, that is, to his apparent concern that women continue to be protected by law from the threat of "molestation" of "this part of the female anatomy."[8]

Two more obvious or real concerns for Payne, however, are that the biological imperatives of species reproduction not be demeaned and that the historical (religious) sanctity associated with women's capacity to nurture or breast-feed children not be tarnished by flagrant exposure or gratuitous displays of female breasts in public. For Payne, the "role" of the female breast "in the sexual life of the female and the male partner, and in the nurturing of children places [the female breast] ... in the community standard to be a part of the anatomy that should not be exposed gratuitously and continuously in public places."[9]

Payne treated the recognized, scientific authorities as effectively more informative of community standards of tolerance than the average man- and woman-on-the-street, even though these materials are silent about such standards. And this evidence was itself meant to address an issue of legislative fact: whether exposure of female breasts to men in public is dangerous. For Payne, technical biological and psychological information about sexual glands and stimulation somehow suggests the danger is real, as does also some non-technical, lay opinion from the community. Yet as already mentioned, the community survey evidence and other opinions from passers-by was considered to be largely useless.

Approximately a year after Jacob's arrest, a whole group of women (and some men) in Kitchener, Ontario, exposed their breasts to public view in formal protest of Jacob's conviction. Some of these women were arrested and took their case to trial in *R. v. Arnold*. By the time this case was tried, Jacob's own conviction appeal had been heard and rejected by the General Division of the Ontario Court of Justice. This development meant that in *Arnold*, Judge Katie McGowan was bound by the rule of law (regarding public exposure of female breasts) laid down by Payne in the *Jacob* case unless she could distinguish the two cases on factual grounds. Accordingly, defence counsel for Arnold and the other accused individuals presented expert opinion evidence about sexuality and nudity specifically directed at the special circumstances of the case.

In particular, the defence called Dr Langevin, the psychologist and "expert in human sexuality" who testified in the various child pornography cases reviewed in chapter 5. As McGowan recalls, Langevin stated that the erotic nature or implications of exposure to the female breast vary depending on the circumstances.[11] More precisely, Langevin remarked, "The bare breast is not of itself erotic ... in order for there to be some sexual arousal there must be some cultural signal that tells the onlooker 'I am looking for sexual behaviour'. Revealing breasts at a civil protest rally is not ... an erotic signal."[12] This very last notion, uttered by a recognized expert in human sexuality, appears to inform most directly McGowan's own finding of legislative fact that public exposure of female breasts at a protest rally is somehow unerotic, and presumably harmless, and therefore not contrary to community standards of decency. Yet Langevin's expert opinion on this point was bolstered by that of Penny Van Esterick, an anthropologist, whose own studies "have focused on social attitudes of breast feeding." McGowan clearly found Van Esterick's evidence convincing, especially her hypothesis that, "since society clearly tolerates some eroticism in the mode of dress of its members, then surely it must tolerate bare breasts without eroticism."[13] Such thinking, McGowan observes, is "consistent with [Van Esterick's] opinion that, in some circumstances, the partially exposed breast is more erotic than the wholly exposed breast."[14]

Now expert anthropological opinion is used both to supplement extant psychological or sexological opinion evidence favouring a woman's freedom to bare her breasts and to rebut or at least qualify Payne's finding in *Jacob*. In this light, McGowan clearly accepted the anthropologist as a new, legitimate, professional player in the battle of the sex- and morality-oriented experts in Canadian constitutional law. As the last chapter revealed, the anthropologist played an even more dominant role in recent and current gay and lesbian constitutional struggles.

One other expert called for the defence in *Arnold* was Kay Armitage, a critically acclaimed filmmaker and an instructor of women's studies. Her expert evidence is worth recalling not so much for what it positively contributed to the discussion in *Arnold*, but for the reasons McGowan gave for rejecting it. In essence, Armitage shared Langevin's and Van Esterick's opinion that the baring of female breasts at a political protest rally is within the community standard of tolerance,[15] but McGowan more or less dismissed Armitage's opinion because it was not properly substantiated and, in effect, appeared to be more in the nature of argument than "impartial," "objective," or "scientific" observation. As McGowan explains, "The focus of [Armitage's] work has been the sexual exploitation of women. Her research is not empirical and has been conducted from a feminist point of view and so may be biased. In addition, her analysis of recent opinion columns is academically novel and its accuracy is untried. In determining the Canadian standard of tolerance (a term with which Dr. Armitage was unfamiliar) the court must be satisfied that the assessment is objective and impartial."[16] Again, McGowan hearkens back to the earliest American and Canadian jurisprudence involving matters of legislative fact, particularly those cases that have been influenced by the advent of feminism across North America. The "average conscience" and its legal corollary, the community standard of tolerance, are capable of assessment, and ideally this must be done scientifically, empirically, methodologically, and where possible, clinically. This is why McGowan points out that "Doctors Van Esterick and [Langevin] have engaged in a more scientific analysis of social attitudes" than Armitage.[17] So far, where artist and "scientist" discuss or argue the same topic in constitutional law, artistic insight is not presumed to be as reliable as scientific knowledge.

Yet McGowan goes further. She expressly discounts the opinion of Armitage because it purports to reflect "a feminist point of view and so may be biased." Here McGowan employs the traditional but clearly problematic dichotomy between expert "opinion" and "argument," and she ironically undermines the very epistemological force behind the feminist-based reforms to Canadian criminal law initiated, for example, in the *Doug Rankine Co.* and *Butler* cases. To recall, it was partly Rowlands's "feminist point of view" that informed a new, judicially-defined, harms-based definition of obscenity in 1983; moreover, it was Donnerstein, Linz, and Penrod's personal aversion to media depictions of sexual aggression against women that partly motivated their influential laboratory research into pornography (Donnerstein, Linz, and Penrod 1987, 196); and, finally, it was a much larger body of radical-feminist theory and feminist-informed research that helped to entrench this definition in the minds of Canada's Supreme Court justices in 1992. In those cases, a feminist point of view was considered reliable and indeed probative of the legislative-fact issue at hand; yet for McGowan, however cogent a feminist view may be in shaping policy, and however consistent it may be with the ultimate finding of fact in the case at bar, it must be left outside the courtroom door if unsupported by non-biased, empirical research.

MORE THAN FIFTY YEARS AFTER *CONWAY*: THE DANCE IS DIRTIER AND EXPERTS SAY INFECTIOUS DISEASES MAY BE SPREADING

In 1988, in *R. v. Tremblay et al.*, the owner of a house in Montreal was prosecuted for operating a commercial bawdy-house named Pussy Cat, in which certain indecent acts were performed. In the establishment, customers (who were typically, if not exclusively, male), would select a "dancer" from a book of photographs, go to a private room furnished with a mattress and a chair, and then for a fee, watch the dancer undress and perform a dance on the mattress. In some cases the dancer would caress herself with a vibrator, simulating (and at times actually performing) self-stimulation. Most of the patrons masturbated while the dancers performed, but in no cases did the patrons touch the dancers, as any such contact was understood by all involved to be strictly prohibited. It is noteworthy also that a peephole was placed in one of the walls of each room to enable the management to maintain security (but not to encourage voyeurism).

At trial the presiding judge applied the 1985 *Fraser Report* findings to the impugned behaviour, listened to testimony from some police officers and a former employee of the Pussy Cat club, and heard expert evidence from Michel Campbell, a psychologist, sexologist, and professor at the Université de Québec à Montréal. In light of all the evidence, the trial judge found that the allegedly indecent "dancing," although it may be considered dirty by some, is something the Canadian public in general is willing to tolerate.

At the Quebec Court of Appeal, Justice Brossard held that the expert evidence introduced at trial was irrelevant to the only issue in the appeal, namely, whether masturbation in a public place was indecent according to Canadian criminal law. Although the acts of the dancer and her client were effectively private, in the sense that only the management could watch them (for the purpose of security), Justice Brossard reasoned that they were public as far the law was concerned because members of the public could attend the Pussy Cat club for a fee. Brossard reasoned further that, as none of the expert evidence before the trial judge addressed the acceptability of public acts of masturbation, such acts must be considered to offend the Canadian community standard of tolerance.

At the Supreme Court of Canada Justice Cory (for the majority) applied the community standard of tolerance test informed by *Butler* and asked whether the impugned acts were harmful. Remarkably, Cory emphasized that the circumstances in which the acts occurred, particularly "the place in which the acts take place *and the composition of the audience*" were germane to this issue.[18] Although Cory did not directly address the opposite contention from *Butler*, dating back to Justice Wilson's decision in *Towne Cinema Theatres*, that the community standard of tolerance should not depend on the "constituency" which observes the impugned material, Cory's thinking is entirely in line with the expert literary evidence introduced in the *Little Sister's* case. Indeed, since Justice Dickson declared in *Towne Cinema Theatres* that the "audience to which the allegedly obscene material is targeted must be relevant,"[19] one can only wonder how the contrary view of Wilson has prevailed to this day.

Once he established the relevancy of the audience, the place, and the general context to the question of indecency, Cory reviewed the evidence introduced at trial. Campbell testified regarding the increased "normalcy" and acceptability of masturbation among men and women (as if the practice, not the self-reporting, has increased). Cory accepted this evidence with the caveat that the legal question of whether the act of masturbation itself is indecent must depend on the "surrounding circumstances." To illustrate the force of Campbell's evidence, Cory displayed some literary acumen akin to that of Judge Woolsey in the *Ulysses* prosecution and commented, "If masturbation can be one of the principal themes of the well-accepted novel, *Portnoy's Complaint*, by the outstanding author Philip Roth, it surely cannot have the same connotation of indecency it possessed in the past."[20] Bearing *Butler* in mind, Cory also recalled, "In the opinion of Dr. Campbell, the acts performed in the Pussy Cat were non-pathological acts of voyeurism and exhibitionism which did not cause harm to anyone."[21]

Most notably, Campbell felt that the acts of self-stimulation performed by the dancers and their clients constituted "safe sex" because as long as the no contact rule was obeyed, no sexually transmittable diseases could be contracted by either participant. Not only does the very substance of this expert opinion appear novel in Canadian anti-obscenity litigation at this time, prompted likely by an emergent public concern with the spread of the potentially lethal AIDS virus, Cory also relates this opinion to the community standard of tolerance principle.

He remarked, "In these times, when so many sexual activities can have a truly fatal attraction, these acts provided an opportunity for safe sex with no risk of any infection. The absence of any risk of harm could properly be taken into account in assessing community standard of tolerance for the act."[22]

Like Justice Brossard at the Quebec Court of Appeal, Justice Gonthier considered Campbell's evidence to be irrelevant because it did not address the Canadian standard of tolerance for masturbation *in public*. Even though Cory reasoned that the social setting in which the Pussy Cat acts were performed were "relatively private," Gonthier argued that technically, as a matter of law, the acts were public, and Canadians were not yet tolerant of public acts of masturbation.

Cory also accepted the trial judge's view that the 1985 Fraser Committee report was applicable to the behaviour occurring in the Pussy Cat club, and that this report would support the tolerability of private acts of nude dancing and self-stimulation. Gonthier disagreed. Again, emphasizing the legally public nature of the activities, he noted that the *Fraser Report* did not canvass Canadians' opinions regarding public acts of masturbation, and he argued that the results of the report could not be extrapolated to this new domain of inquiry.

Two police officers testified in *Tremblay*. One of the officers conceded under cross-examination that the dancers' acts of simulated masturbation and self-stimulation in the Pussy Cat club were not significantly different than those performed in some other strip clubs and that the latter were tolerated by the police. The other officer disagreed, testifying that he had not seen other nude female dancers touch their genitals the way they did at the Pussy Cat club. The fact that police officers testified in this general regard recalls the *Conway* case fifty years prior. There two police officers testified that they were not scandalized by the impugned "tableau" of showgirls, and one of them, to the surprise of the reviewing judge, admitted that he thought the scene was an "artistic arrangement."

Finally, Johanne Totunov, a former employee of the Pussy Cat club and former nude dancer in Montreal, testified that the erotic dancing in the Pussy Cat was more risqué or "*osé*" than that in other strip clubs. Cory observed, however, that Totunov's testimony, combined with that of the police officers, only revealed Montreal police to be generally tolerant of dancers who touched their breasts, buttocks, and at times genitals.

At about the same time in Toronto, undercover police were busy investigating some other kinds of intimate dance styles – table- and lap-dancing. Indeed, in *R. v. Mara and East*, an owner and manager of Cheaters Tavern in midtown Toronto was prosecuted for allowing nude dancers to give indecent performances. In this case, some officers testified that in their undercover roles as tavern patrons they experienced the dancers attempting to masturbate them. They also described many other forms of sexual touching between the dancers and patrons during the table and lap dances. The trial judge concluded that such conduct would be indecent in law, but by comparison to the kind of sexual behaviour at issue in the *Tremblay* and *Hawkins* cases, the table and lap dance activity was "innocuous."

Chief Justice Dubin of the Ontario Court of Appeal disagreed with the trial judge's assessment. Unlike the "relatively private" dances taking place at the Pussy Cat in Montreal, the lap and table dances being performed at Cheaters Tavern were "relatively public," and as *Tremblay* made abundantly clear, the Canadian community is not prepared to tolerate public acts of masturbation. Moreover, whereas the dancer and her client at the Pussy Cat club made no physical contact (at least according to the evidence), the essence of the lap and table dances was sexual contact in various forms. This consideration naturally invited Dubin to emphasize the increased "risk of physical harm" to the dancers posed by lap- and table-dancing and, more notably, the risk of "spreading infectious diseases by oral and genital contact."[23]

Remarkably, no experts were called to testify in *Mara and East*. Dubin referred briefly to the *MacGuigan Report* cited in *Butler* to support his view that the behaviour of the dancers in the course of table- and lap-dancing posed the same threat to women's dignity and equality discussed in *Butler*. Yet the general absence of expert evidence in *Mara and East* appears somehow refreshing. Although such evidence (for example, as provided frequently by the *Fraser Report*) might or might not have benefited the proprietor and manager of Cheaters Tavern, a sweeping review of the history of expert evidence in Canadian obscenity prosecutions shows that the lynchpin concept of the community standard of tolerance is simply not amenable to expert measurement.

The presence of the police officers and the professional dancer in *Tremblay* and *Mara and East* further illustrates the apparently increasing trend of Canadian courts to hear a broader variety of opinion evidence for the purpose of discerning community mores and issues of social harmfulness. This development is welcome as the community standard of tolerance continues to dominate the focus of Canadian obscenity and indecency law. Yet this legal concept cannot avoid importing majoritarian morality into the overall obscenity analysis, even though Justice Sopinka emphasized in *Butler* that one person's morals should not limit another person's freedom to read, write, watch, or publish sexually explicit narratives and imagery, and that Canadian courts should focus their attention on the physical and psychological harmfulness of exposure to and production of pornography. So now the social scientists search for signs of harm but continually come up short, and the phenomenal failure rate results *not* from the real possibility that pornography is harmful in the ways identified in *Butler*, but because the correlations being sought will not reveal themselves in experiments and laboratories.

Conclusion

This book has steered a relatively rocky course through early American and Canadian constitutional review cases in order to show the doctrinal bumps and epistemological bruises that accompany obscenity law when it pulls into shore. Judges are expected merely to confirm or reject the reasonableness of a government's apprehension that sexually explicit reading and viewing materials, and most recently those combining sex and violence, are sufficiently dangerous to the general health and welfare of society that the production and consumption of such materials need to be outlawed. Judges once felt comfortable acting as moral guardians in this respect, and in cases where an impugned, sexually graphic book appeared to serve some "higher" artistic and indeed moral end, judges might consider the opinions of established literati to help them with a difficult decision. More recently in Canada, judges have accepted that they are not to be moral arbiters when it comes to deciding what kind of sexually explicit material can be published and who can read it. Their task is to weigh carefully the importance to a democratic society of promoting unrestricted expression against the value to that same society of ensuring that every single member within it is treated with dignity in everyday civil and domestic affairs. Of course, as Justice Sopinka observed insightfully, albeit peripherally, in *Butler*, the current issue of pornography's harmfulness invariably involves moral considerations, but the epistemological question has clearly shifted from "Does this material promote immoral thoughts and behaviour?" to "Does this material encourage hateful attitudes toward others, and in so doing, pose a real risk of physical danger to those same people?"

Most probably because certain social science methodologies purport to be able to determine, measure, or gauge psychological and behavioural responses to various stimuli, judges consider professionals in particular social scientific domains to be helpful in resolving questions of pornography's alleged harmfulness. This book has attempted to demonstrate, however, that after thirty years of social science research relating to this problem, the jury is *still* out. The tenuous social science foundation laid in *Butler* is beginning to give way to the critical eye of a broader society of social scientists, literary academics, anthropologists, judges, and "ordinary" Canadians. And the problem here is rooted much more in the social scientific approaches to pornography than the lack of consensus within society at large regarding pornography's harmfulness or moral worth.

In a word, the purported dangers of human sexuality and its various depictions in published forms is a non-justiciable issue. Social science research may hold out promise to some judges, but the nagging problem of pornography cannot be redressed by educating judges in the art of social science jargon and methodologies. This would be both impractical and undesirable. It is impractical because proper training in this regard would require judges to spend too much time away from the everyday task of adjudicating cases. It is undesirable because the social sciences should not be seen to bear a particularly more probative or cogent epistemological role in legislative fact-finding than other disciplines. If judges were expected for this purpose to become knowledgeable in the principles of economics, anthropology, sociology, and psychology, why should they not be expected also to become equally versed in comparative literature, history, religious studies, and philosophy?

At the same time, assuming that Canada's tradition of constitutional review is unlikely to be abandoned in the near future, reviewing judges cannot be expected simply to defer to the purported wisdom of the legislature with respect to legislative-fact issues. The notion of assessing the soundness or reasonableness of legislative wisdom requires a critical attitude or eye. This is why reviewing judges are encouraged to consult whatever evidence seems relevant to the social, economic, and probably moral issue at hand. This book has argued that, since the inception of the Canadian *Charter of Rights and Freedoms*, Canadian judges have a mandate to hear evidence from a wide assortment of Canadian citizens in such matters; or that the consultation process in any event should not be dominated by so-called experts. The expert evidence canvassed throughout this book has clearly informed many of the landmark decisions in American and Canadian constitutional law since the turn of the century, but it has not always been trustworthy, and in many cases it has not been very edifying. As some scholars have noted, many of the sociologists and sociologically-minded jurists who were dedicated to progressivist initiatives during the New Deal were nonetheless intellectually and politically conservative. Brockman has pointed out the sexist or "androcentric" character of traditional social scientific approaches to knowledge and has discussed the implications of this for women who rely on social science evidence in court to support their claims of sexual discrimination in the workplace (Brockman 1992, 213) Herman has noted that the social sciences do indeed have their conservative sides – which have been pitted against their liberal sides in recent Canadian family law adjudication – to the detriment of homosexual couples seeking equal treatment before and under the law (Herman 1994, 143–4). And other analysts have clearly shown how the law's understanding of pornography's harmfulness over the years has been shaped as much by politics as laboratory and other kinds of empirical research (Lacombe 1994).

Where expert evidence has expressly supported a judge's or court's ultimate finding of legislative fact, it has either cloaked that finding with an aura of epistemological authority and objectivity, or it has enabled a judge or court to rationalize a finding which rests more on personal conviction and pragmatism than any genuine understanding of the complexity of the matter at hand. In the meantime, laypersons' opinions have gone mostly unheeded, as if they have nothing meaningful to contribute to intelligent public policy, unless of course they are collected and organized, and ultimately interpreted through the lens of further expert-based, social scientific investigation. If, in the context of obscenity litigation, expert evidence seems preferable to lay opinion because the Charter is meant to protect against the opinions of the so-called "moral majority," then the community standards test of obscenity should simply be abandoned. It is illogical in this context, and practically useless anyways.

The historical overview of cases presented in this book ultimately shows that legislative fact-finding in America and Canada is a misnomer, insofar as it is so much more a matter of argument proper than objective, impartial "fact" finding. At the end of the day it is simply difficult to say that, as a matter of fact, women's factory labour bears harmfully upon the female reproductive capacity in general (and for that matter, the perpetuation of the human species); that double-digit inflation is deleterious to the nation's health; that reading pornography either liberates one sexually, empowers one socially and psychologically, or causes another to hate and assault women; or that permitting physician-assisted suicide in limited circumstances will cause some people to die against their own will. From a historical point of view, the experts have not proven themselves to "know" a lot about such issues, so there is no *good* reason why judges charged with constitutional review should continue in the future to consult expertise exclusively in such matters. If and when they do seek expert assistance, they should be encouraged at least to be more critical and less deferential to the relevant expert opinion claims.

Happily, as cases such as *Hawkins* and *Sharpe*, and the British Columbia Court of Appeal decision in *Little Sister's* illustrate, some Canadian judges are beginning to scrutinize claims to expert knowledge very carefully. Remarkably, Justice Souter emphasized in *Washington v. Glucksberg* that where there is "serious factual controversy" and "little experience directly bearing on the issue" before a reviewing court, as there is with the issue of the social costs and benefits of assisted suicide laws, the court should "stay its hand," to permit further legislative consideration and experimentation.[1] This position will not likely satisfy those who, at the moment, are greatly interested in being able to exercise a right to have a deeply painful and undesirable life medically terminated, but it enables further discussion of the issue, which in turn may or may not serve the interests of these and more people in the longer term. As Dworkin observed of Souter's position in *Washington v. Glucksberg*, "Postponement is not what the philosophers' brief urges. But it would be the most statesmanlike way in which the Court could make the wrong decision" (Dworkin, Nagel et al. 1997, 42).

To use Souter's terms, one can readily say that "serious factual controversy" exists about the harmfulness and emancipatory potential of pornography, but it is more difficult to accept that American and Canadian courts have had "little experience" directly bearing on such issues. They have been receiving the opinions of a variety of experts on these issues for at least a century and it is becoming increasingly clear to some judges that the accumulated firmament of research and expert opinions in the area of pornography and media effects is indeed very frail. In light of this understanding, one can reasonably ask whether it would be "most statesmanlike," to use Dworkin's expression, for courts to stay their hands when confronted by further expertise in this area. After all, it has recently been the "wisdom" of courtroom witnesses and the critical evaluation of expert opinions by judges, not the collected views of state-sponsored or government-funded travelling committees on obscenity, that has awakened Canadian politicians and citizens to the real intellectual and constitutional problems with existing anti-obscenity laws.

This book has not concerned itself directly with the question, which institution of democratic government is more appropriately suited to shape obscenity law: the legislature or the courts? It has attempted to show that a real problem with prevailing wisdom about obscenity, even where this is informed by specialists working within a wide variety of disciplines, is that such wisdom is Socratic. Having more information and communication about erotic, pornographic, and violent imagery appears to yield more questions than conclusions about the significance of such imagery to human behaviour. Accordingly, it is not unreasonable to expect that the constitutionality of criminal laws and rules which proscribe the production and distribution of sexual and violent images will continue to be evaluated from time to time. But whether this review process is governed by the mandate of a special parliamentary or government committee, or whether it takes place occasionally in a courtroom, Frank's views about democratizing expertise and Dewey's emphasis on full participation in decision-making should be born in mind. The very process of developing sound public policy in this important aspect of human life will benefit by receiving the opinions of many persons – judges, specialists, tradespeople, and laypersons alike.

Notes

Case references in the notes are in a shortened form. The complete case reference for each case appears in the List of Cases following the Bibliography. For scholarly pupposes, the cases are listed separately for each country.

INTRODUCTION

1 *Little Sister's Book and Art Emporium* v. *Canada (Minister of Justice)*.
2 The case was *R.* v. *Sharpe*.
3 The case was *R.* v. *Butler*.

CHAPTER ONE

1 *Ritchie* v. *People*, at 457–8.
2 *State* v. *Buchanan*, Am. St. Rep. at 931.
3 *W.C. Ritchie & Co.*, at 697; see also *Lochner* v. *People of the State of New York*, at 940.
4 *State* v. *Buchanan*, at 931.
5 It is difficult to identify the exact notion or "theory" of the so-called "state" that judges had in mind when they related the police power to the sovereignty of the state. Melossi discusses some notions of the state available during this period, most notably that which Fries labelled "the German idea of the state." This notion refers to "the state whose origin is in history, whose nature is organic, whose essence is unity, whose function is the exercise of its sovereign will in law, and whose ultimate end is the moral perfection of mankind" (Fries 1973, 391, as quoted in Melossi 1990, 107). According to Melossi, this theory never became popular "outside the classrooms of the Departments of Political Science" as it was "too alien to the Lockean/common law/democratic tradition,

and wholly unable ... to give a conceptual answer to the American crises of those years" (Melossi 1990, 107). It seems, however, that some elements of the "German idea" were at play outside university departments, and inside courtroom discussions of the police power, as vestiges of Lockean notions (such as "political" power) can be gleaned in judges' discussions of the police power, as can aspects of Rousseau's understanding of the social contract, such as "unity" (ibid., 21, 27–9).

6 See *Ritchie v. People*, at 458; and *Territory v. Ah Lim*.

7 An example is *O'Gorman & Young, Inc. v. Hartford Fire Ins.*, at 257–8.

8 *Commonwealth v. Allison*, at 266.

9 See *Ex Parte Jackson*; *U.S. v. Harmon*, at 415; *Commonwealth v. Isenstadt*, at 848; and *State v. Becker*.

10 *Commonwealth v. Allison*, at 266.

11 *Ritchie v. People*, at 458.

12 *Re Jacobs*; emphasis added; see also *Lindsley v. Natural Carbonic Gas*, at 379.

13 *Ritchie v. People*, at 458.

14 Ibid.

15 *Gitlow v. New York*, at 669.

16 Ibid. at 668.

17 *Ritchie v. People*, at 459.

18 Note that Magruder saw the irrelevance of these particular materials to the case at bar. As he explains, the act in question "is not based upon the theory that the manufacture of clothing, wearing apparel, and other articles is an improper occupation for women to be engaged in ...
On the contrary, it recognizes such places as proper for them to work in by permitting their labor therein during eight hours of each day. The question here is not whether a particular employment is a proper one for the use of female labor, but the question is whether, in an employment which is conceded to be lawful in itself, and suitable for women to engage in, she shall be deprived of the right to determine for herself how many hours she can and may work during each day": *Ritchie v. People*, at 459.

19 The case was *R. v. Oakes*.

20 *R. v. Oakes*, at 138.

21 Ibid. at 139–40.

22 American commentators seem to agree, for example, that race-based legislative distinctions will normally involve such a reversal of the burden (and indeed increase in the standard) of proving constitutionality. See Monahan and Walker 1991, 587–9; Karst 1960, 87, n.44; Kohn 1960, 143.

23 Justice Laskin said this in *Reference re Anti-Inflation Act*.

24 *R. v. Butler*, S.C.R. at 502–4 [hereinafter *Butler* cited to S.C.R.].

25 Ibid. at 501–2.

26 This query is meant to recall Hogg's own prophetic concern that as long as the government's opinion regarding the risk of harm posed by some activity or another is supported by *any* expert opinion, it is difficult to see "how the government could ever lose on an issue of legislative fact" (Hogg 1976, 407).

27 See *R. v. Butler*, at 502.

28 The case was *Little Sister's Book and Art Emporium v. Canada (Minister of Justice)*. The evidentiary aspects of this case will be discussed in more detail in chapter 5. The current discussion primarily concerns the "rational basis" principle as it was applied in *Little Sister's*.

29 Of course, the much broader contention was made that Canadian customs officers had been specifically targeting gay and lesbian materials for prohibition and detention for years and that such a practice was blatantly discriminatory. The evidence brought to bear on this particular claim is only tangentially related to that of the alleged "obscenity" of the materials in question. At any rate, it is not legislative-fact evidence.

30 See Kendall 1993.

31 Portions of this expert report were read into evidence by a government lawyer at the *Little Sister's* trial. See Transcript of Proceedings at *Little Sister's* trial (25 November 1994).

32 *Little Sister's*, at 289.

33 *R. v. Sharpe*, at para.157.

34 Ibid. at para.158.

35 Ibid. at paras.182–5.

36 This book bears in mind, however, Swinton's observation that in a constitutional review the simple question of whether a plaintiff's constitutional right has been violated functions as an "adjudicative" issue (Swinton 1987).

37 Much scholarly and critical attention has been devoted to the question of when to introduce legislative-fact evidence. See, for example, Miller and Barron 1975; and Jackson 1993. This book does not address this issue directly.

38 The statement is referred to as "The Social Science Statement" and is published as "The Effects of Segregation and the Consequences of Desegregation: A Social Science Statement" (1953) 37 *Minn. L. Rev.* 427. Shortly prior to this case, expert social science testimony was heard in the very first challenge in America to the constitutionality of segregation in professional schools: *Sweatt v. Painter*. Kohn makes it clear that this testimony was meant to serve as legislative-fact evidence. Some of this testimony involved second-hand information about the psychological effects of segregated education on students generally, and some of the evidence consisted of survey evidence tending to show

the desirability of integrated schooling for educational purposes. It is difficult to tell, however, whether this evidence had any real bearing on the court's decision to uphold the impugned legislation, because no mention was made of it in the judgment (Kohn 1960, 140).

39 *Brown* v. *Board of Education*, at 494, n.11.

40 *Danson* v. *Ontario (A.G.)*, at 1099.

41 Woolhandler has also remarked that a "paradigmatic legislative fact is one that shows the general effect a legal rule will have," and that the "line between adjudicative and legislative facts is indistinct … because decisionmakers use even the most particularized facts to make legal rules" (Woolhandler 1988, 114; footnote omitted). Some of the American literature on this subject does treat legislative facts primarily in Woolhandler's "paradigmatic" way, but this is certainly not how all (and especially how Canadian) literature treats the subject. This book attempts to show how Woolhandler's "paradigmatic" legislative fact is but one of a variety of interpretations of this concept. This book also shows how, at times, the line between adjudicative and legislative facts is indeed fine in Canadian law. The difficulty of drawing a nice line between these two purportedly different kinds of fact does not affect most of the analysis of legislative facts in this book. It is highlighted, however, to undermine the argument of Monahan and Walker that legislative facts bear a certain, natural law–like character, based on their generality.

42 Frank explains that the very enterprise of social science research is concerned with the discovery of "social laws," and these laws, "like those of physics," are meant to be "formulations of 'recurrent patterns or relatively constant configurations of repeatable elements'" (Frank 1950, 209–10; footnotes omitted). So when legislative-fact evidence is tendered in court, it purports (at least implicitly) to understand some segment of society either in causal terms or in the language of probable correlations.

43 *Irwin Toy* v. *Quebec (A.G.)*, at 987.

44 Ibid. at 988.

45 See *Irwin Toy* v. *Quebec (A.G.)*, at 988, quoting *In the Matter of Children's Advertisting*, 34–5.

46 *Butler*, at 501–4.

47 This idea is also implied by the statement of the Canadian *Report on Pornography*, that "the effect of this type of [pornographic] material is to *reinforce* male-female stereotypes to the detriment of both sexes" (*MacGuigan Report* 1978, 18:4; emphasis added).

48 Woolhandler's argument is not inconsistent with Lacombe's analysis of law reform in the area of pornography in Canada (Lacombe 1994). Lacombe's discussion of the "mobilization" of science in this regard will be discussed in chapter 3.

49 Indeed, Woolhandler offers the important insight that broad consensus about legislative facts renders formal procedures for admitting legislative-fact evidence superfluous (Woolhandler 1988, 123, n.75). That is to say, if judges, social scientists, and some sizable cross-section of the general public all agree on certain legislative facts, there is no good reason why a judge should not simply take "judicial notice" of them. If there is real dissensus about relevant legislative facts, however, then presentation of legislative facts in court "will not provide 'answers' of compelling legitimacy" (ibid.). Without going into any more depth on this issue for the moment, suffice it to say that this book also attempts to demonstrate that having *more* legislative evidence in constitutional review does not necessarily improve the "accuracy" of information available to the reviewing court or enhance the "legitimacy" of the court's reviewing function.

50 Conversely, in cases involving a "strict standard" of judicial scrutiny of legislative objectives and means, Monahan and Walker prefer to abandon the language of "presumption of *un*constitutionality" in favour of "assumption of unconstitutionality," and the language of "proof" in favour of "argument" (Monahan and Walker 1991, 587–9).

51 Note also that, in their analysis of prior research into the harmful "effects" of violent pornography, Fisher and Barak remark, "Violent pornography by definition portrays the utility and normativeness of sexual violence against women and as such *might be expected* to foster anti-woman thoughts, attitudes, and acts (Fisher and Barak 1991, 67; emphasis added). Regardless of the varying conclusions obtained from research in this area, Fisher and Barak's remark makes it clear that violent pornography is effectively or operationally *assumed*, not demonstrated, to be a causal factor in this research.

52 At some point, for example, in her linguistic explanation that "a + b" is 'identical' to "b + a," the math teacher will be forced to say, "this is just how we talk," which is an ungrounded behavioural explanation. In other words, if no one in the relevant community of language-users can agree on the meaning of *is, is the same as, is equal to,* or *is identical to,* then it is a wonder that people in that community can talk sensibly to one another at all.

53 Dworkin has in mind here the New York State Task Force on Life and the Law's 1994 report entitled *When Death is Sought: Assisted Suicide and Euthanasia in the Medical Context.* In *Vacco* v. *Quill,* Chief Justice Rehnquist addressed the question of whether or not a distinction that is made by medical professionals – that is, a distinction between assisted suicide and the medical practice of withdrawing or withholding treatment – should also be given effect in law. Although the New York State Task Force report observed that this distinction is consistently made by professional organizations, Rehnquist cited the

same report as supporting the view that "there are differences of opinion within the medical profession on this question" (*Vacco* v. *Quill*, at 842, fn.6).

54 "Brandeis-style briefs" refers to the kind of legal brief that Louis D. Brandeis employed in the case *Muller* v. *Oregon*, which is discussed in chapter 3. This is a legal brief that contains a variety of empirical research conclusions, statistical data, historical information, as well as government committee report findings, to support a lawyer's argument in a constitutional review case.

55 See Transcript of Proceedings at *Little Sister's* trial (13 October 1994, 27).

56 Although Paciocco is concerned here with the use of "social framework" evidence in non-constitutional litigation (such as battered-wife or repressed-memory syndrome evidence presented in criminal trials), the logic of his observation extends nicely to the use of legislative-fact evidence in constitutional adjudication. In this context, the concern becomes greater, because the policy decisions which judges make here directly affect the constitutional rights and freedoms of all citizens. This idea will be explained shortly.

57 Paciocco makes this argument in regard specifically to "social framework" evidence.

58 Of course, judges can become educated in social science principles and methodologies, but this suggestion risks elevating the importance of the social sciences within the legislative fact-finding process to an even higher position than they already occupy. Moreover, it is reasonable to observe that many judges are generally busy enough with developments in substantive and procedural law: requiring them to learn other disciplinary knowledges is impractical.

59 Cahn comments, "In the last two decades, many Brandeis briefs have been conspicuously vulnerable in respect of statistical method, rationality of inferences from assembled data, adequacy of sampling, and failure to allow for – or to disclose – negative instances. Perhaps their quality will improve with a more critical attitude on the judges' part" (Cahn 1955, 154).

CHAPTER TWO

1 In a sense the role of this special jury resembles that of the contemporary expert sociologist or researcher who Monahan and Walker believe should be called to court to apply the findings of the sociological evidence contained in Brandeis-style briefs (Monahan and Walker 1989, 471).

2 Landsman observes more precisely that medical professionals had forged an economic monopoly of medical services early in the nineteenth century (Landsman 1995, 151).

3 See, for example, McLachlin 1993, 4 (citing Taylor 1906); and Phipson 1921, 386.

4 *Phipson on Evidence*, 6th ed., quoted in *Brownlee* v. *Hand Firework*, at 653.

5 Of course, this discussion is not suggesting that the presentation of legislative facts or social science evidence by experts was an issue in the English and American courts at this time. The focus here is on the attitude judges bore toward experts generally.

6 This so-called *Frye* test was articulated in 1923, in *Frye* v. *United States*, at 1014.

7 Landsman also observes that shortly before the *Frye* ruling the administration of justice had been "embarrassed" by "a series of highly charged criminal cases in which clashing expert views about relatively novel questions of forensic science" were presented (Landsman 1995, 152–3).

8 See Nowlin 2001.

9 *R.* v. *Mohan*, C.C.C. at 411.

10 Herman is less categorical and more skeptical in this regard. She proposes that judges respond to experts in different ways but concludes, generally, that experts are unlikely to 'convert' judges who already "bring to court the politics and vested interests that will lead them to certain decisions and not others" (Herman 1994, 140).

11 See *R.* v. *D.(D.)* (2000), at 61.

12 See *Texada Mines* v. *A.G.B.C.*

13 Miller and Barron distinguish this issue of "legitimacy" from that of the "separation of powers" between government and the judiciary (Miller and Barron 1975, 1228). They note that, although "[h]istory and long-continued practice" have conferred some kind of "legitimate" power on the judiciary to resolve disputes concerning "the rights and duties of persons ... either against each other or against the state," the "legitimacy of the Supreme Court's stating norms of general applicability" is "still controversial" (1228–9; footnotes omitted). Certainly in Canada this issue is very much alive: see, for example, Hutchinson and Monahan 1987.

14 For Woolhandler, the number of identifiable socio-economic interests affected by a piece of legislation may be so great as to force the reviewing court into some kind of "pragmatic balancing" of such interests or "ad hoc balancing of the effects of legal rules" (Woolhandler 1988, 124–5). Woolhandler believes otherwise underrepresented interests would receive "better protection from principles and precedent" (125).

15 It does, however, share Woolhandler's concern that, by expanding the scope of "represented" interests as far as possible, reviewing courts may be seen fairly to be duplicating the legislative process, in which case

either the legislative or the judicial function becomes superfluous here (Woolhandler 1988, 125).

16 Hogg provides an excellent discussion of the attempts to prove legislative facts associated with double-digit inflation in the 1976 *Anti-Inflation Reference* in Hogg 1976.

17 It is important to note here that determinations of legislative facts in American and Canadian constitutional cases (including references) are not made by juries but only by judges. In this sense there is a structurally entrenched elitism in Canada's constitutional review process, because the layperson does not have an opportunity to express her or his opinion regarding the legislative-fact evidence presented to the court. In chapter 3, an example demonstrates that this lack of opportunity among laypersons to determine legislative-fact issues in Canadian obscenity cases poses a serious problem for the so-called public accountability of this process. The resolution of such cases has become dependent on some measure of "community standards of tolerance," yet it is a community of highly educated professionals, not laypersons, that decides this measure.

18 Frank himself became the General Counsel of the Agricultural Adjustment Administration around this time (Melossi 1991, 130).

19 The Schwendingers refer to Jefferson's concept of democracy as "patrician," and perhaps more importantly, "elitist" and undemocratic (Schwendinger and Schwendinger 1974, 466). Lasch also discusses the notion that the "Jeffersonian" tradition of democracy was modelled upon a principle of "aristocracy of talent" (Lasch 1995, 74–6).

20 Just a couple of years before Lippmann published *Public Opinion*, E.C. Hayes also commented on the potential for American public education and the popular press to become "propaganda" vehicles (Weatherly 1920, 36). In order to minimize this possibility, Hayes urged that these two institutions "be most zealously purified, and strengthened, and defended by all those who share in that eternal vigilance which is the price of liberty" (ibid.).

21 Of course, as Lasch observes, Lippmann's implied distinction between "fact" and "opinion" had already come under attack from other philosophers (Lasch 1991, 365); chapter 1 of this book demonstrated that such an attack is applicable to the North American legal realm. For the moment it is more important to understand Lippmann's broader argument for technocracy within liberal society.

22 Years later the American judge Jerome Frank made a similar observation in his own terms. His words are well worth noting, mainly because they so eloquently relate the language and concern of Lippmann to that of Dewey, who will be discussed shortly. Frank stated, "Inescapably, we are confined in our 'private' human world, our sub-universe.

Conceivably, we might be able to merge the 'private' worlds of individual men, or groups of men, into a 'public' human world. Perhaps some day we can thus achieve such a 'public' world to this extent: that men everywhere on this planet will confront experience with the combined understanding of our ablest scientists and our wisest philosophers and poets. But it is not conceivable that we can ever rid ourselves of all our human limitations. A thoroughly 'public' world, in that sense, lies beyond our power. The ultimate perfection of our capacities would still leave us provincials" (Frank 1949, 11).

23 Lord Devlin of Great Britain also presumed the jury to be an ideal vehicle for ascertaining the average moral sensibility of a given society. Referring to the legal concept of the "reasonable man," he stated, "I should like to call him the man in the jury box, for the moral judgment of society must be something about which any twelve men or women drawn at random might *after discussion be expected to be unanimous*" (Devlin 1965, 15; emphasis added). Of course, the twelve people who comprise the jury today are not "drawn at random" but selected according to features that lawyers believe will assist their cases, such as sex, physical appearance, occupation, etc.

24 This logic explains the enthusiasm of some social scientists and lawyers for social science survey evidence in matters of community morals, as chapter 4 makes clear.

25 Mouffe borrows the notion of "constitutive outside" from Jacques Derrida (Mouffe 1995, 261).

26 As Melossi clearly shows, Dewey's understanding of the importance of full and effective communication to democracy had firm roots in Cooley's *Social Organization*. Melossi paraphrases this work as saying, "Democratic society could be organized only by virtue of the diffusion and spread of communication." Melossi explains further, "That such communication had to be free, had to be encouraged, and not censored, was due, according to Cooley's analysis, to the very diversity among individuals, and especially among the groups, that made up society" (Melossi 1990, 114).

27 "Republican/communitarian" and "liberal" conceptions of citizenship are not the only existing alternatives to Mouffe's preferred concept. Lasch puts forward a view of citizenship consistent with a "populist" vision of democracy, in direct contrast to that of liberal and republican/communitarian ideals (Lasch 1995, 92–114; Lasch 1991, 366–7).

28 Further support for this view may be gleaned in an observation made by Alan Ryan, who, in the course of reviewing Lasch's posthumously published *Women and the Common Life*, remarked, "Robert Westbrook, a younger colleague of Lasch's, persuaded, or half-persuaded, Lasch at the end of his life that Dewey was better understood as a theorist of

participatory democracy than a defender of a scientific smoothing out of social tensions and conflicts" (Ryan 1997, 48). Perhaps one major difference between Mouffe's and Dewey's visions of democratic citizenship lies in Dewey's uncritical acceptance of the notion of a substantive common good (Dewey 1927, 149) compared to Mouffe's desire to abandon talk of "a substantive and unique vision of the common good" (Mouffe 1992a, 29) in favour of what she calls "allegiance to the constitutive ethico-political principles of modern democracy: liberty and equality for all" (30). Despite Mouffe's efforts to distinguish allegiance to freedom and equality from the kind of substantive good imagined by Dewey, there is, however, very little difference between the two thinkers' positions. This is because the distinction drawn by Mouffe between "common good" and "common bond" or "public concern" (in the form of allegiance to the principles of freedom and equality) cannot ultimately be made clear. Mouffe's "public concern" that others be treated as free and equal citizens in all facets of social life is entirely compatible with a substantive "common good" that embodies the same principles. Again, Dewey's reference to a common "good" recognizes the fact of dissenters – or what Mouffe might call members of the "constitutive outside" (ibid.; Mouffe 1995, 261). Yet Dewey is adamant that the essence of democracy lies in finding some universally accepted means by which all individuals, whether on the "inside" or "outside," can "bring into being a greater liberty to share in other associations." This view, which eschews the 'cramping' and 'depressing' effects of hegemony regarding one's available "modes of association" (Dewey 1927, 194), is entirely consistent with Mouffe's concern that "relations of domination" be "challenged everywhere" (Mouffe 1992a, 32).

29 See also Lasch 1995, 170–2.

30 For his part, Lasch paints a particularly dark portrait of the role of formalized knowledge and technical competence in current "democratic" society. He refers to the "professional and managerial elites" of contemporary America, who can be said to form a "new class" only "in the sense that their livelihoods rest not so much on the ownership of property as on the manipulation of information and professional expertise (Lasch 1995, 34). Moreover, although these elites may be seen to push "relentlessly [for] a program of liberal reforms," they hold a "continuing fascination with the capitalist market" and maintain a "frenzied search for profits" (34–5).

CHAPTER THREE

1 The case was *People* v. *Muller*.

2 Ibid. at 638.

3 The case was *United States* v. *Harmon*.

4 *United States* v. *Harmon*, at 414.

5 The *Hicklin* formulation states that "the test of obscenity is this, whether the tendency of the matter charged as obscene is to deprave and corrupt those whose minds are open to such immoral influences, and into whose hands a publication of this sort may fall": *R.* v. *Hicklin*, at 369.

6 *United States* v. *Harmon*, at 417–18.

7 *People* v. *Eastman*, at 463.

8 *People* v. *Muller*, at 637.

9 See, for example, *People* v. *Eastman*, at 463, as per O'Brien J.; *Konda* v. *United States*, at 93; *United States* v. *Kennerley*, at 121.

10 *United States* v. *Kennerly*, at 121.

11 Ibid.

12 *United States* v. *Harmon*, at 418.

13 See, for example, *Rosen* v. *United States*, at 610, per Harlan, J.; and *United States* v. *Dennett*, at 568, per Augustus N. Hand, C.J. This view is contradicted by Judge Baker in *Konda* v. *United States*.

14 Later Pound raised the same concern by referring to the want of "team play" between "jurisprudence and the other social sciences" before World War I and in the early 1940s (Pound 1945, 334).

15 See also Geis 1964, 273–6.

16 Ward also espoused a highly technocratic vision in his *Applied Sociology*, which was published in 1906. There he contemplated a legislative body either composed entirely of trained sociologists, or at least informed completely by these sociologists (Ward 1906, 338–9; Geis 1964, 274).

17 Pound's own "theory of interests" nevertheless eschewed "sociological questionnaires and other methods of attitude measurement" in favour of "the assertions that persons make in legal proceedings and press in legislative proposals" (Geis 1964, 280).

18 See also Landsman 1995, 151–2; and Freckleton 1987, 233.

19 Lasch writes that Ross's *Social Control* "celebrated the impending rise to power of the intellectuals as a class. Ross based his prediction of the intellectuals' increasing influence on the complexity of society, which gave rise, [Ross] argued, to a demand for specialized knowledge that was greater than the public schools could meet. The result would be to widen the gap between higher education and public education" (Lasch 1965, 173–4).

20 *Ives* v. *South Buffalo Ry.*, at 287.

21 *Lochner* v. *New York*, at 75.

22 Holmes's critique is actually aimed at the suggestion that the application of general propositions to specific facts by judges is "rational."

He says, "General propositions do not decide concrete cases. The decision will depend on a judgment or intuition more subtle than any articulate major premise" (*Lochner* v. *New York*, at 76). In this sense Holmes directly anticipates the so-called "Legal Realism" of Justice Jerome Frank, which will be discussed later.

23 One possible explanation for the general reluctance of lawyers to embrace the emergent sociological wisdom of the day is provided by Lippmann. He proposes that, in contradistinction to the reliability of knowledge obtained in natural scientific research, social science knowledge is almost inherently unreliable, and that this is a matter of public knowledge. Thus he posited the "man of affairs," who observes "that the social scientist knows only from the outside what he knows, in part at least, from the inside, recognizing that the social scientist's hypothesis is not in the nature of things susceptible of laboratory proof, and that verification is possible only in the 'real' world, has developed a rather low opinion of social scientists who do not share his views of public policy" (Lippmann 1922, 235).

24 The case was *Muller* v. *Oregon*.

25 *Muller* v. *Oregon*, at 556.

26 Ibid. at 555; emphasis added.

27 Brewer refers to women's role in the "struggle for subsistence" at least three times on a single page of his reasons for judgment: see *Muller* v. *Oregon*, ibid. at 556.

28 Ibid.

29 The case was *W. C. Ritchie & Co.* v. *Wayman*.

30 *W. C. Ritchie & Co.*, at 701.

31 The case was *United States* v. *One Book Called "Ulysses,"* [hereinafter cited as *Ulysses Trial*].

32 See also Vanderham 1998, 89.

33 Recall that the legal test for determining obscenity at this point in American history was whether the publication in question was obscene according to the "average" reader.

34 Vanderham provides the list of Ernst's arguments for dismissing the case against *Ulysses* at Vanderham 1998, 95. Vanderham explains how some of these arguments were informed by Joyce's new "schema" at Vanderham 1998, 80-1.

35 *Ulysses Trial* at 184.

36 The case was *United States* v. *One Book Entitled Ulysses by James Joyce* [hereinafter referred to as *One Book Entitled Ulysses*].

37 In essence, Judge Augustus Hand reformulated the *Hicklin* test for obscenity, which was the effect of any isolated passage on a particular reader. He substituted the effect of the whole work on the average reader, taking into consideration its theme: *One Book Entitled Ulysses*, at 707-8.

38 Ibid. at 711.

39 Ibid. at 709.

40 *United States* v. *Levine*, at 157.

41 Ibid. at 158. Rembar observes that Learned Hand's preference for
"printed critical opinion over live critics subject to cross-examination"
was "peculiar," in the sense that this suggested approach to the measuring of artistic merit was cited only once before the publication of D.H.
Lawrence's *Lady Chatterly's Lover* was litigated in *Grove Press* v.
Christenberry, and, by 1968, had not been cited again (Rembar 1968, 79).

42 *United States* v. *Levine*, at 158.

43 See, for example, Palys 1992, 196–201.

44 Rose argues that social psychology became increasingly important to
the American government after WW I and through WW II, mainly
because this discipline revealed how group loyalty among soldiers
was crucial to maintaining the desire of individual soldiers to fight,
even when such individuals expressed no committment to the objectives of the war itself (Rose 1989, 40–52).

45 See also Geis 1964, 274.

46 Even eugenics found utility in psychology at this time. As Rose explains,
"Eugenics sought a link between the biological, heritable, variable basis
of mental characteristics and the criteria of social worth. This link ...
was to be forged by psychologists, who measured the senses and related
these measurements with social judgments" (Rose 1989, 138).

47 See *Parmelee* v. *United States*, at 732.

48 Ibid.

49 Ibid.

50 Ibid. at 737.

51 Ibid. at 735.

52 Ibid. at 735–6, n.25.

53 *Commonwealth* v. *Isenstadt*, at 849.

54 Unfortunately, it is not possible to obtain transcripts of the trial
proceedings in this case, which would indicate precisely who said what.
At least the reasons for judgment here provide an idea of what was
said generally and of the kind of experts who appeared to contribute
to the evidence.

55 Indeed, the charge assumes that youths would somehow be exposed to
the impugned book. Qua proposed that young people would be a substantial part of the public who would read *Strange Fruit*, but Justice
Lummus disagreed (*Commonwealth* v. *Isenstadt*, at 845, 850).

56 Ibid. at 848–9. Of course, it should be noted that Qua himself presumes to know much about "community" or public opinion *and* about
literature and psychiatry. Furthermore, Qua makes his observation from
the point of view of a highly educated person, specifically a judge, and
in this sense acts as an elite.

57 Qua also states this "probable effect" measure as the proper test (ibid. at 849).
58 Ibid.
59 Ibid.
60 Ibid.
61 Although Frank is clearly associated with the birth of Legal Realism, it is interesting that in his preface to the sixth printing of *Law and the Modern Mind*, he prefers to describe the so-called realists' approach to legal decision-making as a kind of skepticism, especially "constructive skepticism" (Frank 1963, ix). It is perhaps more noteworthy that he distinguishes between kinds of legal skeptics, mainly between "rule skeptics" and "fact skeptics," and labels himself a "fact skeptic." For Frank, it is impossible (and thus futile) to attempt to predict the course of future legal decisions because the facts on which any given dispute turns are subject to an enormous number of psychological and physical idiosyncracies – that is, on the part of judges, juries, and witnesses (xi–xiv). This observation is directly relevant to the role of expert witnesses who, as human beings, are not immune from the very kind of idiosyncracies, prejudices, and biases considered by Frank.
62 From a taxonomical point of view, it is interesting that Frank saw the development of the social sciences as but "phases of cultural anthropology," insofar as the former produced generalizations relating to "the customs, group beliefs, mores, [and] folkways" of different peoples (Frank 1955, 10; Frank 1950, 210).
63 Despite the reference to Czechoslovakia in the title of the impugned book, Judge Frank believes its various "waggish tales" to be in fact "American-made or shared smoking room jests and stories, obscene or offensive enough by any refined standards and only saved, if at all, by reason of being both dull and well known" (*Roth* v. *Goldman*, at 789).
64 Ibid. at 792.
65 Ibid. In *Censorship: The Search for the Obscene*, Ernst and Schwartz mention that Frank was concerned that the First Amendment allegedly permitted exceptions for prosecution of obscenity in the absence of evidence that exposure to objectionable writing could lead to socially injurious or immoral conduct (Ernst and Schwartz 1964, 202). Frank reviewed the state of the law and discovered that the United States Supreme Court had not yet formally addressed itself to the First Amendment issue. Thus the Supreme Court decision in *Roth* v. *Goldman* addresses this issue directly.
66 *Roth* v. *Goldman*, at 792; footnote omitted.
67 Ibid. at 792, n.17. See also West 1972.
68 Ibid. 793, n.17.
69 Ibid. at 793, nn.18, 19. For a discussion of the sociological surveys, see Alpert 1938.

70 *Roth* v. *Goldman*, n.19.

71 The test for obscenity at this point has become the *likely* behavioural effects on the reader. Frank points out, however, that American law does not require "direct proof" in this respect. This is significant insofar as it is the same principle that the Canadian judiciary applied as late as 1992, in the landmark obscenity case, *R.* v. *Butler*, which will be discussed in the next chapter.

72 *Roth* v. *Goldman*, at 795.

73 Ibid. at 796.

74 Ibid. at 795, 796; footnote omitted.

75 *State* v. *Becker*, at 287.

76 Ibid.; emphasis added.

77 *State* v. *Becker*, at 287; emphasis added.

78 According to this rule, an expert is not entitled, for example, to say whether a particular book is *in fact* obscene, because that is the judge's or jury's responsibility. In this context, a finding that the book in question is in fact obscene provides the "ultimate" fact because it directly informs the "ultimate" legal question: Is the book obscene *in law*?

79 *State* v. *Becker*, ibid. at 287.

80 See *Roth* v. *United States*.

81 *Smith* v. *California*, 4 L. Ed. 2d 205 at 215, 218–19.

82 See *United States* v. *Klaw*, at 165–6 and *United States* v. *Palladino*, at 72–3. For a discussion of these cases, see McGaffey 1974.

83 *Paris Adult Theatre I* v. *Slaton* at 56, n.6.

84 *Miller* v. *California*, at 24; emphasis added.

85 *United States* v. *Groner*, at 579.

86 *Miller* v. *California*, at 24.

87 The case was *Pope* v. *Illinois*.

88 *United States* v. *Groner*, at 587; footnotes omitted.

89 See also Foster 1984 for considerably more material in this respect.

90 See Devlin 1965 and Hart 1963.

91 This approach is based on the concept of extended judicial notice, which is aptly summarized in Kiselbach 1995.

CHAPTER FOUR

1 *Conway* v. *The King*, at 192, 195.

2 Ibid. at 195.

3 *R.* v. *American News*, at 161.

4 Ibid. at 170.

5 Ibid. at 171.

6 Ibid.; emphasis added.

7 The case was *Grove Press* v. *Christenberry*. See also Rembar 1968.

8 In the early stages of interpreting this law, the first question seemed to require some kind of qualitative assessment of the degree to which sex is exploited in the publication in question. The second question appeared to demand a more quantitative response: one that counts how many pages of the book involve the "exploitation of sex," how many develop character, how many advance plot, etc., until it can be said that, at the end of the book, many pages exploited sex (in which case the exploitation of sex was a "dominant characteristic" of that book) or relatively few pages exploited sex (in which case the exploitation of sex was not a dominant part of the book).

9 *R. v. Brodie*, C.C.C. at 179 [hereinafter *Brodie* cited to C.C.C.]. It is interesting to note how Judson's literary experts were considered competent to address the issue of "artistic merit" insofar as it was relevant to a book's "dominant characteristic," whereas Judge Woolsey's literary "assessors" in the American *Ulysses Trial* were considered competent to address the issue of artistic merit insofar as it bore upon the likely psychological and behavioural reaction of a reader of Joyce's *Ulysses*.

10 *Brodie*, at 180.

11 Ibid. at 181.

12 *People v. Muller*, at 637–8.

13 In 1936 Judge Learned Hand suggested that literary reviews are more reliable than the oral opinions of expert witnesses at trial, because the former "[do] not lead far afield and [are] rationally helpful" (*United States v. Levine*, at 158).

14 *Brodie*, at 180.

15 From here on, this book refers to evidence of book sales, movie ticket sales, art gallery attendance numbers, etc., as "marketplace" evidence. Readership or marketplace evidence has been and continues to be heard and admitted regarding community standards to the present day. Justice Cole of the Ontario Provincial Court articulated the state of the jurisprudence in this area well when he remarked, "there is a very substantial and sustained market for explicit sex videos. While the case law has decided that popularity cannot be determinative of legality, it is certainly one factor which I should consider in my judgment" (*R. v. Ronish*, O.J. at 11). Perhaps one of the greatest problems faced by judges who are presented with this kind of marketplace evidence is what social scientists might call the representativeness of the sample involved. In 1993, Justice Paris expressed concern that the distribution and sales of a book entitled *Sex*, which were introduced into court as an indicator of community standards regarding depictions of lesbian, and possibly sadomasochistic, sexuality constituted "too small [a sample] to be a reliable indication of the public's reaction to its distribution": *R. v. Scythes*.

16 It is also important to note that, as late as *Brodie* and for a short while afterward, many judges gave very little, if any, weight to any evidence beyond the literal borders of the book or frames of the pictures in question. By promulgating the notion that the book or picture speaks "for itself," judges have effectively arrogated to themselves not only the capacity to determine community standards but also the competence of experienced literary critics.

17 This is not to say that Edinborough did not comment on the literary merit of the magazines in question. Justice Freedman relates, the witness "described [the magazines] as flippant and saucy, and noted that when they dealt with sex they treated it in a normal and not perverted fashion" (*R. v. Dominion News & Gifts*, C.C.C. at 118) [hereinafter *Dominion News & Gifts* cited to C.C.C.].

18 Justice Schultz emphasized that Edinborough's testimony informed the "*general reaction* of Canadian metropolitan communities to magazines such as Dude and Escapade," although the proper issue before the court was the reaction of the community to the specific volumes of the two magazines in question (ibid. at 114).

19 Ibid. at 108. Edinborough's testimony was not obviously entirely "general," as reflected in the synoptic observation by Justice Freedman that Edinborough found the magazines in question "flippant and saucy."

20 Ibid. at 114.

21 It is also possible that, prior to testifying at the *Dominion News & Gifts* trial, Edinborough gave a single talk on the subject of indecent literature in Winnipeg. See *Dominion News & Gifts*, at 119.

22 *Dominion News & Gifts*, at 118.

23 Ibid. at 121.

24 Ibid.

25 Ibid. at 113, 116.

26 Ibid. at 116.

27 See, for example, *Parmelee v. United States*. In this case, Justice Miller took judicial notice of obscenity, yet articulated the desirability of "expert opinions of psychologists and sociologists" on this point (*Parmelee*, at 732). Justice Vinson criticized his brother's faith in such experts, however, reminding the public that "social scientists do not always reflect, or even intend to reflect, the sentiment of the community" (at 741).

28 *R. v. Cameron*, at 285.

29 Ibid. at 305. Justice Aylesworth was also clearly alert to the importance of civil liberties, but unlike Justice Laskin, he was cautious about granting an artist too much "licence," especially where doing so would clearly offend the broader community standard (ibid. at 288–9). Curiously, the fact that Laskin concerns himself here with artistic endeavour conducted

primarily (if not exclusively) in "serious vein" suggests that he is not prepared to extend the same freedom of expression to artists who are less "seriously" committed. Rembar highlights a similar problem with the trial of *Lady Chatterley's Lover* in America, when he recounts how Cowley, the literary expert called on behalf of the plaintiff, *Grove Press*, "was impelled [via cross-examination] to say that the degree of freedom we were advocating should be reserved for men of Lawrence's caliber" (Rembar 1968, 87).

30 *Cameron*, at 305.

31 Ibid. at 304.

32 Ibid. at 305.

33 *R. v. Great West News, Mantell and Mitchell*, C.C.C. at 315–16 [hereinafter *Great West News* cited to C.C.C.].

34 Ibid. at 316. The reasons for judgment do not indicate precisely where the Child Guidance Clinic is located.

35 Ibid.

36 The trial judge may have simply rejected the relevance of psychological and behavioural evidence here because the aforementioned British *Hicklin* test of obscenity, which invited some measurement of the tendency of a work to "deprave" or "corrupt" its readership, had been strictly superceded by the new Canadian law which focused on the "undueness" of "sexual exploitation" in an impugned work (*Great West News*, at 316). It is also plausible that the trial judge did not accept, for whatever reason, that a psychiatrist was technically trained to express an opinion about such a particular matter.

37 See *Roth v. Goldman*, at 792ff.

38 *Roth v. Goldman*, at 792–3, n.17.

39 Around this time in England, defence lawyers were attempting to introduce psychological and behavioural expert evidence to the effect that a reader's exposure to certain kinds of shocking images or explicit scenes of depravity and degradation could actually repel or discourage that reader from committing the acts portrayed in the offending scenes: see, for example, *R. v. Calder & Boyars Ltd.* and *R. v. Anderson*.

40 *Brodie*, at 186.

41 Fisher and Barak cite various scholarly and clinical-based publications appearing in this field around the early 1970s in America (Fisher and Barak 1991, 69).

42 See also McGaffey 1974.

43 *Cameron*, at 305.

44 *Great West News*, at 308.

45 At the Manitoba Court of Appeal, however, Dickson noted that Rich should have been allowed to testify as an expert in the field of pornography, but that the trial judge's error in this regard was fairly

inconsequential because "Dr Rich testifed at length on matters of which only an expert would testify": *Prairie Schooner News*, ibid. at 267.

46 Kohn provides a sample bibliography of several law journal articles published on this point between 1953 and 1960 (Kohn 1960, 137, n.2).

47 *R. v. Prairie Schooner News Ltd. and Powers*, C.C.C. at 260 [hereinafter *Prairie Schooner News* cited to C.C.C.].

48 Ibid. at 265.

49 Ibid.

50 Ibid.

51 Ibid. at 266.

52 The Alberta case was *R. v. Pipeline News*.

53 *R. v. Times Square Cinema*, C.C.C. at 235 [hereinafter *Times Square Cinema* cited to C.C.C.].

54 Ibid. at 240–1.

55 Ibid. at 235.

56 Chief Justice Gale criticized the "objectivity" of the respondents, claiming that they were motivated to see the film in the first place by its apparently "sensual" nature. Lamont argues that this logic recalls an outmoded legal test (or standard) for obscenity which was concerned primarily with the influence of obscene publications or images on people "whose minds are open to such immoral influences, and into whose hands" such publications might fall (Lamont 1973, 152). See also *R. v. Hicklin*, at 369.

57 This point is made by Bullough's own observation that Alfred Kinsey's massive study of male sexuality (Kinsey 1948) was criticized at the time because it relied exclusively on volunteers. These participants could be viewed as especially uninhibited, and therefore unrepresentative of the American public at large. Although Bullough concedes the possibility of "some truth" in this charge, he does explain how Kinsey attempted to ameliorate the problem of representativeness in his study (Bullough 1994, 176).

58 *R. v. Pipeline News*, at 79.

59 Ibid. at 81–4.

60 Ibid. at 84–5.

61 Ibid. at 85.

62 Ibid. at 86.

63 Ibid.

64 See *R. v. Ronish*, which will be discussed in chapter 5.

65 *Cameron*, at 305.

66 *R. v. Ramsingh*, at 240.

67 See also Roberts 1996.

68 *Cameron*, at 285.

69 *Re Regina and Provincial News*, at 208.

70 Ibid. at 209.

71 R. v. *Odeon Morton Theatres*, at 197. Psychiatric and psychological testimony pertaining to the harmfulness of exposure to such graphic images as presented in *Last Tango in Paris* was notably absent in *Odeon Morton Theatres*. This is probably because, as already suggested, the broader social scientific community at the time could not conclude that such exposure presented any real personal and societal danger.

72 R. v. *Odeon Morton Theatres*, at 203.

73 The Manitoba Provincial Court saw and heard numerous expert literary opinions, including those from Chester Duncan, a professor of English at the University of British Columbia and CBC film critic; Leslie Wedman, a film critic; Alice Poyser, a CBC film critic and commentator; John Hirsch, a theatre director; Elmer Reimer, a professor of English at the University of Winnipeg; J. Pungente, a Jesuit priest and chairman of the Manitoba Film Classifcation Board; Omri J. Silverthorne, a chairman of the Film Censor Board of the Province of Ontario; Gerald Pratley, a film critic; and A.C. Forrest, a minister of the United Church of Canada and editor of *United Church Observer*.

74 *Odeon Morton Theatres*, at 195, as per Justice Freedman.

75 Ibid. at 204.

76 Ibid. at 192.

77 Edinborough was asked, "Does Tango endow and glorify sex, and, in fact, glory in it?" He replied, "I don't think you could say that. I think it's concerned with it and concerned with it at various levels, but glorying in it just for the sake of it, no. It is all part of the psychological torment of the two characters involved" (ibid. at 195).

78 Ibid. at 205.

79 Ibid. at 194.

80 *Re Regina and Provincial News*, at 209.

81 *Prairie Schooner News*, at 254.

82 *Odeon Morton Theatres*, at 196.

83 Ibid. at 200.

84 "Unusual" is a word Justice Monnin uses in his paraphrase of Forrest's testimony (ibid. at 203).

85 Ibid. at 204.

86 As regards the Canadian context see, for example, Lacombe 1994. It should be noted that, although the *Charter of Rights and Freedoms* came into effect in 1982, the equality provisions did not come into effect until 1985.

87 R. v. *Doug Rankine Co. and Act III Video Productions*, at 58.

88 *Doug Rankine Co.*, at 58.

89 Ibid. at 57–8.

90 Ibid.

91 Ibid. at 57. It is also possible in this regard that Borins was concerned with Walker's admission at trial that the National Film Board documentary film *Not a Love Story* influenced her own views on pornography (ibid.).

92 Ibid. at 58.

93 Ibid.

94 *R. v. Arnold*, at 19. This case will be discussed in chapter 6, which addresses expert evidence in indecency proceedings.

95 Transcript of Proceedings at *Little Sister's* trial (26 October 1994, 27). These proceedings are discussed in detail in the next chapter.

96 The kind of disciplinary group bias contemplated here is made obvious in *R. v. Fringe Product* (to be discussed in detail below), wherein Judge Charron recalls social science opinions presented by groups such as the Canadian Psychological Association or behavioural scientists (*R. v. Fringe Product*, at 437).

97 Borins states in this respect, "Of course, Mrs. Rowlands did not conduct any surveys. However, as an elected alderman in the City of Toronto and a member of various committees, organizations and boards in Metropolitan Toronto she had the opportunity to meet and speak to many people and is in a very good position to offer her opinion with respect to community standards in Metropolitan Toronto" (*Doug Rankine Co.*, at 58). The hearsay nature and admissibility of opinion evidence deriving from a witness's participation in such "committees, organizations and boards" is addressed in the very recent *Little Sister's* case, which is discussed in greater detail in the next chapter.

98 Ibid. at 59.

99 See Kiselbach 1995, 10.

100 At the conclusion of his judgment, Borins says that "films which consist substantially or partially of scenes which portray violence and cruelty in conjunction with sex, particularly where the performance of indignities *degrade and dehumanize* the people upon whom they are performed, exceed the level of community tolerance" (*Doug Rankine Co.*, at 70; emphasis added). Borins also finds that "the degree of explicitness of the sexual acts" contained in some of the other films at issue factored into the "undueness" equation, but as will be made evident below, the "degradation and dehumanization" test or principle has become the dominant conceptual threshold against which all pornographic materials are measured in Canadian anti-obscenity cases.

101 See Judge Borins's dicta, *Doug Rankine Co.*, at 65–6.

102 The case was *R. v. Wagner*.

103 *R. v. Wagner*, at para. 69.

104 Ibid. at para. 60.

105 Ibid. at para. 80.

106 Ibid. at para. 67.

107 See, for example, Malamuth and Check 1981; and Malamuth and Donnerstein 1982.

108 *R. v. Towne Cinema Theatres*, C.C.C. at 202 [hereinafter *Towne Cinema Theatres* cited to C.C.C.].

109 Ibid. at 216.

110 Ibid. at 209-10.

111 Ibid. at 210. By 1978, the Ontario Court of Appeal had already held that expert evidence regarding community standards was not necessary and was not a matter of fact that the Crown was obliged to prove in an anti-obscenity prosecution: see *R. v. Sudbury News Service*.

112 *Towne Cinema Theatres*, at 211.

113 Ibid. at 212.

114 Ibid. at 221.

115 Ibid. at 223.

116 In Ontario, for example, the case was *R. v. Metro News*. In Manitoba the case was *R. v. Arena Recreations (Toronto)*.

117 *R. v. Arena Recreations (Toronto)*, at 129.

118 Ibid. at 124-5.

119 Respectively, these are the *Attorney General's Commission on Pornography: Final Report* (1986), *Report of the Special Committee on Pornography and Prostitution*, Vol. 1 (1985), and the *Report of the Joint Selection Committee on Video Material in Australia* (1988).

120 These include James Check, an associate professor of psychology at York University, Edward Donnerstein, a professor of psychology at the University of California, and Taylor Buckner, an associate professor of sociology at Concordia University. Check and Donnerstein provided expert opinion evidence regarding human sexuality and aggression, while Buckner provided expert testimony regarding social science research methodology and design (*R. v. Fringe Product*, at 432).

121 Ibid. at 433. For Check, pornography was limited to sexually explicit and violent material, and non-violent, sexually explicit material which was dehumanizing or degrading.

122 Ibid. at 434-5.

123 Ibid. at 435. This conclusion itself was based on the participation of Donnerstein and "several other leading social scientists" in a 1986 Surgeon General's Workshop on Pornography and Public Health.

124 Ibid. at 435.

125 Ibid. at 436-7.

126 See also *R. v. Fringe Product* at 444; and the report of the Special Committee on Pornography and Prostitution 1985, 1: 98-9.

127 See the report prepared by H.B. McKay and D.J. Dolff for the Fraser Committee: "The Impact of Pornography: An Analysis of Research and Summary of Findings" (1984). This report was subsequently published

by the Research and Statistics Section of Canada's Department of Justice as a working paper on pornography and prostitution entitled *The Impact of Pornography: A Decade of Literature.*

128 See *Fringe Product,* at 438; McKay and Dolff 1984, 85.

129 See *Attorney General's Commission on Pornography: Final Report,* 1: 326; chapter 5, 95–8; West 1987, 701.

130 *Fringe Product,* at 437.

131 See, for example, Indianopolis and Marion County, Ind., Ordinance 35, S2, 16–3(q) Proposal No. 298 (15 June 1984).

132 *R.* v. *Butler,* S.C.R. at 484–5 [hereinafter *Butler* cited to S.C.R.].

133 Ibid. at 501.

134 Ibid. at 485, 502.

135 Transcript of Proceedings at *Little Sister's* trial (26 October 1994, 50).

136 *Butler,* at 479, 484–5.

137 Fuller and Blackley point out that the lawyer for Little Sister's Book and Art Emporium had appeared as an intervenor on behalf of the British Columbia Civil Liberties Association in *Butler* with the intent to "influence" the Supreme Court of Canada's decision along lines favourable to his client in the impending *Little Sister's* trial (Fuller and Blackley 1995, 40).

138 The various cases reviewed in this section were reviewed by the Ontario Court of Appeal together and reported in a single judgment cited as *R.* v. *Hawkins et al.* (1993), 86 C.C.C. (3d) 246 (Ont. C.A.).

139 The trial-level decision of this case is reported and cited as *R.* v. *Ronish* (1993), 18 C.R. (4th) 165, O.J. No. 608 (QL).

140 The trial-level decision of *R.v. Hawkins* is unreported but summarized in (1992), 16 W.C.B. (2d) 377, and *R.* v. *Laliberte* is unreported.

141 *R.* v. *Hawkins et al.,* at 263.

142 Ibid. at 265.

143 Ibid. at 266.

144 *R.* v. *Erotic Video Exchange Ltd. et al.,* at 186.

145 Ibid. at 192.

146 Ibid.

147 See *Prairie Schooner News,* at 254; *Re Regina and Provincial News,* at 209; *Odeon Morton Theatres,* at 194. To recall, "unusual" was the word Justice Monnin used to paraphrase Forrest's characterization of the anal intercourse scenes at issue in *Odeon Morton Theatres.*

CHAPTER FIVE

1 *Canada Customs Memorandum D9–1–1,* "Interpretative Policy and Procedures for the Administration of Tariff Code 9956."

2 Although Little Sister's Book and Art Emporium was challenging the constitutional validity of Canada Customs legislation, that legislation

made reference to Canada's obscenity law, so a Supreme Court of Canada ruling regarding the constitutional validity of Canada's obscenity law could have some bearing on the validity of the legislation.

3 West recalls the argument made by MacKinnon that any enjoyment a particular woman might purport to obtain from the pain or bondage associated with s/m is suspect (or "problematic") to the extent that women and men are acculturated to accept a certain degree of violence and pain as pleasurable or desirable within an already violent and patriarchal society (West 1987, 703–4). See also MacKinnon 1989.

4 Carol Vance provides a good working notion of literalism in her own testimony at the *Little Sister's* trial. She says there "are special problems in a visual image involving literalism, that is, there is a tendency in viewing all photography to take it as a really realistic representation in a way that we would not think of a novel as a realistic representation": Transcript of Proceedings at *Little Sister's* trial (26 October 1994, 37).

5 For those familiar with the lesbian genre, however, it is understood that the masochist or "bottom" actually dictates the scene and, in this sense, controls the dominatrix or "top." This idea will be discussed in detail below.

6 Transcript of Proceedings at *Little Sister's* trial (26 October 1994, 50).

7 The style of cause of these proceedings is *Glad Day Bookshop Inc. v. Deputy Minister of National Revenue (Customs and Excise)*, [1992] 90 D.L.R. (4th) 527, O.J. No. 1466 [hereinafter *Glad Day Bookshop* cited to O.J.]. The appellant, Moldenhauer, first sought a redetermination in 1990 from the Tariff and Values Administrator. This official determined the publications in question to be "obscene" pursuant to the Customs Tariff and the Canadian *Criminal Code*. As a result, Moldenhauer appealed to the deputy minister for another re-determination. This appeal was heard at the General Division of the Ontario Court of Justice in 1992.

8 *Glad Day Bookshop*, at 18–19. See also *Towne Cinema Theatres*, at 217–18.

9 As was suggested earlier, Rowlands's professional position as an alderperson enabled her to comment on local community standards. Rae provides a similar evidentiary function in *Glad Day Bookshop* to the extent that he gives opinions as to the conditions under which gay sexual practices might be considered degrading within the broader gay and lesbian community. Like Rowlands, Rae was a duly elected politician with some 'boardroom' experience, and any professional authority he would appear to have in the eyes of the court would be simultaneously rooted in his popular appeal.

10 This notion is suggested by Rae's own statement at trial that his political constituency encompasses the largest gay community in Canada (*Glad Day Bookshop*, at 20).

11 Specifically, Rae indicated that he had lobbied to get sexual orientation into the *Human Rights Code* (ibid.).

12 *R.* v. *Butler,* S.C.R., at 479.

13 See *R.* v. *Jobidon.*

14 See *R.* v. *Brown.*

15 *Butler,* at 479. Insofar as MacKinnon helped to prepare the government's factum in *Butler,* it is also worth noting her previously published views in this regard. She stated, for example, "The appearance of [women's] choice or consent [in pornography], with their attribution to inherent nature, is crucial in concealing the reality of force. Love of violation, variously termed female masochism and consent, comes to define female sexuality" (MacKinnon 1989, 141; footnote omitted).

16 *Glad Day Bookshop,* at 25–6.

17 This statement is Justice Hayes's paraphrase of Professor Adams's trial testimony (ibid. at 22; emphasis added).

18 This last claim is supported in the discussion of the *Little Sister's* case below.

19 *Glad Day Bookshop,* at 26–7; emphasis added.

20 Indeed, as will be observed shortly, in *Little Sister's* Ross and Kinsman openly challenged the heuristic relevance of Neil Malamuth's laboratory research regarding pornographic imagery to an understanding of gay and lesbian sexual expression.

21 *Glad Day Bookshop,* at 36–7; emphasis added.

22 See *R.* v. *Scythes,* at 2. The characterization of the magazine *Bad Attitude* is taken from the headnote to *Scythes.*

23 *R.* v. *Scythes,* at 3.

24 To be precise, Paris found that the sexual composition of the actors or models in certain kinds of sexual imagery (such as sadomasochistic depictions) is inconsequential to the question of social harmfulness, which is basically the same opinion Malamuth provided in relation to the lesbian materials contained in *Bad Attitude.* Although Paris does not expressly ground his written opinion in Malamuth's testimony, it is clear to Ross that Paris's stated rationale for accepting Malamuth as an expert on lesbian pornography during the qualifications process foreshadowed his written opinion in this matter (Ross 1997, 154).

25 *R.* v. *Scythes,* at 7.

26 Ibid. at 5.

27 Ibid. at 7. The story is called "Wunna My Fantasies" and is contained in the impugned *Bad Attitude.*

28 The case was *Little Sister's Book and Art Emporium v. Canada (Minister of Justice),* (B.C.S.C.) [hereinafter *Little Sister's,* (B.C.S.C.)].

29 Transcript of Proceedings at *Little Sister's* trial (13 October 1994). By way of a technical note, it is possible to trace the roots of semiotics as

far back as the nineteenth century, specifically to the writings of the American scholar Charles Sanders Pierce, but semiotics did not become formally recognized as such until after WW II.

30 Ibid. (13 October 1994). The novelty of Ross's testimony at both *Scythes* and *Little Sister's* is highlighted by the fact that she was the first recipient of a Ph.D. in lesbian studies in Canada.

31 Ibid. (17 October 1994).

32 Ibid. (26 October 1994).

33 Ibid. (19 October 1994).

34 Ibid. (20 October 1994).

35 Ibid. (24 October 1994).

36 *Butler*, at 485.

37 In this respect, Weir uses deconstruction theory to unsettle established definitions of "dehumanization," "degradation," and "pain": Transcript of Proceedings at *Little Sister's* trial (24 October 1994, 49-50; 25 October 1994, 1, 5).

38 Weir's testimony, especially that part involving the application of deconstruction and hermeneutic theory to certain passages in the impugned books, highlights the limited utility of Monahan and Walker's "social fact" concept. Monahan and Walker are clear that their concept captures empirical social science research relevant to community standards of tolerance regarding a particular publication (Monahan and Walker 1988, 469). Weir's evidence, however, is not empirical in the sense imagined by Monahan and Walker; nor is it properly social scientific.

39 Transcript of Proceedings at *Little Sister's* trial (24 October 1994, 34).

40 *R. v. Towne Cinema Theatres*, C.C.C. at 215, 217. This proposition was supported by both Justice Beetz and Justice McIntyre, but not by Chief Justice Dickson. In *Butler* Justice Sopinka appears to have acquiesced in Justice Wilson's opinion (*Butler*, at 478).

41 Transcript of Proceedings at *Little Sister's* trial (24 October 1994, 14).

42 Weir makes this point in her description of a hypothetical reader of Geoffrey Mains's *Urban Aboriginals* (to be discussed below) "who is made very uncomfortable by this book," having "perhaps never read a text of this sort before," or perhaps coming "to the subject with no prior knowledge": ibid. (24 October 1994, 46). Vance's evidence at *Little Sister's* is generally supportive of this hermeneutic approach to understanding s/M imagery. When asked how one knows whether the s/M depictions at issue are fantasy, consensual, or staged, Vance replied, "I think there are some ways to know but that has to do with the viewer's familiarity with the codes of meaning that the participants engage in, and there is no question that someone who is familiar with SM practices would view a film probably quite differently from someone who is not": ibid. (26 October 1994, 69).

43 See, for example, the testimony of Testa: ibid. (13 October 1994, 3–8); and the testimony of Ross: ibid. (13 October 1994, 8).

44 Ibid. (24 October 1994, 32–3).

45 Ibid., 36.

46 Ibid., 36–7.

47 Ibid., 34–6.

48 Ibid. (20 October 1994, 24).

49 Ibid., 40. Kinsman also views the problem from the point of view of the meaning of "degradation" and "dehumanization." He argues in this regard that such terms have been historically and legally associated with some homosexual practices, insofar as these same practices are seen to violate culturally dominant conceptions of human nature and human sexuality (ibid., 36–9).

50 Ibid., 39–41.

51 The issue of class difference within gay social relations and its implications for gay s/m is discussed by Testa: see Transcript of Proceedings at *Little Sister's* trial (13 October 1994, 19).

52 Transcript of Proceedings at *Little Sister's* trial (20 October 1994, 41).

53 Ibid., 42.

54 Ibid., 44.

55 This is the picture Kinsman presents in order to distinguish the effects of gay male pornography on gay male readers and participants (ibid.).

56 Ibid., 46–8.

57 Ibid., 48.

58 Ibid., 77.

59 Ibid., 79.

60 *Little Sister's*, (B.C.S.C.) at 284–5. For the article, see Kendall 1993.

61 Transcript of Proceedings at *Little Sister's* trial (20 October 1994, 83).

62 Ibid., 87–91.

63 This is the question of how lesbian s/m differs from heterosexual s/m from the point of view of those who produce it and those who consume it. This point will be discussed below shortly.

64 Transcript of Proceedings at *Little Sister's* trial (13 October 1994).

65 Ibid. (18 October 1994).

66 Ibid. (13 October 1994, 33).

67 Ibid., 4.

68 This is the expression Testa uses to describe a message which is essentially "literal" or "singular" (ibid., 9–10, 12).

69 Ibid. at 9–10.

70 This example is extracted from the Epilogue of John Preston's *I Once Had a Master*, reproduced by Ricci in Transcript of Proceedings at *Little Sister's* trial (18 October 1994, 19).

71 Transcript of Proceedings at *Little Sister's* trial (13 October 1994, 9–10).

72 Ibid., 9.

73 Ibid., 13.

74 Ibid., 13, 18, 21.

75 Ibid., 21.

76 Ibid. (25 October 1994, 5).

77 Ibid. (13 October 1994, 35).

78 Ibid. (18 October 1994, 3–5, 13–16).

79 Ibid., 17.

80 Ibid., 19.

81 Ibid., 4.

82 Ibid., 14.

83 Ibid., 16.

84 Ibid., 33–4.

85 Ibid., 5.

86 Ibid., 18–19. It is noteworthy that the passages Ricci reads to the court contain completely unsupported, categorical statements about heterosexual sexuality, the nature of which are directly in dispute in *Little Sister's*.

87 Aspects of Ross's testimony in *Scythes* have already been discussed. Aspects from *Little Sister's* will be examined in the next section of this chapter.

88 Vance is also an epidemiologist, and as such testified at *Little Sister's* about the way certain sexual practices (for example, homosexual sexual practices) have become intellectually associated with the spread of disease (mental and physical) at certain times. She then explained the way law and public policy have been formed in response (or at least in relation) to these perceptions: see Transcript of Proceedings at *Little Sister's* trial (26 October 1994, 12–16, 30–2, 65).

89 Transcript of Proceedings at *Little Sister's* trial (26 October 194, 20ff., 76–7).

90 Ibid., 20.

91 Ibid., 71–2.

92 Ibid., 50. See also Vance 1993, 43; and West 1987.

93 Transcript of Proceedings at *Little Sister's* trial (26 October 1994, 61–2).

94 *Little Sister's*, (B.C.S.C.) at 285–6. The rule against hearsay evidence will generally allow testimony about what the witness heard other people say, but only for the purpose of establishing that these people did make such statements, not for the purpose of establishing the truth of the statements themselves.

95 This "rational-basis" notion is synonymous with the reasonable apprehension of harm doctrine.

96 *Little Sister's*, at 285–6.

97 Transcript of Proceeding at *Little Sister's* trial (26 October 1994, 49–50).

98 Ibid., 50.

99 Ibid., 51.

100 Ibid., 76.

101 Ibid., 62–3.

102 Ibid., (17 October 1994, 9).

103 Ibid., 15.

104 Ibid., 13.

105 Ibid.; emphasis added. It is noteworthy that Ross also distinguishes between homosexual erotica (specifically lesbian) and heterosexual erotica in terms of "the relations of production" involved in each enterprise: see Transcript of Proceedings at *Little Sister's* trial (13 October 1994, 9). Both Ross and Waugh want to suggest that the production of homosexual erotica, unlike that of heterosexual or mainstream pornography, is somehow culturally affirmative or at any rate not sexually or economically exploitative.

106 Transcript of Proceedings at *Little Sister's* trial (17 October 1994, 14).

107 Ibid.

108 Ibid.

109 Ibid., 24–5.

110 Ibid., 39; emphasis added.

111 Ibid. (26 October 1994, 37–8).

112 Ibid. (17 October 1994, 39).

113 Ibid., 49.

114 Ibid. (13 October 1994, 8).

115 Ibid. (17 October 1994, 49–50).

116 Ibid., 50.

117 This picture of heterosexual structural inequality informed the idea (reiterated by Justice Sopinka in *Butler*) that the appearance of a woman's "consent" to some act of male sexual aggression committed upon her effectively reinforces the stereotypical image of women as enjoying or desiring their place of sexual-social subordination. It is noteworthy here that, as far as the genre of heterosexual s/m imagery is concerned, depictions involving a female dominatrix (or "top") and a male submissive (or "bottom") are very popular among readers: see Transcript of Proceedings at *Little Sister's* trial (26 October 1994, 72–3).

118 Transcript of Proceedings at *Little Sister's* trial (13 October 1994, 3).

119 Again, Ross was the first person in Canada to receive a doctorate degree in lesbian studies.

120 Transcript of Proceedings at *Little Sister's* trial (13 October 1994, 8–9).

121 Ibid. (20 October 1994, 12).

122 Ibid. (24 October 1994, 23).

123 Ibid. (19 October 1994, 47).

124 As will be explained shortly, Ross herself gives some indication of what this condition might be when she discusses the differences between

some so-called lesbian s/m spreads in an issue of *Hustler* magazine and others in a volume of *Bad Attitude*.

125 Transcript of Proceedings at *Little Sister's* trial (17 October 1994, 50).

126 Transcript of Proceedings at *Little Sister's* trial (13 October 1994, 9–10). In her post–*Little Sister's* publication, Ross argued similarly that "in lesbian s/m fantasy, the 'bottom' actually 'runs the fuck' – a fact that throws into chaos the legally codified (yet highly subjective) notions of 'harm' and 'degradation' enacted via (male) dominance and (female) submission. By orchestrating the sexual encounter, the bottom disrupts popular conceptions that she is passive, subjugated, and exploited" (Ross 1997, 160; endnote omitted).

127 Some relevant aspects of MacKinnon's view have been discussed above and more will be discussed shortly. Scales's perception of lesbian s/m as presented in *Little Sister's* will be discussed below. For Ross's own critique of Scales's view as presented in the *Scythes* case, see Ross 1997, 184–5.

128 Transcript of Proceedings at *Little Sister's* trial (13 October 1994, 10).

129 The cogency of Ross's analysis in this respect depends in part on various philosophical assumptions about the nature of "activity" and "passivity," or "aggression" and "compliance," as applied to sexual imagery generally. Yet it is difficult in some cases to say decisively that a particular sexual posture or position appears "active" or "passive." This book clearly relies on such notions but accepts that they may be interpreted or understood differently within separate pictorial and textual contexts.

130 Transcript of Proceedings at *Little Sister's* trial (13 October 1994, 13).

131 Ibid. This testimony is almost verbatim the same testimony Ross gave in the *Scythes* case (see Ross 1997, 166).

132 Transcript of Proceedings at *Little Sister's* trial (13 October 1994, 13); emphasis added.

133 Ibid., 13–14. See also Ross 1997, 167.

134 Ibid., 15.

135 Ibid., 16.

136 Vance has pointed out that "there are special problems in a visual image involving literalism," such as "a tendency in viewing all photography to take it as a really realistic representation in a way that we would not think of a novel as a realistic representation": Transcript of Proceedings at *Little Sister's* trial (26 October 1994, 37).

137 Ibid. (13 October 1994, 16).

138 Ibid., 9.

139 Ross's analysis seems inherently problematic even by her own terms. Reflecting upon her experience in the *Scythes* trial, she describes as "surreal" one moment where she had to "clarify" for the Crown and the judge that "a photograph of a butch/femme couple was of two

women, not a man and a woman" (Ross 1997, 168). Presumably the Crown and the judge were too inattentive or unacculturated to see past the sophisticated sexual guise or ruse presented by the photograph. Yet this is disingenuous, for "butch/femme" role playing clearly draws on traditional and recognizable "masculine" and "feminine" figures, in which case a plausible argument can be made for the derivative, as opposed to radically specific, nature of lesbian sexual expression. As will be made clear below, Califia's testimony in the *Little Sister's* case supports this argument.

140 *Little Sister's,* (B.C.S.C.) at 308.

141 It is important to note here that Smith also quoted from Pat Califia's book *Macho Sluts* in support of his finding that homosexual sado-masochist literature is important "in furthering the principles and values that underlie freedom of expression" (ibid. at 307). Califia's evidence in the *Little Sister's* trial will be discussed below.

142 According to Fuller and Blackley, the government lawyers in *Little Sister's* were not particularly attuned to Scales's ability to make a damning case against the LSBAE if she wanted (Fuller and Blackley 1995, 63).

143 Transcript of Proceedings at *Little Sister's* Trial (25 November 1994, 27).

144 See Miller and Barron 1975, 1203.

145 The plaintiffs' lawyer also suggested that Scales was competent to deter-mine whether some principled or rational basis exists for distinguishing between different books in terms of obscenity: Transcript of Proceed-ings at *Little Sister's* trial (25 November 1994, 37). Given that this question is almost impossible for anyone to answer, whether expert or lay, it is surprising, to say the least, that Scales was tendered as an expert on this issue.

146 Ibid., 45–6. This is a particularly significant claim in light of the fact that, when asked to talk about the various themes *Doc and Fluff* addresses, Califia herself mentioned several, only one of which was vio-lence against women. Califia's testimony in this respect will be addressed in the next section.

147 Ibid., 47–50.

148 Ibid., 39.

149 Ibid., 52–3.

150 Ibid., 41–2.

151 Ibid., 43.

152 Ibid., 57.

153 See Ross 1997, 184–5; Scales 1994, 375.

154 Transcript of Proceedings at *Little Sister's* trial (25 November 1994, 58–9).

155 In reference to heterosexual pornography generally, Scales says, "Every piece of pornography seriously expresses the most serious of political

themes: consuming women sustains male superiority. The better pornography does its job, the more protected it is" (Scales 1994, 369–70; footnotes omitted).

156 Transcript of Proceedings at *Little Sister's* trial (20 October 1994, 14).

157 Ibid., 17–18.

158 Ibid. (19 October 1994, 46–7).

159 Ibid. (20 October 1994, 15–16).

160 Ibid., 21.

161 Fuller and Blackley also indicated that the plaintiffs' lawyer wanted Califia to "counterbalance the strong, pro-censorship accent of feminism, especially in light of *Butler*" (Fuller and Blackley 1995, 59–60). This rationale does not explain, however, why the qualified expert, anti-censorship advocate, and lesbian author, Jane Vance Rule was also asked to testify about the literary merit and/or artistic purpose of Califia's novel, *Doc and Fluff*, when Califia could do so herself. It is noteworthy in this respect that, for Rule, *Doc and Fluff* was written with a serious artistic and indeed moral purpose – mainly about coming to terms with power, hatred, violence, etc. – even though Califia herself is a "crude stylist," who is sometimes "sentimental" and "oversimplistic": Transcript of Proceedings at *Little Sister's* trial (24 October 1994, 26–7). Califia did not expressly concede these latter literary limitations in her own testimony, but she did say "within the limits of my gifts as a writer I do attempt to create work that will engender a multitude of responses in the reader and work that can hopefully be read more than once that contains enough detail, enough nuances and enough twists in plot that the reader can come away with a different perspective": ibid. (20 October 1994, 14).

162 Smith quoted passages from Califia's introduction that expressed her reasons for writing and her feelings as a sadomasochist and found that these supported the plaintiffs' argument that homosexual sadomasochist literature contributed to the self-affirmation and empowerment of gay and lesbian communities and sub-communities: see *Little Sister's*, (B.C.S.C.) at 307.

163 *Little Sister's*, (B.C.S.C.) at 281–2. For a detailed discussion of Smith's application of the doctrine of "relevance" to the facts of the *Little Sister's* case see Nowlin 1996.

164 *Little Sister's*, (B.C.S.C.) at 128.

165 I have outlined some of these problems elsewhere (Nowlin 1996, 342, n.38). For example, Smith's reasoning must assume that gay and lesbian sexually explicit writing and imagery contains relatively more obscenity, quantitatively speaking, than heterosexual sexual depictions. It does not consider the possibility that, despite the relatively greater importance of sexuality to gays and lesbians than to heterosexuals,

heterosexuals produce relatively more obscene sexual depictions than gays and lesbians. This possibility is entirely consonant with Smith's finding that, given the social, cultural, and political importance of gay and lesbian sexual expression (including gay and lesbian s/M imagery) to gay and lesbian lives, "a society committed to the values underlying freedom of expression ... cannot defend the *automatic* prohibition of descriptions and depictions of homosexual sadomasochism": *Little Sister's*, (B.C.S.C.) at 308; emphasis added. Perhaps closer analysis will reveal that most gay and lesbian sexually explicit writing and imagery is not obscene, and most heterosexual sexual expression is. In any case, the evidence introduced in *Little Sister's* was far from establishing this point.

166 Transcript of Proceedings at *Little Sister's* trial (25 November 1994, 34).

167 *Little Sister's*, (B.C.S.C.) at 298.

168 Transcript of Proceedings at *Little Sister's* trial (18 November 1994, 28).

169 Ibid., 29.

170 This trial is technically cited as *R. v. Scythes* [1993], O.J. 537, but it is often informally recognized as the *Bad Attitude* trial, in reference to the name of the publication at issue there.

171 Transcript of Proceedings at *Little Sister's* trial (13 October 1994).

172 Ibid., 35.

173 Ibid. (20 October 1994, 90). See also Fuller and Blackley 1995, 102.

174 *Little Sister's Book and Art Emporium v. Canada (Minister of Justice)*, (B.C.C.A.) at 506 [hereinafter *Little Sister's*, (B.C.C.A.)].

175 Ibid. at 541. The "concluding sentence" mentioned by Justice Finch reads as follows: "To the extent that one can conclude that the messages within heterosexual pornography might affect attitudes regarding the acceptability of some behaviors (e.g., sexually violent portrayals affecting attitudes regarding sexually aggressive acts), it may be reasonable to assume that similar processes and effects would occur when such messages are incorporated within homosexual pornography" (ibid. at 540).

176 *Little Sister's*, (B.C.S.C.) at 308.

177 Ibid. at 305.

178 Ibid. at 304–7.

179 *Little Sister's Book and Art Emporium v. Canada (Minister of Justice)*, (S.C.C.) at 1184 [hereinafter *Little Sister's*, (S.C.C.)].

180 Ibid. at 1188.

181 See Nowlin 1996.

182 *Little Sister's*, (S.C.C.) at 1165–6, 1223–4.

183 Arvay made this point in a forum discussion he gave at the University of British Columbia Faculty of Law shortly after Justice Smith rendered his decision in *Little Sister's*.

184 *Butler*, at 485.
185 *R. v. Langer*, at 210.
186 Ibid. at 213.
187 Ibid. at 215.
188 Ibid. at 216.
189 Ibid. at 218.
190 Canadian child obscenity law captures two kinds of child pornography. Section 163.1(1)(b) of the *Criminal Code* defines child pornography as printed or visual depictions that advocate or counsel unlawful sexual activity with persons under eighteen years of age. Section 163.1(1)(a) defines child pornography as either photographic and other visual depictions of children under eighteen years of age engaging in sexual activity or photographic and other visual depictions of the sexual organs or anal regions of persons under the age of eighteen years where the purpose of the depictions is predominantly sexual. The latter, but not the former, is limited by the community standard of tolerance test. The former operates logically on the assumption that the material in question probably poses a risk of harm of the kind identified in the *Butler* case. Where it does, writers or producers of child pornography can evade prosecution in Canada by demonstrating that their writings or works in some "objective" way have artistic merit: [*R. v. Sharpe*, (S.C.C.) at 88–9
191 *R. v. Langer*, at 233.
192 Ibid.
193 Ibid. at 234.
194 Ibid.
195 Ibid. at 215.
196 Ibid.
197 Ibid. at 213.
198 *R. v. Stroempl*, at 190.
199 *R. v. Sharpe*, (B.C.S.C.) at 136 [hereinafter *Sharpe*, (B.C.S.C.)].
200 Ibid. at 137–8.
201 Ibid. at 138.
202 See *Sharpe*, (B.C.S.C.) at 138.
203 *Sharpe*, (B.C.S.C.) at 138. See Carter, Prentky, et al. 1987, 197.
204 *Sharpe*, (B.C.S.C.) at 139.
205 The study by Marshall that Collins used states at p.284: "Slightly more than one third of the child molesters and rapists claims to have at least occasionally been incited to commit an offense by exposure to one or the other type of the sexual materials specified in this study" (Marshall 1988, 284; emphasis added). See *Sharpe*, (B.C.S.C.) at 137. The idea that "slightly more than one third" of the child molesters and rapists studied claimed to have at least "occasionally" been incited to commit

an offence by exposure to hard-core pornography implies that nearly two-thirds of the same subject group have either never been so incited or have been thus incited several times. For this study to be even remotely interesting or probative, an analyst would want to know the variety of psychological, physical, biological, emotional, social, economic, and cultural conditions under which each subject belonging to the "one third" group became exposed to hard-core pornography, and how the exposure incited him or her to commit an offence; and the analyst would also want to know the same variety of conditions under which each individual in the group representing the other two-thirds became exposed to the same pornography (if this occurred at all), and how each of these individuals reacted to the exposure.

206 *Sharpe*, (B.C.S.C.) at 138; emphasis added. This quoted passage is taken directly from p.207 of the published study by Carter, Prentky et al. 1987.

207 *R. v. Langer*, at 240.

208 *Sharpe*, (B.C.S.C.) at 145.

209 Ibid. at 140–1. The new test was articulated in *Dagenais* v. *Canadian Broadcasting Corp.*

210 *Sharpe*, (B.C.S.C.) at 145–6.

211 *R. v. Sharpe*, (B.C.C.A.) at 152 [hereinafter *Sharpe*, (B.C.C.A.)].

212 Ibid. at 139.

213 Ibid. at 160.

214 Ibid. at 167–8.

215 *R. v. Sharpe*, (S.C.C.) at 85, 103–4; [hereinafter *Sharpe*, (S.C.C.)].

216 *Sharpe*, (S.C.C.) at 96–101.

217 Ibid. at 135–6.

218 Transcripts of Trial of *R. v. Sharpe* , vol. 1: 40–1 (9 November 1998).

219 See ibid. 101 (12 November 1998).

220 *Sharpe*, (S.C.C.) at 135–6.

221 Transcripts of Trial of *R. v. Sharpe*, vol. 1: 135 (9 November 1998).

222 *Sharpe*, (S.C.C.) at 152–3.

223 *Sharpe*, at para. 19.

224 Ibid. at paras. 23–5.

225 Ibid. at paras. 9–10.

226 Ibid. at para. 97.

227 Section 163.1(1)(b) of the *Criminal Code*.

228 *Sharpe*, (S.C.C.) at 84.

229 *Sharpe*, at paras. 33–4.

230 Ibid. at para. 98.

231 Ibid. at paras. 83–6, 90–1.

232 Ibid. at paras. 93–6.

233 In such a case, the moral aspect is limited to the question posed in the *Butler* case: will the creation, production, or publication of an

impugned work tend to foster misogyny or hatred, or in some other way violate the rights of Canadian citizens to be treated as equals and with dignity?

234 *Sharpe*, at para. 104-5.

235 Ibid. at para. 10.

236 Ibid. at para. 103.

237 Ibid. at paras. 8-9.

238 Ibid. at para. 61; emphasis added.

239 Ibid. at paras. 64, 66; emphasis added.

240 At one point in his written reasons, Shaw makes the very curious observation that Sharpe's writings "simply describe morally repugnant acts" (ibid. at para. 35). Shaw makes this observation to counteract the proposition that perhaps Sharpe's stories are thinly disguised exhortations to the seduction or exploitation of children. Nonetheless, it appears entirely at odds with the nature of the defence expert opinion evidence, which attributed aspects of parody, irony, and allegory to Sharpe's writings, and which Shaw appeared to accept more or less without reservation.

241 This "aversion" type of argument was made, for example, in relation to certain depictions in Hubert Selby Jr's novel *Last Exit to Brooklyn* when that novel was the subject of criminal proceedings in England: see R. v. *Calder & Boyars Ltd.*

242 *Sharpe*, at para. 103.

243 Ibid. at para. 71.

244 Ibid. at paras. 80-1.

245 Ibid. at para. 9.

246 Ibid. at para. 103.

247 It must not be forgotten here that Sharpe himself made clear in his correspondence that his writings were created partly for erotic purposes.

248 *Sharpe*, at para. 72.

249 It is worth asking in this respect whether as a book or film begins to appear to a trained eye to be advocating or ennobling racism, sexism, or some indefensible hatred, it also begins to lose its literary merit, despite how much artistry and knowledge is brought to it.

CHAPTER SIX

1 R. v. *Jacob*, (Ont. Ct J., Prov. Div.) at 2.

2 Ibid. at 2-3.

3 Ibid. at 3.

4 R. v. *Jacob* (Ont. C.A.) at 6.

5 *Jacob*, (Ont. Ct. J., Prov. Div.) at 2; emphasis added.

6 Ibid. at 10.

7 Ibid.

8 Ibid. at 14. It is entirely possible that Kinsey himself would draw a completely different conclusion from the quoted passage, so it is difficult to see just how this same passage "supports" Payne's conclusion in any way.

9 Ibid. at 13.

10 *R. v. Arnold*, at 7.

11 Ibid. at 7–8.

12 This is also McGowan's paraphrase of Langevin's evidence.

13 This is McGowan's paraphrase of Van Esterick's testimony.

14 *R. v. Arnold*, at 6–7.

15 Ibid. at 9.

16 Ibid. at 19–20.

17 Ibid. at 20.

18 *R. v. Tremblay et al.*, at 117; emphasis added.

19 *R. v. Towne Cinema Theatres*, at 205.

20 Ibid. at 123.

21 Ibid. at 120.

22 Ibid. at 125.

23 *R. v. Mara and East*, at 156.

CONCLUSION

1 *Washington v. Glucksberg*, at 830–1.

Bibliography

Adler, A. 1996. "What's Left?: Hate Speech, Pornography, and the Problem for Artistic Expression." 84 *California Law Review* 1499.

– 1993. "Why Art is on Trial." 22 *The Journal of Arts Management, Law, and Society* 322.

– 1990. "Post-Modern Art and the Death of Obscenity Law." 99 *Yale Law Journal* 1359.

Allen, R., and J. Miller. 1993. "The Common Law Theory of Experts: Deference or Education?" 87 *Northwestern University Law Review* 1131.

Alpert, L. 1938. "Judicial Censorship of Obscene Literature." 52 *Harvard Law Review* 40.

Appendix to Appellants' Briefs. 1953. "The Effects of Segregation and the Consequences of Desegregation: A Social Science Statement, Brown v. Board of Educ., 347 U.S. 483 (1954)." 37 *Minnesota Law Review* 427.

Ariens, M. 1992. "Progress is Our Only Product: Legal Reform and the Codification of Evidence." 17 *Law & Social Inquiry* 213.

Attorney General's Commission on Pornography: Final Report. 1986. Washington, DC: U.S. Department of Justice. (*Meese Report*)

Benjamin, J. 1988. *The Bonds of Love: Psychoanalysis, Feminism, and the Problem of Domination.* New York: Pantheon Books.

– 1980. "The Bonds of Love: Rational Violence and Erotic Domination." In *The Future of Difference.* Ed. H. Eisenstein and A. Jardine. Boston: G.K. Hall and Co.

Bates, F. 1978. "Pornography and the Expert Witness." 20 *Criminal Law Quarterly* 135.

Berkowitz, L. 1971. "Sex and Violence: We Can't Have It Both Ways." 5 *Psychology Today* 14.

Bikle, H.W. 1924. "Judicial Determination of Questions of Fact Affecting the Constitutional Validity of Legislative Action." 38 *Harvard Law Review* 6.

Borovoy, A. 1988. *When Freedoms Collide: The Case for Our Civil Liberties.* Toronto: Lester and Orpen Dennys.

Brannigan, A. 1991. "Obscenity and Social Harm: A Contested Terrain." 14 *International Journal of Law and Psychiatry* 1.

Brockman, J. 1992. "Social Authority, Legal Discourse, and Women's Voices." 21:2 *Manitoba Law Journal* 213.

Bullough, V.L. 1994. *Science in the Bedroom: A History of Sex Research.* New York: Basic Books.

Burk, D.L. 1993. "When Scientists Act Like Lawyers: The Problem of Adversary Science." 33 *Jurimetrics Journal* 363.

Busby, K. "LEAF and Pornography: Litigating on Equality and Sexual Representations." 9 *Canadian Journal of Law and Society* 165.

Cahn, E. 1956. "Jurisprudence." 31 *New York University Law Review* 182.

– 1955. "Jurisprudence." 30 *New York University Law Review* 150.

Cain, M. 1988. "Beyond Informal Justice." In *Informal Justice?* Ed. R. Mathews. London: Sage Publications.

– 1983. "Gramsci, the State and the Place of Law." In *Legality, Ideology and the State.* Ed. E. Sugarman. London: Academic Press.

Canada. 1985. *Pornography and Prostitution in Canada: Report of the Special Committee on Pornography and Prostitution,* vol. 1. Ottawa: Supply and Services. (*Fraser Report*)

Caputi, M. 1994. *Voluptuous Yearnings: A Feminist Theory of the Obscene.* Boston: Rowman & Littlefield Publishers.

Cardozo, B.N. 1924. *The Growth of the Law.* New Haven: Yale University Press.

Carter, D.L., R.A. Prentky, et al. 1987. "Use of Pornography in the Criminal and Developmental Histories of Sexual Offenders." 2 *Journal of Interpersonal Violence* 196.

Charles, W.H.R., T.A. Cromwell, et al. 1989. *Evidence and the Charter of Rights and Freedoms.* Toronto: Butterworths.

Clark, J.T. 1993. "The 'Community Standard' in the Trial of Obscenity Cases – A Mandate for Empirical Evidence in Search of the Truth." 20 *Ohio Northern University Law Review* 13.

Committee on Sexual Offences Against Children and Youth. 1984. *Sexual Offences Against Children.* Ottawa: Department of Supply and Services. (*Badgley Report*)

Cossman, B., and B. Ryder. 1996. "Customs Censorship and the Charter: the *Little Sister's* case." 7 *Constitutional Forum* 103.

Cross, R. 1967. *Evidence.* 3rd ed. London: Butterworths.

Davis, K.C. 1942. "An Approach to Problems of Evidence in the Administrative Process." 55 *Harvard Law Review* 364.

Davis, P.C. 1987. "'There is a Book Out': An Analysis of Judicial Absorption of Legislative Facts." 100 *Harvard Law Review* 1539.

Davison, J.F. 1938. "The Constitutionality and Utility of Advisory Opinions." 1 *University of Toronto Law Journal* 254.

Devlin, P. 1965. *The Enforcement of Morals.* London: Oxford University Press.

Dewey, J. 1927. *The Public and Its Problems.* Denver: Henry Holt and Company.

Dingwall, R., and P. Lewis, eds. 1983. *The Sociology of the Professions: Lawyers, Doctors, and Others.* New York: St Martin's.

Donnerstein, D., D. Linz, and S. Penrod. 1987. *The Question of Pornography: Research Findings and Policy Implications.* New York: The Free Press.

Downs, D. 1987. "The Attorney General's Commission and the New Politics of Pornography." 4 *American Bar Foundation Research Journal* 641.

Doyle, W.E. 1977. "Can Social Science Data Be Used in Judicial Decisionmaking?" 6:4 *Journal of Law and Education* 13.

Duggan, L., N. Hunter, and C.S. Vance. 1985. "False Promises: Feminist Antipornography Legislation in the U.S." In *Women Against Censorship.* Ed. V. Burstyn. Vancouver: Douglas & McIntyre at 130.

Duncan, O.D., ed. 1964. *William F. Ogburn on Culture and Social Change: Selected Papers.* Chicago: University of Chicago Press.

Duval Hesler, N. 1995. "The Role of the Expert in Environmental Litigation." In *Filtering and Analyzing Evidence in An Age of Diversity.* Ed. M.T. MacCrimmon, and M. Ouellette, Montreal: Les Éditions Thémis.

Dworkin, R. 1997. "Assisted Suicide: What the Court Really Said." 44:14 *The New York Review of Books* 40.

– 1977a. *Taking Rights Seriously.* Cambridge: Harvard University Press.

– 1977b. "Social Sciences and Constitutional Rights – The Consequences of Uncertainty." 6:4 *Journal of Law and Education* 3.

Dworkin, R., T. Nagel, et al. 1997. "Assisted Suicide: The Philosophers Brief." 44:5 *The New York Review of Books* 41.

Ernst, M.L. 1955. "The Lawyer's Role in Modern Society: A Round Table." 4 *Journal of Public Law* 1.

Ernst, M.L., and A.U. Schwartz. 1964. *Censorship: The Search for the Obscene.* New York: Macmillan.

Faigman, D.L., E. Porter, et al. 1994. "Check Your Crystal Ball at the Courthouse Door, Please..." 15 *Cardozo Law Review* 1799.

Fiedler, L. 1984. "To Whom Does Joyce Belong? *Ulysses* as Parody, Pop and Porn." In *Light Rays: James Joyce and Modernism.* Ed. H. Ehrlich. New York: New Horizon.

Fisher, W.A., and A. Barak. 1991. "Pornography, Erotica and Behavior: More Questions than Answers." 14 *International Journal of Law and Psychiatry* 65.

Foster, H. 1984. "Against Pluralism." In *Art After Modernism.* Ed. B. Wallis. New York: New Museum of Contemporary Art in association with D.R. Godine Inc., Boston.

Foucault, M. 1990. *The History of Sexuality: An Introduction, Vol. 1.* Trans. R. Hurley. New York: Vantage Books. Original work published in French · in 1976.

– 1982. "The Subject of Power." In H.L. Dreyfus and P. Rabinow. *Michel Foucault: Beyond Structuralism and Hermeneutics.* Chicago: University of Chicago Press.

Frank, J. 1963. *Law and the Modern Mind.* Garden City, NY: Anchor Books.

– 1955. "The Lawyer's Role in Modern Society: A Round Table." 4 *Journal of Public Law* 8.

– 1950. *Courts on Trial: Myth and Reality in American Justice.* Princeton: Princeton University Press.

– 1949. "The Place of the Expert in a Democratic Society." 16 *Philosophy of Science* 3.

Freckleton, I. 1987. *The Trial of the Expert.* Oxford: Oxford University Press.

Friedson, E. 1986. *Professional Powers.* Chicago: University of Chicago Press.

Fuller, J., and S. Blackley. 1995. *Restricted Entry: Censorship on Trial.* Vancouver: Press Gang Publishers.

Gatowski, S.I., S.A. Dobbin, et al. 1996. "The Diffusion of Scientific Evidence: A Comparative Analysis of Admissibility Standards in Australia, Canada, England and the United States, and their Impact on Social and Behavioral Sciences." 4:3 *Expert Evidence: The International Digest of Human Behaviour Science and Law* 86.

Geis, G. 1964. "Sociology and Sociological Jurisprudence: Admixture of Lore and Law." 52 *Kentucky Law Journal* 267.

Goldman, C.S. 1974. "The Use of Learned Treatises in Canadian and United States Litigation." 24 *University of Toronto Law Journal* 423.

Gottel, L. 1997. "Shaping *Butler*: The New Politics of Anti-Pornography." In Cossman, B., S. Bell, et al. *Bad Attitude/s on Trial: Pornography, Feminism, and the* Butler *Decision.* Toronto: University of Toronto Press.

Hagan, J. 1987. "Can Social Science Save Us? The Problems and Prospects of Social Science Evidence in Constitutional Litigation." In *Charter Litigation.* Ed. R.J. Sharpe. Toronto: Butterworths.

Hand, L. 1901. "Historical and Practical Considerations Regarding Expert Testimony." 15 *Harvard Law Review* 40.

Hart, H.L.A. 1963. *Law, Liberty and Morality.* Stanford: Stanford University Press.

Harvard Law Review Editors. 1995. "Confronting the New Challenges of Scientific Evidence." 108 *Harvard Law Review* 1481.

Haskell, T., ed. 1984. *The Authority of Experts.* Bloomington: Indiana University Press.

Herman, D. 1994. *Rights of Passage: Struggles for Lesbian and Gay Legal Equality.* Toronto: University of Toronto Press.

Hite, S. 1981. *The Hite Report on Male Sexuality.* New York: Knopf.

Hogg, P. 1976. "Proof of Facts in Constitutional Cases." 26 *University of Toronto Law Journal* 386.

Huber, P. 1992. "Junk Science in the Courtroom." 26 *Valparaiso University Law Review* 723.

Hutchinson, A.C., and P. Monahan. 1987. "Democracy and the Rule of Law." In *The Rule of Law: Ideal or Ideology.* Ed. A.C. Hutchinson, and P. Monahan, Toronto: Carswell.

Jackson, J.F. 1993. "The Brandeis Brief – Too Little, Too Late: The Trial Court as a Superior Forum for Presenting Legislative Facts." 17:1 *American Journal of Trial Advocacy* 1.

Jasanoff, S. 1992. "What Judges Should Know About the Sociology of Science." 32 *Jurimetrics Journal* 345.

Jasanoff, S., and D. Nelkin. 1981. "Science, Technology, and the Limits of Judicial Competence." 214 *Science* 1211.

Karst, K.L. 1960. "Legislative Facts in Constitutional Litigation." *Supreme Court Review* 75.

Kaye, D.H. 1992. "Proof in Law and Science." 32 *Jurimetrics Journal* 313.

Kelly, J. 1998. *Our Joyce: From Outcast to Icon.* Austin: University of Texas Press.

Kendall, C. 1993. "'Real Dominant, Real Fun!': Gay Male Pornography and the Pursuit of Masculinity." 57 *Saskatchewan Law Review* 22.

Kinsey, A.C., W.B. Pomeroy, and C.E. Martin. 1953. *Sexual Behavior in the Human Female.* Philadelphia: Saunders.

– 1948. *Sexual Behavior in the Human Male.* Philadelphia: Saunders.

Kiselbach, D. 1995. "Preparing and Tendering Section 1 *Charter* Evidence: *Little Sister's Book and Art Emporium* v. *The Minister of Justice.*" Vancouver: Department of Justice.

Kohn, J.G. 1960. "Social Psychological Data, Legislative Fact, and Constitutional Law." 29 *George Washington Law Review* 136.

Kuhn, T.S. 1970. *The Structure of Scientific Revolutions.* 2nd ed. Chicago: University of Chicago Press.

Lacombe, D. 1994. *Blue Politics: Pornography and the Law in the Age of Feminism.* Toronto: University of Toronto Press.

Lamont, J. 1973. "Public Opinion Polls and Survey Evidence in Obscenity Cases." 15 *Criminal Law Quarterly* 135.

Landsman, S. 1995. "Of Witches, Madmen, and Products Liability: An Historical Survey of the Use of Expert Testimony." 13 *Behavioral Sciences and the Law* 131.

Larson, M.S. 1984. "The Production of Expertise and the Constitution of Expert Power." In *The Authority of Experts.* Ed. Thomas Haskell. Bloomington: Indiana University Press.

Lasch, C. 1995. *The Revolt of the Elites and The Betrayal of Democracy.* New York: W.W. Norton and Company.

– 1991. *The True and Only Heaven: Progress and Its Critics.* New York: W.W. Norton and Company.

– 1965. *The New Radicalism in America.* New York: W.W. Norton and Company.

Laumann, E.O., J.H. Gagnon, et al. 1995. *The Social Organization of Sexuality: Sexual Practices in the United States.* Chicago: University of Chicago Press.

Lester, G.S. 1995. *Some Notes on Expert (Opinion) Evidence.* Ottawa: Department of Justice, Canada.

Lewontin, R.C. 1997. "Billions and Billions of Demons." 44:1 *The New York Review of Books* 28.

– 1995a. "Sex, Lies, and Social Science." 42:7 *The New York Review of Books* 24.

– 1995b. "Sex, Lies, and Social Science: An Exchange." 42:8 *The New York Review of Books* 43.

Linz, D., S.D. Penrod, and E. Donnerstein. 1987. "The Attorney General's Commission on Pornography: The Gaps Between 'Findings' and 'Facts.'" 4 *American Bar Foundation Research Journal* 713.

Lippmann, W. 1922. *Public Opinion.* New York: The Free Press.

Llewellyn, K. 1931. "Some Realism About Realism: Responding to Dean Pound." 44 *Harvard Law Review* 1222.

– 1930. "A Realistic Jurisprudence – The Next Step." 30 *Columbia Law Review* 431.

Lowman, J., M.A. Jackson, et al., eds. 1986. *Regulating Sex.* Burnaby: School of Criminology, Simon Fraser University.

MacCormick, N. 1978. *Legal Reasoning and Legal Theory.* Oxford: Clarendon Press.

MacDonald, V.C. 1939. "Constitutional Interpretation and Extrinsic Evidence." 17 *Canadian Bar Review* 77.

MacDougall, C.A. 1984. "The Community Standards Test of Obscenity." 42 *University of Toronto Faculty of Law Review* 79.

MacKinnon, C.A. 1989. *Toward A Feminist Theory of the State.* Cambridge: Harvard University Press.

– 1984. "Not a Moral Issue." 2 *Yale Law & Policy Review* 321.

Malamuth, N.M. 1984. "Aggression Against Women: Cultural and Individual Causes." In *Pornography and Sexual Aggression.* Ed. N.M. Malamuth and E. Donnerstein. Orlando, Fl.: Academic Press.

Malamuth, N.M., and E. Donnerstein. 1982. "The Effects of Aggressive-Pornographic Mass Media Stimuli." In *Advances in Experimental Social Psychology*, vol. 15. Ed. L. Berkowitz. New York: Academic Press.

Malamuth, N.M., and J.V.P. Check. 1981. "The Effects of Mass Media Exposure on Acceptance of Violence Against Women: A Field Experiment." 15 *Journal of Research in Personality* 436.

Manfredi, C.P. 1993. *Judicial Power and the Charter: Canada and the Paradox of Liberal Constitutionalism*. Toronto: McLelland & Stewart.

Marshall, W.L. 1988. "The Use of Sexually Explicit Stimuli by Rapists, Child Molesters, and Non-offenders." 25 *Journal of Sex Research* 267.

Masters, W.H., and V.E. Johnson. 1966. *Human Sexual Response*. Boston: Little Brown.

McGaffey, R.A. 1974. "A Realistic Look at Expert Witnesses in Obscenity Cases." 69 *Northwestern University Law Review* 218.

McKay, H.B., and D.J. Dolff. 1984. *The Impact of Pornography: A Decade of Literature*. Canada: Department of Justice, Research and Statistics Section.

McLachlin, B. 1993. "The Use and Misuse of Expert Evidence." Paper presented to the Canadian Bar Association, Civil Litigation Section, in Edmonton, Alberta, on 21 June 1993, and in Vancouver, British Columbia, on 22 June 1993.

Melossi, D. 1990. *The State of Social Control: A Sociological Study of Concepts of State and Social Control in the Making of Democracy*. Cambridge, UK: Polity Press.

Mezibov, M. 1992. "The Mapplethorpe Obscenity Trial." 18:4 *Litigation* 12.

Miller, A.S., and J.A. Barron. 1975. "The Supreme Court, The Adversary System, and the Flow of Information to the Justices: A Preliminary Inquiry." 61 *Virginia Law Review* 1187.

Moenssens, A. 1993. "Symposium On Scientific Evidence: Forward – Novel Scientific Evidence in Criminal Cases: Some Words of Caution." 84 *Journal of Criminal Law and Criminology* 1.

Monahan, J., and L. Walker. 1994. "Judicial Use of Social Science Research After Daubert." 2:2 *Shepard's Expert and Scientific Evidence Quarterly* 327.

– 1991. "Empirical Questions Without Empirical Answers." 1991 *Wisconsin Law Review* 569.

– 1988. "Social Science Research in Law: A New Paradigm." 43:6 *American Psychologist* 465.

– 1986. "Social Authority: Obtaining, Evaluating, and Establishing Social Science in Law." 134 *University of Pennsylvania Law Review* 477.

Mouffe, C. 1995. "Post-Marxism: democracy and identity." 13 *Environment and Planning D: Society and Space* 259.

– 1992a. "Citizenship and Identity." 61 *October* 28.

– 1992b. "Democratic Citizenship and the Political Community." In *Dimensions of Radical Democracy: Pluralism, Citizenship, Community*. Ed. C. Mouffe. London: Verso.

– 1988. "Radical Democracy: Modern or Postmodern?" In *Universal Abandon? The Politics of Postmodernism*. Ed. A. Ross, trans. P. Holdengraber. Minneapolis: University of Minnesota Press.

Nowlin, C. 2001. "Should Any Court Accept the 'Social Authority' Paradigm?" 14 *Canadian Journal of Law and Jurisprudence* 55.

– 1999. "Where is the Rhyme in the 'Reasoned Apprehension of Harm' Doctrine?" 57 *The Advocate* 843.

– 1996. "The Relevance of Stereotypes to s.15 Analysis – *Little Sister's Book and Art Emporium* v. *Canada (Minister of Justice)*." 30 *University of British Columbia Law Review* 333.

Ogburn, W.F. 1934. *On Culture and Social Change*. Chicago: University of Chicago Press.

Paciocco, D., and L. Stuesser. 1996. *The Law of Evidence*. Concord, Ont.: Irwin Law.

Paciocco, D. 1995. "Evaluating Expert Opinion Evidence for the Purpose of Determining Admissibility: More Recent Lessons from the Law of Evidence." Paper prepared for the Criminal Law Intensive Study Program at the National Judicial Institute, Canada.

Palys, T.S. 1992. *Research Decisions: Quantitative and Qualitative Perspectives*. Toronto: Harcourt Brace Jovanovich.

Palys, T., and J. Lowman. 1984. "Methadological Meta-Issues in Pornography Research." Paper presented to the annual meeting of the Canadian Psychological Association, held in Ottawa, Ontario, 31 May–2 June 1984.

Peirce, M. 1994. *Argument and Evidence Under Section 1 of the Canadian Charter of Rights and Freedoms*. Ottawa: Department of Justice Human Rights Law Section.

Philosopher's Brief. 1997. "The Brief of the Amicus Curiae" 44:5 *The New York Review of Books* 43.

Phipson, S.L. 1921. *The Law of Evidence*. 6th ed. London: Sweet and Maxwell.

Plato. 1964. *Gorgias*. Reprinted in *The Dialogues of Plato*, vol. 2. Trans. A. Jowett. London: Oxford University Press.

Pound, R. 1945. "Sociology of Law." In *Twentieth Century Sociology*. Ed. G. Gurvitch and W.E. Moore. Freeport, NY: Philosophical Library.

– 1922. *An Introduction to the Philosophy of Law*. New Haven: Yale University Press.

– 1920. "A Theory of Social Interests." 15 *Publications of the American Sociological Society* 16.

– 1912. "The Scope and Purpose of Sociological Jurisprudence." 25 *Harvard Law Review* 489.

– 1910. "Law in Books and Law in Action." 44 *American Law Review* 12.

– 1908. "Mechanical Jurisprudence." 8 *Columbia Law Review* 605.

Power, A. 1974. *Conversations with James Joyce*. Ed. C. Hart. New York: Harper and Row.

Razack, S. 1991. *Canadian Feminism and the Law*. Toronto: Second Story.

Rembar, C. 1968. *The End of Obscenity*. New York: Random House.

Roberts, P. 1996. "The Admissibility of Expert Evidence: Lessons from America." 4:3 *Expert Evidence* 93.

Roesch, R., S.L. Golding, et al. 1991. "Social Science and the Courts: The Role of Amicus Curiae Briefs." 15 *Law & Human Behavior* 1.

Rose, A.M. 1956. "The Social Scientist as an Expert Witness." 40 *Minnesota Law Review* 205.

Rose, N. 1989. *Governing the Soul: The Shaping of the Private Self.* London: Routledge.

Ross, E.A. 1919. *Foundations of Sociology,* 5th ed. New York: Macmillan.

Ross, B.L. 1997. "'Its Merely Intended for Sexual Arousal': Interrogating the Indefensibility of Lesbian Smut." In Cossman, B., S. Bell, et al. *Bad Attitude/s On Trial: Pornography, Feminism, and the* Butler *Decision.* Toronto: University of Toronto Press.

Ryan, A. 1997. "The Prophet." 44:17 *The New York Review of Books* 47.

Saks, M.J. 1993. "Improving A.P.A. Science Translation Amicus Briefs." 17 *Law and Human Behavior* 235.

Samaras, C. 1993. "Feminism, Photography, Censorship, and Sexually Transgressive Imagery: The Work of Robert Mapplethorpe, Joel-Peter Witkin, Jacqueline Livingston, Sally Mann, and Catherine Opie." 38 *New York Law School Law Review* 75.

Scales, A. 1994. "Avoiding Constitutional Depression: Bad Attitudes and the Fate of *Butler.*" 7 *Canadian Journal of Women and the Law* 349.

Schiff, S. 1963. "The Use of Out-of-court Information in Fact Determination at Trial." 41 *Canadian Bar Review* 335.

Schroeder, T.A. 1972. *"Obscene" Literature and Constitutional Law.* New York: DeCapo. Originally published 1911.

Schwendinger, H., and J. Schwendinger. 1974. *The Sociologists of the Chair.* New York: Basic Books.

Scott, J.E., D.J. Eitle, and S.E. Skovron. 1990. "Obscenity and the Law: Is it Possible for a Jury to Apply Contemporary Community Standards in Determining Obscenity?" 14 *Law and Human Behavior* 139.

Scott, J.E. 1991. "What is Obscene? Social Science and the Contemporary Community Standard Test of Obscenity." 14 *International Journal of Law and Psychiatry* 29.

Small, A.W. 1910. *The Meaning of Social Science.* Chicago: University of Chicago Press.

Sopinka, J., S. Lederman, and A. Bryant. 1992. *The Law of Evidence in Canada.* Vancouver: Butterworths.

Standing Committee on Justice and Legal Affairs, House of Commons. 1978. *Report on Pornography.* Proceeding No. 18, 3rd Sess., 30th Parl., 1977–78. (*MacGuigan Report*)

Strayer, B. 1968. *Judicial Review of Legislation in Canada.* Toronto: University of Toronto Press.

Swinton, K. 1987. "What do the Courts Want from the Social Sciences?" In *Charter Litigation.* Ed. R.J. Sharpe. Toronto: Butterworths.

Tomkins, A.J., and J.S. Cecil. 1994. "Treating Social Science Like Law: An Assessment of Monahan and Walker's Social Authority Proposal." 2:2 *Shepard's Expert and Scientific Evidence Quarterly* 343.

Tushnet, M. 1990. "The Politics of Constitutional Law." in *The Politics of Law: A Progressive Critique* (rev. ed.) ed. D. Kairys. New York: Pantheon Books.

Vance, C. 1993. "Negotiating sex and gender in the Attorney General's Commission on Pornography." In *Sex Exposed: Sexuality and the Pornography Debate*. Ed. L. Segal and M. McIntosh. New Brunswick, NJ: Rutgers University Press.

Vanderham, P. 1998. *James Joyce and Censorship: The Trials of Ulysses*. Washington Square: New York University Press.

Vidmar, N. 1995. "How Many Words for a Camel? A Perspective on Judicial Evaluation of Social Science Evidence." In *Filtering and Analyzing Evidence in an Age of Diversity*. Ed. M.T. MacCrimmon and M. Ouellette. Quebec: Les Éditions Thémis.

Wallace, W. 1971. *The Logic of Science in Sociology*. Chicago: Aldine Atherton.

Ward, L.F. 1906. *Applied Sociology (A Treatise on the Conscious Improvement of Society by Society)*. Boston: Athenaeum Press.

Weatherly, U. 1920. "Democracy and Our Political Systems." 14 *Publications of the American Sociological Society* 23.

West, R. 1972. *Conscience and Society*. Westport, Conn.: Greenwood Press, Publishers. Originally published in 1945.

West, R. 1987. "The Feminist-Conservative Anti-Pornography Alliance and the Attorney General's Commission on Pornography Report." 4 *American Bar Foundation Research Journal* 681.

White, G.E. 1972. "From Sociological Jurisprudence to Realism: Jurisprudence and Social Change in Early Twentieth-Century America." 58 *Virginia Law Review* 999.

Wigmore, J.H. 1923. *On Evidence*. 2d ed. Boston: Little, Brown and Company.

Wilson, J. 1986. "Decision-making in the Supreme Court." 36 *University of Toronto Law Journal* 227.

Wittgenstein, L. 1983. *Philosophical Investigations*. Trans. G.E.M. Anscombe. Oxford: Basic Blackwell. Originally published in 1958.

– 1979. *On Certainty*. Trans. D. Paul. and G.E.M. Anscombe. Oxford: Basic Blackwell.

Woolhandler, A. 1988. "Rethinking the Judicial Reception of Legislative Facts." 41 *Vanderbilt Law Review* 111.

List of Cases

Ritchie v. People, 155 Ill. 98, 46 Am. St. Rep. 315, 40 N.E. 454 (1895).

Roth v. Goldman, 172 F. 2d 788 (1949).

Roth v. United States, 354 U. S. 476, 1 L. Ed. 2d 1498, 77 S. Ct. 1304 (1957).

Rosen v. United States, 161 U.S. 29, 40 L. Ed. 606 (1896).

Smith v. California, 361 U.S. 147, 4 L. Ed. 2d 205, 80 S. Ct. 215 (1959).

Shenck v. United States, 249 U.S. 47, 63 L. Ed. 470, 39 S. Ct. 247 (1919).

State v. Becker, 272 S. W. 2d 283 (1954).

State v. Buchanan, 29 Wash. 602, 70 Pac. 52, 59 L.R.A. 342, 92 Am. St. Rep. 930 (1902).

Sweatt v. Painter, 339 U.S. 629 (1950).

Territory v. Ah Lim, 1 Wash. 156, 24 Pac. 588 (1890).

United States v. Clarke, 38 Fed. 500 (1889).

United States v. Dennett, 39 F. 2d. 564, 76 A.L.R. 1092 (1930).

United States v. Groner, 479 F. 2d 577 (5th Cir. 1973).

United States v. Harmon, 45 F. 414 (1891).

United States v. Kennerley, 209 F. 119 (1913).

United States v. Klaw, 350 F. 2d 155 (2d Cir. 1965).

United States v. Levine, 83 F. 2d 156 (1936).

United States v. One Book Called "Ulysses," 5 F. Supp. 182 (1933).

United States v. One Book Entitled Ulysses by James Joyce, 72 F. 2d 705 (1934).

United States v. Palladino, 475 F. 2d 65 (1973).

Vacco v. Quill, 521 U.S. 793, 138 L. Ed. 2d 772, 117 S. Ct. 2258 (1997).

Washington v. Glucksberg, 521 U.S. 702, 138 L. Ed. 2d 772, 117 S. Ct. 2258 (1997).

W.C. Ritchie & Co. v. Wayman, 91 N.E. 695 (1910).

CANADIAN CASES

Brownlee v. Hand Firework (1930), 65 O.L.R. 646 (C.A.).

Canada Post Corp. v. Smith (1994), 118 D.L.R. (4th) 454.

Conway v. The King (1943), 81 C.C.C. 189 (Que. K.B.).

Co-operative Committee on Japanese Canadians v. A.G. Canada, [1947] A.C. 88.

Dagenais v. Canadian Broadcasting Corp. (1994), 94 C.C.C. (3d) 289 (S.C.C.).

Danson v. Ontario (A.G.), [1990] 2 S.C.R. 1086.

Eskimos Reference, [1939] S.C.R. 104.

Fort Frances Pulp and Power v. Manitoba Free Press, [1923] A.C. 695.

Glad Day Bookshop v. Deputy Minister of National Revenue (Customs & Excise), [1992] 90 D.L.R. (4th) 527, O.J. No. 1466 (QL) (Ont. Ct. (Gen. Div.)).

Irwin Toy v. Quebec (A.G.), [1989] 1 S.C.R. 927.

Knodel v. B.C. (Medical Services Committee) (1991), 58 B.C.L.R. (2d) 356 (B.C.S.C.).

Little Sister's Book and Art Emporium v. Canada (Minister of Justice) (1996), 18 B.C.L.R. (3d) 241 (B.C.S.C.), aff'd (1999), 54 B.C.L.R. (3d) 306, 125 C.C.C.

R. v. *Ramsingh* (1984), 14 C.C.C. (3d) 230.

R. v. *Ronish* (1993), 18 C.R. (4th) 165, O.J. No. 608 (QL) (Ont. Ct. (Prov. Div.)).

R. v. *Scythes* [1993] O.J. No. 537.

R. v. *Sharpe* (1999), 22 C.R. (5th) 129, B.C.J. No. 54 (QL) (B.C.S.C.), aff'd (1999), 136 C.C.C. (3d) 97 (B.C.C.A.), aff'd [2001] 1 S.C.R. 45, 150 C.C.C. (3d) 321.

R. v. *Sharpe*, 2002 BCSC 423 (B.C.S.C.)

R. v. *Springer* (1975), 24 C.C.C. (2d) 56, 31 C.R.N.S. 48.

R. v. *Stroempl* (1995), 105 C.C.C. (3d) 188.

R. v. *Sudbury News Services* (1978), 39 C.C.C. (2d) 1 (Ont. C.A.).

R. v. *Times Square Cinema* (1971), 4 C.C.C. (2d) 229, 3 O.R. 688 (Ont. C.A.).

R. v. *Towne Cinema Theatres*, [1985] 1 S.C.R. 494, 18 D.L.R. (4th) 1, 45 C.R. (3d) 1, 18 C.C.C. (3d) 193.

R. v. *Tremblay et al.* (1993), 84 C.C.C. (3d) 97.

R. v. *Wagner*, [1985] A.J. No. 570 (QL) (Alta. Q.B.).

Texada Mines Ltd. v. *A.G.B.C.*, [1960] S.C.R. 713, 24 D.L.R. (2d) 81.

Transcript of Proceedings at *Little Sister's* trial, Oct.–Nov. 1994.

Transcript of Proceedings at *Sharpe* trial, Nov. 1998.

Willick v. *Willick* (1994), 6 R.F.L. (4th) 161.

ENGLISH CASES

R. v. *Anderson* [1972] 1 Q.B. 304.

R. v. *Brown* (1992), 97 Cr. App. R. 44, [1993] 2 All. E.R. 75 (H.L.).

R. v. *Calder & Boyars Ltd*, [1968] AC 706.

R. v. *Hicklin* (1868), 3 L.R. 359.

R. v. *Martin Secker & Warburg Ld.* (1954), W.L.R. 1138.

R. v. *Penguin Books Ltd.* [1961] Crim. L.R. 176.

Index